THE AMERICAN
ECONOMY
IN CONFLICT

THE
AMERICAN
ECONOMY
IN CONFLICT

Robert B. Carson
State University College
Oneonta, New York

D. C. HEATH AND COMPANY
Lexington, Massachusetts

Preface

TO THE STUDENT

Long ago, as a not very inspired undergraduate suffering through his first economics course, I recall that my instructor required the class to purchase, along with the textbook, a book of readings. For some weeks after the course began, I kept looking at the readings text as it lay on my desk, promising myself that I would sooner or later get around to doing the assignments in it. I also remember that, at least once or twice, I actually made an effort to keep this pledge. But the collection was extremely dull and quite irrelevant to a first-year economics student. The essays and articles were fairly theoretical, written to be sure by all the great men in economics (of course, I really didn't know or care then who was or wasn't "great"). To me, the readings seemed to be lifeless, not very well organized, and horribly obscure footnotes to the basic text. I responded to them accordingly.

Since then, collateral readings texts in basic economics have improved and greatly grown in number; but as a teacher, I am still doubtful that very many succeed in stimulating the student's interest. I also know from my own experience that all too few students make a serious effort to do their assigned readings. With these reservations in mind, I set about to put together this collection.

The student should note that the readings are organized around current economic and social issues. The emphasis is on understanding problems rather than mastering economic theory, although the student should quickly realize that a grasp of theory is basic to analyzing problems. The selections are readable and alive, not the obscure writings of academic economists who so avidly employ curious language and mysterious thought patterns. The issues chosen for analysis are not issues that simply attract the attention of the economists; instead they are questions that should be meaningful to all thoughtful citizens.

The student must be warned that there is no attempt to resolve the issues or problems that are presented. That cannot be the responsibility of any textbook but rather is the obligation of the student himself. The selected articles represent a spectrum of diverging views. The student should use his growing knowledge of economic theory and fact to discern which views, which resolutions to the problems, are most reasonable and desirable.

TO THE INSTRUCTOR

My own preference in teaching an introductory economics course is to make the maximum use of controversy over social and political issues. This is not to say that I don't think economic theory and analysis are important but rather that they become more important if shown to be relevant to the "gut" issues of our contemporary society. This collection of readings is intended as a means of bringing to life the controversies that run just below the surface of economic analysis.

This collection can be used in a number of different ways. The reading of the various issues does not need to follow any particular sequential pattern. Each section is complete and stands by itself. The order of selection of issues should, it seems to me, be based on the instructor's use of the textbook and the classroom introduction of particular economic concepts. The readings will stimulate some desire for discussion of the issues by students. To stimulate such discussion, regularly or occasionally according to the instructor's wishes, there is a series of questions listed after each section of articles. Since this is a survey text, footnotes have been deleted; those wishing a more complete reference should check the original source.

Robert B. Carson

Contents

PART FOUR

The Performance of the National Economy

THE AMERICAN
ECONOMY
IN CONFLICT

A Place to Begin

PART ONE

The Economic Problem

Robert L. Heilbroner

Man, it is repeatedly said, does not live by bread alone. Indeed, when we look back over the pageant of what is usually called "history," the humble matter of bread hardly strikes the eye at all. Power and glory, faith and fanaticism, ideas and ideologies are the aspects of the human chronicle that crowd the pages of history books. If the simple quest for bread is a moving force in human destiny, it is well concealed behind what one philosopher-historian has called "that history of international crime and mass murder which has been advertised as the history of mankind" [Karl Popper].

Obviously, man cannot live without bread. Like every other living thing, as the imperious first rule of continued existence, the human being must eat. And this first prerequisite is less to be taken for granted than at first appears, for the human organism is not, in itself, a highly efficient mechanism for survival. From each one hundred calories of food it consumes, it can deliver only about twenty calories of mechanical energy. On a decent diet, man can produce just about one horsepower-hour of work daily, and with that he must replenish his exhausted body. With what is left over, he is free to build a civilization.

In many countries, the basic expectation of human continuity is far from assured. In the vast continents of Asia and Africa, in the Near East, even in some countries of South America, brute survival is the problem which stares humanity in the face. Millions of human beings have died of starvation or malnutrition in our present era, as countless hundreds of millions have died over the long past. Whole nations are acutely aware of what it means to face hunger as a condition of ordinary life: it has been said, for example, that the Egyptian *fellah*, from the day he is born to the day he dies, never knows what it is to have a full stomach. In many of the so-called underdeveloped nations, the life span of the average person is less than half of ours. Not many years ago, an Indian demographer made the chilling calculation that of one hundred Asian and one hundred American infants, more Americans would be alive at sixty-five than Indians at *five!* The statistics, not of life, but of premature death throughout most of the world are overwhelming and crushing.

THE INDIVIDUAL AND SOCIETY

For most Americans, these considerations are apt to seem tragic but remote. None of us is conscious of a struggle for existence to anything resembling

From *Robert L. Heilbroner,* The Making of Economic Society, © *1962. Reprinted by permission of Prentice-Hall, Inc., Englewood Cliffs, New Jersey.*

a life-or-death degree. That it might be possible for us to experience severe want, that we might ever know in our own bodies the pangs of hunger experienced by an Indian villager or a Bolivian peon is a thought which it is nearly impossible for us to entertain seriously.

Short of a catastrophic war, it is highly unlikely that any of us ever will know the full meaning of the struggle for existence. Nonetheless, even in our prosperous and secure society, there remains, however unnoticed, an aspect of life's precariousness, a reminder of the underlying problem of survival. *This is our helplessness as economic individuals.*

It is a curious fact that as we leave the most impoverished peoples of the world, where the human being with his too few calories of energy scratches out for himself a bare subsistence, we find the economic insecurity of the individual many times multiplied. The solitary Eskimo, Bushman, Indonesian, Nigerian, left to his own devices, will survive a considerable time. Living close to the soil or to their animal prey, the peoples with the lowest standards of living in the world can sustain their own lives, at least for a while, almost single-handed. With a community numbering only a few hundred, they can live indefinitely. Indeed, a very large percentage of the human race today lives in precisely such fashion—in small, virtually self-contained peasant communities which provide for their own survival with a minimum of contact with the outside world. This large majority of mankind suffers great poverty, but it also knows a certain economic independence. If it did not, it would have been wiped out centuries ago.

When we turn to the New Yorker or the Chicagoan, on the other hand, we are struck exactly by the opposite condition, by a prevailing ease of material life, coupled at the same time by an extreme *dependence* of the individual in his search for the means of existence. In the great metropolitan areas where most Americans live, we can no longer envisage the solitary individual or the small community surviving, short of looting warehouses or stores for food and necessities. The overwhelming majority of Americans have never grown food, caught game, raised meat, ground grain into flour, or even fashioned flour into bread. Faced with the challenge of clothing themselves or building their own homes, they would be hopelessly untrained and unprepared. Even to make minor repairs in the machines which surround them, they must call on other members of the community whose business it is to fix cars, or repair plumbing, or whatever. Paradoxically, perhaps, the richer the nation, the more apparent is this inability of its average inhabitant to survive unaided and alone.

We survive in rich nations because the tasks we cannot do ourselves are done for us by an army of others on whom we can call for help. If we cannot grow food, we can buy it; if we cannot provide for our needs ourselves, we can hire the services of someone who can. This enormous *division of labor* enhances our capacity a thousandfold, for it enables us to benefit from other men's skills as well as our own.

Along with this invaluable gain comes a certain risk. It is a sobering thought, for example, that we depend on the services of only 180,000 men— fewer than one out of every three hundred people working in the nation—to provide us with that basic commodity, coal. An even smaller number of workers—less than 75,000—are responsible for running the locomotives which haul all the nation's rail freight and passenger service. A still smaller number— under 15,000—comprises our total commercial aircraft pilot and navigator crew. A failure of any one of these very small groups to perform its functions would cripple us: in the case of airplane pilots, slightly; in the case of locomotive engineers, badly; in the case of coal miners, perhaps disastrously. As we know, when from time to time we face a bad strike, our entire economic machine may falter because a strategic group ceases to perform its accustomed tasks.

Along with the abundance of material existence as we know it goes a hidden vulnerability: our abundance is assured only insofar as the organized cooperation of huge armies of people is to be counted upon. Indeed, our continuing existence as a rich nation hinges on the tacit precondition that the mechanism of social organization will continue to function effectively. *We are rich, not as individuals, but as members of a rich society, and our easy assumption of material sufficiency is actually only as reliable as the bonds which forge us into a social whole.*

ECONOMICS, SCARCITY, AND SOCIAL ORGANIZATION

The problem of how societies forge and maintain the bonds which guarantee their material survival is the basic problem of economics.

We know very little of how those bonds may have been originally constituted. Man appears on the scroll of history as a member of a group, and as such, the beneficiary of a rudimentary division of labor. Yet it is noteworthy that even his simplest familial cooperation is not achieved instinctually as is the case with communities of insects or of animals, but must be buttressed with magic and taboo and maintained by more or less repressive laws and traditions.

Strangely enough, then, we find that man, not nature, is the source of most of our economic problems. To be sure, the economic problem itself—that is, the need to struggle for existence—derives ultimately from the scarcity of nature. If there were no scarcity, goods would be as free as air, and economics, at least in one sense of the word, would cease to exist as a social preoccupation.

And yet if the scarcity of nature sets the stage for the economic problem, it does not impose the only strictures against which men must struggle. For scarcity, as a felt condition, is not solely the fault of nature. If Americans today, for instance, were content to live at the level of Mexican peasants, all our material wants could be fully satisfied with but an hour or two of daily labor. We would experience little or no scarcity, and our economic problems would virtually disappear. Instead, we find in America—and indeed in all industrial societies—that as the ability to increase nature's yield has risen, so has the reach of human wants. In fact, in societies such as ours, where relative social status is importantly connected with the possession of material goods, we often find that "scarcity" as a psychological experience and goad becomes more pronounced as we grow wealthier: our desires to possess the fruits of nature race out ahead of our mounting ability to produce goods.

Thus the "wants" that nature must satisfy are by no means fixed—while, for that matter, nature's yield itself is not a constant, but varies over a wide range, depending on the social application of human energy and skill. Scarcity is therefore not attributable to nature alone but to "human nature" as well; and economics is ultimately concerned not merely with the stinginess of the physical environment, but equally with the appetite of the human temperament.

Hence we must begin a systematic analysis of economics by singling out the functions which social organization must perform to bring human nature into social harness. And when we turn our attention to this fundamental problem, we can quickly see that it involves the solution of two related and yet separate elemental tasks:

1. A society must organize a system for producing the goods and services it needs for its own perpetuation.

2. It must arrange a distribution of the fruits of its production among its own members, so that more production can take place.

These two tasks of economic continuity are, at first look, very simple. But it is a deceptive simplicity. Much of economic history . . . is concerned with the manner in which various societies have sought to cope with these elementary problems; and what strikes us in surveying their attempts is that most of them were partial failures. (They could not have been total failures, or society would not have survived.) Hence it behooves us to look more carefully into the two main economic tasks to see what hidden difficulties they may conceal.

THE PRODUCTION PROBLEM

What is the difficulty which the production problem poses? What are the obstacles which a society encounters in organizing a system to produce the goods and services it needs?

Since nature is usually stingy, it would seem that the production problem must be essentially one of engineering, or technical efficiency. It would seem to revolve around the effort to economize, to avoid waste and apply social effort as efficaciously as possible.

This is indeed an important task for any society, and a great deal of formal economic thought, as the word itself suggests, is devoted to economizing. Yet this is not the core of the production problem. Long before a society can even concern itself about using its energies "economically," it must first marshal the energies to carry out the productive process itself. That is, *the basic problem of production is to devise social institutions which will mobilize human energy for productive purposes.*

This basic requirement is not always so easily accomplished. For example, in the United States in 1933, the energies of nearly thirteen million people—one quarter of our work force—were not directed into the production process. Although these unemployed men and women were eager to work, although empty factories were available for them to work in, despite the existence of pressing wants, somehow a terrible and mystifying breakdown short-circuited the production process, with the result that an entire third of our previous annual output of goods and services simply disappeared.

We are by no means the only nation which has, on occasion, failed to find work for willing workers. In the very poorest nations, where production is most desperately needed, we frequently find that unemployment is a chronic condition. The streets of the Asian cities are thronged with people who cannot find work. But this, too, is not a condition imposed by the scarcity of nature. There is, after all, an endless amount of work to be done, if only in cleaning the filthy streets or patching up the homes of the poor, building roads, or planting forests. Yet, what seems to be lacking is a social mechanism to put the unemployed to work.

Both these examples point out to us that the production problem is not solely, or perhaps even primarily, a physical and technical struggle with nature. On these "scarcity" aspects of the problem will depend the speed with which a nation may forge ahead and the level of well-being it can reach with a given effort. But the original mobilization of productive effort itself is a challenge to its social organization, and on the success or failure of that social organization will depend the volume of the human effort which can be directed to nature.

Putting men to work is only the first step in the solution of the production problem. Men must not only be put to work; they must be put to work *in the right places.* They must produce the goods and services which society needs. In addition to assuring a large enough quantity of social effort, the economic institutions of society must also assure the *proper allocation of that social effort.*

In a nation such as India or Brazil, where the great majority of the population is born in peasant villages and grows up to be peasant cultivators, the solution to this problem offers little to vex our understanding. The basic demands of society—food and fiber—are precisely the goods which its peasant population "naturally" produces. But in an industrial society, the proper allocation of effort becomes an enormously complicated task. People in the United States demand much more than bread and cotton. They need, for instance, such things as automobiles. Yet no one "naturally" produces an automobile. On the contrary, in order to produce one, an extraordinary spectrum of special tasks must be performed. Some people must make steel. Others must make rubber. Still others must coordinate the assembly process itself. And this is but a tiny sampling of the far from "natural" tasks which must be performed if an automobile is to be produced.

As with the mobilization of its total production effort, society does not always succeed in the proper allocation of its effort. It may, for instance, turn out too many cars or too few. Of greater importance, it may devote its energies to the production of luxuries while the majority of its people are starving. Or it may even court disaster by an inability to channel its productive effort into areas of critical importance. In the early 1950's, for instance, the British suffered a near economic collapse because they were unable to get enough of their workers to mine coal.

Such allocative failures may affect the production problem quite as seriously as a failure to mobilize an adequate quantity of effort, for a viable society must produce not only goods, but the *right* goods. And the allocative question alerts us to a still broader conclusion. It shows us that the act of production, in and of itself, does not fully answer the requirements for survival. Having produced enough of the right goods, society must now *distribute* those goods so that the production process can go on.

THE DISTRIBUTION PROBLEM

Once again, in the case of the peasant who feeds himself and his family from his own crop, this requirement of adequate distribution may seem simple enough. But when we go beyond the most primitive society, the problem is not always so readily solved. In many of the poorest nations of the East and South, urban workers have often been unable to deliver their daily horsepower-hour of work because they have not been given enough of society's output to run their human engines to capacity. Worse yet, they have often languished on the job while granaries bulged with grain and the well-to-do complained of the ineradicable "laziness" of the masses. At the other side of the picture, the distribution mechanism may fail because the rewards it hands out do not succeed in persuading people to perform their necessary tasks. Shortly after the Russian Revolution some factories were organized into communes in which managers and janitors pooled their pay, and from which all drew equal allotments. The result was a rash of absenteeism on the part of the previously better-paid workers and a threatened breakdown in industrial production. Not until the old unequal wage payments were reinstituted did production resume its former course.

As was the case with failures in the production process, distributive failures need not entail a total economic collapse. Societies can exist—and indeed, in the majority of cases, do exist—with badly distorted productive and distributive efforts. It is only rarely, as in the instances above, that maldistribution actively interferes with the actual ability of a society to staff its production posts. More frequently, an inadequate solution to the distribution problem reveals itself in social and political unrest or even in revolution.

Yet this, too, is an aspect of the total economic problem. For if society is to insure its steady material replenishment, it must parcel out its production in a fashion that will maintain not only the capacity but the willingness to go on working. And thus again we find the focus of economic inquiry directed to the study of human institutions. For a viable economic society, we can now see, is not only one which can overcome the stringencies of nature, but one which can contain and control the intransigence of human nature.

THE THREE SOLUTIONS TO THE ECONOMIC PROBLEM

Thus to the economist, society presents itself in an unaccustomed aspect. He sees it essentially as an elaborate mechanism for survival, a mechanism for accomplishing the complicated tasks of production and distribution necessary for social continuity.

But the economist sees something else as well, something which at first seems quite astonishing. Looking not only over the diversity of contemporary societies, but back over the sweep of all history, he sees that man has succeeded in solving the production and distribution problems in but three ways. That is, within the enormous diversity of the actual social institutions which guide and shape the economic process, the economist divines but three overarching *types* of systems which separately or in combination enable humankind to solve its economic challenge. These great systemic types can be called economies run by Tradition, economies run by Command, and economies run by the Market. Let us briefly see what is characteristic of each.

Tradition. Perhaps the oldest and, until a very few years ago, by far the most generally prevalent way of solving the economic challenge has been tradition. It has been a mode of social organization in which both production and distribution were based on procedures devised in the distant past, rigidified by a long process of historic trial and error, and maintained by heavy sanctions of law, custom, and belief.

Societies based on tradition solve the economic problems very manageably. First, they deal with the production problem—the problem of assuring that the needful tasks will be done—by assigning the jobs of fathers to their sons. Thus a hereditary chain assures that skills will be passed along and that the ongoing jobs will be staffed from generation to generation. In ancient Egypt, wrote Adam Smith, the first great economist, "every man was bound by a principle of religion to follow the occupation of his father and was supposed to commit the most horrible sacrilege if he changed it for another." And it was not merely in antiquity that tradition preserved a productive orderliness within society. In our own Western culture, until the fifteenth or sixteenth centuries, the hereditary allocation of tasks was also the main stabilizing force within society. Although there was some movement from country to town and from occupation to occupation, birth usually determined one's role in life. One was born to the soil or to a trade; and on the soil or within the trade, one followed in the footsteps of one's forebears.

Thus tradition has been the stabilizing and impelling force behind a great repetitive cycle of society, assuring that society's work would be done each day very much as it had been done in the past. Even today, among the less industrialized nations of the world, tradition continues to play this immense organizing role. In India, until very recently at least, one was born to a caste which had its own occupation. "Better thine own work is, though done with fault," preached the *Bhagavad-Gita,* the great philosophic moral poem of India, "than doing other's work, even excellently."

Tradition not only provides a solution to the production problem of society, but it also regulates the distribution problem. Take, for example, the Bushmen of the Kalahari Desert in South Africa who depend for their livelihood on hunting prowess. Elizabeth Marshall Thomas, a sensitive observer of these peoples, reports on the manner in which tradition solves the problem of distributing their kill.

> The gemsbok has vanished . . . . Gai owned two hind legs and a front leg, Tsetchwe had meat from the back, Ukwane had the other front leg, his wife had one of the feet and the stomach, the young boys had lengths of intestine. Twikwe had received the head and Dasina the udder. . . . It seems very unequal when you watch Bushmen divide the kill, yet it is their system, and in the end no person eats more than any other. That day Ukwane gave Gai still another piece because Gai was his relation, Gai gave meat to Dasina because she was his wife's mother . . . . No one, of course, contested Gai's large share, because he had been the hunter and by their law that much belonged to him. No one doubted that he would share his large amount with others, and they were not wrong, of course; he did.

The manner in which tradition can divide a social product may be, as the illustration shows, very subtle and ingenious. It may also be very crude and, by our standards, harsh. Tradition has often allocated to women, in non-industrial societies, the most meager portion of the social product. But however much tradition may accord with or depart from our accustomed moral views, we must see that it is a workable method of dividing society's production.

Traditional solutions to the economic problems of production and distribution are most commonly encountered in primitive agrarian or nonindustrial societies, where in addition to serving an economic function, the unquestioning acceptance of the past provides the necessary perseverance and endurance to confront harsh destinies. Yet even in our own society, tradition continues to play a role in solving the economic problem. It plays its smallest role in determining the distribution of our own social output, although the persistence of such traditional payments as tips to waiters, allowances to minors, or bonuses based on length of service are all vestiges of old traditional ways of distributing goods, as is the differential between men's and women's pay for equal work.

More important is the place which tradition continues to hold, even in America, as a means of solving the production problem—that is, in allocating the performance of tasks. Much of the actual process of selecting an employment in our society is heavily influenced by tradition. We are all familiar with families in which sons follow their fathers into a profession or a business. On a somewhat broader scale, tradition also dissuades us from certain employments. Sons of American middle-class families, for example, do not usually seek factory work, even though factory jobs may pay better than office jobs, because "blue-collar employment" is not in the middle-class tradition.

Even in our society, which is clearly not a "traditional" one, custom provides an important mechanism for solving the economic problem. But now we must note one very important consequence of the mechanism of tradition. *Its solution to production and distribution is a static one.* A society which follows the path of tradition in its regulation of economic affairs does so at the expense of large-scale rapid social and economic change.

Thus the economy of a Bedouin tribe or a Burmese village is in few essential respects changed today from what it was a hundred or even a thousand years ago. The bulk of the peoples living in tradition-bound societies repeat, in the daily patterns of their economic life, much of the routines which characterized them in the distant past. Such societies may rise and fall, wax and wane, but external events—war, climate, political adventures and misadventures—are mainly responsible for their changing fortunes. Internal, self-generated economic change is but a small factor in the history of most tradition-bound states. Tradition solves the economic problem, but it does so at the cost of economic progress.

Command. A second manner of solving the problem of economic continuity also displays an ancient lineage. This is the method of imposed authority, of economic command. It is a solution based not so much on the perpetuation of a viable system by the changeless reproduction of its ways, as on the organization of a system according to the orders of an economic commander-in-chief.

Not infrequently we find this authoritarian method of economic control superimposed upon a traditional social base. Thus the Pharaohs of Egypt exerted their economic dictates above the timeless cycle of traditional agricultural practice on which the Egyptian economy was based. By their orders, the supreme rulers of Egypt brought into being the enormous economic effort which built the pyramids, the temples, the roads. Herodotus, the Greek historian, tells us how the Pharaoh Cheops organized the task.

[He] ordered all Egyptians to work for himself. Some, accordingly, were appointed to draw stones from the quarries in the Arabian mountains down to the Nile, others he ordered to receive the stones when transported in vessels across the river. . . . And they worked to the number of a hundred thousand men at one time, each party during three months. The time during which the people were thus harassed by toil lasted ten years on the road which they constructed, and along which they drew the stones; a work, in my opinion, not much less than the Pyramid.

The mode of authoritarian economic organization was by no means confined to ancient Egypt. We encounter it in the despotisms of medieval and classical China, which produced, among other things, the colossal Great Wall, or in the slave labor by which many of the great public works of ancient Rome were built. Of course, we find it today in the dictates of the communist economic authorities. In less drastic form, we find it also in our own society, for example, in the form of *taxes*—that is, in the preemption of part of our income by the public authorities for public purposes.

Economic command, like tradition, offers solutions to the twin problems of production and distribution. In times of crises, such as war or famine, it may be the only way in which a society can organize its manpower or distribute its goods effectively. Even in America, we commonly declare martial law when an area has been devastated by a great natural disaster. On such occasions we may press people into service, requisition homes, impose curbs on the use of private property such as cars, or even limit the amount of food a family may consume.

Quite aside from its obvious utility in meeting emergencies, command has a further usefulness in solving the economic problem. Unlike tradition, the exercise of command has no inherent effect of slowing down economic change. Indeed, the exercise of authority is the most powerful instrument society has for *enforcing economic change*. One example is, of course, the radical alterations in the systems of production and distribution which authority has effected in modern China or Russia. But again, even in our own society, it is sometimes necessary for economic authority to intervene into the normal flow of economic life to speed up or bring about change. The government may, for instance, utilize its tax receipts to lay down a network of roads which brings a backwater community into the flux of active economic life. It may undertake an irrigation system which will dramatically change the economic life of a vast region. It may very considerably affect the distribution of income among social classes.

To be sure, economic command which is exercised within the framework of a democratic political process is very different from that which is exercised by strong-arm methods: there is an immense social distance between a tax system controlled by Congress and outright expropriation or labor impressment by a supreme and unchallengeable ruler. Yet, whilst the means may be much milder, the *mechanism* is the same. In both cases, command diverts economic effort toward goals chosen by a higher authority. In both cases it interferes with the existing order of production and distribution, to create a new order ordained from "above."

This does not in itself serve to commend or condemn the exercise of command. The new order imposed by the authorities may offend or please our sense of social justice, just as it may improve or lessen the economic efficiency of society. Clearly, command can be an instrument of a democratic as well as of a totalitarian will. There is no implicit moral judgment to be passed on this second of the great mechanisms of economic control. Rather, it is important to note that no society—certainly no modern society—is without its elements of command, just as none is devoid of the influence of tradition. If tradition is the great brake on social and economic change, so economic command can be the great spur to change. As mechanisms for assuring the successful solution to the economic problem, both serve their purposes, both have their uses and their drawbacks. Between them, tradition and command have accounted for most of the long history of man's economic efforts to cope with his environment and with himself. The fact that human society *has* survived is testimony to their effectiveness.

The Market. There is also a third solution to the economic problem—that is, a third solution to the problem of maintaining socially viable patterns of production and distribution. This is the *market organization of society,* an organization which, in truly remarkable fashion, allows society to insure its own provisioning with a minimum of recourse either to tradition or command.

Because we live in a market-run society, we are apt to take for granted the puzzling—indeed, almost paradoxical—nature of the market solution to the economic problem. But assume for a moment that we could act as economic advisers to a society which had not yet decided on its mode of economic organization. Suppose, for instance, that we were called on to act as consultants to one of the new nations emerging from the continent of Africa.

We could imagine the leaders of such a nation saying, "We have always experienced a highly tradition-bound way of life. Our men hunt and cultivate the fields and perform their tasks as they are brought up to do by the force of example and the instruction of their elders. We know, too, something of what can be done by economic command. We are prepared, if necessary, to sign an edict making it compulsory for many of our men to work on community projects for our national development. Tell us, is there any other way we can organize our society so that it will function successfully—or better yet, more successfully?"

Suppose we answered, "Yes, there is another way. Organize your society along the lines of a market economy."

"Very well," say the leaders. "What do we then tell people to do? How do we assign them to their various tasks?"

"That's the very point," we would answer. "In a market economy no one is assigned to any task. The very idea of a market society is that each person is allowed to decide for himself what to do."

There is consternation among the leaders. "You mean there is *no* assignment of some men to mining and others to cattle raising? No manner of selecting some for transportation and others for cloth weaving? You leave this to people to decide for themselves? But what happens if they do not decide correctly? What happens if no one volunteers to go into the mines, or if no one offers himself as a railway engineer?"

"You may rest assured," we tell the leaders, "none of that will happen. In a market society, all the jobs will be filled because it will be to people's advantage to fill them."

Our respondents accept this with uncertain expressions. "Now, look," one of them finally says, "let us suppose that we take your advice and let our people do as they please. Now let's talk about something important, like cloth production. Just how do we fix the right level of cloth output in this 'market society' of yours?"

"But you don't," we reply.

"We don't! Then how do we know there will be enough cloth produced?"

"There will be," we tell him. "The market will see to that."

"Then how do we know there won't be *too much* cloth produced?" he asks triumphantly.

"Ah, but the market will see to that, too!"

"But what *is* this market that will do all these wonderful things? Who runs it?"

"Oh, nobody runs the market," we answer. "It runs itself. In fact, there really isn't any such *thing* as 'the market.' It's just a word we use to describe the way people behave."

"But I thought people behaved the way they wanted to!"

"And so they do," we say. "But never fear. They will want to behave the way you want them to behave."

"I am afraid," says the chief of the delegation, "that we are wasting our time. We thought you had in mind a serious proposal. But what you suggest is madness. It is inconceivable. Good day, sir." And with great dignity the delegation takes its leave.

Could we seriously suggest to such an emergent nation that it entrust itself to a market solution of the economic problem? . . . The very perplexity which the market idea would rouse in the mind of someone unacquainted with it may serve to increase our own wonderment at this most sophisticated and interesting of all economic mechanisms. How *does* the market system assure us that our mines will find miners, our factories workers? How does it take care of cloth production? How does it happen that in a market-run nation each person can indeed do as he wishes and, withal, fulfill the needs which society as a whole presents?

ECONOMICS AND THE MARKET SYSTEM

Economics, as we commonly conceive it . . . , is primarily concerned with these very problems. Societies which rely primarily on tradition to solve their economic problems are of less interest to the professional economist than to the cultural anthropologist or the sociologist. Societies which solve their economic problems primarily by the exercise of command present interesting economic questions, but here the study of economics is necessarily subservient to the study of politics and the exercise of power.

It is a society which solves its economic problems by the market process that presents an aspect especially interesting to the economist. For here, . . . economics truly plays a unique role. Unlike the case with tradition and command, where we quickly grasp the nature of the economic mechanism of society, when we turn to a market society we are lost without a knowledge of economics. For in a market society it is not at all clear that the problems of production and distribution will be solved by the free interplay of individuals without guidance from tradition or command.

The Organization of the American Economy

PART TWO

How Well Does American Capitalism Work?

Modern American capitalism bears little resemblance to the economic system laid down by the venerable Adam Smith and the classical economists. Their prescription for an ideal economy, characterized by a freely competitive market without interference from government and without the concentration of economic power in monopolies or trade unions, has little literal application to the United States today. As a matter of fact, it may be debated as to whether any nation very rigorously followed the dictates of classical laissez faire, even in the obscure "good old days." Americans have always shown a highly pragmatic attitude toward their economic system rather than acting slavishly under a very rigid ideology; despite its deviations from the ideal typology of "capitalism," however, the American economy is clearly capitalistic with its emphasis on private enterprise, capital accumulation, and substantial market determination of prices and resource allocation.

To pose the question, "How well does American capitalism work?" is likely to strike most readers as incredibly naive. Through nearly two hundred years as a nation the system has proved, by any known standard of production and output, to be phenomenally successful. To Americans, who characteristically appraise things quantitatively, if something is bigger, or stronger, or there is more of it, there is general consensus that it has to be better. Quantitatively, the American economy seems to be almost above question. Even its occasional shortcomings, as adaptations were made to new economic conditions, pale before its long-run performance. The general economic stability, the level of affluence of most, if not all, of its citizens, and the wide range of consumer products are only a few of the more obvious examples of this quantitative dimension. The question of how well the system works has another side to it—an estimate of the qualitative performance as well as the quantitative. On this point there has been, in recent years, much less positive agreement. Perhaps, as a result of our evident affluence, we have recently begun to ponder questions about the "quality of life" produced by our economic system, whereas in the past Americans took for granted that the existence of more goods, more income, and greater stability meant greater happiness. Nevertheless, a considerable body of criticism on the qualitative performance of the economy developed during the decade of the sixties, precisely at a time of high and sustained economic growth.

The following two articles are contrasts in response to the question set forth here. The first is a highly laudatory estimate of American capitalism, emphasizing the obvious quantitative successes of the economy and concluding that the system has been able to produce "the good life" for most of its citizens. The second article, by two well-known and respected Marxist scholars, lays out a "New Left" critique, arguing that American capitalism is neither rational nor humane and that the quality of life in America has been degraded by the system's preoccupation with production and consumption as ends in themselves. While the second article might have been ignored a few years ago by economists, its cutting edge seems to have become uncomfortably sharper.

The Case of American Capitalism

Nathaniel Stone Preston

THE PRACTICE OF CAPITALISM

The United States is, by agreement of friend and foe alike, the leading exponent of capitalism and example of a capitalist nation. To the extent that any deny this, they generally deny that any nation still practices a predominantly capitalistic method of economic organization. And it is true that only a few nations do practice something approaching pure capitalism, principally because the cultural traits . . . providing a favorable environment for it and the economic, social, and political conditions conducive to its operation have not been characteristic of most of the countries of the world. Because substantially all of our examples of capitalism in action will be drawn from the United

States, it is well to deal briefly with these background conditions, bearing in mind that not all countries that enjoy capitalism have reached it by the same route.

The United States was the third major country in the world to undergo industrialization, and although the process was interrupted by a tearing civil war, there were many factors that rendered it the least painful of all of the early industrial revolutions. There was less of a social upheaval because there had existed no feudal class structure to be torn down to make way for it. It occurred in a society already oriented in large measure to economic goals, an orientation that is often obscured by the historical attention given the Pilgrim Fathers in New England as against the adventurers who colonized Virginia, the trading Dutch in New York, and the mercantile purposes that underlay the majority of the companies that organized and supported colonization. There were all of the usual horrors of early factory life, but escape from them was possible and wages were higher, because unclaimed land at the frontier was available to which the unemployed and the disenchanted could repair. There were not, as there were in England, wandering armies of dispossessed peasants whose search for work drove wages down and bred insecurity and fear. Because they were among the first peoples to industrialize, Americans did not suffer the stresses of forced-draft development that characterize many parts of the world today. England and France were far enough away, and their goods sufficiently difficult to bring across the ocean, that America's growth was not distorted by a too early appearance of an intense desire for goods the economy was not ready to produce itself. When growth did occur, however, a vast and seemingly limitless market, unbroken by tariff walls, gave opportunity and reward to those who dared to offer it new things.

It should not be thought that the process was painless. It was not. No perusal of American history from the 1840s onward would fail to reveal misery, dirt, slums, sweatshops, depressions, and all of the other plagues that attended industrialization in England and elsewhere. They were less horrible, however, and more strongly overbalanced by buoyant growth, the excitement of sudden wealth, and the other bearers of an aggressive optimism. Straight up through modern times no other country so frequently portrayed examples of the rags-to-riches story, and in no other was a competitive individualism so strongly nurtured, not only on the frontier, but in the cities and factories where fortunes were built. It is a very trite story, this, but a conscientious comparison of the United States in the nineteenth century, and even as far as the 1920s, with other nations cannot but reveal a difference that could only bring a different outlook and a different set of values to dominate popular thinking.

Two expressly political factors need to be mentioned as well before we can summarize the effects of these developments. . . . The franchise had been extended without serious opposition (except in a few of the original states) to all white male adults before the Industrial Revolution started, thus removing a possible cause for the growth of intense class feeling during the process. Secondly, the United States enjoyed a happy immunity from armed invasion. A threat of invasion tends to emphasize the State as protector of the people and draws energies away from the productive task in hand. The Civil War did the latter, but neither its slogans nor its results operated to endear governmental power to the people. This, and perhaps the confusion of loyalties brought about by the existence of a federal system, tended to weaken the already low prestige of governmental power in general—power that had once belonged to the colonial ruler across the sea, and power of which the framers of the Constitution had shown their fear and dislike by dividing and scattering it about in a way designed to make it largely unusable.

In no other country has the ground been prepared so well for capitalism. Not only its economic success, which a great many other nations have shared, if less impressively, but every facet of its political and social experience tended to produce a people lacking in affection for government, optimistic about their own possibilities of self-betterment, free of class antagonisms, and aggressively individualistic. With all of these were combined certain attitudes of a milder, kinder sort: The cooperation on a community scale that was necessary in frontier life, religious attitudes that bespoke charity and concern for the weak, tolerance of differences (except in the scarifying matter of race), and generosity bred of confident self-sufficiency. These were to have their effect in modifying the application of the principles of capitalism, and were, in fact, the ones that were transferred to and expressed in the political order.

The Political and Economic Orders Under Capitalism. The principles of capitalism require a limitation of the impact of the political order on the economic order, but actual practice has shown that that limitation is far from absolute. Political intervention has never been absent and has often been rather massive. At least five major (but overlapping) forms can be distinguished. First, government has been called upon by the various competitors in economic struggles to give them an advantage or to counter an advantage held by their opponents. Secondly, government is responsible for the framework of law within which the capitalist system operates. In that capacity it has had to make adjustments of that framework from time to time as the system evolved in order to help it continue under new conditions or to improve its operation where defects were discovered. Thirdly, the political order has intervened to correct and supplement the effects of the market in meting out rewards and allocating power. It has registered society's refusal to abide by the results of the play of market forces within the particular market structure that existed. Fourthly, efforts have been made to correct the so-called business cycle—the great alternation of prosperity and depression that came to attend the unregulated market. Finally there are the occasions and conditions in which the government has stepped in to control and even supplant the market in the performance of the economic function, suspending, limiting, or replacing the capitalist system entirely. The first two of these five forms of intervention arise from the necessary connection that exists between the political and economic orders in any society. The last three grow out of the government's function as custodian for what is often called the general interest—those values so widely shared that it is not felt amiss to express them authoritatively if need be, and to which every order of society must, in the last estimate, conform if it is to be allowed to function otherwise undisturbed. . . .

Summary. Despite the really remarkable number of points of contact between the economic and political orders in American capitalism, the general nature of them with the understandable exception of war supports our view of the United States as a thoroughly capitalist nation. By and large the market is left as the guide to production and the register of people's wants; governmental action merely supplements it and seeks to keep it from damaging excesses. The decentralization of economic power that underlies the concept of private ownership continues, although the decentralization is less than that envisioned in the theory of pure competition, and is certainly weakened by the new mixed enterprise developments in the fields of military production, aerospace, atomic power, and communications. The economic decisions of American society are still made largely outside of the political order, at least insofar as the allocation of resources to civilian production and the very important matters of prices, profits, wages, rents, and interest are concerned. Government action to affect these (including interest, through central banking operations and handling of Treasury borrowings) has remained largely permissive in nature, and despite not infrequent national emergencies caused by strikes, the temptation to substitute compulsory arbitration for the pulling and hauling of the collective bargaining process has been resisted. Finally, competition based on the expectation of gain remains as the motivating force in the economy, however much transformed by the development of the corporation, the growth of unions, and the other phenomena that have marked the evolution of capitalism.

EVALUATION OF CAPITALISM

Abundance. How well has this system succeeded in fulfilling [certain necessary economic] objectives . . . ? On the matter of abundance the answer is apparently clear: The United States has the highest per capita income of any nation in the world, clearly exceeding the others. . . .

In the second highest per capita income group is Switzerland, a small country substantially lacking in all of the specifically economic advantages of the United States (natural resources, a huge domestic market), but one that stands with the United States as a nearly completely capitalist society.

On the question of whether or not the abundance is *increasing* at what might be deemed a satisfactory rate, a more cautious answer must be given. In absolute terms, the wealth of the nation has been increasing at an irregular but impressive rate throughout the period for which good economic statistics exist. . . . The frightening decline in productivity that took place during the Depression, however, and the higher rate of increase that has marked productivity in other nations since the Second World War have caused doubts to be raised concerning the ability of the capitalist economy to sustain a high rate of growth once a rather comfortable affluence has been achieved. . . . Many nations have improved their output at higher rates since the Second World War. There are some indications, however, that tend to dispel these doubts. In the period 1960 to 1965, a new and radical upswing has been observed with an average growth rate of 4.5 percent per year for the period. Many of the trends that were supposed to account for a tapering off, specifically a decline in the rate of population growth and a drying up of new investment opportunities, have been reversed. Population in the United States, which seemed to be leveling off in the 1930s, has resumed, not merely as a result of the "baby boom" after the Second World War, but in a sustained fashion ever since. Invention and risk-taking have been spurred not only in the new fields of atomic power, electronics, and drugs, but in quite unexpected places. Such unpromising fields as cosmetics and the sale of miscellaneous articles for use in the home, including brushes, cleaning solutions, waxes, and the like, have witnessed the rapid growth of new, or previously small, firms that have had astonishing successes. Their principal techniques have not been product innovation, but improvements in marketing—an element . . . of increasing fundamental importance for the economy.

A point that might occasion surprise is the fact that the capitalist method of economic organization has not, in the United States at least, diverted an unusually large share of the growing national wealth from employees and given it to stockholders, landowners, and business proprietors. Among countries whose shares of the total national income are analyzed by the International Labour Office, the United States ranks third in the total shares given in wages and salaries and other forms of compensation to employees. As is the case with most statistics giving international comparisons, these are not reliable as to detail, but relative position shows the United States and Canada ranking at the top with the considerably more socialized United Kingdom, Sweden, and Norway.

Less impressive is the performance of the economy in extending its benefits to all segments of society. A continuing trouble spot lies in the effects of technological displacement, and this has been exacerbated in recent years by the development of automation. The new economy requires fewer workers in many industries to provide an increasing output, and it is more demanding of higher skills than it is of unskilled labor. . . .

Those without skills find it increasingly difficult to find employment, and a recently increasing rate of high school drop-outs has added to precisely this segment of the labor force. In addition, the decay of once-important employment industries such as coal mining has brought economic blight to entire regions of the country. Unemployment hovered around 5.5 percent, or four million unemployed, from 1960 to 1964, only falling below 4 percent in 1966 as a consequence of a sustained boom to which the Viet Nam war was a contributing factor. These matters have not gone unnoticed in the political order, however, and increasingly greater effort is being made to extend training to those who need it and to seek new industries for regions where old ones have declined. Under the impact of the Manpower Development Training Program, begun in 1962, Federal funds for adult vocational and technical training increased sixteenfold in three years, nearing the half-billion-dollar mark in 1965. Relief for depressed areas has been instituted, and a variety of experiments has been undertaken in the so-called war on poverty.

Looking at the broader pattern of income distribution, the picture is much brighter. There has been a distinct leveling upward, as shown in the following table:

TABLE 1

PERCENT DISTRIBUTION OF U.S. FAMILIES HAVING GIVEN MONEY INCOME IN CONSTANT (1964) DOLLARS, 1947–1964

Income Level	Percent of Families		
	1947	1955	1964
Under $3,000	31	24	18
$3,000–4,999	31	24	17
$5,000–6,999	19	24	20
$7,000–9,999	12	18	23
$10,000–14,999	}7{	8	16
$15,000 and over		2	6

Adapted from *Statistical Abstract of the United States*, 1966, Table 473, p. 337. Table lists families only, not unrelated individuals.

Put another way, the average incomes received by the lower income groups in the nation have risen at a markedly higher rate in terms of constant dollar buying power than those of the higher income groups:

TABLE 2

INCREASE IN AVERAGE FAMILY INCOME, UNITED STATES, 1935–1962

	Percent Increase in Average Income (1950 dollars)		
Rank by Size of Income	*1935/36 to 1941*	*1935/36 to 1962*	*1941 to 1962*
Lowest fifth of households	23	120	79
Second fifth of households	28	136	84
Third fifth of households	36	131	70
Fourth fifth of households	33	115	62
Highest fifth of households	18	74	48
Top 5%	13	47	30
National average	25	98	59

Adapted from *Statistical Abstract of the United States*, 1965, Table 465, p. 340.

The cause of this does not lie in the graduated income tax, which is not deducted in these figures, but reflects such factors as higher wages gained in collective bargaining and in the enforcement of minimum wage laws. In addition, there has been a decrease in the number of hours in the work week, which is a way of distributing the benefits of affluence to the lower economic strata. This decline is not paralleled as closely in the number of hours worked by responsible management personnel. Certainly, the overall performance of the capitalistic economy has not denied the promises of abundance held out for it, given the guidance that the political order has offered.

Freedom Versus Power. The objective of freedom of choice with its concomitant purpose of restraint of arbitrary power has been met only partially. Economically, the range of choice in occupation, investment, and consumer goods is unparalleled. Americans are often accused of a deadening conformity, and the example most commonly cited is the automobile. Even leaving aside all imported car styles, however, the range of choice is almost too broad. The lower price ranges of 1966 models included 57 body styles of Plymouths, 52 Fords, 50 Chevrolets, and 26 American Motors cars. To gain some idea of the magnitude of choice, Ford offered its models in 44 colors, Plymouth offered four different transmissions throughout its line, and engine choices and optional features such as air conditioning and radios made it at least conceivable that no two identical cars would be sold. It can be argued that the purpose thus served is trivial, but it is a reflection of the market principle that popular desires, as reflected in consumer buying choices, shall determine production. Capitalism responds to those desires, whether one chooses to call them trivial or not. It thus fulfills its own objectives and serves its own values possibly at a cost to values that noncapitalistic societies would prefer. It may be noted that where consumer choices do not reflect urgent public needs, the political order may still undertake to supplement them by regulation. The weakness of consumer demand for safety features in automobiles is a case in point. Congressional legislation aimed at requiring safety standards for car manufacturers sought to meet this problem in 1966.

The question of power is more disturbing. American industry displays a high degree of concentration, as does also American labor through its union organizations. Substantial agglomerations of economic, social, and political power exist in the hands of a relatively small number of managers, owners, and labor leaders, as well as in government. The number of mergers among American corporations, after a long period in which it was believed that concentration had substantially reached its limit, has begun to rise again.

The nature of the problem is apparently clear. Some five to six hundred corporations control about two thirds of American industry. Approximately 30 percent of all nonagricultural employees are members of the 130 unions affiliated with the AFL-CIO. The decisions made by these giants could thrust the economy into inflation or depression, or bring it to a halt through work stoppages or shutdowns. They make the principal decisions on the directions new investment will take. Individual firms could and sometimes do destroy the economies of cities by moving their operations elsewhere. To add to the problem, the stockholders, numerous as they are, no longer actively control their companies, and the largest stockholders, the pension funds, trusts, and insurance companies, generally refuse to exercise their voting control to hold management accountable. (If they did, they would still represent highly concentrated control.) Does this mean that these concentrations of economic power can and do control American society?

Curiously enough, it is Professor [Adolf A.] Berle . . . who supplies the negative answer. Restraint of economic power comes partly from the fact that it is not monolithic—that within the economic realm in markets, wage negotiations, and the like, power is restrained by countervailing power, overseen by government agencies that attempt to see to it that no one achieves a monopoly of any form of power. More important, however, is the central fact of capitalism itself, the separation of the institutions for wielding economic power from the institutions of government that wield political and military power. Berle likens this to the separation of powers in the American Constitution. People whose demands are not heeded in the economic order can make them heard in the political order, as the catalogue of government restrictions, regulations, and interventions . . . has shown. The economic giants operate within the framework of what he calls a "public consensus" of which, however indefinite may be its prescriptions, they are most clearly aware. That consensus establishes limits that serve to confine the exercise of economic power largely to the purposes for which it was established: the pursuit of economic growth. When those limits have been violated, that consensus has been enforced by government through revision or reinterpretation of the law, and neither corporate managers nor the labor union officials can and do ignore it. Experiences such as the seizure of the steel mills by President Truman in 1952 and government intervention in the railway labor dispute in the 1960s indicate that neither labor nor management will be allowed to use its power in a way that will interrupt the basic flow of economic activity. Increasing evidences exist that corporate managements, particularly the managements of the larger corporations, are actively concerned with their social responsibility in the performance of their corporate functions, however much they might privately wish that this were not added to their other cares. The readiness with which American industry responded in 1965 to President Johnson's call for a limitation on foreign spending to help the balance of payments suggests a combination of willingness to accept responsibility and a fear that it will otherwise be enforced. Similar calls to both labor and management to avoid inflationary wage and price rises have been given increasing attention as the willingness of government to follow up a voluntary request with firm action has been demonstrated.

An area in which this pattern of separation and restraint is weakest is the troublesome one of the aerospace industries, atomic research and development, and the other elements of the "civil-military complex." Here there is a power problem that has not been solved, and it is notable that one of the elements of difficulty is its involvement in the international competition for scientific prestige and the military demand for secrecy. . . . War is no friend to capitalism, and cold war is not different from "hot war" in that respect. The absence of separation between the two orders in this field is, however, the underlying problem and although it is largely confined to one sector of the economy, that sector is the most rapidly advancing one in technology. The political processes in the United States are not accustomed to this burden of responsibility, but they will need to develop effective checks over this growing cluster of power.

If, in capitalism, government is a restraint on economic power, so also do economic organizations serve to restrain governmental power. Through the organization of interest groups and the mobilization of popular support, business and labor both can, on occasion, veto contemplated government action. The veto plays a large role in political activity under capitalism, especially in America. The American political system facilitates its use by its own fragmentation. A veto is, however, a characteristic expression of capitalism's presumption against any increase in government activity above the level already undertaken.

But the limitation of governmental power does not take place only through lobbying. It occurs through the electoral system and public opinion as well. The funds exist to oppose the government of the day, and the private media of communications are at least as often critical of public officials as not. No power center is, in fact, safe from the possibility of attack by critics financed out of funds accumulated in private enterprise. Not so long ago great foundations that bear some of the illustrious names from American industrial history—Rockefeller, Ford, and Carnegie among them—were subjected to congressional investigation on the grounds that they were supporting research and writing that was sharply critical (and alleged to be subversive) of the American political system and the economic system as well. It is through their support of the foundations and of great private universities where academic freedom is held sacred, and through the individual support of unpopular and even unlikely causes, that capitalist managers and owners help maintain a climate of critical discussion that holds the state accountable for its actions, and holds the wielders of economic power themselves accountable also.

The goal of freedom is, then, not badly served, although there is far less decentralization of power than might have been expected at the start. The political order, too, plays a much greater role in preserving that freedom than was suggested in the outline with which we began.

Rewards and Recognition. The least measurable of all of the objectives of capitalism is that of reward according to merit, for merit is an ethical standard and will be judged on a slightly different basis by each observer. What can be measured is the degree to which capitalist society affords opportunities for workers to change jobs and rise to higher (or fall to lower) occupations. In this, American experience is impressive. Of all men twenty-five to sixty-four years old in the active labor force in 1962, less than one quarter were in the same occupational class as their fathers. Even more striking is the fact that nearly three quarters of them had changed their occupational category since their first jobs. . . . There is literally no limit to the possible rise or fall of an American worker. Some of those who began their working careers in even the lowest occupational categories rose to the top of the occupational hierarchy, and some who began at the top ended as common laborers. In most cases only a small minority of those who started in a given job remained there. American mobility rates are not . . . markedly different from those in other countries at a comparable level of industrialization. However, that they are as high as they are suggests not only a system that discriminates on the basis of ability rather than heredity, but one in which positions of leadership, and therefore of power, are not likely to remain in the same families from generation to generation. The immediate *cause* of high mobility is apparently industrialization, but the significant finding here is that, contrary to the claims of Marxists, capitalism does not stifle mobility under a rigid class structure.

Further substantiation of mobility in American life, and an indication that it is, if anything, increasing, comes from a comparison of the education of fathers and sons in 1962. In that year, 43 percent of men fifty-five to sixty-four years old exceeded the educational level of their fathers, while 62 percent of the younger group, twenty-five to thirty-four years old, did so. Because education correlates closely with earnings and occupational level, this change is most significant. The occupational figures are statistical indications only and do not prove that merit was the principal cause for occupational rise and fall. However, the conclusion is not unreasonable that the capitalist system of the United States does meet the test of providing wide opportunities very well. . . .

The Irrational System

Paul A. Baran and Paul M. Sweezy

It is of the essence of capitalism that both goods and labor power are typically bought and sold on the market. In such a society relations among individuals are dominated by the principle of the exchange of equivalents, of *quid pro quo*, not only in economic matters but in all other aspects of life as well.

Not that the principle of equivalent exchange is or ever has been universally practiced in capitalist society. As Marx showed so convincingly in the closing chapters of the first volume of *Capital*, the primary accumulation of capital was effected through violence and plunder, and the same methods continue in daily use throughout capitalism's dependent colonies and semi-colonies. Nevertheless the ideological sway of *quid pro quo* became all but absolute. In their relations with each other and in what they teach those over whom they rule, capitalists are fully committed to the principle of *quid pro quo*, both as a guide to action and as a standard of morality.

This commitment reflected an important step forward in the development of the forces of production and in the evolution of human consciousness. Only on the basis of equivalent exchange was it possible to realize the more rational utilization of human and material resources which has been the central achievement of capitalism. At the same time, it must never be forgotten that the rationality of *quid pro quo* is specifically capitalist rationality which at a certain stage of development becomes incompatible with the underlying forces and relations of production. To ignore this and to treat *quid pro quo* as a

From *Paul A. Baran and Paul M. Sweezy*, Monopoly Capital (*New York: Monthly Review Press, 1966*). *Reprinted by permission of Monthly Review Press. Copyright* © *1966 by Paul M. Sweezy.*

universal maxim of rational conduct is in itself an aspect of bourgeois ideology, just as the radical-sounding assertion that under socialism exchange of equivalents can be immediately dispensed with betrays a utopian view of the nature of the economic problems faced by a socialist society.

But even during the life span of capitalism itself, *quid pro quo* breaks down as a rational principle of economic and social organization. The giant corporation withdraws from the sphere of the market large segments of economic activity and subjects them to scientifically designed administration. This change represents a continuous increase in the rationality of the parts of the system, but it is not accompanied by any rationalization of the whole. On the contrary, with commodities being priced not according to their costs of production but to yield the maximum possible profit, the principle of *quid pro quo* turns into the opposite of a promoter of rational economic organization and instead becomes a formula for maintaining scarcity in the midst of potential plenty. Human and material resources remain idle because there is in the market no *quid* to exchange against the *quo* of their potential output. And this is true even though the real cost of such output would be nil. In the most advanced capitalist country a large part of the population lives in abysmal poverty while in the underdeveloped countries hundreds of millions suffer from disease and starvation because there is no mechanism for effecting an exchange of what they could produce for what they so desperately need. Insistence on the inviolability of equivalent exchange when what is to be exchanged costs nothing, strict economizing of resources when a large proportion of them goes to waste— these are obviously the very denial of the rationality which the concept of value and the principle of *quid pro quo* originally expressed.

The obsolescence of such central categories of bourgeois thought is but one symptom of the profoundly contradictory nature of monopoly capitalism, of the ever sharpening conflict between the rapidly advancing rationalization of the actual processes of production and the undiminished *elementality* of the system as a whole. This conflict affects all aspects of society. While rationality has been conquering ever new areas of consciousness, the inability of bourgeois thought to comprehend the development of society as a whole has remained essentially unchanged, a faithful mirror of the continuing elementality and irrationality of the capitalist order itself.

Social reality is therefore conceived in outlived, topsy-turvy, and fetishistic terms. Powerless to justify an irrational and inhuman social order and unable to answer the increasingly urgent questions which it poses, bourgeois ideology clings to concepts that are anachronistic and moribund. Its bankruptcy manifests itself not so much in the generation of new fetishes and half-truths as in the stubborn upholding of old fetishes and half-truths which now turn into blatant lies. And the more these old fetishes and half-truths lose whatever truth content they once possessed the more insistently they are hammered, like advertising slogans, into the popular consciousness.

The claim that the United States economy is a "free enterprise" system is a case in point. At no time was enterprise really free in the sense that anyone who wanted to could start a business of his own. Still the concept conveyed an important aspect of the truth by pointing up the difference between the relative freedom of competitive capitalism on the one hand and the restrictions imposed by the guild system and the mercantilist state on the other. Having long ago lost this limited claim to truthfulness and referring as it now does to the freedom of giant corporations to exercise undisturbed their vast monopoly powers, "free enterprise" has turned into a shibboleth devoid of all descriptive or explanatory validity.

Of a similar nature is the incessant repetition that the political regime in the United States today is a democracy. In the United States, as in all other capitalist countries, the propertyless masses have never been in a position to determine the conditions of their lives or the policies of the nation's government. Nevertheless as long as democracy meant the overthrow of monarchial despotism and the ascent to power of a relatively numerous bourgeoisie, the term focused attention on a major change in the life of society. But what is left of this truth content in a society in which a tiny oligarchy resting on vast economic power and in full control of society's political and cultural apparatus makes all the important political decisions? Clearly the claim that such a society is democratic serves to conceal, not to reveal, the truth. . . .

Adam Smith saw in the division of labor the key to the wealth of nations, and he was of course right. Many before and after him saw a darker side, and they were right too. In Marx's words, "the division of labor seizes upon not only the economic but every other sphere of society and everywhere lays the foundation of that all-engrossing system of specializing and sorting men, that development in a man of one single faculty at the expense of all other faculties, which caused A. Ferguson, the master of Adam Smith, to exclaim: 'We make a nation of helots and have no free citizens.' ". . .

Marx thought that such a high degree of labor productivity could be realized only in a "higher stage of communist society." We can now see that this was an illusion, that from the point of view of raising the productivity of labor, capitalism had a much greater potential than Marx, or for that matter contemporary bourgeois social scientists, imagined. The giant corporation has proved to be an unprecedentedly effective instrument for promoting science and technology and for harnessing them to the production of goods and services. In the United States today the means already exist for overcoming poverty, for supplying everyone with the necessities and conveniences of life, for giving to all a genuinely rounded education and the free time to develop their faculties to the full—in a word for escaping from that all-engrossing system of specializing and sorting men of which Marx wrote.

In fact, of course, nothing of the sort has happened. Men are still being specialized and sorted, imprisoned in the narrow cells prepared for them by the division of labor, their faculties stunted and their minds diminished. And a threat to their security and peace of mind which already loomed large in Marx's day has grown in direct proportion to the spreading incidence and accelerated speed of technological change under monopoly capitalism. . . .

"There is," Paul Goodman writes, " 'nearly full employment' (with highly significant exceptions), but there get to be fewer jobs that are necessary and unquestionably useful; that require energy and draw on some of one's best capacities; and that can be done keeping one's honor and dignity." Goodman is certainly right to stress that this "simple objective fact" is important in explaining the troubles of young people in this society. But it is more than that: it is important in explaining the alienation from work, the cynicism, the corruption which permeate every nook and cranny of monopoly capitalism and which anyone with a sense of history cannot fail to recognize as characteristic features of a society in full decline.

Asked if he liked his job, one of John Updike's characters replied, "Hell, it wouldn't be a job if I liked it." All but a tiny minority of specially lucky or privileged workers would undoubtedly agree. There is nothing inherently interesting about most of the narrowly sub-divided tasks which workers are obliged to perform; and with the purpose of the job at best obscure and at worst humanly degrading, the worker can find no satisfaction in what his efforts accomplish. As far as he is concerned, the one justification is the paycheck.

The paycheck is the key to whatever gratifications are allowed to working people in this society: such self-respect, status, and recognition by one's fellows as can be achieved depend primarily on the possession of material objects. The worker's house, the model of his automobile, his wife's clothes—all assume major significance as indexes of success or failure. And yet within the existing social framework these objects of consumption increasingly lose their capacity to satisfy. Forces similar to those which destroy the worker's identification with his work lead to the erosion of his self-identification as a consumer. With goods being sought for their status-bearing qualities, the drive to substitute the newer and more expensive for the older and cheaper ceases to be related to the serviceability of the goods and becomes a means of climbing up a rung on the social ladder.

In this way consumption becomes a sort of extension and continuation of the process of earning a livelihood. Just as the worker is always under pressure to get ahead at the expense of his fellows at the shop or office, so the consumer pursues the same goals at the expense of his neighbors after work. Neither worker nor consumer is ever really satisfied; they are always on the lookout for a new job, always wanting to move to a better neighborhood. Work and consumption thus share the same ambiguity: while fulfilling the basic needs of survival, they increasingly lose their inner content and meaning.

Nor are matters any better when it comes to another aspect of the worker's non-work life—the expenditure of leisure time. Leisure has traditionally been thought of as serving the purpose of "recreation," that is to say the revival and refocusing of mental and psychic energies from their compulsory commitment to work to genuinely interesting pursuits. Now, however, the function of leisure undergoes a change. As Erich Fromm has observed, leisure becomes a synonym of time spent in passivity, of idleness. It no longer signifies doing what a person *wants* to do, as distinct from doing, at work, what he *must* do; to an ever-increasing extent it means simply doing nothing. And the reason for doing nothing is partly that there is so little that is humanly interesting to do, but perhaps even more because the emptiness and purposelessness of life in capitalist society stifles the desire to do anything.

This propensity to do nothing has had a decisive part in determining the kinds of entertainment which are supplied to fill the leisure hour—in the evenings, on weekends and holidays, during vacations. The basic principle is that whatever is presented—reading matter, movies, radio and TV programs—must not make undue demands on the intellectual and emotional resources of the recipients: the purpose is to provide "fun," "relaxation," a "good time"—in short, passively absorbable amusement. Even the form and organization of the material is affected. The show is continuous, the movie theater can be entered at any time; the book can be read from front to back or from back to front; skipping a few installments of a serial does not matter; the TV can be switched from channel to channel without loss of coherence or comprehension.

Other forms of "killing time"—what a revealing expression!—are hardly more exacting. Being a sports fan does not involve participation in any activity or acquiring any skill. Events are provided for all seasons, and it is not even necessary to attend in person since giant corporations find it a profitable form of advertising to sponsor radio and TV broadcasts of games and matches. Elaborate statistical records are compiled and regularly published in specialized books and periodicals, enabling even fans who have never played a game in their lives to discuss the various teams and players with all the assurance of experts. Being interested at different times of the year in the sports appropriate to the season turns into something people have in common. Like the largely imaginary good and bad points of different makes and models of automobiles, the strengths and weaknesses of teams and players become topics of conversation which the inherent triviality of the theme transforms into mere chatter. . . .

With the increasing specialization and rationalization of the part processes of the capitalist economy, calculation has come to pervade all aspects of life. The individual is pressed from the very beginning into one of the available prefabricated molds—depending on the social class and stratum to which he, or rather his family, belongs—and the normal outcome is a standardized, rationalized human product systematically checked by means of statistical quality controls administered by innumerable testing services from nursery school on. This "product's" reactions and responses become increasingly automatic and predictable. Smiling is to be expected from receptionists and airline hostesses, from sales clerks and gas station attendants—regardless of their mood, their physical condition, their attitude toward the other party. A sustained display of cheerfulness is a necessity in dealing with workers and employees, suppliers and customers—equally regardless of the content and meaning of these dealings as such. Similarly, whether a person, a landscape, a musical composition is judged beautiful depends not on its specific characteristics but on its market success, relation to the latest fad, cost, newness, its capacity to purvey "fun" and "relaxation." . . .

Behind the emptiness, the degradation, and the suffering which poison human existence in this society lies the profound irrationality and moral bankruptcy of monopoly capitalism itself. No outraged protests, no reforms within the monopoly capitalist framework can arrest the decay of the whole. And as becomes clearer every day, this decay makes increasingly problematical the rationality of even the most spectacular advances in scientific knowledge and technical and organizational skills. Improvements in the means of mass communication merely hasten the degeneration of popular culture. The utmost perfection in the manufacture of weapons of destruction does not make their production rational. The irrationality of the end negates all improvements of the means. Rationality itself becomes irrational. We have reached a point where the only true rationality lies in action to overthrow what has become a hopelessly irrational system.

Will such action be forthcoming in sufficient volume and intensity to accomplish its purpose? The future of the United States and of monopoly capitalism obviously depends on the answer. So also, though more indirectly, does the future of mankind itself for a long time to come.

The answer of traditional Marxian orthodoxy—that the industrial proletariat must eventually rise in revolution against its capitalist oppressors—no longer carries conviction. Industrial workers are a diminishing minority of the American working class, and their organized cores in the basic industries have to a large extent been integrated into the system as consumers and ideologically conditioned members of the society. They are not, as the industrial workers were in Marx's day, the system's special victims, though they suffer from its elementality and irrationality along with all other classes and strata—more than some, less than others.

The system of course has its special victims. They are the unemployed and the unemployable, the migrant farm workers, the inhabitants of the big city ghettos, the school dropouts, the aged subsisting on meager pensions—in a word, the outsiders, those who because of their limited command over purchasing power are unable to avail themselves of the gratifications, such as they are, of consumption. But these groups, despite their impressive numbers, are too heterogeneous, too scattered and fragmented, to constitute a coherent force in society. And the oligarchy knows how, through doles and handouts, to keep them divided and to prevent their becoming a lumpen-proletariat of desperate starvelings.

If we confine attention to the inner dynamics of advanced monopoly capitalism, it is hard to avoid the conclusion that the prospect of effective revolutionary action to overthrow the system is slim. Viewed from this angle, the more likely course of development would seem to be a continuation of the present process of decay, with the contradiction between the compulsions of the system and the elementary needs of human nature becoming ever more insupportable. The logical outcome would be the spread of increasingly severe psychic disorders leading to the impairment and eventual breakdown of the system's ability to function even on its own terms.

QUESTIONS FOR DISCUSSION

1. *In what ways does Preston believe that, overall, American capitalism has proved to be a highly productive and workable economic system? Do you agree? Why or why not?*
2. *Does the article by Baran and Sweezy contradict any points raised by Preston?*
3. *What is the basis of Baran's and Sweezy's conclusion that the system is irrational? What do they mean by "irrational"?*
4. *Implicit in the Preston article is the assumption that, overall, American capitalism has proved to be highly adaptable. Do you think it will eventually adapt to the criticisms of Baran and Sweezy? Need it adapt to these charges?*

The Working of Markets

PART THREE

Is Business Getting Too Big?

Although conventional economic analysis elaborates a theory of pure competition, few economists would hold that the theory has any literal application in describing the structure and organization of American business enterprise. The competitive model provides us only with a yardstick by which we can judge or compare real market behavior. Without many exceptions (realistically, we should say without *any*), the American business system is dominated by large units of production and by market arrangements which abridge any theory of pure competition. Strictly speaking, this is not a recent development. The tendency toward combination and "bigness" has been basic to the structure of the American economic system from its very beginnings. Nevertheless, this tendency has never quite been reconciled with the American political and economic ethic of individualism and "free" enterprise, and probably no contemporary economic issue has been debated by economists and other social scientists, as well as politicians and ordinary citizens, for such a long period of time. The charge of excessive business concentration had its origin in the era of the trusts at the close of the nineteenth century, grew to a shrill cry during the progressive administrations of Theodore Roosevelt, Taft, and Wilson, and was, from the public's point of view, most popular during Franklin Roosevelt's New Deal.

Over the years an impressive array of antimonopoly legislation has been written into law for the alleged purpose of controlling "bigness." Both its effectiveness and its desirability are frequently challenged and, at any rate, it is certain that this legislation has not halted the tendency toward "bigness." Between 1909 and 1928, the two hundred largest United States corporations grew two and a half times faster than all others; and between 1947 and 1958, their share of value added to product by manufacturing grew from 30 percent to 38 percent. Since

1960, mergers have been proceeding at an average rate of nearly two thousand per year.

Despite the awesome evidence of "bigness" in American business, it is important to answer two further questions before condemning it. First, is the concentration of market power, as distinct from the number of mergers, actually increasing? And, second, does bigness *ipso facto* mean evidence of "badness"?

To the first question, there is no easy answer. Economists have constructed a number of models in examining this question and have reached a number of different conclusions as to whether there is significantly increasing concentration of market power. On the second question, the article by the late Senator Estes Kefauver holds that monopoly behavior in the auto industry has meant considerable hardship for the American consumer. While this article contends that "bigness" is growing and it is undesirable, the second article, a well-known piece by the late Sumner H. Slichter, is a defense of bigness in business. The last article, by the Federal Reserve Bank of Cleveland, notes "official" concern with the new wave of conglomerate mergers.

Clearly these articles do not exhaust the rather immense question posed here, but they are a beginning toward arriving at an understanding of the issues involved.

Monopoly and Waste

Senator Estes Kefauver

THE EXTENT OF CONCENTRATION

Of this country's major industries, automobile manufacture represents the apex in economic concentration. In recent years the four largest companies producing passenger cars have accounted for about 99 percent of the output. Even this figure does not reveal the full extent of the concentration that exists. In 1963, one company produced over half of the cars manufactured in the United States. General Motors' share in 1963 was about 53 percent, as contrasted with 26 percent for Ford, 14 percent for Chrysler, and 6 percent for American Motors.

In terms of new car registrations, this general relationship is only slightly different when imports are considered. In 1963 General Motors had about 51 percent of U.S. sales. Ford had 25 percent, Chrysler, 12 percent, and American Motors, about 6 percent. The remaining 6 percent was divided among Studebaker, Checker, and, particularly, foreign imports.

This structural imbalance is relatively new. In 1921 there were 88 firms in the automobile industry. This was the era that E. B. White, the noted essayist, termed "paradise" for the consuming public. "Thirty or forty years ago, when a man wanted a car, he had a fabulous assortment to choose from—everything from a jackrabbit to a bearcat. Big cars, medium-size cars, cheap cars, expensive cars, moderate-priced cars, high cars, low cars, open cars, closed cars, gas cars, steam cars, electric cars; it was paradise." In those days the new industry was in the throes of creation, and a vigorous competitive and experimental spirit characterized its activities.

As compared with the situation today, prices varied enormously. In late 1923 a Ford Model T touring car could be purchased for $380; the Chevrolet Superior and Overland 91 models were going for around $500. The Maxwell, Dort, and Studebaker—each produced by an independent company—were priced at around $1000. Touring cars such as the Hudson, Hupmobile, and Willys-Knight were a little more, but were still under $1500. Another group, including the Marmon and the Cadillac, were in the $3000 range. Then, for the more affluent of our society, there were such showcases as the Duesenberg and the Pierce-Arrow in the $5000 class.

The sedan, which was just coming into vogue, was also available in a wide price range. The Ford Model T was the lowest priced, selling for $685. Chevrolet and Overland models were available for $795. A number of cars—including Oakland, Cleveland, Buick, Gardner, and Jewett—were in the $1500 range. Then came the Hudson and Chalmers, selling for around $2000; and from there, there was a steady climb to such models as the Lafayette for $6500 and the Duesenberg for $7500.

In those days rivalry among auto manufacturers occurred on all fronts. Not only was there unremitting effort, through improved engineering and design, to provide greater comfort, safety, reliability and performance; there was also intense price competition, resulting in good part from the aggressive competitive behavior of Henry Ford. In 1909 the Ford touring car was selling for $950; by 1912 the price had been reduced to $600; and by 1916 it was available for $360. World War I sent the price up again to around $600, but by 1920 a sagging economy resulted in a sharp curtailment of automobiles sales and Ford announced drastic price cuts on his products. The touring car was reduced from $575 to $440, the sedan from $975 to $795.

The first response of his competitors was hostile. Several—including General Motors, Dodge, Hudson, Maxwell-Chalmers, and Paige—took the position that sales are not stimulated by price reductions. Buyers, it was argued, would suspend purchases, waiting for even further reductions. Henry Ford was unconvinced: "It was said that we were disturbing conditions," Ford is reported to have remarked later; "that is exactly what we were trying to do."

At one time it appeared that the extraordinary Seldon patent could be used to curb this business revolutionary. As early as 1879, George B. Selden, as enterprising patent attorney in Rochester, New York, filed a patent application on the entire automobile. At this time the automobile was in a state of embryonic development; numerous European and American inventors, professional and amateur, were making improvements in the construction and arrangement of components. Specific patents were being secured on the new combinations, but none of these inventors attempted to secure a patent on the entire vehicle in the belief that the concept was so well known as to be in the public domain.

A patent would have served little purpose in 1879, since the automobile had not yet reached the stage of profitable commercial production. By a series of delays and intricate maneuvers in handling his patent application, Selden managed to prolong the proceedings for 16 years in the Patent Office. Then in 1895—to the vast astonishment of the burgeoning automobile industry—Selden received a patent. An alliance was quickly formed between the patentee and a group of Eastern financiers who saw in the patent an opportunity to impose private monopoly control over a new, swiftly growing industry. One by one the automobile manufacturers succumbed to pressure and secured a license under the Selden patent; such licenses contained production limitations as well as price-fixing requirements.

In 1903, Ford made application for a license but was refused. His continuance in the industry resulted in the institution of an infringement action under the Selden patent. The legal battle, which lasted for eight years, ended in victory for Ford, and the industry was freed to develop in a competitive environment. Perhaps in consequence of this litigative history, the automobile industry was one of the first to recognize the problems created by a mass of patents in separate hands on an interlocked technology. Very early, therefore, the industry established a patent pool under which patents were freely licensed to all comers.

During most of the period from World War I to the depression of the early 1930's, Ford was the leading producer. The cause was not difficult to find. Not only were the Ford cars lowest in price; they had an established reputation for reliability. As one historian remarked, "Nobody ever called the Model T handsome, much less beautiful; nobody ever rhapsodized over its silhouette; nobody ever praised its comfort. It could plow through bogs, surmount hills, skitter along slopes, and take stumps and rocks in its stride. Summer cloudbursts and winter blizzards merely gave it stronger heart."

By the beginning of the 1930's, Ford's position as leader was in jeopardy. In 1929, Ford and General Motors each held about a third of the market;

in 1930, Ford's share rose to over 40 percent. This was its last year as the country's top producer. In 1931 General Motors took the lead with 43 percent—never to lose it again. Throughout this period it became increasingly clear that the public wanted something more than sheer utility. Given the choice between an economic and dependable but rather ungainly Ford and a Chevrolet which, for a hundred dollars more, offered not only a better appearance but greater speed and better transmission, cooling, lubrication, ignition, and springs, the public was willing to pay the added price.

General Motors was well equipped to take command of the automobile industry. As early as 1917, when the company was in financial difficulties, the duPont Company had made substantial investments in General Motors and even, for a time, assumed responsibility for the financial policies of the automobile company. In the relationship of these two companies reciprocity in buying and selling was developed into a fine art, for each of these giant corporations manufactures products that are useful to the other. The effect, of course, is to provide, on the one hand, assured markets for certain products; and, on the other, assured sources of supply. Large quantities of goods are removed from the marketplace; the flow is channeled exclusively between the parties, and outsiders are denied access to the market. It was in this context—its effect upon competition—that the Antitrust Division sought and recently secured severance of the partnership between duPont and General Motors in the courts. Undoubtedly, one of the consequences of this corporate alliance was to provide General Motors with the financial resources to assert its dominance in the automobile industry.

Indeed, its association with duPont was a significant element in the development of General Motors as one of the world's greatest conglomerate concerns. Regularly, in the *Fortune* listing of the 500 Largest Industrial Corporations, this company has ranked first, with annual sales now in excess of 15 billion dollars. The Subcommittee's report on the automobile industry in 1958 shows that approximately 35 percent of all sales—then 11 billion dollars—involved activities *other than* the manufacture and sale of passenger cars and trucks. This contrasts markedly with the situation for Ford and Chrysler. Of Ford's total sales of 5.6 billion dollars, only 18 percent—1.2 billion dollars—involved areas other than the manufacture of passenger cars and trucks. In the case of Chrysler, the smallest of the "Big Three," with annual sales of about 2 billion dollars, almost all of that figure came from automobile manufacture.

Most of General Motors' widespread activities appear to be confined to industries in which the degree of concentration is relatively high and in which the company itself ranks among the top producers. It is one of the four largest companies producing diesel engines, trucks and truck tractors, motor buses, railroad locomotives and switchers, bicycles, and aircraft engines and propellers.

It is a major producer of household refrigerators, service and household machines, cast-iron heating boilers, household electric ranges, and the like. And it is, of course, a leading supplier of equipment and parts for these products.

A question of particular interest to the Subcommittee during the hearings was the manner in which this vast economic power has been used. For example, were profits enjoyed in a sheltered market used to subsidize losses in more competitive areas? In these latter industries, were prices deliberately driven down to such levels that smaller firms were forced out of business? What devices were employed to discipline competitors whose activities were confined to just one industry? In a word, how does a giant conglomerate, with substantial monopoly power in some industries, throw its weight around in the competitive areas in which it operates?

The answer of General Motors' officials provided little clarification. Information showing a breakdown of profits by operating divisions was held to be "confidential." Subsequent to the hearings a statement was filed by the company to clarify testimony by its officials, but was phrased in such generalities as to intensify, if anything, the confusion that already existed. The net result was to suggest that, insofar as General Motors was concerned, its actual exercise of the vast economic power in its hands was a sensitive subject that preferably should remain undiscussed.

Over and beyond its conglomerate operations are other important sources of General Motors' dominance in the automotive field. It has a strong dealer organization embracing the largest number of dealerships of any automobile company in the world. Its advertising and sales efforts are unparalleled. It has been a beneficiary of substantial Government contracts, both for production and for research and development work. Because of the manner in which used car prices are arrived at, the prices of GM used cars—and, thus, their "trade-in" values—are higher than the comparable models of its competitors. This, of course, greatly aids dealers in swelling the sales of new GM cars. Any catalog of the operations of GM should also include General Motors Acceptance Corporation, the wholly owned automobile financing company. The auto finance company is the most costly way of financing the purchase of a car; its "6 percent add-on finance charge" over a three-year period adds up to an interest rate of over 11 percent annually. For the ten-year period 1950–60, GMAC's net profit, after taxes, regularly exceeded 15 percent.

THE STRANGE PATTERN OF COMPETITION

The imbalance between General Motors and its smaller competitors determines the competitive pattern in the automobile industry. A single event will highlight the present scene. In the fall of 1956, rumors were abroad in the industry that prices on the 1957 models would be increased 5 to 7 percent to help maintain "a competitive pricing position for higher cost producers such as Chrysler, American Motors, and Studebaker-Packard." However, the first announcement was made by Ford, and the average increase was only 2.9 percent. At the time a Ford representative explained that the increases were "no more than our actual costs for materials and labor have gone up." Two weeks later General Motors announced its prices on its new Chevrolet models only. The average price increases amounted to 6.1 percent. Ford waited one week, and then revised its prices upward to be in line with those of General Motors. With the situation clarified, Chrysler then made its announcement of prices which conformed to those of its larger rivals.

This episode illustrates the almost complete replacement of price competition with price leadership accompanied by non-price competition. In autos as in steel, lesser companies may make the first announcement of a price increase, but it does not become effective until the leader acts. . . .

CAR FANCIFICATION—COMPETITIVE WASTE

The disappearance of price competition has engendered the socially wasteful competition embodied in annual style changes. To an extent unparalleled by any other durable goods industry, this type of rivalry represents a concerted, unrelenting effort to make quickly obsolescent a product which, by its very nature, is designed to give service for many years. To convert a durable type of consumer product into an ephemeral perishable of fashion is a difficult art. Every conceivable form of pressure and inducement is invoked to make the consumer dissatisfied with his old car while it is still a useful instrument of transportation. An endless stream of "improvements" is presented which have little or no real significance insofar as the public is concerned. Each new offering, however, is hailed as "revolutionary," and every advertising device is skillfully employed to shame the consumer into discarding his current automobile in the interest of presenting a more prosperous appearance to the world with the latest automotive fashion.

A number of experts appearing before the Subcommittee stressed the unsuitability of the automobile as a style guide. Dr. Ruby Turner Morris, in remarking that the annual model changes are "wasteful of our natural resources," stated that "Automotive engineers themselves must regret when perfectly good dies, capable of putting out millions of more excellent cars, have to be thrown in the dust heap as a sacrifice to the great god of fashion and change for change's sake." Indeed, one of the difficulties involved in annual change is that no company can anticipate all of the problems that arise when a pilot model is translated into a mass-produced product; some "bugs" are inevitable. Where the model is kept standard for some years, design errors or mechanical defects can be corrected. Under the present system, however, there is little incentive to make these corrections, particularly if they involve substantial alterations in jigs or dies, because in a few months the equipment will be discarded for a different model.

In consequence, it is not surprising that many experts feel there has been actual deterioration in the quality of cars now being produced. In part, this has been due to the fact that emphasis on styling is so dominant that function is sacrificed. Speaking on this point, the automotive consultant of Consumers Union, a testing service for consumers, remarked that it often appears that "modern styling was created only to hinder both car and driver." He added that "when a styling feature vies with a practical feature, or a safety feature, styling usually wins."

As an example he cited the fact that, back in 1937, Chrysler had the idea of flattening off the dashboard by recessing all knobs. This important safety feature did not, however, survive the vicissitudes of new styling changes. Most of the new cars of today are characterized by highly decorative dashboards containing protruding objects which are a hazard to front-seat occupants.

Industrial designers frequently draw a distinction between style and innovation. The stylist is concerned with superficial changes to give the appearance of newness where the reality is absent. Innovation occurs when advances take place which affect both the product itself and its visual appearance. In the latter instance there is genuine progress when the two essential factors—function and style—are combined. The problem faced by the stylist is that he has a limited palette; the number of acceptable variations can easily be exhausted, and little by little he is pushed into creating ridiculous changes. In the automobile industry this has been reflected in the rise and fall of fins, the multitudinous lighting components, gingerbread chrome and glitter, bucket seats, ornate but functionless bumpers with protruding lights, and the like.

The cost of annual model changes can only be described as staggering. Recently a trio of college professors presented to the American Economic Association a paper on the costs of automobile model changes in recent years. For the five-year period 1956–60, they estimated that these changes contributed about 25 percent to the average price of four-door sedans currently available in the market. Over-all expenditures for the entire industry for model changes amounted to about 3.9 billion dollars annually during this period.

But this is not the whole story. Accompanying the annual model changes has been the horsepower race which started in the early 1950's. The ever-larger power plants have necessitated bigger and heavier cars; this situation, in turn, has created greater expense which is not exhausted with purchase of the car but is expended throughout its life. Important among these is increased gasoline consumption. These economists estimated that the owner of the average 1956–60 car pays for gasoline about $40 more per 10,000 miles than would have been necessary if models had remained constant as of the period just prior to the horsepower race. This represents another 20 percent increase in total gasoline costs, or an additional annual expenditure of about 968 million dollars. And this increased cost is bound to continue during the useful lives of the existing stock of cars. For all cars built through 1961 the economic team estimated that the cost to the public of additional gasoline consumption would run to about 7.1 billion dollars.

Altogether, their estimates of costs of model changes run to about 5 billion dollars annually over the 1956–60 period, as compared with the prehorse-power-race years of 1949 or 1950. And they emphasize that these figures are, if anything, underestimates. No attempt was made to assess the higher costs to the public of repair bills and replacement parts, the added costs arising out of the increased use of highly skilled mechanics and the complex tools made necessary by the huge automotive mechanisms, and the frightful expense involved in the repair of bodywork damage. Nor, of course, could any monetary values be placed upon the heavy social costs arising out of the parking problems created by these larger vehicles in areas already heavily congested. . . .

In the course of the 1958 automobile hearings, General Motors officials expressed great pride in the "styling leadership" of their company. At one time, major style changes involving some advances in technology were made every four or five years; intervening years were marked by superficial "face lifts" designed to give the appearance of change. Under the leadership of General Motors, however, this period has been shortened until now the companies boast of completely new models each year. Alone among the major manufacturers, GM has the financial resources to play this costly game successfully—a game which both Ford and Chrysler have felt compelled to follow. According to Mr. Romney of American Motors, this situation developed after the postwar period when the two companies could easily have been eliminated from the industry; in an effort to solve their dilemma "they simply. adopted the GM product philosophy, and the result is all three of them began to build products based on the same product idea." This was not conspiracy, he thought; GM's competitors were simply doing "what the champ had done" with proved success.

Neither the officials of Ford nor those of Chrysler revealed much enthusiasm for the annual style change. Mr. Yntema of Ford explained simply that his company had no choice; it would like to lower tooling and other costs but when "the competition" comes out with a new model, Ford is compelled to do likewise or lose business. Chrysler officials took the same view; if their company presented the same car year after year "when General Motors or Ford or both of them are changing to new cars each year, you'd pretty soon be out of business." Thus both feel themselves caught in a real dilemma. Major model changes are necessary to maintain sales, yet the staggering costs such changes entail are a threat to the companies' continuing survival.

At the time of the Subcommittee's hearings in 1958, the new compacts had yet to make their appearance. However, foreign imports of small cars were making threatening inroads in the United States market. From 1 percent of new passenger car registrations in 1955, the figure for this group had risen to over 5 percent by 1958 and was to reach 6½ percent in 1959. Yet American cars, bigger and fancier, were being produced each year. Who dictated these styles? Who decreed the social waste involved in the enormous expenditures for annual model changes?

General Motors' response was prompt. "Fancification," said the president of GM (and he used that term), "is the result of the demand on the part of the public." When asked whether the consumer took the initiative or was receptive to auto companies' advertising, he replied, "I would say that the customer now has the pressure on us to make changes." He went on to explain that consumer preference was determined by surveys constantly being conducted, and added significantly, "There is no indication that there will be a change in the trend in the near term."

Officials of the other auto companies were less dogmatic with respect to the origin of style changes. An official of Ford pointed out that, unlike most consumer-goods industries, there is a "4-year gestation period" on automobile production; the 1962 models, for example, were worked up in 1958. This time factor, of course, presents serious problems; there is always the danger that one may produce cars consumers wanted four years earlier. Indeed, according to one authority, this is exactly what happened in the case of the Edsel. Richard S. Latham, industrial designer, told the Subcommittee that "The Edsel, a wholly new product said to have cost 250 million dollars to develop, is the result of four years' research into 'what the consumer really wanted in a middle-bracket car.' The conclusion that one cannot fail to reach, for its apparent and proven lack of success, is that it was, indeed, research in what people wanted—four years ago."

Testimony by Ford officials indicated that the role of the consumer is not that of dictator of style changes, but rather of final arbiter in the marketplace. To a large extent, styling is a guessing game; the risks are extraordinarily great and "a few wrong decisions can wreck a company." The Chrysler position was very similar. "You decide what the consumer wants at the time and you do your best to adjust yourself to what you think he is going to want, and if you guess wrong, you are in bad shape."

George Romney of American Motors pointed out that the introduction of a significant change in design is very difficult for the smaller producers; they lack the large volume necessary to secure immediate acceptance by the public. A company of the size of General Motors can, however, create public adoption of the new style immediately. With saturation advertising and a strong dealer organization, the public can quickly be prevailed upon to believe that the change represents a substantial improvement over the older models. As an example Romney cited the wraparound windshield introduced by General Motors. This development did not significantly improve vision but immediately became high style. As he put it, "A small company could not have made the wraparound windshield a successful thing because when you get right down to the guts of it, it has no basic advantages over the straight windshield, and yet through advertising and promotion you can make an item of that type become absolutely the hallmark of a modern car, if you have got a large enough percentage of the total market to do it."

To further illustrate his point, Romney likened the automobile business to the millinery trade. If one milliner had over half the country's hat business, his decision to put cherries on ladies' hats would determine high fashion for that year. All other milliners would have to think twice before omitting cherries from their models if they expected to get some business. The introduction of cherries by a small milliner, however, might well be disregarded as an unattractive, if not ridiculous, adornment. Thus, he suggested, the introduction of the wraparound windshield by a small manufacturer "probably would have been a flop, but the fact that it was put on cars by a company doing as much business as the company that put it on helped to make the thing a success, because in the field of fashion, Senator, familiarity brings acceptance."

The introduction of the compact car represented a triumph of public demand for smaller and more economical instruments of transportation. The burgeoning of foreign imports and the success of American Motors were a direct refutation of the GM position, in the Subcommittee's 1958 hearings, that "there is no indication that there will be [a] change in the trend [in] the near term." Instead, in a flurry of activity, the large automobile manufacturers suddenly reversed their accustomed course and adopted the philosophy of one of their smaller, upstart competitors.

Yet the new compacts had hardly made their appearance before the pressure began anew for bigger and fancier versions. At the present time the major manufacturers are vociferously vying with each other in P. T. Barnum's term for the "biggest little midgets in the world." Indeed the talk is now in terms of the "fresh new compact in the large economy size." A supercharged version of Chevrolet's compact Corvair has been given the imposing name of Corvair Monza Spyder, the last two names suggestively referring to an Italian race course and a West German racing sports car. The new models enjoy the delightful contradiction of being "too roomy to be a compact" but "too darn thrifty to be anything else."

Reflecting the extent to which the 1957 agreement to ban speed and horsepower promotion has been abandoned, these "sleek, sparkling newcomers" in the automotive field are also "spirited." In the case of the Dodge Dart, you no longer have to settle for "weak-sister power"; "you get the kind of standard horses you pay extra for in most other compacts." And you have the best of two possible worlds, for Dart not only "saves with the rest of 'em," it "outstrides the best of 'em." And the Pontiac Tempest 4 "goes around acting like a V-8," as you will realize when you get those "horses atrotting." All accounts indicate that the horsepower race has been moved to a war footing by the major manufacturers. The stepping up of power has extended from the more modest compacts to the fanciest models. . . .

The situation in the automobile industry epitomizes the kinds of problems that develop when price competition has atrophied and rivalry among firms is limited to non-price forms. The public, allegedly the impetus for the annual style changes, is in reality the victim. It is called upon to foot the bill for a kind of competition that is neither healthy for the industry nor useful to the consumer. Indeed, in the aggregate, the social wastes involved may be more important than the pecuniary costs, great as they are. Unfortunately, the social losses—absence of the real technological progress that could have been achieved, loss of human life arising out of the industry's emphasis on speed and power, the traffic problems that have multiplied in the wake of today's automotive monsters—are not susceptible of ordinary measurement. Nor, indeed, is the loss to society of the benefits that would have arisen were this highly important industry constantly revitalized by the free play of industrial rivalry in all its forms, including price competition.

In Defense of Bigness in Business

Sumner H. Slichter

The 1957 decision of the Supreme Court in the duPont-General Motors case suggests the desirability of a review and an appraisal of American policy toward competition, monopoly, and bigness in business. The decision reveals the strong determination of the court to prevent competition from being weakened and the court's willingness to resort to controversial interpretations of the law in order to implement the public policy of preventing restraints on competition.

But the decision also reminds us that much thinking on the relation of bigness to competition is out of date and unrealistic. Hence, the adaptation of

From The New York Times Magazine, *August 4, 1957,* © *1957 by The New York Times Company. Reprinted by permission.*

traditional American antitrust policy to the facts of modern industry requires that we take a fresh look at the role of large enterprises in American business—particularly the role of large enterprises as a source of vigorous and dynamic competition.

When one compares the economy of the United States with the economies of other advanced industrial countries, four characteristics stand out conspicuously.

1. The government of the United States endeavors through broad and drastic laws to prevent restraints on competition and to forestall the growth of monopoly. Most other advanced industrial countries either tolerate considerable restraint on competition or even encourage organizations of businessmen that are designed to control competition.

2. Competition in American industry is far more vigorous and pervasive than in the industries of any other advanced industrial country. Indeed, the vigor of competition in the United States almost invariably attracted comment from the European productivity teams that visited this country in the years following the war.

3. The United States has many more huge business enterprises than any other country. Several years ago this country had more than 100 corporations (exclusive of purely financial ones) with assets of more than $250 million each. General Motors produces far more cars than the combined British, German, and French automobile industries, and the United States Steel Corporation produces more steel than the entire British steel industry.

4. Production in many American industries (especially those requiring large capital investment) is highly concentrated in the hands of a few large concerns. As a general rule, the concentration of production in other industrial countries is far less than here.

These four characteristics of the American economy are not unrelated. It would be wrong to ascribe the widespread and intense competition in American industry *solely* to the strong public policy against restraint of trade, monopolization, and interference with competition. Conditions in the United States—the absence of class lines, the abundance of opportunity, the weakness of tradition—have long made life here highly competitive in all its aspects, and competition in business is just one manifestation of this general competitive spirit. But America's unique and firm public policy against restraints on competition has undoubtedly helped greatly to keep industry here strongly competitive.

This strong policy, however, has paradoxically encouraged the development of giant industrial corporations and the concentration of production in many industries among a few large concerns. The growth of enterprises in Europe has been limited by the practice of forming cartels—a practice which governments have tolerated and even encouraged. The cartel or trade association divides markets among its members, limits the growth of the most efficient concerns, and assures the weak, high-cost concern a share of the market.

In the United States, where cartels are illegal, each concern is pretty completely exposed to competition from all other firms, and business goes to the firms that can get it. This means that in many industries production is gradually concentrated in the hands of a few industrial giants, and only a small part of the business is left for small firms.

The trend toward corporate bigness in industry has led many students of anti-monopoly policy to believe that the American policy of encouraging competition and discouraging monopoly is turning out to be a failure and to conclude that steps need to be taken to limit the influences of large enterprises in American industry. Of many proposals that have been made, two principal ones are of particular interest.

One proposal is that new restrictions be placed on mergers. Some have urged that no merger be permitted which cannot be justified by technological reasons. Some have proposed that mergers involving a corporation above a given size be prohibited unless found by the Federal Trade Commission to be in the public interest.

The second proposal deals with the concentration of production in various industries into a few enterprises. It is urged that the government undertake a comprehensive survey of American industry to determine whether enterprises exceed the size required by modern technology and that the government be authorized to break up firms that are unnecessarily large.

Both of these proposals are based on fallacy. They rest upon a mistaken conception of the role of large corporations in American business and particularly upon the relation of large corporations to competition. Each, if put into effect, would weaken rather than strengthen competition. In fact, in order to stimulate competition, existing restrictions on mergers should be relaxed, not tightened, and large enterprises, instead of being threatened with breakup, should be given a clear mandate to grow, provided they use fair means. Let us examine more completely each of these two proposals to restrict the growth of enterprises.

The proposal that new restrictions be placed on mergers arises from the fact that the United States in recent years has been experiencing a great wave of mergers. But recent mergers have not weakened competition. On the contrary, and they have indirectly strengthened it because they have enabled managements to build more diversified and better-integrated enterprises—enterprises which are more capable of reaching all parts of the vast domestic market, of adapting themselves to market shifts and changes in technology, of riding out the ups and downs of business, and of supporting technological research and development. Many large firms and firms of moderate size have acquired small firms, but the acquisitions by the very largest firms have not been numerous.

The specific circumstances surrounding each merger are unique, but a case-by-case examination shows how mergers are helping to build stronger enterprises, better able to complete and to hold their own in competition.

Let us consider a few examples. A maker of cans bought a concern manufacturing plastic pipe in order to get a foothold in the plastic pipe business. A maker of railroad freight cars bought companies making electrical equipment, truck trailers, and dairy supplies in order to shift from a declining business to expanding businesses. A food manufacturer bought a West Coast manufacturer of salad seasoning in order to give nation-wide distribution to its product. A maker of household wares bought a supplier in order to have a source of pressed wood handles for its appliances.

Unusually competent managements often buy other concerns so that they can spread good administrative methods to less efficiently operated enterprises.

The many advantages produced by mergers show that the proposal that mergers be prohibited unless they can be justified by technological reasons does not make sense. There are good reasons for mergers that have nothing to do with technology.

Moreover, it would be unwise to require government approval of all mergers involving an enterprise above a specified size. That would be substituting the decision of government officials for the decision of businessmen on matters that the businessmen are better able to understand. The public interest is amply protected by the present drastic provision of Section 7 of the Clayton Act.

Indeed, the fact that mergers often make for more vigorous competition by helping managements build stronger and more efficient business enterprises indicates the need for relaxing the present severe restrictions on mergers contained in Section 7 of the Clayton Act. This section prohibits any merger which is likely to lessen competition substantially in *any* line of commerce. The fact that the merger may increase the intensity of competition in *other* lines of commerce makes no difference. As Section 7 now reads, the *total effect* of the merger on competition is irrelevant. If it is likely to lessen competition substantially in any one line of commerce, it is illegal.

Obviously the section, as it now reads, conflicts with the national policy of encouraging competition. It should be rewritten to make the legality of mergers depend upon the *total* effect [on] competition, thus permitting any merger that has the net effect of increasing competition.

The second proposal—to remake the structure of American industry by breaking up the largest enterprises—rests upon the mistaken view that, where output is concentrated among a few concerns, effective competition does not occur. The error of this view is shown by the vigorous competition in various industries in which most of the output is made by a few firms—in such industries as the automobile, tire, refrigerator, soap, cigarette, paper products, television, and many others.

There are two principal reasons why competition tends to be vigorous when production is concentrated among a few large concerns. One is that such enterprises keep close track of their rank in sales and fight hard to move ahead of rivals or to avoid being surpassed by rivals. The second reason, and one that is rapidly gaining in importance, is the fact that competition among large firms is being stimulated by the growth of technological research.

It is only within the last several decades that managements have generally discovered the big returns yielded by technological research. As a result, the outlays by private industry on research and development increased nearly six-fold between 1940 and 1953. In 1957, the total research and development expenditures of private industry, exclusive of the aircraft industry, which is a special case, are running about 71 percent greater than they were in 1953. By 1960 outlays on research are expected to be 21 percent above 1957.

No expenditures are more competitive than outlays on research, for the purpose of these expenditures is to improve products, develop new products, and cut costs. More than 70 percent of the outlays on research and development are made by firms with 5000 or more employees because concerns with large sales can best afford this overhead expense. Hence the rapidly mounting outlays on research indicate both the growing competitiveness of American industry and the increasingly important role large enterprises are playing in making competition more intense.

Incidentally, competition among large firms is superior in quality to competition among small firms and serves consumers more effectively. This is because the greater research by the large firms gives the consumers a wider range of choice over a period of years than competition among a much larger number of small firms that can afford little or no research. In general, the wider the range of choice open to consumers, the more effectively is the welfare of consumers advanced.

In view of the growing importance of large enterprises as a source of competition and the superior quality of this competition, a move to break up large concerns would be a blunder. There is much to be said, however, in favor of incentives for enterprises to split themselves voluntarily, if the managements consider a split desirable. The resulting increase in the number of top managements with independent authority to make policies and to try experiments would be favorable to technological progress—provided the concerns are large enough to support extensive research. A good incentive for voluntary splits would be created by relieving stockholders from liability for the capital gains tax on the appreciation of their holdings from the time they purchased the stock up to the date of the split.

But enforced splitting of enterprises, except as a remedy for flagrant monopolizing of trade by unscrupulous methods, would be another matter. In fact, the present law needs to be clarified in order to encourage a few of the very largest concerns to strive harder for a bigger share of the market. The managements of a few very large and efficient concerns apparently feel that efforts to get more business by cutting prices will be held to be attempts to monopolize. There is need to make clear that efforts to win business by giving consumers the benefits of low costs will not be regarded as monopolistic.

Americans need to understand that a variety of conditions—rapidly changing technology, the growing importance of industrial research, the growing strength of trade unions—tend to increase in many industries the size of the enterprise that is able both to compete and to survive in competition. Hence, we are likely to see a spread of the tendency for production to be concentrated in a few large or fairly large firms.

But this trend, if it occurs, should not disturb us. It will simply represent an adaptation of industry to the conditions of the time.

Mergers, Concentration, and Public Policy

Federal Reserve Bank of Cleveland

Merger activity in the United States soared to a record high in 1968 (see Table 1). The rising number of industrial mergers has raised concern over the effects of mergers on economic concentration, as well as over the adequacy of existing antitrust legislation.

Antitrust enforcement agencies fear that recent changes in industrial structure are not consistent with traditional goals of public policy toward business structure. Since the passage of the Sherman Act in 1890, the goal of public policy has been to maintain competition and to check economic concentration. The philosophy underlying that goal reflects distrust of any concentrated power. The same philosophy is reflected in the political structure of the United States, where power is separated among three branches of the Federal government and distributed between Federal and state governments. However, the public goal of maintaining numerous competing firms to disperse economic power may be inconsistent with other goals, such as efficiency and scale of operations. According to some observers, these other goals should receive serious consideration despite their possible anticompetitive effects.

MERGERS AND CONCENTRATION

Market concentration ratios are considered significant by antitrust enforcement agencies and the courts in evaluating competitive effects of mergers. It is

From the Federal Reserve Bank of Cleveland, weekly commentary of May 12, 1969. John J. Erceg, the bank's senior economist, had primary responsibility for preparing this commentary.

TABLE 1
FIRMS ACQUIRED IN MANUFACTURING AND MINING, UNITED STATES, 1950–1968

Year	Number
1950	219
1951	235
1952	288
1953	295
1954	387
1955	782
1956	824
1957	730
1958	737
1959	936
1960	966
1961	1,117
1962	1,033
1963	985
1964	1,065
1965	1,125
1966	1,106
1967	1,639
1968	2,655

NOTE: Date [sic] for 1950–1954 are not strictly comparable to 1955–1968.
Source: Federal Trade Commission.

generally accepted that market structure (the number, size, and size distribution of firms in an industry) affects competition among firms within an industry. One measure of market structure is the share of assets accounted for by the top firms in an industry (generally the top four or eight firms). In turn, industries are often classified by market structure, ranging from those characterized by many sellers to those with a single seller that dominates the industry. Some economists have associated low concentration ratios with a competitive market structure and high ratios with a noncompetitive structure. Although there are a number of highly concentrated industries in manufacturing, the level of market concentration for all manufacturing industries was, on balance, unchanged from 1947 to 1966. In the first half of the period, market concentration tended to decline, while in the latter half of the period, market concentration rose, largely because of stepped up merger activity. In addition, from 1947 to 1966, the level of concentration among producers' goods industries tended to fall, while among consumer goods industries, concentration tended to rise.

Although the level of market concentration has been relatively unchanged, the level of aggregate concentration in manufacturing has risen substantially in the past two decades. According to the Federal Trade Commission, the share of total manufacturing assets held by the top 200 firms rose from 49% in 1950 to 59% in 1967, with the sharpest increase occurring in recent years. Aggregate concentration, i.e., the share of assets held by the largest industrial firms in the United States (generally the top 100 or 200 firms), has little significance for antitrust policy, but antitrust enforcement agencies watch aggregate concentration trends closely.

The apparent discrepancy in concentration trends reflects the fact that horizontal and vertical mergers, which affect market structure, have dwindled sharply in response to antitrust enforcement, while conglomerate mergers, which cut across many markets and thus affect the level of aggregate concentration,

TABLE 2

PERCENT DISTRIBUTION OF LARGE MANUFACTURING AND MINING ACQUISITIONS BY TYPE, UNITED STATES, SELECTED PERIODS, 1948–1968

Type of Merger	1948–1953	1960–1965	1968
Horizontal	31%	12%	7%
Vertical	10	16	9
Conglomerate	59	72	84
Total	100%	100%	100%

Source: Federal Trade Commission.

have risen dramatically.* Conglomerate mergers have dominated merger activity in recent years. Antitrust enforcement agencies have had less difficulty in establishing the probable anticompetitive effects of horizontal and vertical mergers than for other types. Accordingly, in 1968, horizontal and vertical mergers accounted for only 7% and 9%, respectively, of all "large" mergers, down sharply from previous years (see Table 2). On the other hand, conglomerate mergers have soared in recent years and accounted for nearly 84% of all large mergers in 1968. The fact that antitrust enforcement agencies have not challenged

---

* Horizontal mergers involve firms that produce the same products; vertical mergers involve firms that have a buyer or seller relationship. There are three classes of conglomerate mergers: (a) product extension conglomerates involving firms that produce different but related products; (b) market extension conglomerates involving firms that produce the same products but sell in different geographic markets; (c) "pure" conglomerates involving firms that produce unrelated products.

mergers involving firms that produce unrelated products, i.e., the "pure conglomerate" merger, partially accounts for the phenomenal rise of such mergers in the last few years.

Neither economic theory nor antitrust laws have established the probable competitive effects of the conglomerate, which, according to some observers, has its strength in several different markets rather than a single market. Moreover, until recently, the existing body of antitrust legislation had been held to be inadequate by antitrust agencies.

PUBLIC POLICY TOWARD MERGERS

At present, antitrust legislation includes four major laws plus amendments to each. The most effective legislation has been the Celler-Kefauver Act, which amended the Clayton Act of 1914. Congressional hearings that preceded passage of the Celler-Kefauver Act of 1950 made it clear that Congress intended to cover in the Act all types of mergers "where in any line of commerce, in any section of the country, the effect of such acquisition may be substantially to lessen competition or tend to create a monopoly," even though conglomerate mergers were not specifically defined. Moreover, Congress intended the Act to apply to incipient lessening of competition.

In recognition of traditional Congressional concern over concentration and maintenance of competition, the Supreme Court in the landmark Brown Shoe case decision in 1962 stated, "we cannot fail to recognize Congress' desire to promote competition through protection of viable, small locally owned businesses. Congress appreciated that occasional higher costs and prices might result from the maintenance of fragmented industries and markets. It resolved that there is competing consideration in favor of decentralization."

Since the Celler-Kefauver Act was passed, judicial opinions, particularly Supreme Court decisions, have had a major influence on the formation of antitrust policy. Courts have had to define a relevant market as well as determine the probable effects of an acquisition on market structure. Since the Brown Shoe case in 1962, the Supreme Court applied definitions in several key decisions that were sympathetic to Congressional intent to maintain competition. To date, court decisions have affected horizontal and vertical mergers, but only certain types of conglomerate mergers.

CONCLUDING COMMENTS

The firm stand of Assistant Attorney General McLaren toward conglomerate mergers appears consistent with the mainstream of legislative and judicial tradition that has characterized United States economic history since the enactment of the Sherman Act. That tradition is based on diffusion of economic power through maintenance of numerous firms operating in a competitive market structure so that no one firm can influence output and prices. It is apparent that antitrust policy has played an important role in protecting competition, and that continued vigorous enforcement may be necessary in light of the growing number of conglomerates in manufacturing, transportation, banking, and elsewhere. According to antitrust enforcement agencies, such conglomerates may represent a threat to traditional goals of public policy toward business structure.

QUESTIONS FOR DISCUSSION

1. *What factors have contributed to the growth of "Big Business"?*
2. *What problems does "bigness" pose?*
3. *In what ways does Senator Kefauver see bigness in the auto industry actually harming the consumer? Do you agree with his analysis? Why or why not?*
4. *On what grounds does Slichter's article defend "bigness"?*
5. *What do you think Slichter means by arguing that businesses should be free to grow to whatever size is practical if "they use fair means"?*
6. *On what basis does Slichter argue that competition still exists even with bigness?*
7. *How do conglomerate mergers differ from the past trend in American business consolidations?*
8. *What special problems do conglomerate mergers pose for public policy?*

What Relationship Between Government and Business?

Discussions of the proper relations for business and government in the American economy usually are noteworthy in generating more heat than light. The question is scarcely one that produces neutrality and, too often, it fails to produce objectivity. To many staunch proponents of "a free enterprise business system," government has grown too large. It regulates business affairs too broadly and too rigorously through a proliferation of regulatory agencies as well as through its pursuit of fiscal, monetary, and social welfare policies. On the other hand, a large body of opinion (by far the largest among economists) holds that the expansion of government authority in the economy has been necessary to correct the deficiencies of a "free" market. Too frequently, both views tend to accept the idea that greater government involvement is a comparatively recent phenomenon, with the economic crisis of the 1930's roughly the watershed for this change.

From the outset, however, government has always played a large role in the American economy. Throughout the nineteenth century, by means of tariffs, cash subsidies, land grants, and miscellaneous pieces of favorable legislation, government, especially the federal government, acted positively and forcefully in spurring business development. While the expanded role of government in the economy, beginning with the "Progressive" administration of Theodore Roosevelt and then maturing during and after Franklin Roosevelt's New Deal, is usually cited both by friends and foes of these policies as a new direction for business-government relations, such an interpretation is too simplistic. This interpretation implies an antibusiness bias in the "new" role of government in the economy. It must be clear to even the casual observer that the expanded role of government has not meant the actual replacement of private enterprise by rigorous public control, nor is there evidence to support the idea that profits have been, in the aggregate, reduced. There is considerable opinion among business leaders that the expanded role of government may be in the distinct favor of business. The "new direction" may not be new at all but, examined broadly, it may well be a continuation of the traditional "pro-business" attitude of government.

The three articles in the selection offer widely differing interpretations on this question. The first, by a businessman of the self-made type, strongly attacks the expansion of government regulation of business. The piece by Michael Reagan is a partisan attack upon a "free market" economy and clearly anti-business in its implication. These two articles represent the extremes of the debate over this question. Henry Ford II, author of the third article, is a leading member of the American business community and influential in shaping business opinion. It should be noted that he served as a leader of a "Business for Johnson" movement in the 1964 Goldwater-Johnson election, apparently indicating a preference for the emerging pattern of business-government relations and a repudiation of the laissez faire ideas of the Republican candidate. Ford's article clearly follows this line of argument.

Freedom's Last Frontier

Lawrence H. Rogers II

Briefly and seriously, I want to examine with you what I conceive to be the clear and present danger of the decline and fall of the American free private enterprise system.

For the moment at least, let's forget the past. Let's deal only in the present.

Only a moment ago . . . as history's flight is reckoned . . . John Kennedy soared into the White House on the wings of the New Frontier. He inspired what he felt to be a jaded and complacent populace with his colorful characterization of the challenges and fulfillments of our exciting age. It was to be our destiny to realize the rewards of Valley Forge and Gettysburg; to fulfill the dreams of Woodrow Wilson; to conquer space for peace; and to

From an address by Lawrence H. Rogers II, President, Taft Broadcasting Company, before the Television Bureau of Advertising, Inc., Twelfth Annual Dinner, Chicago, Illinois, November 17, 1966. Reprinted by permission from Vital Speeches of the Day, *March 15, 1967.*

extend to all people the blessings of the most affluent society. Alas, many of the highest motives and brightest hopes died with Jack Kennedy. But a dynamic nation feeds upon its history, and ere long we were harnessed by LBJ into another utopian dream known as the Great Society.

The President has characterized the Great Society as a land free of fear; free of want; and free of labor . . . goals which can be described as noble only if you consider effort ignoble . . . goals which are utopian only to the extent that no one need worry. Frankly, I worry about any circumstance free of worry. Isn't slavery free of worry?

Nevertheless, in a sort of spooky real-life version of Ayn Rand's *Atlas Shrugged,* the dizzy modern Robin Hood notion of forcing the productive to provide equally for the nonproductive has introduced a disquieting note in our land. Suddenly we are confronted with the quixotic notion that noneffort is productive; that productivity is antisocial; that up is down; that black is white . . . and this is the crux of it: that the lifeblood of our entire free enterprise society—profit—is a dirty word.

To be too productive is to be the target of the social planners. But the social planners would take the proceeds of our productivity to give them to the nonproductive. In this way, they tell us, they will achieve the ultimate in the democratic ideal: a static euphoria in which everyone enjoys the comforts and rewards of those who were privileged to produce them!

As that noted American philosopher, Peanuts, would no doubt observe, "Good grief!"

Do we have to go through all this again? Yes, we do. In fact we're going through it now. And if we are resourceful, tough, resilient, determined, dedicated, and charitable, we may survive it.

If I have been too abstruse, let me rephrase the problem in words of one syllable: TO BE FREE IS BAD.

All words of one syllable. Yet they accurately describe the danger. Freedom, dear friends, is under attack. The free enterprise society is having its last day in court. Our country, its ideals, its accomplishments, and its future are in trouble, deep trouble. And it is up to you and me and all of us to get us out.

Symptomatic of the concerted and growing attack upon the very concept of free enterprise is the increasing use among economists, academicians, and bureaucrats of the phraseology dividing the nation's productive apparatus into what are known euphemistically as the "private sector" and the "public sector." The very words are a semantical attack on freedom, inasmuch as there is no such thing as a public sector of the economy that is not itself supported by the tax base of private property and free enterprise wages and profits. But we tend to be lulled into a false sense of well-being by the passage of time. The TVA was a hot political issue thirty years ago. Now TVA competes with tax-paying utility companies from a plant entirely financed by tax dollars wrung from you and me and those same companies, and we remain blissfully unaware of the dangerous growth of socialized power.

Bringing the concept quickly up to date, the Eighty-ninth Congress indulged in a display of deficit spending that made the New Deal of the thirties look like a Ben Franklin frugality program by comparison.

In the recent election campaign the administration and its supporters stumped the land crying, "You never had it so good! Look at all the money we pumped into your economy!"

Whose money? It was ours . . . and, thank God, a large part of the American public reacted by throwing the rascals out!

The administration had unashamedly promoted a "Guns and Butter" economy . . . loudly declaiming we can fight an undeclared war while we go right on with enlarged deficit financing of social programs at home. All the while, any college freshman economics student could tell you the inevitable result is inflation. But what was the response from Washington?

Blame it on business!

Businesses are making too much profit! So increase the interest rates! Increase the taxes on profits and incomes! Let the unions get higher wages to be able to buy the higher-priced products. Repeal the 7 percent tax credit originally set up to spur business to the creation of more jobs!

Increase the minimum wage. Increase the social security benefits. Never mind that these two things alone will aggravate the inflation. Politics as usual. A whole army of welfare state Neros, fiddling while Rome is in flames . . . no, not fiddling. Pouring fuel on the flames!

Medicare. Lots of propaganda about how good it is and how free it is. Not one word about how incomplete it is and how it makes the inflation worse. A cruel political hoax at best.

Auto safety. The august Senate of the United States flies into a panic over a possibly libelous book by a clever publicity hound. New legislation in time for election that inevitably and immediately causes a sharp increase in the cost of autos. Not one simple provision which strikes at the root cause of 50,000 terrible fatalities a year on the highways: the nut behind the wheel. . . .

Reduced to the lowest economic denominator, this creeping excursion into socialism which has been foisted off on us by the do-gooders in Washington can accomplish nothing except to aggravate the very problems it is dedicated to solve. For every dollar of valuation that is siphoned off from productive private enterprises into the so-called "public sector" there is a corresponding reduction in the tax base from which dollars are drawn with which to finance the "public sector." There is no way on earth in which these dollar valuations can be replaced except by inflation or devaluation. This constitutes nothing more dignified than a government stealing from its citizens. Its inevitable result is self-destructive. . . .

The old, old claim harking from the days of the Trust Busters is that Big Business has too much economic power, and that this power is used to hurt consumers and keep other producers out of the market.

Therefore it is necessary for the Government to protect the consumer. The consumer must be protected not only from evil business practices, but also from himself, primarily because the consumer is sometimes stupid or thoughtless enough to place convenience or quality above price! . . .

What all social engineers fail to see is that the very controls they propose, and the burdensome tax structure that finances them, make smallness in business a practical impossibility. Today a business must either expand or die. The little fellow with a great product or a unique system will sooner or later sell out to a giant for his capital gains treatment, thus enabling the giant to improve its product performance and its operating efficiency. . . .

When I cry out against the invasions of the social planners I am not overestimating their strength and their brilliance. I consider most of them weak and dull. My warning is against the inactivity that allows such unimaginative people to occupy an enormously influential part in shaping the destiny of our nation and the lives of all Americans.

We might all hark back to our grade school general science. "Nature abhors a vacuum," they started out by telling us. It is no less true among men and nations. Government and crusaders, no less than nature, abhor vacuums. Where there is a social vacuum, you may be sure a centralized government planner will rush into it.

I have . . . some vivid examples, among them the sad plight of Britain. It's true that England is about gone. But only part of it was the fault of the socialist planners. By far the greatest part was the rock-ribbed resistance to change on the part of the whole British establishment . . . political, business, and military . . . that made such an upheaval inevitable. Had the inventiveness of private business been used to better the lot of the working classes of England, I daresay they very likely would never have taken that first fatal step of nationalizing steel.

You can apply the same thing to any number of problems that face us.

Had the auto manufacturers made their safety devices standard instead of optional some years ago, that silly Ralph Nader business would have never happened. I urge you to consider getting behind a tough campaign in your state to improve the licensing laws and make for stricter driver law enforcement. Unsafe cars don't kill 50,000 people a year. Unsafe drivers do. And unless we do something about it—you and I—there will be more bad laws before there are some good ones. And a lot more people killed.

Take Medicare. Had the insurance industry and the medical profession been sensitive to obvious social needs over the past twenty years, and had they been properly responsive to them, there would have been no vacuum in health care for the aged. And there would have been no taxpayer supported Medicare program.

Although there are some that will claim this address is political, it certainly is not anti-labor union. I have yet to see a very bad union labor problem that was not in the first place created by inept management. The responsibilities of leadership are every bit as important as the rewards. More so, really.

So far we don't have the interference of the FCC or the FTC in the matter of Television Code business for only one simple reason: The television industry started to do something about self-regulation before it was forced down our throats.

I can't resist the comment that unless we look very carefully at the state of our self-regulation, which contains a vacuum here and there, the government is likely to be right in there with both feet . . . and soon.

Sixty years ago Congress passed anti-trust laws because there were abuses that needed correction. There was a vacuum, and the government filled it.

Last month Congress rushed into a vacuum created by too little under-standing of the importance of brand competition and packaging with a restraint called the "truth in packaging" law. Largely through the efforts of manu-facturers, including P&G, and some broadcasters . . . some of the more onerous and unnecessary aspects of that legislation were eliminated. But the fact that we, all of us, were too little and too late with cogent commentary on this issue cost us another piece of expensive and unnecessary legislation that chips off another precious piece of our freedom.

No matter that the government already had laws and machinery to protect the public from fraudulent packaging: we sleep on while they added more machinery on top of it. . . .

To finish this circuitous route back to the subject that was assigned to me for this meeting, the first Business of Business is Business!

Let us all return to our respective part in it, dedicated to tell its story as it should be told.

Of this you may be certain: free private enterprise is not really free. The price we all must pay . . . and it's the greatest bargain in the world . . . is the constant vigilance and effort on all our parts to keep it alive and flourishing.

The Expanding Economic Role of Government

Michael D. Reagan

WHY GOVERNMENT'S ROLE HAS EXPANDED

The reasons for expanding governmental economic activity are a mixture of circumstantial development, increased knowledge of how an economy functions, and changing community values, each related to and reinforcing the others.

The rise of industrialization and its social corollary, urbanization, represent the circumstantial development. Perhaps the broadest effect of industrialization has been to substitute formal social controls for the informal ones of earlier society and to create new controls to handle problems that did not exist in the simpler and less interdependent technology of agricultural society.

As an example of new formal controls, we have the pure food and drug statutes and the Federal Trade Commission replacing the old attitude of *caveat emptor*. When consumer goods were largely limited to food and fiber products, "let the buyer beware" was not an impossible rule, for the consumer could easily be as knowledgeable as the seller regarding the desirable qualities in a vegetable or a pair of trousers made of natural fibers. But when industrialization and technological progress introduced a new and vastly extended range of products, complex in their mechanism and often artificial in their materials, common knowledge became a poor basis for purchase. The informal control by consumer information then required supplementation by formal protection. The Pure Food and Drug Act established an agency and a set of rules to guard the hopeful and gullible consumer from harmful remedies and contaminated foods. Today we are moving toward additional protection: to ensure against the great economic waste and personal financial distress caused by purchase of products which are ineffective though innocuous, by requiring that the producer prove his remedy has beneficial effect. The Kefauver hearings on the drug industry, whatever they prove about profits, have certainly demonstrated the necessity to safeguard the consumer against medically meaningless though commercially profitable innovations in prescription and proprietary drugs. President Kennedy's 1962 consumer protection message to Congress and his establishment of a Consumer Advisory Council exemplify the increasing activities on the part of government in areas where lack of consumer knowledge needs to be compensated for by formal social control.

Or consider antimonopoly legislation. When production was agricultural and producers were many and small, the consumer was protected by the market mechanism itself, which enabled the retail distributor to have a choice of suppliers. With the rise of national markets and industrial producers, the maintenance of competition became a matter for conscious policy as concentration of production in a few firms came to typify the situation. It was not a change from no regulation to government regulation, but from market regulation to government regulation.

To illustrate the need for new controls where no controls previously existed, we can cite the development of traffic rules, motorcycle policemen, and traffic courts and, in quite another sphere, blue-sky laws and the Securities and Exchange Commission. Also zoning and land-use regulations are the by-product of industrial urbanization, which makes my neighbor's use of his property a matter of economic, esthetic, and hygienic concern to me.

In addition to supplying the supporting framework for business, government in industrial society is also necessarily called upon to provide a supporting framework for individuals and families. This is not the result of an alleged loss of "moral fiber" in the people, but of the living pattern of urban culture and the specialization and interdependence of industrial employment. In the pre-industrial society, people were literally more self-sufficient than it is possible for them to be today: the farm family grew its own food, made some of its own clothing, and built its own house and outbuildings. Families were large, and children contributed economically by working in the fields or the house at an early age. Because there was a minimum of exchange and minimal use of cash, there was not the dependence upon cash income that there is today. The grandparents could be cared for within the home, and usually could continue to be useful members of the family, not a drain on their children's resources. When industrialism began to make some headway, and a son went off to the city to become a factory worker, it was still possible for him to return to the family farm if he lost his city job or became ill. Family responsibility for each member was then more feasible than it can be today.

Contrast with this picture the situation today, and the underlying causes for the expansion of economic welfare activities by government become quickly apparent. Production and consumption are divorced. The man does not work on his own farm but for an organization. He does not produce his own food, let alone clothing and housing, but performs a specialized task for a cash income, which he then exchanges for all of his family's needs. Loss of cash thus means loss of all sustenance. The family farm is no longer there to fall back on in rough times, nor would the urban-raised man know how to do farm work if it were available. Children in the city are economically unproductive; they cannot perform small tasks on their father's assembly line or in his office, as they could on the farm. Urban housing and the concentrated living patterns of the city do not easily accommodate three generations under one roof, so the grandparents require separate housing at separate expense. Furthermore, industrial employment is subject to fluctuations against which no individual can protect himself. Given the consequences of unemployment, and this inability to guard against it, income-support programs by government, such as unemployment compensation, disability compensation, health insurance, and old age pensions, can be seen as simply the modern equivalent of protections once, but no longer, provided by the socio-economic system itself.

While agricultural societies had good and bad seasons, and incredible human suffering might be the price of the latter, they could still not have the complete collapse of economy that happened in 1933, when one-fourth of the work force was unemployed. The business cycle did not originate with industrialization, but its consequences were so vastly magnified that the price paid for a self-adjusting economy became intolerable. Hence changed circumstances called forth another whole area of governmental function: the stabilization of employment, production, and prices.

Yet it was not just changed circumstance, for when we say that a situation becomes intolerable we are making a value judgment, not just describing a situation. Community value changes were just as essential a part of the expanding economic role of government as changes in the objective situation. When unemployment was thought of, in Spencerian terms, as the justly deserved punishment of the shiftless and lazy, no one thought to provide governmental protection. When "the devil take the hindmost" and *caveat emptor* were the slogans of the day, the social and economic costs of the crude early brand of capitalism were ignored with good conscience—at least by those whose opinions counted politically. In short, when doctrines of individualism held a monopoly on the operative ideals of the community, collective economic action was by definition anathema. There were critics who posed more humane values—like Disraeli and Dickens in England, Lincoln Steffens and Ida M. Tarbell in the United States—but their impact was felt only belatedly.

Concepts of social justice began to receive more articulate support, and wider public awareness and acceptance around the turn of the century. The almost Marxian criticism of capitalism embedded in Pope Leo XIII's encyclical, *Rerum Novarum;* the growth of an industrial working class for whom the individualist precepts of the Horatio Alger literature had a distinctly hollow ring; the development of the Brandeis brief to break down with factual recitations of suffering and inequity the Supreme Court's dogmatic assumption of economic harmony under laissez faire; and the beginnings of sociological analysis of power relationships—all these were forces undermining the Spencerian-Darwinian scheme of values.

Simultaneous change in conditions and in values provided the elemental forces necessary for development of new governmental roles; the catalytic agent was often a crisis or a catastrophe. The Triangle Shirtwaist Company fire in New York in 1911, in which 146 workers died, led to much factory legislation in 1912–14; ship losses led to radio requirements and legislation; and the depression of 1929–39 led to a whole range of programmatic and institutional innovations patterned on an industrially oriented scheme of values: the Securities and Exchange Commission, Home Owners' Loan Corporation, Old Age and Survivors Insurance, and the Council of Economic Advisers—just to list a few.

Nor is the conflict of values over yet. Roughly speaking, what Galbraith called the conventional wisdom and what Barry Goldwater and the NAM preach in the name of individualism represent vestiges of pre-industrial thinking, which are still quite lively, unfortunately. Such thinking contends for the power to shape public policy with what may be called the liberal-labor ideology, which accepts industrialization and recognizes its social imperatives—indeed, it overstresses them, say conservatives. The recent and continuing conflict over the means test versus the social-insurance approach to publicly provided medical care is a perfect case in point. The means-test philosophy dates back hundreds of years. Its view of man is that his dignity counts only when he is self-supporting; its view of the economy is that no one ever lacks adequate means of support except through his own shiftlessness or inadequacy. The social-insurance approach emphasizes the technical concept of risk-sharing, the ethical concept that dignity resides in all humans, not just the fortunate ones, and the economic concept that social costs and benefits are not synonymous with private costs and benefits as measured by the market. Pictures of the situation and systems of values are thus fused into total approaches to socio-economic problems, approaches with quite different implications for the range of public policy.

Two other developments were highly instrumental, and in some respects requisite, to expansion of government's economic role of social control. There was a recognition of socio-economic institutions as man-made rather than divinely ordained, and, concurrently, the technical development of economic analysis as a social-scientific discipline. When social and economic systems were thought of as divinely ordained or as natural growths, it was popularly supposed that men neither could nor should make changes in the framework. If some men starved, it was regrettable; but nothing could be done in the face of "natural law." Although the early factory wage system reeked of injustice, one could not tamper with the "iron law of wages." Such crude doctrines of natural law, widely believed, for a long time effectively stopped social and economic reform measures, for "interference" with nature was immoral and, by definition, futile because "unnatural."

As the scientific spirit began to invade the sphere of moral philosophy and men began to doubt the finality of social institutions which showed great variation between cultures, it gradually came to be understood that social arrangements are what we make them, that within bounds set by resources and knowledge there are a great variety of ways in which goods production can be handled. And men began to demand that governments act as instigators of change to produce institutional patterns more in keeping with an enlightened humanist image of man. Although social science has become heavily self-conscious about its self-imposed role of analysis without prescription in recent years, its early growth came largely through men committed to engineering a better world. The draft of objectives circulated by Richard T. Ely in 1885 as a prospectus for an American Economics Association, for example, began with an explicit rejection of the laissez faire doctrine: "We regard the state as an educational and ethical agency whose positive aid is an indispensable condition of human progress. . . . We hold that the doctrine of laissez-faire is unsafe in politics and unsound in morals." Not all the economists of that time agreed with Ely, yet a milder version of this statement was incorporated into the original constitution of the Association. And some men would have made the Association's role even more activist. Simon Patten, for example, felt that the Association membership "should give in some specific form our attitude on all the leading questions where State intervention is needed."

Use of governmental power to achieve reform objectives was made socially feasible by the social scientists' demonstration that economic and other institutions were not the immutable creations of nature but the conscious and unconscious creations of man. What once had to be accepted, though regretted, could now be attacked: men could be blamed and held responsible; their behavior could be required to conform to standards other than those enshrined in the market mechanism; and institutions could be reformed to accord with humanistic aims.

The best will in the world will accomplish little, however, if objective analysis of the problem is faulty or techniques have not been developed for directing social forces toward the desired goal. Advances in economic theory and in techniques of measuring performance of the economy were therefore prerequisite to the translation of humane ideals into programs of public economic policy. Concretely, the Keynesian revolution provided an essential key to understanding the nature of the business cycle and the failure of conventional budget-balancing economics to pull the economy out of a slump once begun. President Roosevelt's initial attempts to cut government spending are a leading example of the perils of action on the basis of faulty analysis. The development of the national income model and its accompanying analysis of the flow of funds and the relationships among savings, investment, and consumption are the intellectual basis for policies aimed at growth and full employment. While our understanding of economic behavior still appears to lag far behind our understanding of the physical world, and our institutional arrangements for using economic knowledge are about as well adapted to our needs as the old wagon trail would be to a high-speed automobile, we do know enough now to avoid the grosser fluctuations of the business cycle. In fact, these and similar technical developments in economic science have probably been themselves a causative factor in the change in values from acceptance of adversity as God-given to community demands that the economy be controlled in the interests of the general public.

For all of these reasons then, the economic role of government has been enlarged many times over in our day. The ubiquity of this development in all economically advanced or advancing nations is sufficient proof against the unenlightened conservative's easy explanation that it is all the fault of "that man in the White House," whether Roosevelt, Truman, Eisenhower, or Kennedy. And the nature of the forces catalogued suggests that the limits of essential intervention have not yet been reached. . . .

Are Government and Business Enemies?

Henry Ford II

If anyone were to keep track of the top 10 subjects for business banquet speeches, Government and business would probably be No. 1, year in and year out.

My interest in reviving this familiar topic is prompted in part by the well-publicized differences between Washington and Detroit in recent months. But it is prompted also by my conviction that the relations between Government and business have been changing in basic ways and for basic reasons—ways and reasons that affect all business, and should be considered carefully by all businessmen.

The most obvious aspect of this change is the rapid penetration of Government into all the activities of business. This, too, may sound familiar, but I think you would all agree that Government involvement in business has been expanding more rapidly in recent years than at any time since the 1930s.

It would be a mistake, however, to draw further parallels between the 1960s and the 1930s. What is happening now is happening in a different climate and largely for different reasons.

Before I get into reasons, however, let me first sketch the extent of Government's recent penetration into business activities.

As the result of recent traffic-safety and air-pollution legislation, the Federal

Full text of an address which Mr. Ford, chairman of the board of Ford Motor Company, gave in New York City on January 12, 1967.

Government will now be deeply involved in the design and construction of cars and trucks. And there are strong signs that this may be only the beginning. It has been suggested by people in important Government positions that the public interest may soon require severe restrictions on the use of automobiles, a total ban on the internal-combustion engine, the development under Government auspices of alternative power sources, and public policies to force people in metropolitan areas out of private cars and into public transit facilities.

Putting aside the merits of these measures, it is plain that they would have a profound effect on a society that does 90 percent of its traveling in automobiles, and relies on the automobile and related industries for at least one job in every seven.

Such developments are by no means unique to our business. Similar things are happening in the food and drug industries, in finance and insurance, in advertising and retailing. In virtually every industry, Government looms increasingly large between business and its customers, its employees, its shareholders and the general public.

In the name of consumer protection, we now have federal regulation of packaging, and so-called truth-in-lending legislation is sure to be introduced again. The Federal Trade Commission and the Food and Drug Administration are policing advertising with growing rigor. The Federal Trade Commission is now engaged in a massive investigation into the heart of the automobile industry's relations with its customers—our warranty and service policies and practices.

A high Government official has suggested that the advertising budgets of big companies are a monopolistic force that should, in some circumstances, be curtailed. Last week, Senator Hart of my own state suggested that the Government should try to reduce prices, curb the growth of big business, stimulate competition, and finance the "Great Society" through a series of tax-law changes, including a progressive tax ranging up to 75 percent of corporate profits. There have also been proposals that the Federal Government go into the business of testing, evaluating, grading, and recommending consumer products.

The governmental presence also looms bigger and bigger between business and its employees. Witness the recent extension of minimum-wage coverage and the raising of the minimum-wage level, frequent intervention in labor disputes, the enlargement of the scope of bargainable issues by the National Labor Relations Board and the courts, and current proposals to extend the emergency strike provisions of the Taft-Hartley Act and provide for closer Government regulation of private pension plans.

Under the heading of business relations with shareholders we have the recent Securities and Exchange Commission report on mutual funds, and SEC studies of a possible requirement that diversified companies publish financial results by product lines.

And, finally, under the heading of business and the public at large, we have growing governmental concern in such matters as air and water pollution by industrial plants, and regulation of roadside billboards. Under this same heading we have seen in recent years the burgeoning of governmental guidelines for wages, prices, certain exports and imports, foreign investments, and international financial transactions.

Although I disagree with many of these measures, my purpose in setting out this abbreviated catalogue of growing Government intervention is not to suggest that every step taken or proposed by the Government is mistaken. Even less do I suggest that business had better mount its white charger and do battle with the forces of galloping socialism. On the contrary, when a trend is this strong and this pervasive, something fundamental must lie behind it. No matter how misguided some Government policies may be, in the judgment of many of us in business, it would be folly to charge blindly into the fray. What we had better do first is consider carefully what we are confronted by and what lies behind it.

What lies immediately behind every particular issue of this kind is a host of conflicting and confusing pressures, interests, ambitions, irritations and philosophies. But if we look at the forest rather than the trees, it seems to me that what lies fundamentally behind the explosive growth of Government in our day are two other explosions—the knowledge explosion and the population explosion.

The progress of science and technology has given us the material resources to accomplish unprecedented tasks—to reach the moon, to fight a good-sized war, and to raise our standard of living simultaneously. Moreover, our capacity to solve the most difficult problems has been vastly enlarged by advances in computer science, in new problem-solving methods, and in our knowledge of man and society.

The inevitable result of our growing ability to reach new goals has been the raising of our national sights. If we can reach the moon, then why can't we abolish poverty? If we can have both guns and butter, then why can't we also have safe highways, clean air, pure water, honest advertising, full employment, competent auto mechanics, stable prices, peaceful labor relations, good television programs, and all the other things that go to make a "Great Society"?

Of course, there are good reasons why we can't solve all our problems all at once. One of them is that the combination of rising affluence and rising population multiplies our problems along with our problem-solving capacities. More people driving more cars more miles means more traffic congestion, more parking problems, more highway accidents. More people consuming more goods of all kinds means more waste products to be disposed of in the only three available repositories—the air, the water, or the ground. Like Lewis Carroll's Alice, we must run faster and faster merely to stand still.

It seems clear, however, that the American people have no more patience with these new problems than they have with the older ones. The more progress our country makes, the more progress it demands. To paraphrase a well-known advertising slogan, we expect more from life, and we are determined to get it. Barring some drastic setback that saps our national confidence, I would expect Americans to go right on demanding more from life—and I, for one, would have it no other way.

To say that people expect more from life really implies that they expect more from all the major institutions of society, including especially business and Government. Business firms, Government agencies, and legislatures are all operating today under stricter and more-demanding public standards than ever before.

By and large, I think both business and Government have made a strong effort to respond to the national demand for progress on all fronts. As it happens, however, there are few major problems that can be solved by Government alone, without business, or by business alone, without Government.

Take your pick of the problems I listed a moment ago—from poverty to traffic accidents, from water pollution to labor strife—not one of them is exclusively a governmental problem, nor exclusively a business problem. Each of them overlaps both areas by a very considerable margin.

Here, I think, is where we finally locate the basic source of the growth of Government involvement in business affairs. As Government and business both respond to the major problems of our day, as each of them enlarges the scope of its responsibilities to the public, they inevitably move into the no man's land where functions overlap and boundaries are ill-defined. And therefore they are bound to bump into each other more and more frequently, and more or less violently.

From all of this I draw two conclusions: First, the quality of business-Government relations is crucial to the future progress of our nation. None of our major problems can be solved, and none of our major goals can be reached unless business and Government learn to pull together rather than at cross purposes.

My second conclusion is that there is really only one way to get business and Government to pull together. To keep them from constantly colliding with each other as they work on common problems, we have to draw boundaries between them. We have to decide more rationally, more consistently, and more clearly than we are now doing what functions and responsibilities belong to Government, and what can better be left to private initiative.

It seems to me that there are two ways to go about making these distinctions:

The wrong way is what might be called the good guys vs. the bad guys approach. There are still a lot of businessmen—though, fortunately, fewer than there used to be—who think that the main difference between business and Government is one of virtue and wisdom. From this point of view, the average Government official is a bumbler, a bureaucrat, an opportunist or worse. Government, in short, is the enemy.

On the other hand, there are still a lot of Government people—though again fewer than there used to be—who simply turn this assumption around. From their point of view, the average businessman is a selfish, shortsighted, ruthless profiteer. Business serves only private aggrandizement, while Government serves only the public interest. Business, in short, is the enemy.

This may seem like a caricature, but it seems to me that most people in business and in Government suffer at least a little bit—some of us a great deal—from the tendency to overlook our own failings and exaggerate those on the other side. We could all do with a bit more humility and a stronger effort to see ourselves as others see us.

When you come right down to cases, there is probably very little to choose between business and Government on the score of virtue and wisdom. Let's take a few examples.

Although the Federal Trade Commission may have some doubts, you and I know that the business world is intensely competitive.

We must also admit that in the heat of competition, businessmen sometimes do things they shouldn't do, and leave undone some things they ought to do. That, after all, is why we need commercial law and regulatory agencies.

On the other hand, it's difficult to think of any business that is more competitive than politics. Like businessmen, legislators and Government officials sometimes do things in the heat of competition that they should not do, and leave undone things they ought to do. If businessmen sometimes place short-run profit ahead of higher considerations, I suspect that once in a while politicians give greater weight to their own immediate political advantage than to the public interest.

Advertising has been under especially heavy attack lately. The recently published report of the President's Consumer Advisory Council was strongly critical of automobile advertising because it is emotional and persuasive rather than coldly factual and informative. The use of pretty girls in car ads was especially deplored.

It seems to me there is a fair comparison to be made between business advertising and political campaigning. I don't recall that I heard a single campaign speech last fall that consisted strictly of the facts, all the facts and nothing but the facts. It seems to me there were even a few pretty girls in some of the campaign parties. And I wonder when was the last time a political party made good on all the promises in its platform.

Just before Christmas, the four federal agencies that regulate banks sent a letter to all banks whose deposits are insured by the Government. The letter banned misleading claims about interest rates paid on deposits. Among other things, the Government instructed the banks to state the fact if an advertised rate of interest is payable only on accounts held for a specified length of time.

Then somebody asked an embarrassing question. What about Government advertising of Government savings bonds? Shouldn't the Treasury Department point out that bonds must be held for seven years to earn the advertised rate of 4.15 percent? Shouldn't it state that after one year the interest is only 2.24 percent?

The treasury doesn't think so. In fact, an unnamed spokesman was rather indignant at the suggestion, according to the press reports. He was quoted as saying that he saw nothing wrong with the Treasury's ads, and he doubted that there was any major amount of public misunderstanding.

Defenders of consumer interests are very much concerned over the bewildering variety of items on the retailer's shelves these days. How, they ask, can the customer possibly choose wisely among so many similar products?

To get back to the last election, I was somewhat bewildered myself when I faced the voting machine, and I doubt that I really made all the wisest choices among all the similar candidates. It may be that something could be done to simplify both sets of choices, but it may also be that the difficulty is at least in part the price we pay for the right to choose.

The automobile manufacterers have taken their lumps for being slow to require all their customers to pay for safety features that the customers were not exactly eager to have. On the other hand, we in the industry think that governments have been slow to enforce the laws against drunken driving and to impose other unpopular traffic-safety measures such as tighter licensing standards and compulsory vehicle inspection. Perhaps both sides have been guilty of expecting the other to take steps that are necessary, but risky.

While the Government is pressing us, in the name of safety, to make some changes in our products that cannot possibly be made by the time we begin producing 1968 models, the Government is also cutting back on highway construction although new and improved highways are one of the surest ways to reduce accidents and injuries. The recently announced 1.1-billion-dollar cut in federal highway funds has already crippled road building in many parts of the country. It will certainly offset some of the life-saving potential of the federal vehicle-safety standards that will go into effect with our 1968 models. The car manufacturers have been accused of putting dollars before lives, but the Government seems to feel that sometimes it is necessary to count dollars, even when lives are at stake.

I think the point is evident. Neither business nor Government has a monopoly on virtue and wisdom. Both are made up of fallible people who generally do their best in a mixed-up world. Sometimes they do well, sometimes not. But by and large, American Government and American business work reasonably well—better than in most other places, and better than they used to.

There are also several other points to be made. The good guys vs. bad guys approach to business-Government relations is as fruitless as it is harmful. It is harmful because it poisons the atmosphere and leads both sides to take hard-and-fast positions. It is harmful because each side is likely to lose sight of the public interest in its anxiety to gain the advantage over the other.

It is fruitless because it provides no real boundaries that can keep business and Government from colliding with each other. If people in Government regard business as the enemy, then their only logical conclusion is that the responsibilities of Government are without limit.

If businessmen regard Government as the enemy, then their only possible conclusion is that Government should be kept to the barest minimum, and everything else should be left to private initiative.

Neither conclusion is consistent with the interests of a progressive democracy. We cannot expect Government or business to provide all the answers to all the problems our nation faces.

In the face of new problems and new goals, the traditional division of responsibilities between Government and business is no longer adequate. The most urgent need in business-Government relations right now is the development of a new division of responsibilities between them. The more care and the more wisdom we put into this task, the better those relations will be, and the more effectively business and Government will work together in the common interest.

Businessmen sometimes think that the way to stem the growth of Government is to have business take on the responsibility for meeting all the nation's problems and all the nation's needs before Government starts to worry about them. I would agree that business must enlarge its responsibilities for solving some problems and meeting some needs. But if we place no limit on our responsibilities, we only invite censure for failing to do what we cannot do and should not really be expected to do.

If there is little to choose between business and Government on the score of virtue and wisdom, there is much to choose between them on the score of special abilities. There are many tasks that business cannot do well, because it has neither the resources, the abilities, nor the incentives. And, likewise, there are some things Government does well, other things it does less well.

I have neither the competence nor the time to spell out these distinctions, but I would like to make a few closing observations about how they should be made.

By and large, Government does well when it works in harmony rather than at cross purposes with the dynamic forces of free enterprise.

By and large, it does well when it sets the broad rules of the game, and it does poorly when it seeks to control business activities in detail.

By and large, business does well when it sticks to what it knows best and has the strongest incentives for accomplishing. Business cannot solve the race problem, but each business can make sure that it does not discriminate.

Business cannot eliminate unemployment, but each business can do its competitive best to expand its own sales and employment. Business cannot stop inflation, but every business can strive for greater efficiency and lower costs.

One more of the many things that business can do is support rather than oppose well-considered Government programs to accomplish what Government can do and business cannot do.

The real question for businessmen is not how to stop the growth of Government. To meet our nation's growing problems and aspirations, both Government and business must expand their responsibilities and activities. The only real question is which of them should do what?

It is imperative that we find better answers to this question, and that we find them soon. We should not delude ourselves, however. By the nature of the question, the answers can never be final or definitive. With the progress of our country comes a steady flow of new challenges to business and Government, and new questions about which of them should do what.

Even more important, therefore, than the answers of the moment is the attitude we bring to the search for new answers. With a bit of humility and a great deal of common sense, better answers should not be too hard to find. And when we have them, business and Government can get on with the job of working together toward the better life that all Americans expect.

QUESTIONS FOR DISCUSSION

1. *What does Rogers see as producing the "decline and fall of the American free private enterprise system"? Do you agree or disagree? Why?*
2. *Do we have "creeping socialism" in the United States?*
3. *Is laissez faire only a myth, as Reagan charges, or might it work if given a chance?*
4. *How do you react to the statement: "Government must act to produce reforms because no one else is able to"?*
5. *What are Ford's views toward the future of government-business relations? Do such developments work for or against basic economic and social values of our economic system?*

What About Labor Unions?

The historical importance of labor unions in the development of the American economy is a well-known story. Very clearly, labor unions have had a number of positive effects in the growth of a more equitable sharing of economic power between business and labor. After a stumbling period of development in the nineteenth century, when labor unions were vigorously opposed by business, impeded if not outright prohibited by government actions, and ignored by the great majority of American workers, the union movement began to flourish in the first half of this century. Given legal recognition by the Clayton Act of 1914 and official encouragement by a number of New Deal legislative enactments and executive actions, the American union movement could boast of about eighteen million members by 1968.

Defenders of unions point to union effectiveness in raising wages and improving working conditions in American industry generally, arguing that such improvements could not have been counted upon if competitive labor market conditions and the "largesse" of business had been the only factors at work. While labor unions are admittedly an attempt to form a monopoly over labor supply, defenders argue that this is absolutely necessary to deal with the monopsonistic and oligopsonistic conditions on the buyer's (industry's) side of the market. To argue that labor unions destroy competitive markets must be admitted but it must also be noted that competition does not characterize business organizations either.

Despite the existence of considerable anti-union sentiment and a large body of economic theory which holds that unions interfere with efficient resource allocation and the distribution of market power, relatively few Americans see unions as truly inimical to the American economic system. Unionism, except in a very few cases, has not opposed the essentially capitalist bias of the nation's economic institutions.

Unions have sought to rationalize their existence within the framework of a "free enterprise" system.

Since the end of World War II, there has been a growth of anti-union sentiment in the nation. Generally, this has not meant an effort to destroy unions outright, although some staunch union members may hold to this interpretation, but rather a series of attempts to curtail their powers and regulate their activities. This position is set forth in the first article, which offers a fairly traditional anti-union analysis, although the writer clearly does not favor the outright abolition of unions.

The second article argues that for all of their shortcomings unions are "worth it," that despite the growth of anti-union feeling and the frequent charges that union leaders have become "fat" and complacent, they remain an asset in the American political economy.

Unions Are Too Powerful

Donald R. Richberg

We are facing now the need of applying a rule of law in the domain of what have been called economic conflicts between management and labor. This necessity has come about because of the inevitable trend of the presently increased power of organized labor toward what must be in the end a class rule, which must be in the end a dictatorial rule.

Under our democratic republican form of government with its preservation of individual liberty, the standard of living and the general welfare in the United States have risen beyond even the dreams of previous generations. To preserve these we must put brakes upon the power of the rulers of organized labor to dominate the entire economy and politics of the nation. Those rulers of organized labor, if they were wise, would themselves approve of putting brakes upon powers which are rapidly getting beyond the capacity of any rulers to wield wisely, or even safely.

Wide publicity has been given to proposals which the writer made not long ago to restrict the powers of organized labor, particularly in the matter of striking. So it seems worth while now to explain further what was offered

From *Donald R. Richberg,* Labor Union Monopoly (*Chicago: Henry Regnery Co., 1957*). *Reprinted by permission.*

as "a practical program of obvious remedies for intolerable abuses of labor's powers of collective action"—powers which "should be preserved but in particular uses must be restrained."

Proposition 1. "The creation and exercise of monopoly powers by labor unions should be made unlawful." The reason for the exemption of labor from the prohibitions and penalties of the antitrust laws was not because anyone contended that labor unions should be permitted to exercise monopoly powers. It was because in their normal efforts to establish uniform terms and conditions of employment unions might be and often were held to be technically "conspiracies in restraint of trade." Hence the provision was written into the law that in the legitimate exercise of their legitimate functions labor unions should not be held conspiracies in restraint of trade.

Unfortunately, aided by judicial constructions, this limited exemption of labor unions has been unduly extended into a wholesale exemption of all their activities from prosecution as monopolistic. As a result, the unions openly take the position that their now declared object to monopolize all employments has been legalized and that they have a right to exercise monopoly controls over jobs and wages, and over the quality, quantity, and price of products. This means that the greater the power of the unions, the greater becomes their monopoly control of the entire economy, with the eventual destruction of a competitive economy becoming inevitable with the constant rise of labor power. There is no possibility of preserving a free economy unless the exercise of such monopoly powers by organized labor is clearly made unlawful.

Proposition 2. "Compulsory unionism, a form of involuntary servitude, should be abolished by law. This is a duty of Congress under the Thirteenth Amendment."

Fifty years ago, when the closed shop was only an agreement between a single employer and a group of employees, the requirement that every employee in one plant should be a member of a local union would not impose involuntary servitude on any one, because there were plenty of competing enterprises where a man could get a job without joining a union. The closed shop was then an exception and the open shop the rule.

Today, when unions have enlarged to huge numbers and the coverage of union contracts is often industry-wide, the requirement that a man must join a union in order to obtain a particular employment has become in fact a requirement that he must join a union, a private organization, in order to be able to work. In one industry after another the door has been closed to the employment of any except union members.

It is a simple fact today that compulsory unionism is a denial to millions of men of any ability to earn a living except by agreeing to pay dues and submit to the discipline of a private organization. They cannot even withdraw from a labor union if violently opposed to its economic or political policies without losing the ability to earn a livelihood. This is in reality an involuntary servitude which it is not only the right but the duty of the Congress under the Thirteenth Amendment to forbid by law.

Proposition 3. "The right to strike should be qualified and limited by defining the lawful objects, the lawful methods, and the lawful occasions for strikes." Strikes should be held unlawful which are:
"Strikes against the public health, safety, and welfare.
"Strikes to compel political action.
"Strikes without a preceding reasonable effort to avoid a strike.
"Strikes conducted with the aid or toleration of criminal violence."

It may be easy to make the foregoing statements, but the question immediately arises: Suppose a law is passed making such wrongful strikes unlawful? In the first place, how will the law be enforced? In the second place, how will the economic conflicts be settled which will still inevitably arise?

The answer to the first question is not a difficult one. Senator Taft once asked me, in a discussion about outlawing certain strikes, how you were going to put ten thousand men in jail. I answered him that that would never be necessary. A large effective strike requires organization and leadership. There are very few spontaneous mass uprisings. Generally, even rioting has organization behind it. To prevent lawless collective action, all that is necessary is to strike at the leadership and centers of organization of any such mass movement.

Certainly the communists have taught us this lesson, even if they have done it in a most vicious and indefensible manner. But, the government antistrike action against John L. Lewis and the United Mine Workers should have settled the question for all time that a vigorous government can, with due process of law, peacefully prevent, or at least make ineffective, any unlawful strike.

The second question is a much more serious one. Certainly a strike against the public health, safety, and welfare should be subject to prevention. On the other hand, those who are engaged in rendering services, as in public utilities, which are essential to the public health, safety, and welfare, should not be left subject to the dictation of a private management as to the terms and conditions of their employment. Their grievances should have a full opportunity of just settlement.

Here, however, we find a curious inconsistency in public thinking. It has been long accepted that the rates and conditions of public service can be regulated by government tribunals. Why, therefore, should not the wages and conditions of employment be likewise regulated? The stock answer is that "property rights," such as payments for, and protection of capital can be submitted to judicial tribunals, but that "human rights" to wages and working conditions should not be subject to any such determination.

In the first place, it should be pointed out that fixing rates and service conditions in a public utility is not merely determining the rights of investors, but also the very important rights, the "human rights," if you will, of thousands of consumers who are absolutely dependent upon public utility services. They are certainly as vitally interested in proper utility rates as wage earners are in proper wages. Furthermore, the standards by which fair wages for labor can be determined are about as easily ascertained and can be as impartially applied as the standards fixing payments for capital and fair rates for utility service.

As a final answer, however, to all those who object to any judicial settlement of wages and working conditions in industries of public necessity, I may suggest that anyone who engages as his livelihood in an industry of vital necessity has taken for himself the security of an employment upon which his fellow citizens are definitely dependent. He should accept an obligation to give continuous service. Furthermore, even public utility services are competitive to some extent with other services. Prices should not be forced up indefinitely by increased labor costs. Consumers use more electricity because it is cheap. They use less coal and more oil for fuel partly because John L. Lewis and his followers have used monopoly power so unwisely as to price their product out of many markets. Milk is a necessity to some, but a luxury, as the price goes up, to others.

However, it is not my proposition that any law should require the compulsory arbitration of all labor disputes in essential industries. Representatives of management and labor should not only have opportunity, but be required to make every reasonable effort, to agree upon terms and conditions of employment. But if, because of disagreement and the absence of a contract under which cooperation can continue, the public is threatened with a stoppage in production or distribution of an essential commodity or service, then there should be a recognized public right to intervene and to insure for a brief period, such as six months or one year, a continuation of production either with or without modification of the existing contract.

Such a law would not impose any involuntary servitude because no worker would be required to continue his employment. But it should be a provision of the law that any worker quitting his work would be acting as an individual, resigning all present and future rights, as he would in any permanent quitting of employment. It would also be unlawful to conduct or maintain any concerted withdrawal of employment or boycott of the business involved. As a practical matter, we may be sure that the vast majority of American workers, unionized or nonunionized, would welcome and live happily under a law which lifted from them the burdens and losses of strikes. I venture the prophecy that those industries in which striking had been practically outlawed would become rapidly among the most preferred of employments.

Political Strikes. There should be no argument among believers in the American form of government that strikes to compel political action should be outlawed. The idea of converting an economic organization into a political organization has grown recently, but has still not grown to the point where the American worker desires to find himself hazarding his livelihood from time to time and stopping his earning power in the effort to compel a political action regarding which he may be far from enthusiastic. Furthermore, the attempt to coerce public officials by concerted attacks on the public welfare is a subversive attack upon our form of government.

Quickie Strikes. As a principle, most persons will agree that strikes without a preceding reasonable effort to avoid a strike are an intolerable wrong on all three parties concerned. First of all, on the worker; second, on the management; and third, on the consuming public. Nevertheless, in recent years there have been plagues of petty strikes throughout industries, which clearly show the need for putting a brake upon the abuse of power by little men vested with a brief authority. Penalizing such strikes should be a matter of easy legislation and prosecution.

Lawless Violence. What to do about a strike conducted with the aid or toleration of criminal violence is a more complicated problem. It is entirely possible for agents provocateurs or outsiders to take advantage of a strike situation and to "frame" a law-abiding labor organization with charges of criminality. Nevertheless, it is not unreasonable to require that any organization conducting a strike take every reasonable means of preventing criminal violence. Nor is it difficult, as a rule, to distinguish a labor organization which lives by and with the aid of violence from one which is essentially law-abiding.

Under the cloak of unionism, so many vicious, intolerable criminal organizations have flourished that it should be made to the interest of all legitimate labor organizations to dissociate themselves from such criminality. Contrariwise, at the present time there is far too close association and cooperation between organizations of a fundamentally criminal character and those which are primarily law-abiding, but entirely willing to be the beneficiaries of lawlessness.

Fifty years ago, when labor unions were struggling even to gain the right of recognition and struggling against vicious lawless tactics of many employers and employer organizations, there was much excuse if not justification for the use of hoodlums, sluggers, and even worse criminals by those who felt they were fighting for the underdog against overwhelming respectable but tyrannical power. Today, there is little excuse for criminality in support of the legitimate activities of labor unions. It would be far better for the health of labor and for its public relations if outstanding labor leaders supported instead of opposed laws intelligently designed to prevent racketeering and criminality under cloak of labor organizations.

There is a principle which may be regarded as legal as well as moral, which is that, as private power over the welfare of others increases, public responsibility for the welfare of others also increases as a legal and enforceable obligation. It is now well recognized that the conduct of the great industries in a modern nation involves such power over the national welfare that the managers of those industries have a public responsibility for the national welfare represented by an increasing number of legal obligations. Among these are a great number and complexity of obligations to their employees.

In the same way, it must be recognized that the labor organizations in the great industries of the country have such vast power over the welfare of those industries, and hence over the public welfare, that they should likewise be subject to legal obligations to fulfill that public responsibility. In these circumstances, the conduct of labor relations as a form of civil warfare becomes as vicious and antiquated as the practice of dueling.

Centuries ago civilized men began establishing courts to settle all disputes, even of the most personal character, by a peaceful administration of justice instead of by trial by combat. Only gangsters, outlaws, and crazy people today resort to guns and fists to decide their business disagreements. In practically all social and business relations (except in the lunacy of labor relations) good citizens either use peaceful pressures or apply to the courts to adjust their conflicting interests.

Why do we still attempt to settle big and little disputes between employers and employees by force and violence? Why do workers go on strike, depriving themselves of wages they need, injuring the employers who provide them with work, and often imposing great hardship on an innocent public? Why do employers and employees waste enormous amounts of money and energy preparing for warfare and waging wars against each other?

Why do we, here in the United States, tolerate the waging of civil warfare as the means of settling industrial disputes, although we have full power to enact and enforce laws forbidding such warfare and providing the means for peaceful settlement of all industrial conflicts? Why is it that even in wartime we not only refuse to draft men to work for their country, but we actually legalize and support organizations that prevent men from working?

The answer is that we have been fed a mental poison for years which is responsible for the prevailing lunacy of our labor relations. That poison is that there is an irreconcilable conflict between the interests of employers and employees. Yet our whole history shows that there is a community of interest between employers and employees which is much more important to both of them than their competitive interest in sharing the rewards of their common effort.

First, they must work together to produce something of value to someone else. No one can do this job for them and their community of interest lies in producing and selling goods and services that others want and can buy. They are their own best judges of the fair conditions of their joint work and the fair sharing of its rewards. But, if self-interest blinds them to the point where they cannot agree, surely here is the obvious place to bring in the objective judgment of an impartial arbitrator. But a public arbitrator can only decide a simple dispute as a temporary action: he cannot tell employers and employees how to work together and make a success of their joint undertaking. Politicians are not trained or equipped to plan and manage business enterprises.

Yet, strange to say, those who shrink from the idea of calling in a public arbitrator to decide a particular disagreement between experienced management and experienced labor are the very ones who propose as an alternative the socialization of industry. In other words, they propose to substitute for the operation of industry by experienced management and experienced labor an ultimate control by inexperienced unqualified politicians!

As we see our political economy sliding down from the uplands of a free economy into the morasses of state socialism, we may well ask ourselves why we tolerate the constant disruption of industry by strikes, why we do not try for once in our economic history to insist upon the peaceful cooperation of management and labor.

The legal principle to be applied is a simple one. Labor relations, like all other social relations, should be based on voluntary agreement. If parties in association cannot agree, and the public is concerned in their disagreement, public tribunals should be available to settle their dispute temporarily for them. If they are unwilling to accept this public judgment, they may cease peacefully to have relations with each other. The only thing they should not be permitted legally to do is to resort to violence and coercion to force their will upon others—to deny the civil rights of individuals and to inflict injuries on opponents and on the public.

We should not tolerate the increasing menace of industrial warfare that is today simply a legalized form of civil warfare. A rule of law to preserve peace and to establish justice should prove to be as fruitful of human happiness in labor relations as it has been proved to be in all other human relations.

Labor Unions Are Worth the Price

Max Ways

The effort toward giving union members a sense of participation in the control of their working life is and always has been at the heart of American unionism. Accelerated technological change increases the pressure from below on the leaders to provide the protection workers want; at the same time it increases the danger that the steps the unions take to fulfill their function will exact too great a price from the U.S. economy.

This dilemma—and not the cost of strikes—is today's and tomorrow's real "labor problem," and much union energy in recent years has been directed toward dealing with the difficulties posed by the pressures of rapid industrial change. To handle this task unions themselves have had to change, to improvise new devices in dealing with employers, with one another, and with their own members. Although accused of stagnation, the unions are, in fact, teeming with innovation and efforts toward internal improvement.

The Steelworkers, for example, is not a model union; some of its old friends complain that the fire and enthusiasm of its early years have been frozen into a bureaucracy. But bureaucracy can be another name for competent, functionalized administration, and this union has constructed working channels of two-way communications running from the plant floor to the top of a vast (900,000-member) structure. It does much of its bargaining on a national basis, yet it is able to handle effectively the host of individual grievances that arise in the plants. This is no small achievement. Many British unions that bargain nationally have lost touch with the shop stewards, who often disrupt production by acting independently of the national body; on the Continent national unions have, in general, even less top-to-bottom structure than in Britain. In consequence, workers' specific grievances, instead of being resolved within a contractual framework, melt into an ugly lump of politicized class grievance against the bosses and the system.

The Steelworkers and management are now [1963] trying to remove a wide range of issues from the pressures of deadline negotiations. The Human Relations Committee is a year-round joint study group investigating such questions as seniority and work rules. These matters can be of immense importance to individual workers, but, unless the rules are knowledgeably and carefully written, they can impose inefficiencies that cost much more than the benefits are worth. It's too early to say whether steel's Human Relations Committee will do any real good, but at least a sane and novel approach has been made. More interesting is the recent agreement worked out between the Steelworkers

Reprinted from the May 1963 issue of Fortune Magazine *by special permission;* © *1963 Time, Inc. Mr. Ways is a member of* Fortune Magazine's *Board of Editors.*

and Kaiser Steel Corp. Groups of Kaiser workers now receiving incentive pay may vote to give this up (each getting a substantial lump-sum payment for a transitional period); these workers and all others will receive a third of cost savings Kaiser makes by automation or in any other way; to minimize the displacement of workers that may result from cost cutting, workers will be protected by new job-security provisions and strengthened seniority rules. None of the authors of this plan hails it as "the" answer for industry in general or even for the whole steel industry. It is to be a four-year experiment in one company where management and workers, apparently, are acutely aware of the need for cutting costs in the face of competition, while giving the workers as much protection as possible.

Walter Reuther's United Automobile Workers is another union that can hardly be accused of stagnation either in collective bargaining or in efforts to improve the quality of its internal organization. For years the U.A.W. has vainly proposed to the automobile companies that joint study groups be set up in advance of negotiations. This year for the first time the automobile companies seem interested in exploring the plan. Meanwhile, in the way it runs its own affairs the U.A.W. has made a novel approach to the protection of individual members aggrieved by union decisions. Such cases are bound to occur where unions are large, their contracts and procedures complex, their staffs expert, and their officers possessed of the self-confidence that comes with experience in which the rank and file cannot share. Reuther, than whom there is no more self-confident man, is proud these days of having established in the U.A.W. a "supreme court" of seven eminent men, not members of the union, who can decide appeals by aggrieved members against U.A.W. organs or officers, including Reuther. This "court" has heard 122 cases, and its existence is said to have had a substantial effect in making U.A.W. leaders at all levels more careful of the rights of dissidents.

The four biggest unions in the U.S.—the outcast Teamsters, the Steelworkers, the U.A.W., and the Machinists—account for a highly significant quarter of all organized workers, and these are all exceedingly lively unions. But the vigor and change reach further down. Even the unions of the building trades, usually the prime example of reactionary, restrictive "business unionism," show signs of effort toward internal improvement. In recent years they have reduced the damage done by interunion conflict over job jurisdiction.

The plumbers' union, not in the past a progress-minded group, has responded to the challenge of changing technology by operating one of the best training programs of any union. Purdue University helped to train instructors. Scores of locals have set up their own classrooms. Journeymen as well as apprentices are the students. Not long ago the union's president, Peter T. Schoemann, presented diplomas to a group of trainees whose average age was sixty. "What are you old birds going to school for?" asked Schoemann, who is sixty-nine. He was told, "We got tired of holding the pipe while the young men made the weld. Now we've learned to make the weld and they can hold the pipe." Strictly "selfish," of course—but the kind of motivation that built a great nation.

Heart of the training program is lavishly illustrated textbooks that cost several hundred thousand dollars to develop. Union leaders hold out the pipe fitters' manual, inviting the awe and admiration usually reserved for the *Book of Kells*. When the plumbers go all starry-eyed about a training book, it is certain that not all sense of progress has disappeared from the American labor movement.

Management will be deluded if it accepts the widespread opinion that the unions' failure to increase their proportion of the total work force is a sign of weakness. Membership figures must be read against the background of union history and in the framework of present United States employment trends.

In the first place, the labor movement—unlike the telephone business and the diaper-wash industry—is not comfortably pinned to the population curve. Membership in American unions . . . has always advanced in sprints and these sprints are connected more with broad changes in United States life than with the quality or energy of labor leadership. The biggest numerical gains, in fact, have been associated with wartime or postwar labor shortages. In terms of percentage of the labor force, the unions have done better at holding their World War II gains than they did in the years after 1920. American unionism since 1945 has passed through searing vicissitudes—struggles in some unions over Communism, the effects of the Taft-Hartley law, the McClellan investigation—without any substantial exodus of members. (By contrast, the postwar struggles over Communist leadership in some French unions lost millions of members who have never reappeared in French unions.)

Moreover, United States unions have been working against a tide: production workers, among whom unionism has always been strongest, have been declining in proportion to the total work force. Some liberal intellectuals, in their present anti-union mood, will not accept this excuse for union "stagnation"; they demand that unions make more strenuous efforts to break out of their old strongholds and organize the unskilled (especially Negroes) and the growing number of white-collar workers. But in both categories the obstacles to union progress are too deep-seated to be overcome by mere improvement of union leadership or a surge of union organizing "energy."

Before the mid-thirties unskilled industrial workers were mainly white—and unions made little headway in organizing them. Many unskilled production workers—along with skilled and semiskilled—were enrolled during the rapid progress of industrial unionism from 1936 to 1945. But this still left outside of unions many unskilled workers in the service trades, which are now expanding, and in numerous pockets of employment not accessible to industrial unionism. These unskilled workers today have a high proportion of Negroes, Puerto Ricans, and Mexicans, but race is not among the main reasons why more are not organized. Unskilled workers are so easy to replace that they have little inherent bargaining power—the stuff unionism can mobilize and make more effective, but which it cannot create. Moreover, service workers, rarely concentrated in large groups, tend to be harder to organize than factory workers.

In some quarters the idea seems to be that the 1,750,000 Negroes now in unions could be multiplied if labor leaders took a much stronger stand in championing Negro rights and aspirations. In fact, union leadership has a good recent record of anti-discrimination—a record that has undeniably hurt union organizing drives among southern white workers. Whatever may be the ethical merits of the case for even stronger union policies favoring underprivileged groups, there is little chance that adoption of such policies would result in a big net gain in union membership. Those at the bottom of the social escalator may "need" unionism most, but unionism has been most effective within a middle band of workers who have substantial pre-union bargaining power.

Above the middle band lies the unions' other area of frustration, the white-collar workers, of whom less than 15 percent are unionized. Market demand for white-collar workers has been stronger than for production workers. Just before, during, and just after World War II, however, production workers apparently were closing the pay-and-working-condition gap between themselves and the white-collars. This overtaking movement has ceased, and the white-collars may be drawing away again.

Many of the fringe benefits (e.g., sick pay, vacations) on which blue-collar unions are now concentrating have for years been standard in much white-collar employment. The main white-collar advantage—and the one that makes this group hard to unionize—is continuity of job, "the annual wage." Hourly paid production workers, subject to layoff at management discretion, are less reluctant than white-collar workers to interrupt their pay by striking. Where a very high proportion of a white-collar group has been organized (e.g., actors) there is often a background of discontinuous employment. The upper levels of white-collar workers have one other pertinent advantage over production workers: a measure of built-in control over the pace and pattern of their own work. Managers usually don't need a union to tell them that "overbossing" of technicians results in lost efficiency.

The majority of white-collar workers are not likely to be organized unless there are major shifts in the terms of their employment. Such shifts may appear. Years ago, when white-collars were a small minority in most businesses, it was easy to provide them with continuous employment; today the growing proportion of white-collar workers represents in many companies a cost rigidity that is hard to take when business is slack. If management tries to meet this difficulty with white-collar layoffs, or if office automation is too rapid, or if white-collar jobs become overbossed, there may be huge union gains among this group. But in the absence of such changes it is hard to believe that a mere stepping up of union "energy" is going to organize millions of workers who have, without unions, an increasing market power already superior to that of unionized production workers.

In sum, the odds are that in the near future total union membership will not increase or decline sharply.

The present wave of anti-union feeling raises again the question of what effect unions have on the economy. In such an appraisal there are some bear traps for the unwary. The two groups that sound off most loudly about the effect of unions are labor leaders and labor baiters; they tend to agree with each other in rating the impact of unionism very high. The labor leader gives unions credit for a generation of rapid gains by workers, and the labor baiter says almost the same thing when he fixes upon unions the chief blame for rising costs and prices. The truth seems to be that the economic impact of unions is not so great as either group asserts.

In a remarkably clear, concise, and balanced . . . book, *The Economics of Trade Unions,* Albert Rees of the University of Chicago, working from a number of detailed studies, has arrived at some sophisticated opinions about the cost of unions. One way of getting at the wage effect is to compare the wage rates of union members with those of unorganized employees doing comparable tasks. Rees's educated guess is that the over-all difference at any point in time amounts to between 10 and 15 percent. In some industries that are almost completely organized, unions reach periods when they are unable to raise the relative wages of workers at all. An example is the Amalgamated Clothing Workers, once one of the most effective unions. Since the war it has been stymied, and the usual cries have been raised of tired, old leadership. But the Amalgamated had excellent leadership in depth, and it is hardly plausible that the sudden lowering in the union's effectiveness is traceable mainly to leadership. The explanation, according to Rees, is that market factors heavily condition union effectiveness. In the men's clothing field, the postwar market has been soft and many employers are in trouble. In such a situation, even the strongest union must choose between scaling down its wage demands or accepting greater unemployment among its members.

Following the late Henry C. Simons and others, Rees believes that union action in raising wages tends to decrease employment opportunities. (Even where the number of jobs increases, the expansion of employment is slower than it would have been if wage rates had not been pressed upward by union action.) Usually, unemployment in an industry acts as a brake on wage demands. The great exception to this for years has been the United Mine Workers, which forced up wage rates while making no effort to slow the mechanization that was spurred by rising labor costs. The number of coal miners declined from about 450,000 in 1947 to 119,000, while hourly earnings almost doubled.

Rees says that it cannot be proved that unions measurably increase "the workers' share" of total income at the expense of the owners of capital. Union gains are probably paid for by other workers or consumers. On the other hand, Rees defends unions against the charge that they are solely or mainly responsible for "cost-push inflation." Unions can aggravate inflationary dangers arising from monetary or other causes, but their "push" on costs becomes inflationary only when wrong policies are pursued elsewhere in the economy.

The chief cost of unions is not strike losses or cost-push, but the distortions and rigidities that unionism introduces into the market system. Rees says: "If the union is viewed solely in terms of its effect on the economy, it must in my opinion be considered an obstacle to the optimum performance of our economic system."

He has, however, more to say. Although he is an economist, Rees knows that life is not an exercise in economics. American unions rose not in response to an economic theory, but as a complex institutional form of expressing the complex reactions of workers to the pressures of industrial society. "By giving workers protection against arbitrary treatment by employers, by acting as their representative in politics, and by reinforcing their hope of continuous future gain, unions have helped to assure that the basic values of our society are widely diffused and that our disagreements on political and economic issues take place within a broad framework of agreement." He notes that American manual workers are committed to the preservation of a political democracy and a free-enterprise economy and that they are not, "as in many other democracies, constantly . . . attempting to replace it with something radically different." Rees concludes: "The economic losses imposed by unions are not too high a price to pay" for the psychological, social, and political benefits.

Even if this judgment is true about the past and present, what are the prospects? Are the future costs imposed by unions on the economy likely to become "too high"?

In recent years direct union pressure on wage rates has slowed down a bit. But a great deal of present labor activity and conflict is on fronts other than wages; most of these issues are connected with adjustments to technological change; many of them involve the possibility of high economic loss by union infringement on management's "right to manage."

While this danger is real, the actual picture is more complex and more balanced than is generally supposed. In the first place, unions in many industries have had the effect of speeding up the pace of technological improvements. One railroad executive put it this way: "If it wasn't for those damn unions, we'd be using as many man-hours to do every job as we did twenty years ago. Every time they get an increase, we have to get off our duffs and find a cheaper way to do things."

This quote represents an important hidden truth about "the right to manage." If it is assumed that complete managerial control exists prior to any union infringement on management power, then every concession to unions in the form of work rules and other limitations represents a diminution of management power. Examination of the masses of these limitations that have been written in the last fifty years—and are still being written—might lead to the conclusion that management is gradually being pushed into a corner where it has less and less control of the enterprises for which it is legally responsible. But anybody who observes the American business scene knows that picture to be false; management has, in fact, a greater degree of control than it had fifty years ago, and its control increases year by year.

The explanation lies in the falsity of the original assumption that "complete management" preceded union interference. Complete management, the total subjection of action to rational control, never exists. Whether confusion be attributed to original sin or to the undomesticated Freudian id, the truth is that in human affairs, individual or group, the segment of unmanaged activity exceeds the segment of managed activity. (Saints and the Bell Telephone System may be exceptions to this rule.) Masters never exercise complete rational control over slaves, nor parents over children, nor any man over himself, nor managers over a work process.

For example, the imposition by unions of seniority rules in layoffs seems to be an encroachment on the right to manage. But before the unions interfered, the selection of the particular individuals to lay off was often not really a management decision (i.e., it was not worked out rationally in terms of the interest of the enterprise). Foremen and supervisors, unguided by policy from above, selected by favoritism or at random the workers to be retained or laid off. Nobody in his right mind would argue that seniority was the most efficient or economically rational way of selecting workers for continuous employment or for promotion. But in many cases what seniority rules replaced was not rational management but merely power exercised in a way that seemed unfair and arbitrary to workers. It seemed so because that's what it was.

The struggle over the control of labor is not simply management vs. unions. The older struggle is that of management vs. chaos, or unmanagement. Unions make it a three-cornered fight. Nobody can promise that union encroachments upon "the right to manage" will not advance faster than management's ability to win from chaos new frontiers of rational control. In industries where that has happened the costs of unionism may be disastrous. But the general record of a hundred years of unionism indicates that—so far—union power and management effectiveness have *both* advanced together.

When they encroach upon the right to manage, American unions are not trying to take over enterprises; they are trying to restrict or cushion change or to give the workers a sense that some power over the job is in their hands. Since American unions are themselves immersed in market psychology, every union encroachment has a price at which it may be traded for some other potential union advantage.

A most remarkable example of this occurred on the West Coast in 1961. For thirty years Harry Bridges had built up a fantastically restrictive set of work rules. Unneeded men were required for all sorts of specific jobs around the docks. When Bridges was asked what these supernumeraries should be called, his cynical humor answered: "Witnesses." The burden was becoming so intolerable to employers that they "bought" all the restrictive work rules in a single package in return for large employer payments into a special fund that will make possible earlier retirement and larger pensions for longshoremen. The agreement endangered some hundreds of dock-worker jobs, but these were held by "B-men" without voting rights in Bridges' union. The employers have obtained, at a price, a free hand to improve productivity on the West Coast wharves.

What Bridges did in a wholesale deal, other unions do all the time on a retail basis. Much has been heard lately about the printers' insistence on "setting bogus" or "dead horse." But it is less widely known that "dead horse" is often stored up, unset, on the spike and then traded off at the end of a contract term for small additions to wage or other concessions. After the East Coast longshoremen's strike was settled in February, there was a sudden flare-up on a Manhattan pier, where an employer had introduced an unusual distribution of the work gang between the pier, the deck, and the hold. The workers considered this a violation of an agreement to maintain local work patterns unchanged; apparently they had it in mind that the right to change the pattern could be "sold" in some future negotiation. Union officials had to tell them that on this particular pier the right had already been conceded to the shipowner.

The proliferation of specific work rules in American union contracts is not paralleled in other industrial countries—but the actual situation in other countries is not necessarily better from management's point of view. British managers are conscious of worker resistance to automation and change even though that resistance has not been embodied in specific contractual provisions. One result is that the hidden worker resistance in Britain is used by managers to reinforce their own inertia, with the consequence that the pace of industrial change in Britain is slower than in the United States. One rogue whale of a shipowner in New York holds that the slowness of technological change on the waterfront there is attributable mainly to the inertia of shipowners, who for decades were dealing with a weak and racket-ridden union. Now that the East Coast longshoremen are somewhat stronger they may make wage and other bargaining gains; squeezed, the shipowners may be forced into cost-cutting improvements.

The United States practice of writing specific rules into contracts at least exposes the featherbedding to view where it can be argued about, bargained about, and sometimes traded off. It is somewhat more difficult for management to deal with the deep-seated worker resistance, which surfaces only in unofficial slowdowns and general foot-dragging.

The extreme untidiness, the messiness, of collective bargaining in the United States is apparent on all sides. One union is deciding to stress wages while another decides to deemphasize wages and stress security; or the same union reverses its emphasis from one year to another. But these shifting decisions do not express mere whim; they are responses to changing conditions in various industries, and changing fears and desires of particular groups of workers. So untidy, so shifting, so relative is the American labor scene that it *must* be deeply involved in that most untidy, shifting, and relative of all human institutions, the market.

This involvement is no accident but the development of the character that Samuel Gompers imprinted on American unions as boldly as his signature, which adorns the charters that hang in Washington union offices. For Gompers' great invention was the word "more" as a description of what the unions wanted. Usually this word is recalled as an example of the unions' unappeasable voracity; but in its original context and its long-range effect its significance is different. On New York's East Side when Gompers was young, a hundred ideologies of labor competed with one another. His predecessor as head of the Cigar Makers, Adolph Strasser, rebelled against the belief that unions should be considered instruments for gaining utopian goals. In 1873, testifying before a United States Senate committee, Strasser was asked, "What are your ultimate ends?" And he answered: "We have no ultimate ends. We are going on from day to day. We are fighting only for immediate objects—objects that can be realized in a few years." Gompers, accepting the thought, boiled it down to "more, now."

Thereby the United States labor movement committed itself to the United States market system. Again and again ideologues, many of them Marxists, have tried vainly to turn American unions from their "purposeless" pursuit, their concentration on responding to immediate pressures and on improvement within a short perspective of a few years. Gompers' "more" was a non-utopian acceptance of limits rather than an arrogant demand. He didn't want to get to an ideal society; where he wanted the workers to go was merely ahead.

In its refusal to define an ultimate goal of its activity, the labor movement Gompers shaped is not so different from business. Because of the limited ends they have in common, because of their involvement in the messy quicksands of the market, both the businessman and the labor leader have drawn upon themselves the antagonism of modern intellectuals. Unions, whenever they can be hopefully interpreted as instruments toward ideological goals, attract the affection and support of intellectuals; but when they descend into the obscure specifics of practical bargaining, their highbrow friends—and not the Marxists alone—desert them.

This is understandable if not excusable. After all, one of the highest functions of an intellectual is to imprison the buzzing fly of life in the clear amber of definition. The service is indispensable if society is to understand itself, even a little. But the service is difficult to perform, and many modern intellectuals slothfully insist that the fly crawl into the amber of its own accord. This demand is the featherbedding of the intellectuals.

Anybody who wants to understand the labor movement had better start with the object itself in all its historical complexity and the multiple contradictions and defects of its present position. He had better not start with a preconceived notion of what a labor movement, considered as an instrument for attaining the ideal society, ought to be. An example of the latter approach is the complaint of a liberal intellectual, disillusioned with unions, who declared that government intervention must increase because "collective bargaining has failed to solve the labor problem." Indeed, it has failed—and in a free society there can never be any "solution" to the labor problem, the price problem, the investment problem, or the woman problem.

QUESTIONS FOR DISCUSSION

1. *Do you think unions are too powerful today? If so, why and in what ways?*
2. *If you were a union official, how would you respond to the three propositions advanced by Richberg for the "control of union power"?*
3. *Do you see any problems for unions if their power to strike is seriously reduced?*
4. *What are some of the reasons offered by Ways to account for labor's alleged decline in power? Do you agree with his assessment?*
5. *Are unions worth the price?*

Is Automation a Boon or a Threat?

Automation is ". . . the technique of making an apparatus, a process, or a system operate automatically." However, that definition by Webster's New Collegiate tells us very little about what automation really is and what effects it is having on our economy and society. The idea of "automatically" producing goods calls up diverse impressions, ranging from the poor sorcerer's apprentice at the mercy of his own magical broom or pathetic Charlie Chaplin caught in the gears of some monstrous machine, to man's old and practically universal dream of producing goods with little or no human effort.

On the credit side automation has brought about great gains in productivity. There can be little doubt that the current high level of per capita output by the national economy would not have been possible without the recent expanded use of laborsaving machines. Moreover, the expansion of the technology of automation has made possible the development of new goods and services. Our increased use of technological advances cannot be separated from the growth of our affluence.

On the other hand, automation has posed serious questions. First, it has proceeded at a very rapid pace in the past twenty to thirty years, producing much confusion and ignorance about its effects—both those beneficial and those detrimental to the national economy. Second, automation has created real hardships at the same time it has produced gains. A few years ago the Department of Labor calculated that the employment effect of automation advances was to eliminate about two hundred thousand jobs each year. Others, including a spokesman for business, have put the figure as high as two million jobs per year. Unless new jobs are to be found for these workers, plus jobs for the normal new entrants into the work force, the gains of automation may be canceled by the losses in employment.

Clearly the advance of technology may be a boon to us all. Few

Americans would support efforts to halt its advances as the English weavers sought to destroy the hated machines that were introduced in the cloth industry in the nineteenth century. The advances of automation are having a profound impact on the nature of work, the demand for skills, and the overall organization of production. One of the following articles, by the Ad Hoc Committee on the Triple Revolution, even sees automation and cybernation (defined as the automatic programming of output) destroying the traditional work-reward system of a capitalist economy. According to this view, unless income is separated from jobs and received independently of work, automation will create greater income and social problems than the system can bear.

Automation holds out many problems for the economic system and for conventional economic theory and whether or not it will ultimately be a boon or a threat depends upon our ability to understand its full implications. The following readings present only a few of the issues involved. The reader will note that the problem of automation is closely tied to two later sections in this book— one on problems of maintaining full employment and another on poverty and economic disadvantage.

What Is Automation?

Walter Buckingham

It is as hard for businessmen to define automation as for preachers to define sin. D. S. Harder, vice president of the Ford Motor Company and probable originator of the term automation, calls it a "philosophy of manufacturing." Dr. Gordon Brown of M.I.T. terms it an "open ended issue," meaning a "big thing—one of the biggest in history—whose horizons are still expanding as we learn more of its potentialities." It has been called an intellectual revolution, a new system of thought, the mechanization of judgment, machine control by nonhuman means, and, like Boston, a state of mind. Milton Aaronson, editor of *Instruments and Automation,* describes automation as "the substitution of mechanical, hydraulic, pneumatic, electric and electronic devices for human organs of decision and effort." Facetiously, it has been labeled the "substitution of mechanical error for human error." Still other definitions are in terms

From pp. 5–15 in Automation: Its Impact on Business and People (*Hardbound Ed.*) by *Walter Buckingham. Copyright* © *1961 by Walter Buckingham. Reprinted by permission of Harper & Row, Publishers.*

of electronic control devices, automatic assembly lines, the integration of these two, transfer machinery, industrialization in general, a rapid *rate* of industrialization, and even completely automatic economic and social systems. Peter Drucker says, "Above all, there can be little doubt that automation is not 'technocracy' under another name and that the 'push button factory' is not its symbol. Automation is not gadgeteering, it is not even engineering! It is a concept of the structure and order of economic life, the design of its basic patterns integrated into a harmonious, balanced, and organic whole."

For the purpose of analysis, automation can best be defined as any continuous and integrated operation of a production system that uses electronic or other equipment to regulate and coordinate the quantity and quality of production. In its broadest usage it includes both the manufacturing and administrative processes of a firm. These processes can be distilled into four fundamental principles: mechanization, continuous process, automatic control, and rationalization. Each of these four elements has evolved separately. The novelty of automation as a distinct technology is that it is a synthesis of all four, emerging since World War II from a unique combination of scientific breakthroughs and economic conditions.

Mechanization. The industrial revolution of the eighteenth century was introduced by the fusion of several new concepts into the technology of production. This combination, called mechanization, was destined to grow into what has become the most powerful economic and social force in history. It was based on the principles of machinery, particularly standardization of equipment and specialization of tasks.

Mechanization means the use of machines to perform work. Sometimes mechanization substituted machinery for animal or human muscle. The steam engine did this. More recently mechanization has substituted machinery for human sense organs and brainwork at the lower, routine levels. Machinery is now able to measure, do arithmetic, and control other machinery according to information provided by the measuring and calculating devices. The electronic computer does these. Because of the power, compactness, and speed of machine operation, mechanization frequently permits tasks to be performed that could never be done by human labor alone no matter how much labor was used or how well the operation was organized and managed.

The first industrial revolution was based primarily on the principle of specialization. In Adam Smith's famous declaration of economic independence, the *Wealth of Nations* (published, significantly, in 1776) the division of labor concept was dramatically presented in his celebrated "pin factory" example. Several medieval craftsmen pinmakers could produce a certain number of pins in a day. Each had learned the job through years of apprenticeship. But by breaking the pinmaking job into several component parts, such as drawing wire, cutting, grinding a point, hammering a head, polishing, and so on, each worker could specialize. After a short while the production of pins, using the same number of man hours, would multiply enormously. The extra output came from the high skills which could be developed where jobs and labor were highly specialized.

A classic example is said to be that of Humphrey Potter, a twelve-year-old boy employed in the early eighteenth century in England to operate a handle that admitted steam to the cylinder of Newcomen's first steam engine. Potter, being a person of considerable intelligence, yet having nothing else to do but open and close steam valves, noted that whenever the piston was at one end of the cylinder he opened one valve, and whenever it was at the other end he opened another to let the steam into the other side of the piston. He observed the piston-valve relationship, hooked the valve to the piston so that the piston operated the valve automatically, and thereby invented the slide valve mechanism which is still in use today. Incidentally he worked himself out of a job and into a better one.

Machinery and other capital assets, when properly combined by management with labor and natural resources, are able to multiply like families of rabbits, creating enough economic values to repay all the costs of the equipment plus a reward for the owners. The phenomenon of certain circumstances causing technological changes which, in turn, lead to other circumstances which cause more technological change is not an endless circle of nonsensical reasoning but a continuous, developing process of interactive growth. New machinery requires new skills of labor and new knowledge and abilities of management, which, if properly developed, lead to further technological improvement. Machinery also tends to become more highly specialized causing labor and management to specialize further. This self-sustaining upward spiral of productivity can transform a stagnant subsistence society, [as in] medieval Europe or modern Africa, into a progressive, industrial nation with high living standards. The process is not perpetually cumulative because bottlenecks and diminishing returns eventually retard it but usually not until after great economic growth has taken place.

Since World War II some spectacular discoveries in the fields of electronics and communications have permitted the manufacture of various types of automatic electronic computing machinery. These machines are capable of translating a large body of previously developed, theoretical, economic and business principles into practical significance. They are capable of processing data with almost unbelievable speed. When information is fed into them, usually on tapes, they can perform a series of logical operations and can choose among several previously anticipated courses of action based on built-in criteria. They even adjust automatically for errors. Although these computers are, in part at least, merely an extension of mechanization to clerical work, their operation to solve scientific or commercial problems is often referred to as automation.

The essential difference between modern electronic computing machinery and conventional machinery arising out of the eighteenth century industrial revolution is that electronic devices perform decision-making and control functions whereas the older machines merely did physical labor. While earlier machines replaced only forms of human and animal labor, the new machines take over some tasks that have been performed by management. Automation embodies the principles of mechanization but it is so much more than this. It is a vast extension and integration of several particular forms of machine technology and is more than any of them alone.

Continuous Process. The early twentieth century witnessed a second technological revolution based on the principle of mass production. Essential to the mass production system was implementation of the concept of continuous flow or process. Mass production technology is often referred to as a second stage of the industrial revolution and is sometimes confused with automation itself. However, like mechanization, mass production embodying the continuous process concept is only a part of automation. The unique feature of mass production technology is that it permits an enormous increase in productivity, or output per man hour, not through the use of any new machines or the development of any new power sources as did mechanization, but mainly through a new system of organizing the production process itself.

The continuous flow concept was known in the eighteenth century and occasionally applied to industry, as in flour mills, but it was not until this century that it became widely used. The first innovation of mass production was a discovery which occurred independently and almost simultaneously in the infant automobile industries of Europe and the United States around the turn of this century. It was found that if skilled workers moved from one car to another performing the same task over and over again this specializing of jobs alone, without any new machinery, would speed production enormously. In the United States both Ford and Olds are credited with this discovery although it was discovered independently in England, France, and possibly other countries which had developed to about the same technological stage.

The second innovation quickly followed the first. Why not let the workers stay put and have the job move by them? This assembly-line idea was borrowed from the meat-packing industry in Chicago, where, as early as the 1870s, a moving conveyor had been in use. Although better called a dissembly line, since beef carcasses moved by while workers took them apart, the principle was borrowed for assembling, first, magnetos and then entire automobiles. By merely changing the way in which labor and machinery were combined, productivity was enormously increased again.

Between the world wars the assembly line spread to a host of industries while the automobile industry, where it was used first and most effectively, mushroomed into one of the largest industries in the world. World War II introduced a further innovation which completed the evolution of mass production technology. This was the development of automatic transfer machines which integrated the various stages of production so that a continuous flow or process could be secured without the intervention of human labor. These machines handle a piece of work, put it in proper position, fasten it in place, perform some operation on it, release it, move it on to the next stage, and receive the next piece. All this is without any direct human intervention. The whole line of machines is run from a remote electronic control panel.

Since World War II mass production in the automobile and other industries has been greatly speeded up through supplementing conventional assembly-line operations with these new automatic and semi-automatic transfer devices. Hundreds of individual mechanical functions are now being performed without any direct human intervention. The operation of these integrated assembly lines is called Detroit Automation although, like mechanization, this is only another part of the whole automation picture. Actually, automatic transfer equipment was first used by the Morris Motor Company in Great Britain in 1923. At that time it was technically successful but not economical because capital was expensive relative to labor. So the machines were set aside. Now that real hourly wages have doubled and machinery costs have fallen relatively (due to technological advance and freer world trade), the use of this equipment is expanding rapidly in Britain, the United States, and many other countries.

For some industries which process fluids (like oil, milk, or beer) or homogeneous pulverized, mixed, or finely divided solids (like flour, paper, or cement) transfer machines are not necessary for automation. But for industries dealing with the manufacture or assembly of separate units such as automobiles, television sets, or electric motors, the automatic transfer machine permits many separate partial assembly lines to be combined into one continuous process. Thus, transfer machines can make what had formerly been a series of separate, individual job operations into a single, integrated, automatically controlled process. The application of continuous flow technology has a growing importance because the concept itself is spreading from many individual production processes to the business enterprise and on to the entire economy. Mass production, increased interdependence, and now automation embody this principle which is leading to a concept of the business enterprise as an endless process. Business for the most part has ceased being an operation that can be started and stopped with small loss. The regulation of a constant flow of goods has become a major concern of management.

Automatic Control. The third principle of automation is automatic control, or feedback. This is a concept of control whereby the input of machines is regulated by the machine's own output so that the output meets the conditions of a predetermined objective. As in a simple, thermostatically controlled heating system, the conditions created by the output automatically control, in turn, the amount of input and hence the performance of the machine. When controlled by the feedback principle, machines start and stop themselves and regulate quality and quantity of output automatically. Unlike the mechanization and continuous process concepts, feedback is unique to automation.

There are countless examples of feedback in nature. One is the well-known fur cycle in Canada whereby the number of rabbits and lynxes oscillates regularly. This is due to the fact that lynxes depend on rabbits for food. When the rabbit population rises, so does the survival rate of lynxes, who then deplete the supply of rabbits, causing a decline of lynxes and so on.

Over a century ago, Darwin used a feedback concept to explain why so many bumblebees were found in English towns. The Napoleonic Wars had reduced England's male population. There was an increase in unmarried females—old maids—who typically lived in small towns and kept many cats. Cats feed on mice. Mice, in turn, eat bees. Hence, an increase in cats caused a decline in mice, and since mice eat bees, an increase in bees. More cats led to more bees. The war upset the natural feedback or equilibrium in the animal world. There are many other examples of feedback such as the blood system of animals, the oxygen-carbon dioxide cycle in the atmosphere, general price-output equilibrium in classical economic theory, and the level of employment in Keynesian economic analysis. The control of national economics and of economic and technological progress as well is governed increasingly by feedback principles.

Feedback principles have been known and applied mechanically for centuries. Windmills in the seventeenth century used feedback devices to keep their blades always facing the wind. James Watt's familiar flyball governors were automatically controlling steam engine speeds in 1788 just as they control engines today. Charles Babbage devised an analytical engine—the first calculating machine—using feedback principles in 1840. There are other early examples of feedback technology but, like Babbage's calculating machine, the skills, tools, and materials needed to perfect these devices on a large scale and expand them to other uses were not available. It was not until World War II that breakthroughs in the field of electronics permitted truly automatic control devices to be manufactured which had wide applicability and highly efficient operation.

Feedback is used today in combination with mechanization and continuous process technology to produce results that were impossible only ten years ago. Electronic computers are fed cards or magnetic tapes containing information upon which machines are to act. Production problems encountered by machines regulate or determine the information fed into the computer at a later stage. The machines can control output, choose between alternative courses of action, and correct themselves for changes in inputs, outputs, machine wear, and so on. With automation machines can start, stop, accelerate, decelerate, count, inspect, test, remember, compare and measure the dimensions of space, time, sound, temperature, and other physical qualities. With feedback all these can be accomplished automatically.

Rationalization. This is the principle that ties the engineering aspects of automation to the economic, social, and managerial aspects. Rationalism is the application of reason to the solution of problems or to the search for knowledge. It leads to the development of objective criteria, the judicious selection of the most efficient procedures, the logical evaluation of performance, the conservation of resources and energy, the elimination of waste; in short, the optimum combination of means for the most efficient attainment of clearly understood ends. In a production system it means that the entire process from the raw material to the final product is carefully analyzed so that every operation can be designed to contribute in the most efficient way to the achievement of clearly enunciated goals of the enterprise.

Actually, rationalistic philosophy is nothing new having become an important force in the world with the Renaissance. The rationalists turned their back on authority, revelation, and superstition and relied on their minds to uncover the secrets of the universe. Their first great impact was on the natural sciences. They changed alchemy into chemistry and astrology into astronomy. A great leader in the rationalist movement was Francis Bacon who introduced accurate observation and experimentation into scientific procedures. He died in 1626 from a cold caught while stuffing a chicken carcass with snow to discover how long it could be preserved. Later, Isaac Newton discovered gravity and gave a rational key to the universe, setting the stage for the new belief that the world operates in a reasonable way and can be understood by the reason of man.

There is evidence today of a great upsurge of knowledge about man himself that may equal the developments of physical science of the past. There is an acceleration of growth of knowledge and development of new theories in economics, psychology, and other social sciences. Whole new behavioral sciences are on the horizon.

The scientific, rationalist philosophy takes on numerous new implications for understanding and perhaps controlling man when it can be implemented by modern electronic machinery. The rise of electronic computers has led to a new fascination with the possibility that super-rationalism in the business and scientific spheres might spill over and transform society into an exact mechanism in which all elements of chance, risk, capriciousness, and free will, as well as spiritual values, would be eliminated.

Some doubts about rationalism had already been raised. Marx, with his theory of inevitable historical changes, Freud, with this theory that the unconscious mind determines man's actions, and Pavlov, with his experiments on conditioned reflexes, all cast doubts on the rationality and reliability of man's mind. Now come popular writers dwelling on the possibility that a rationalization of human values may lead to a dehumanized society characterized by unenjoyable wealth, totalitarian security, and the cold, deadly religion of efficiency.

The apparent similarity and the historical connection between automation and earlier technological changes have caused considerable speculation on such questions as "Must democracy and individualism be replaced by a collectivism?" and "Must the risk of unemployment and poverty increase?" The advertising brochures of large automation component manufacturers have contributed to a burgeoning literature suggesting the possibility of integrating administrative and manufacturing processes into a single, silent, automatic monster that would grind out an endless chain of products without a man in sight. These awesome speculations have charged the imaginations of some and struck terror in the hearts of others.

In this flood of verbiage, there is no shortage of imagination, but there is a notable lack of the kind of critical thought and careful documentation which yields quantitative, scientifically accurate results. There is a great need to collect, sift, classify, and evaluate the empirical evidence which alone can best refute the fantastic predictions and generalizations of these writings. It is not enough to scoff at such pessimism. The arguments must be refuted or proved with evidence and logic. These speculations may be exaggerated but they should be taken seriously so that such horrible possibilities can be avoided. The impact of technology should be anticipated so that while we encourage its growth we also plan in advance to avoid the pitfalls that could destroy all of its great advantages.

Does Automation Threaten Our Work-Wage System?——Yes.

The Ad Hoc Committee on the Triple Revolution

A new era of production has begun. Its principles of organization are as different from those of the industrial era as those of the industrial era were different from the agricultural. The cybernation revolution has been brought about by the combination of the computer and the automated self-regulating machine. This results in a system of almost unlimited productive capacity which requires progressively less human labor. Cybernation is already reorganizing the economic and social system to meet its own needs. . . .

From "The Triple Revolution" (Washington, D.C.: The Ad Hoc Committee on the Triple Revolution, March 1964).

Cybernation is manifesting the characteristics of a revolution in production. These include the development of radically different techniques and the subsequent appearance of novel principles of the organization of production; a basic reordering of man's relationship to his environment; and a dramatic increase in total available and potential energy.

The major difference between the agriculture, industrial, and cybernation revolutions is the speed at which they developed. The agricultural revolution began several thousand years ago in the Middle East. Centuries passed in the shift from a subsistence base of hunting and food gathering to settled agriculture.

In contrast, it has been less than two hundred years since the emergence of the Industrial Revolution, and direct and accurate knowledge of the new productive techniques has reached most of mankind. This swift dissemination of information is generally held to be the main factor leading to widespread industrialization.

While the major aspects of the cybernation revolution are for the moment restricted to the United States, its effects are observable almost at once throughout the industrial world and large parts of the non-industrial world. Observation is rapidly followed by analysis and criticism. The problems posed by the cybernation revolution are part of a new era in the history of all mankind but they are first being faced by the people of the United States. The way Americans cope with cybernation will influence the course of this phenomenon everywhere. This country is the stage on which the Machines-and-Man drama will first be played for the world to witness.

The fundamental problem posed by the cybernation revolution in the United States is that it invalidates the general mechanism so far employed to undergird people's rights as consumers. Up to this time economic resources have been distributed on the basis of contributions to production, with machines and men competing for unemployment on somewhat equal terms. In the developing cybernated system, potentially unlimited output can be achieved by systems of machines which will require little cooperation from human beings. As machines take over production from men, they absorb an increasing proportion of resources, while the men who are displaced become dependent on minimal and unrelated government measures—unemployment insurance, social security, welfare payments. These measures are less and less able to disguise a historic paradox: that a growing proportion of the population is subsisting on minimal incomes, often below the poverty line, at a time when sufficient productive potential is available to supply the needs of everyone in the United States.

The existence of this paradox is denied or ignored by conventional economic analysis. The general economic approach argues that potential demand, which if filled would raise the number of jobs and provide incomes to those holding them, is underestimated. Most contemporary economic analysis states that all of the available labor force and industrial capacity is required to meet the needs of consumers and industry and to provide adequate public services: schools, parks, roads, homes, decent cities, and clean water and air. It is further argued that demand could be increased, by a variety of standard techniques, to any desired extent by providing money and machines to improve the conditions of the billions of impoverished people elsewhere in the world, who need food and shelter, clothes and machinery and everything else the industrial nations take for granted.

There is no question that cybernation does increase the potential for the provisions of funds to neglected public sectors. Nor is there any question that cybernation would make possible the abolition of poverty at home and abroad. But the industrial system does not possess any adequate mechanisms to permit these potentials to become realities. The industrial system was designed to produce an ever-increasing quantity of goods as efficiently as possible, and it was assumed that the distribution of the power to purchase these goods would occur almost automatically. The continuance of the income-through-jobs link as the only major mechanism for distributing effective demand—for granting the right to consume—now acts as the main brake on the almost unlimited capacity of a cybernated productive system.

Recent administrations have proposed measures aimed at achieving a better distribution of resources, and at reducing unemployment and underemployment. A few of these proposals have been enacted. More often they have failed to secure Congressional support. In every case, many members of Congress have criticized the proposed measures as departing from traditional principles for the allocation of resources and the encouragement of production. Abetted by budget-balancing economists and interest groups, they have argued for the maintenance of an economic machine based on ideas of scarcity to deal with the facts of abundance produced by cybernation. This time-consuming criticism has slowed the workings of Congress and has thrown out of focus for that body the interrelated effects of the triple revolution.

An adequate distribution of the potential abundance of goods and services will be achieved only when it is understood that the major economic problem is not how to increase production but how to distribute the abundance that is the great potential of cybernation. There is an urgent need for a fundamental change in the mechanisms employed to ensure consumer rights.

FACTS AND FIGURES

No responsible observer would attempt to describe the exact pace or the full sweep of a phenomenon that is developing with the speed of cybernation. Some aspects of this revolution, however, are already clear:

The rate of productivity increase has risen with the onset of cybernation.

An industrial economic system postulated on scarcity has been unable to distribute the abundant goods and services produced by a cybernated system or potential in it.

Surplus capacity and unemployment have thus co-existed at excessive levels over the last six years.

The underlying cause of excessive unemployment is the fact that the capability of machines is rising more rapidly than the capacity of many human beings to keep pace.

A permanent impoverished and jobless class is established in the midst of potential abundance. . . .

NEED FOR A NEW CONSENSUS

The stubbornness and novelty of the situation that is conveyed by these [statements] is now generally accepted. Ironically, it continues to be assumed that it is possible to devise measures which will reduce unemployment to a minimum and thus preserve the overall viability of the present productive system. Some authorities have gone so far as to suggest that the pace of technological change should be slowed down "so as to allow the industrial productive system time to adapt.

We believe, on the contrary, that the industrial productive system is no longer viable. We assert that the only way to turn technological change to the benefit of the individual and the service of the general welfare is to accept the process and to utilize it rationally and humanely. The new science of political economy will be built on the encouragement and planned expansion of cybernation. The issues raised by cybernation are particularly amenable to intelligent policy-making: cybernation itself provides the resources and tools that are needed to ensure minimum hardship during the transition process.

But major changes must be made in our attitudes and institutions in the foreseeable future. Today Americans are being swept along by three simultaneous revolutions while assuming they have them under control. In the absence of real understanding of any of these phenomena, especially of technology, we may be allowing an efficient and dehumanized community to emerge by default. Gaining control of our future requires the conscious formation of the society we wish to have. Cybernation at last forces us to answer historic questions: What is man's role when he is not dependent upon his own activities for the material basis of his life? What should be the basis for distributing individual access to national resources? Are there other proper claims on goods and services besides a job?

Because of cybernation, society no longer needs to impose repetitive and meaningless (because unnecessary) toil upon the individual. Society can now set the citizen free to make his own choice of occupation and vocation from a wide range of activities not now fostered by our value system and our accepted modes of "work." But in the absence of such a consensus about cybernation, the nation cannot begin to take advantage of all that it promises for human betterment. . . .

Does Automation Threaten Our Work-Wage System?——No.

William H. Peterson

So one of man's oldest economic delusions rises to blind him again—namely, the notion that machines, technology, science and invention destroy more jobs than they create, that hand-in-hand with the march of science must go the shuffle of the unemployed. To be sure, a flood of books and studies advancing this theory in the past have been proved false. But now it seems these dire predictions, clothed in the new scare words "automation" and "cybernation," are somehow about to become true.

The roots of the superstition reach deep. The Greek mythology of Prometheus and Icarus, the science fiction classics of Mary Shelley and Karel Capek, all testify to man's age-old fear that technological prowess would lead to tragedy. This is mythology and fiction, of course, but still the belief persists that the price of machines is unemployment in the real world, that mechanization or automation—or the . . . word, "cybernation"—constitutes a threat.

If rigorously applied to economic history, however, this belief leads to absurd conclusions. The primitive who invented the wheel, the caveman who discovered fire, the aborigine who made the first flint axe, the long-ago boatman who discovered that wind pocketed in a sail could do away with muscle power applied to an oar—all these early technologists would then be malefactors of mankind, crassly stealing jobs and livelihoods from their fellow men for millennia to come.

From William H. Peterson, "Automation and Unemployment—An Oft-Exploded Myth Revives" Barron's National Business & Financial Weekly, *March 5, 1962. Reprinted by permission.*

Or so working people have frequently thought. From 1811 to 1816, for example, the Luddites—mostly displaced hand-loom weavers from Lancashire and landless croppers from Yorkshire—rioted in public squares, burned down factories and systematically wrecked machinery which, they agreed, was wiping out jobs—a charge which overlooked the more likely source of unemployment stemming from the Enclosure Laws and the inflation-induced depression of the time.

When new stocking frames were introduced during the Industrial Revolution, displaced stocking knitters not only rampaged but also sought out the inventors and caused them to flee for their lives. Yet stocking-making machinery created far more jobs than it destroyed, as indeed was the case with the entire British textile industry, which, thanks to the technology of Arkwright, Hargreaves, Cartwright, Crompton and others, has increased manyfold the number of textile workers since the start of the Industrial Revolution.

Similarly, in the United States, as David A. Wells noted in his book, *Recent Economic Changes* (1889), the Industrial Revolution simultaneously destroyed and created jobs, with full employment being the rule rather than the exception. Mr. Wells noted that in 1885, 600 men did the work that fifteen or twenty years before would have called for 2145 men—a displacement of 1545. In 1845 the boot and shoemakers of Massachusetts averaged 1.52 pairs per working day. In 1886 they were turning out an average of 4.2 pairs daily, while in highly mechanized Lynn and Haverhill the daily average per worker came to 7.0 pairs a day—a gain in productivity of better than 400% in 40 years.

The ways of the twentieth century are more sophisticated than in the time of the Luddites. Inventors nowadays need not tremble in their laboratories; arson is infrequently resorted to; yet the attempted muzzling of technology persists. Automation becomes the excuse by which the Government moves into the "retraining" business. Electricians in New York seek to nullify the efficiencies of automation by enforcing a 25-hour week. "Firemen" still grace railroad Diesel cabs.

Most if not all of these restrictive practices are granted social respectability by influential writers, politicians and social commentators. Thus the waste of restrictionism persists because the public either believes that the unions and their intellectual and political supporters are right, or is too baffled to understand why they are wrong. . . .

Most classical economists—Ricardo, Say, Senior, Bastiat, Mill, along with Smith—saw the fruits for the workingman growing out of technology, capital formation and division of labor. At the same time, however, they were conscious of business cycles—of "gluts" and "trade revulsions." An early French interventionist by the name of Jean Sismondi attributed gluts to overproduction caused by machinery. Sismondi would have met technological unemployment with an official machinery and invention clearance board to restrict the adoption of labor-saving equipment.

Rodbertus, Marx and Engels went even further. In *Das Kapital* (1867), Marx argued that machinery could only result in the lengthening of hours, the shortening of pay and the increase of unemployment. He wrote: "Machinery is the surest means of lengthening the working day." "The constant tendency of capital is to force the cost of labor back towards zero." "Official pauperism is the absolute general law of capitalist accumulation." "The demand for labor falls progressively with the increase of capital." An ever-increasing army of permanently unemployed is "a condition of existence of the capitalist mode of production." How wrong could one man be!

In this country, Thorstein Veblen followed in the philosophical footsteps of Sismondi and Marx. In his book, *The Engineers and the Price System* (1921), Veblen argued that the "mechanical state of the industrial arts will not long tolerate the continued control of production by the vested interests . . . ." Veblen called for technological experts—"production engineers without a commercial interest . . . a Soviet of technicians"—to run industry. Businessmen "working at cross purposes for private gain" were clearly incompetent to maintain full employment.

This theme of running industry by planners and engineers, which Lenin and Stalin were putting into practice in Russia, was picked up by Stuart Chase, the Technocrats, quite a few of F.D.R.'s braintrusters, and other disciples of Veblen during the thirties. Stuart Chase, for example, published a best seller in August 1932, *A New Deal,* which argued that machines and national planning had to be integrated.

Other influential intellectuals of the time joined the attack on technology. John Maynard Keynes in 1930 defined technological unemployment as "due to our discovery of means of economizing the use of labor out-running the pace at which we can find new uses for labor." In his major opus, *The General Theory of Employment, Interest and Money,* published in 1936, Keynes developed his theory of secular stagnation, in which he held that a "mature" economy would tend increasingly to find fewer investment opportunities for its savings, thereby leading to greater unemployment.

Clearly what believers in the technological theory of unemployment fail to take into account is that technology, while it may displace labor, does not in any sense destroy labor, even if it may destroy obsolete jobs and skills. Technology, in other words, serves to allocate labor to its most efficient use. Indeed, not only does technology not destroy labor, but also in a sense it creates labor: technology, when linked to capital formation, actually permits the expansion of population and hence the working force. It is inconceivable that England could have expanded its population from 11 million in 1801 to more than 50 million today were it not for massive capital accumulation and the advance of technology.

What is more, technology made possible the high living standards we enjoy. Walter Reuther's well-publicized story of his visit to the Ford engine plant in Cleveland marks a clever retort but fatuous thinking. A member of

Ford management noted: "Well, you won't be able to collect dues from all of these automated machines." Reuther replied: "You know, that is not what is bothering me. What is bothering me is, how are you going to sell cars to all of these machines?" Even Mr. Reuther should be able to see that machines and scientific advancement boost all real incomes, including those of workers.

To be sure, machines can lead to a reduction in the work week. But the division of increased output between more goods or shorter hours—and the ratio in which productivity gains should be distributed—ought to be decided by a free market and not arrived at under any form of union or Government coercion. For a reduction of hours clearly involves a diminution in production and a lowering of real income. The choice boils down to, then, greater leisure or more goods, or some combination of the two—a linkage which capitalism has abundantly achieved. . . .

In sum, the United States requires not less productivity but more: not fewer hours in the work week but greater assiduity and superior workmanship; not less saving and investment but more—more machines, computers, automation, and yes, more "cybernation." At the same time, the country needs not more Government omnipotence, but less. Labor leaders must see the Marxist fallacy of capital supposedly exploiting labor, for the exact opposite is true: labor exploits capital. Hence, the greater the capital, the higher the wages and the greater the job opportunities. . . .

QUESTIONS FOR DISCUSSION

1. *On the basis of your reading, do you believe automation creates or destroys jobs? How did you reach this conclusion?*
2. *According to the Ad Hoc Committee, automation and cybernation will require the abandonment of our "work-reward" system and the creation eventually of great amounts of leisure. What is your reaction to this analysis?*
3. *The article by William Peterson urges greater use of automation advances. Do you agree with this view or do you think advances should be controlled or regulated? Why?*
4. *What economic and occupational groups are most profoundly affected by automation? What should we do for these groups?*

The Consumer—
Sovereign or Forgotten?

The model of consumer behavior presented in the textbooks presupposes a dominant role for the consumer in the economic system. Presumably, in this model, all buyers are rational and calculating people who always attempt to buy cheaply and to maximize their satisfaction in their spending patterns. According to this view, the consumer's expenditures are "ballots" cast for or against commodities offered for sale; and as consumers vote in the market, their ballots determine acceptance or rejection of goods offered for sale. To talk about a consumer being sold "bad" merchandise or being "exploited" is simple nonsense in this world of rational and economic consumers. All in all, the consumer, in theory at least, is given a crucial, perhaps a dominant, role in a market economy. This conventional analysis supposes other conditions such as the existence of a competitive market and a comparatively simple market structure without such devices as advertising, consumer credit, trading stamps, and the other paraphernalia created to stimulate sales.

While everyone understands that the nature of the market faced by the ordinary consumer is, in reality, quite different from the textbook model, there is by no means agreement as to whether or not the American consumer fares well or badly. The first article in the following section, by Professor Max E. Brunk, while not simply a piece of rhetoric extolling the virtues of a free market system, is nevertheless a defense of the proposition that the consumer is his own best protector and that he is largely sovereign in the marketplace. Brunk suggests that there is no way to construct governmental machinery which will protect the interests of a diverse two hundred million consumers. This argument follows from his belief that the consumer, acting in his own interest along with businessmen "demonstrating their responsibility," will assure his own happiness.

Arguments positing the view that the consumer needs additional protection have in recent years become more common, leading a few years ago to the creation of a special federal agency on consumer affairs. In general, these arguments rest upon a depiction of the consumer as a helpless individual caught up in a basically irrational and exploitive market. Businesses are seen as manipulators of consumer action and choice through the use of clever advertising, managed obsolescence, and confusing and sometimes deceptive standards of packaging and labeling. The article by Ralph Nader attacks business for its contempt for the consumer and for its obvious efforts to obtain profits at whatever cost to the consumer. He also asserts that existing consumer protection legislation is almost useless since it is easily evaded and enforced only sporadically and disinterestedly by the government.

A Case Against Government Regulation

Max E. Brunk

How can the interests of 200 million American consumers best be served? What are the interests, who are the consumers and who best speaks in their behalf? How much protection and how much freedom of choice in the market-place should consumers have? What are the values sought by consumers, how much deception is there and by what process do we seek to create a "better informed" consumer? How much conflict of interest truly exists between the business community and the consumer? To what extent should consumer wants and needs be legislated, supervised and controlled by government? As we ponder these questions, without definitive answers, a mushrooming movement of consumer protection is sweeping our country.

This movement finds its expression in many forms. We have commissions studying the performance of our manufacturing and distributive industries and making recommendations for reform. We witness congressional action on a host of regulatory issues such as packaging, labeling, credit, housing and auto safety. The President constantly calls for greater consumer discretion in spend-

From "Who Best Speaks for the Consumer?" address delivered by Max E. Brunk at annual meeting of the American Meat Institute in Chicago, September 20, 1966. Reprinted by permission of the author.

ing. And we hear increasing talk about the need for organized consumer education and for a new Department of Consumer Affairs. Indeed the entire movement seems destined to destroy the basic tenet on which our government is formed—personal liberty, individual responsibility and freedom of choice.

As government prescribes values, both social and economic, *for* its people what does it do *to* its people? Is it not time that we give attention to the problems already created by consumer protection legislation which prescribes judgment values for all and limits freedom of choice? Are we indeed to eliminate the right of man to make a mistake? . . .

At the present time consumer interests in government are served in a wide variety of ways. A recent congressional study reveals that no less than thirty-three Federal departments are engaged in various phases of consumer protection. This study revealed that these agencies were involved in 118 different consumer protective activities requiring the services of 6500 full-time employees. In addition there were 178 other programs indirectly related to the consumer interest. . . .

And this is but a small part of the activity that goes on in Washington and at the state and local level where we also have extensive policing of a wide variety of marketing processes extending from weights and measures to sanitation and trade practices. This all adds up to a highly protected consuming public and it raises a number of questions. Would the consumer interest better be served by concentrating these activities in a new Department of Consumer Affairs? Can such a department serve as an effective spokesman for the consumer in the promulgation of new laws and regulations? What interest groups would be most influential with such a department? To what degree should such a department act as intermediary between buyers and sellers?

In the past government has established consumer protection laws and regulations in response to needs as they arise. The administration of these activities has been delegated to agencies and departments accustomed to working with the special businesses involved, be it agriculture, finance, commerce, drugs, labor, housing or whatnot. The proposal for a Department of Consumer Affairs shifts the audience center from supplier to buyer and by this process cuts across our total economy. Because almost every issue of consumer protection is related to the operational idiosyncrasies of the supplier involved, such a department would encounter both conflict and duplication of effort with every other department of government. Certainly it is questionable that such a department could effectively administer without bias all the diverse interests involved.

Implicit in serving as spokesman for consumer needs is the identification and interpretation of consumer values and needs. I submit that it is impossible to identify, classify and catalog the consumer value concepts and needs of 200 million Americans. Any businessman knows this. At very best he as an individual can only hope to serve the wants of a small sector of our population part of the time. I say part of the time simply because the values and needs of any individual consumer also change with each purchasing decision. On top of this, consumer values are both tangible and intangible. If indeed these are truths is it any wonder that we stand at a loss to rationalize the purchasing behavior of our people? Is it any small wonder that we say people sometimes act irrationally? What we really mean is irrational in terms of defined values and being only mortals, at any one time, under any one circumstance, we focus on singular material and economic values. My point is simply this. Efforts to reduce the purchasing behavior of man to social common denominators through either education or legislation will serve more to deprive than to enable man to fulfill his wants. It is very important that we distinguish between the proper role of government in protecting its consumers from deceptive practices and the inappropriate role of serving as intermediary between buyers and sellers in making value judgments. A Department of Consumer Affairs geared to an audience of consumers will be concerned more with the latter than the former. With ever expanding regulation of our markets there is perhaps a growing need to protect consumers against governmental actions which restrict the business community from responding fully to the wants of consumers but this is not likely to be forthcoming from a Department of Consumer Affairs.

How effective a spokesman for the consumer the proposed department might be is demonstrated by the past activities of the President's Special Assistant for Consumer Affairs. While it is true that this office does not hold the administrative powers normally entrusted to a cabinet post, it is nevertheless true that much effort has been made to gain consumer, business and labor support for the program during its gestation period. Talks were given, professionally managed press conferences held and consumer meetings scheduled. It should be apparent to the most ardent supporter of the program that consumer interest failed to develop. Participation in the publicly held meetings is indicative of the interest groups from which a new department could be expected to gain its support. They were largely professionals from other government offices, from the colleges and schools, from the press, from labor groups and organizations of various kinds engaged in consumer matters. Characteristically, spokesmen at these meetings seldom spoke as consumers—when they spoke, it was usually in behalf of someone else. Is it not logical that the same representatives will be the influencing force around a Department of Consumers Affairs? At least the evidence strongly suggests that it will not be the consumer.

THE CONSUMER'S ROLE

Apparently the consumer already knows that any remedial action he deems necessary is most directly accomplished as a result of his actions in the marketplace. He also knows that the marketplace respects his actions either when he is in the minority or with the majority. He does not expect to impose his consumption values on his neighbor any more than he expects his neighbor's values to be imposed on him. He clearly sees the so-called proliferation of products in a multitude of package shapes, sizes and design not as deception but as a simple response to his many minority requirements as a consumer. Can you imagine what a canned ham would look like if it were designed to conform to specifications laid down by a democratic consensus of 200 million consumers? To what proportion of the voters would it be acceptable . . . to what proportion deceptive?

In spite of all our efforts to treat them so we must recognize that there is not one universal body of consumers possessing common values. To the contrary the market consists of an endless number of minority groups each seeking special attention. No one law, no one regulation, no one bureau, no one manufacturer, no one retailer can serve them all with equal fairness and satisfaction. Much of the success of a manufacturer or retailer lies in his ability to identify and structure his product to the particular market segment he seeks to serve . . . an action often misinterpreted by those who would apply universal values of consumption to all. Each new protective market regulation reduces the capacity of industry to respond to minority interests. Flexibility to respond to the varied and changing consumer wants is the hallmark of a free market. These are but a few simple reasons a Department of Consumer Affairs can never truly speak for the consumer.

That the Congress serves as spokesman for the voter at the polling place does not mean that it can, or should, serve as spokesman for the consumer in the marketplace. In serving the marketplace, the legislative process at best can only establish general guidelines for all to follow in the prevention of fraud and the maintenance of competition. When these boundaries are violated, Congress finds itself in the hopeless business of determining universal consumer values which transcend the multitude of minority interests previously discussed. Any detailed actions in regulating the marketplace serve to deprive consumer minority groups. This identifies an important distinction between the polling place which rigidly imposes the will of the majority and the marketplace which responds dynamically to all minority interests. . . .

Whenever Congress attempts to regulate the market to serve specific consumer values . . . whenever Congress attempts to speak for the consumer, it ends by delegating the responsibility to some agency of government which it assumes has the omnipotence to do the job. Such contributions to the maze of vague, administratively determined, prohibitive regulations surrounding the marketplace are indeed not the product of one who best speaks for the consumer. . . .

THE ROLE OF BUSINESS

Lastly in our search we turn to the business community—to the manufacturers and retailers who are directly involved in supplying goods and services to the consumer. Not only [do] the manufacturer and retailer have the benefit of the advice and [counsel] of government officials, politicians, academicians, consumer groups and their own market research and experience but also they get the first and most forceful reading on consumer response in the marketplace. Unlike the politician who goes to the polls every few years to get a performance reading the marketer gets his reading each day.

Surely now we have identified who best speaks for the consumer. But if this be true why do the manufacturer and marketer make so many mistakes? Why do you sit here trying to figure out what it is that the consumer wants? Why do you produce so many goods and services that won't sell? Why do you spend so much of the "consumer's money" trying to convince her in every conceivable way to buy your product or shop at your store?

I believe that the answer is simple. There is no true spokesman for the consumer other than the actions of the consumer herself. Try as she might she will rationalize her actions but she cannot explain them in full. That is why she cannot tell you what new or modified goods and services would better serve her needs. In marketing research I have spent the better part of my life ringing consumer doorbells in a futile effort to get them to tell me how some product or market service can be improved or what new products or services they want only to find that in response they failed either to visualize their alternatives or identify the true values to which they in final analysis respond. The consumer, in her mute but effective way, can only bring all her value considerations to bear in response to what is offered her. She has her own built-in protective device. If you displease her . . . if you do not offer her the best alternative . . . if indeed you deceive her in terms of her own values, she simply and quickly votes "no" in the marketplace. That is the miracle of the free market. Those who argue that the consumer acts irrationally or is continually deceived in the marketplace simply fail to identify or accept the true values which the consumer deems important. It takes far more than economic rationality to explain consumer behavior.

In serving the consumer interest the real question is not who best speaks for but rather who best answers the consumer. The reply can only be the manufacturer and distributor . . . those who actually serve her consumption needs . . . those who have given this nation the highest standard of living the world has ever known. . . .

A Case for More Government Protection

Ralph Nader

The rhetoric of consumer protection in recent years has been as impressive as the reality of the consumer interest's expendability. The thunderous acclaim for such legislation or pending legislation as the truth-in-lending bill, the cigarette-labeling law, the truth-in-packaging bill is not measured commensurately by the forcefulness of the legislation in fact. I sometimes think that industry is perfectly willing to trade off a particular name with a particular legislation, such as truth-in-lending, in return for very effectively gutting its adequate provisions. The threat is very often not so much whether we have consumer-protection legislation but whether or not we have a law or a no-law law—a no-law law which simply deludes the consumer, deludes the public into thinking it receives a protection when in fact it is the industry which receives the protection by a bizarre, ironic twist.

The cigarette-labeling act is a perfect case study here. This act effectively excluded any action for five years by the states and cigarette-protection legislation. It effectively excluded the Federal Trade Commission from any action. It effectively excluded any attendance to the problem of advertising in cigarettes. And it effectively provided a convenient defense in civil liability suits for the cigarette industry by requiring a warning on the package that [smoking] may be hazardous to health. This was a bill which the tobacco industry simply could not do without. And yet it was touted as . . . consumer-protection legislation.

I think that it is important to recognize that, even when laws are passed that are adequately drafted, the administration of these laws can effectively render them impotent. A good example here, in terms of abundant authority and not so abundant administration and enforcement, affects the Federal Trade Commission, which I think can be called the Government's better business bureau with all that implies.

A MYTH PERPETUATED

One of the sad by-products of the Federal Trade Commission's pronouncements and activities, with some outstanding exceptions, is that the Commission has perpetuated a myth over the years that deceiving the consumer or harming the consumer is primarily a fly-by-night phenomenon in terms of the fringe

From "Ralph Nader Faces the Nation's Business," address by Ralph Nader to the National Consumer Assembly, Washington, D.C., November 1967. Reprinted by permission of the author.

participants of American business that really isn't the mainstream of solid, upstanding businessmen—it is those near-bankrupt firms that are besmirching the reputation of American business in general.

I find this rather difficult to appreciate in the light of the facts. I don't think the packaging problem in this country just affects a few fringe marketeers. I don't think the credit practices in this country just affect a few corner pawn shops. I don't believe that the electric price-fixing conspiracy which bilked the consumers to the tune of hundreds of millions of dollars over the three decades of the conspiracy, ending in 1961, simply was a result of a few fly-by-night electric firms. I don't think the lack of safety in automobiles is due to a few small garages who hand-make some hazardous automobiles. I don't think the adverse effects of drugs and lack of adequate disclosure is due to makeshift pharmaceutical houses in the back of a large pharmacy or two. I think in effect that the problem of consumer protection is very much the problem of American business in general, very much the problem of the largest industry and the largest company, very much the problem of those who should be able to perform far better and far more responsibly than those fringe businesses who might be up against the wall in terms of their sheer economic survival.

A recent example is the Greyhound Bus Company, which has been routinely using, until very recently, bald regrooved tires, regrooving them again and again, leading to accidents in which people were killed and injured—leading to accidents whose investigations remain secret within our Department of Transportation, because the motor carrier industry wrote that secrecy into legislation years ago—the kind of practices by Greyhound which have never received enforcement. . . . The first enforcement process is now underway in New Jersey for a Greyhound fatal accident involving regrooved tires. The maximum penalty on conviction is $500.

Now, are we dealing with a company—a small bus company—whose back is against the wall, and for sheer survival is trying to cut costs on tires? No. We are dealing with the largest bus company in the world—a bus company whose liquid capital is so embarrassingly ample that it owns outright 27 Boeing 707/727 planes, which it leases to the airlines.

INADEQUATE FULFILLMENT

I think another problem of the Federal Trade Commission as an example of the inadequate fulfillment of its authority comes in areas where there is absolutely no doubt, where there are absolutely no shades of judgment possible in terms of the course of action that should be pursued. For years the odometers have been overregistered—that is, they have been designed in a way to make you think . . . you are traveling more than you are. Now there is . . . far more than a mere psychological consequence to this rigging of a basic measurement device. When an odometer is rigged to the plus side, you tend in the aggregate to trade in your car faster. You think your car is a little older. Your warranty runs out in terms of mileage. You tend to pay more to a rent-car-company which, of course, collects on the mile. You also tend to think you are getting better gas mileage, which is something the auto companies want desperately to convey to their buying public. And yet this problem of odometer deception, which has been going on for years with the knowledge of the Federal Trade Commission, did not achieve attention until about 1964 when the National Bureau of Standards decided to rewrite the standard. Now, even though the standard was rewritten, odometers are still capable of being overregistered and still capable of meeting the new standard. But the important point in the history of the odometer is the statement finally conveyed by an old hand at the Federal Trade Commission, who when confronted with the suggestion that it was the National Bureau of Standards who took the initiative, not the Federal Trade Commission, blurted out, "That is utter nonsense. Why, we have been concerned with odometer problems since the Hoover Administration."

MEAT INSPECTION

Another problem dealing with laws, their adequacy in drafting and their administration and the responsibility of a consumer protection agency or department in government deals with the recent meat inspection controversy. Here we have the Department of Agri-Business, misnamed the Department of Agri-culture, which . . . has had the responsibility—since Upton Sinclair wrote the book, The Jungle—for roughly sixty-one years to inspect meat packaging, meat processing, slaughter houses that trade in interstate commerce. Unfortunately, over the years, there has been a substantial traffic in intrastate meat shipment, and at present 25 percent of all processed meat in this country does not cross state boundaries and therefore escapes the Federal inspection service. This is eight billion pounds a year.

The surveys of the Department of Agriculture in 1962 on a state-by-state basis revealed what everybody in the industry knew all along, but revealed it authoritatively—that there were three basic and endemic problems affecting the intrastate meat industry. The first was a kind of Gresham's law: believe it or not, bad meat is good business. And bad meat drives out good meat in some of these local markets. Bad meat, meaning the 4-D animals: trafficking in dead, dying, diseased or disabled animals, where, for example, the cancerous portions of the cow are simply cut out and the rest of the carcass sent to market.

The second problem: unsanitary, grossly unsanitary, conditions in the meat-processing plant. The reports here are so nauseating—and they are not made by laymen, they are made by veterinarians or inspectors—the reports here are so nauseating on a state-by-state basis that nobody could ever read them through at one sitting and remain with his equanimity. These descriptions reveal, for example, the prevalence of roaches, flies and rodents having free play of the meat-processing plant and willingly or unwillingly finding their way off into the meat vats, the paint flakings from the ceilings dripping and dropping onto exposed food. There was some indication that some of these inspectors couldn't get close to the plants because of the overwhelming potency of the odor, and sometimes they did get close enough, but they couldn't talk clearly with the manager because of the flies that screened out visibility.

The third problem deals with what do you do to make this product—this 4-D product—presentable to the consumer. Of course, here the ingenious misuse of modern chemistry comes into play. Seasoning agents, preservatives and coloring agents do the job, and the basic natural detection processes of the consumers are masked. He is no longer able to taste, smell or see diseased or contaminated meat. And he pays out his money accordingly. This problem was documented in 1962, and our friendly Department of Agriculture felt it was more important to protect the meat-packing industry than to protect the consumer. So for five years they have sat on these reports—for five years they did nothing until there were hearings at the congressional level and new reports were forthcoming to confirm the 1962 reports.

With all of these problems, with all of these disclosures, the House of Representatives by a vote of 140 to 98 passed a weak and meaningless meat inspection act, as far as the control of intrastate plants is concerned. The alternative bill, called the Smith-Foley Amendment, would have brought roughly 98.5 percent of all the meat processing in the country under Federal inspection. That bill was defeated.

LOBBY SEEKS MONEY

The interesting aspect of the situation is the immediate disclosure after the passage of the legislation that a large meat-packing trade association had recommended in a letter to its members . . . that they make contributions to the political campaigns of friendly congressmen (mind you, at the same time, these congressmen were considering the meat inspection bill and its alternative); the recommendation was that the contributions be from $25 to $99—$99 so that the individual contributors need not be disclosed. Now this situation was brought to the attention of the chairman of the House Agriculture Committee, who favored the weak bill. He immediately replied to the director of this trade association that it was a terrible thing to have done—it placed the meat industry in a potentially untenable situation, . . . it jeopardized the meat bill which the meat industry favored. In other words, all his concern was directed towards the welfare of the meat industry and being able to escape Federal inspection of its intrastate activity.

Not a word in these letters, mind you, as to the welfare of the consumer.

Not a word [of] the need to publicize this impropriety the moment it was located. In effect, the entire effort of some of these friendly congressmen at the House Agriculture Committee was to sweep it under the rug, to squash it, to keep it from being disclosed so that nobody learned exactly what [was] going on.

I think it's time to look into this situation with a far greater degree of thoroughness. A congressman who is not known to make very flippant and unsubstantiated remarks has said that he has never seen a bill where so much money was involved in the negotiation. I would think a congressional investigation particularly in the context of the campaign-financing reform that is now pending in Congress would be well advised.

There are other aspects of the meat bill which I think give us good lessons to ponder. These are the kinds of lessons, incidentally, which are similar to the battles over . . . water pollution, soil contamination, chemical and radiation hazards, inadequately tested and prescribed drugs and so forth. At first, it is a [mistake] to think that the meat problem is one of tiny, filthy meat-packing plants. Swift and Armour are involved here—they have plants which operate exclusively within state boundaries. Surveys of these plants have shown very substandard conditions and it's quite clear that Swift and Armour as well as their smaller colleagues have been engaging in marketing of meat which has no place in being sold to the American consumer.

NOT ONLY LIP SERVICE

The role of the Administration is interesting here as well. At the last hour the Administration finally neutralized the Department of Agriculture, with no small achievement, and came out basically through its consumer office and Miss Furness with a stronger version of legislation. That is very encouraging, but obviously that is only the first step in the position which I think the Administration should reflect. The Administration should not only be on the record for consumer protection; it should be on the ramparts. It should not only give lip service. It should give muscle service. It often intrigues me why the administration is so successful[ly] and so powerfully lobbying for the supersonic transport, that great sensational mass alarm clock that is on the horizon, and so ineffective, so reticent and so inhibited when it is asked or expected to lobby for meat inspection laws and for auto safety appropriations, to give just two recent examples. I think it is encouraging that next year will be the first year that the Federal Government will spend more money on traffic safety than the safety of migratory birds. But I don't think it says much for our allocation of our resources in this land. Not when we can spend some $45 million next year for a problem that is killing 53,000 Americans and injuring over 4.5 million at the same time that a nuclear submarine is costing $110 million. That's just one nuclear submarine.

I think, in other words, that it is time not just to give a serious look at the Administration policy on consumer protection but to [ask to] what extent it is going to really begin to effectively advocate it beyond rhetoric and to effectively reallocate some of our resources to this area. The legislation doesn't mean much if you don't have money to administer it with. I think, for example, it is a reflection of a distorted sense of values when we can spend last year $150 million on highway beautification and about $10 million on highway safety. The presumption here against that kind of allocation of resources is that the best way to get more money for traffic safety is to see that the blood gets on the daisies. . . .

It is necessary to stop concentrating exclusively on the syndromes of the consumer protection phenomena, and penetrate through to the more basic preconditions which give rise to the syndrome. I think, to be more specific, that one side of the coin may be consumer protection but the other side of the coin is, inescapably, corporate reform. I think it's important to go to the roots of the problem so we don't place ourselves in the situation of running around trying to plug the holes in the dike before it overflows. And in this sense, in the sense of the controllability of catching these problems before they arise, that focus on corporate reform is a must. For example, corporations now should be required to meet much stiffer disclosure requirements. They should be required to tell specifically the safety performance of their products so that the marketplace can be put to work in a way which they will not perhaps fail.

I think that it is an important distinction to make, that however much lip service corporations give to the free market, they are really more interested in the control market. If they were interested in the free market they would tell you the safety performance of their products, such as automobiles, so that the consumer [could] go to the marketplace and compare make and model and make his choice on the basis of quality and in this way generate the feedback mechanism of the marketplace by rewarding good workmanship and penalizing shoddy workmanship. This is the kind of disclosure requirement that really puts the market to work to a higher degree of efficiency.

PENALTIES NEEDED

Another requirement, I think, is to beef up our sanction for corporate violations. We are reaching a point in this country where it is no longer possible to sweep under the rug the tremendously wide double standard operating between the penalties imposed on individual behavior and the penalties imposed on corporate behavior. Corporate behavior, more and more, is being immunized from legal accountability. You see the decline in criminal penalties in safety legislation for knowing and willful violation. And look at the disparity. A driver negligently driving down the highway kills an individual. He can be subjected to manslaughter charges and put in jail for negligence. But a manufacturer can willfully and knowingly leave a defective product on the market . . . in such a way that it can take human life, under the new auto safety legislation, and there is no criminal penalty whatsoever. Only civil penalties—the kinds of penalties that don't penetrate the corporate framework[—exist]. A perfect and recent example here is the Lake Central Airlines crash in March [1966] with thirty-eight people killed in a crash directly attributed to a soft piston problem, with the propeller coming off and ripping into the fuselage. It so happens that Allison, the division of General Motors that builds the engine and propeller, had known about this defect some time before the crash, and instead of advising all operators to immediately ground this plane and disassemble it, which is the only conclusion that could be reached once a defect of that seriousness is located—instead of doing this, they sent a vague advisory saying why don't you have an oil check to see if the oil's contaminated by metal filings. And the doomed plane was given an oil check and the result was negative. And thirty-eight people died because the Allison Division was worried about its corporate image and was worried about facing up to this problem. The fine by the Federal Aviation Agency was $8,000—about $200 a head. Perhaps one must not be too harsh with the FAA; they resisted General Motors pressure to reduce the fine to $4,000.

RESEARCH A NECESSITY

Another area deals with research and development, which is no longer a luxury on the part of the large corporations, it is an absolute necessity, because simple inaction can bestow on the public welfare and safety immense cruelty. Simple inaction [in] researching ways to clean up the internal combustion engine, or find an alternative, has resulted in a critical air pollution problem in our cities, inaction stemming back many, many years by industry leaders. And so, the problem of research and development, the problem of requiring them to shoulder a responsible portion of this innovative input is one that is on the first agenda, in my judgment.

STANDARDS MOST IMPORTANT

And a final area deals with standards, and I think this is probably the most important one; [I urge] that when safety bills are passed, when standards are set for products, that these standards be set by government, that they not be set by private standards groups, who have succeeded in insinuating into legislation their particular standards and codes. That is, government must make these standards, allowing democratic access to the administrative process on the part of both industry and public groups. This is an extremely critical problem.

It is one which will be more critical the next year, as the United States Standards Institute of America begins its campaign to receive a congressional charter, take on the aura of a quasi-governmental agency and in effect begin to determine the level of standards of safety in product after product. . . .

PROTECTION REQUIRED

I think a stake here in the whole consumer movement is not just the quality of the goods, not just honest pricing, which of course improves our allocation of resources, but also in my judgment the most critical area of all—an area which might be termed as the area of bodily rights. The right of one's physiological integrity from being invaded, assaulted or destroyed by the harmful by-products of industrial products and processing.

Now against this threat we have something to be encouraged by. Unlike prior [eras] in history we now have a technological period where we can actually program innovation in human welfare and safety. We can invent the technological future if we will to do so. And no better was this stated than by the vice president of Ford Motor Company, Donald Frey, who said of his industry that basically our engineers can do anything we want them to do; they "can invent practically on demand." Now with an increased capability like this the ethical imperatives to act become all the more insistent because I think it is fair to say that to a substantial degree . . . what we should do proceeds from what we can do. And as the capability increases . . . so does our ethical requirement to follow through.

It is a serious disservice to consumerism, if I may use a recent term coined in a deprecatory manner by one of our large business executives last year[—it] is disservice to consumerism to view this as a threat to the private enterprise economy or to big business. It is just the opposite. . . . Of course, the upshot of consumer protection, when it succeeds, is simply to hold industry to higher standards of excellence, and I can't see why they should object to that kind of incentive. And hopefully, as it gains momentum, the consumer movement will begin to narrow the gap between the performance of American industry and commerce and its bright promise.

QUESTIONS FOR DISCUSSION

1. *According to Brunk, how well has government performed as a protector of the consumer?*

2. *Would Brunk advocate the ending of all government consumer activity? What is it that he seems to want?*
3. *Brunk thinks the consumer can speak for himself. Do you agree?*
4. *Do you think the consumer needs more protection? If so, what kind?*
5. *Nader suggests that "consumer protection" as a philosophy and as practiced is a myth. What does he mean?*
6. *On what grounds does Nader charge that business "controls" its own product regulation?*
7. *What consumer protection program does Nader urge? What do you think of this program?*
8. *Do you support Brunk's view that businesses are essentially responsible, or Nader's assertion that they are irresponsible? On what grounds do you justify your opinion?*

What Balance Between
the Public and the Private?

A crucial question that has been suggested but not directly dealt with in our readings so far is "What is the proper balance between the public and the private sectors?" The issue is not an especially new one among economists, and considerable literature on the topic has been developed over the past fifteen or twenty years. The present and continued urgency of the problem must be obvious to any serious observer of American affairs. Almost all the issues raised in this collection of readings in some way connect to this problem.

The problem can be approached a number of different ways. It may be examined from the point of view of the economics of resource allocation—emphasizing the study of costs and benefits of public versus private resource utilization and economic decision-making. It can also be approached as a problem of planning—whether or not central as opposed to decentralized economic undertaking leads to maximization. The issue, of course, may also be studied as a largely ideological problem, detached from a purely economic analysis. All these approaches are considered in one form or another in the following two essays.

The first is a classic discussion by John K. Galbraith, arguing that the built-in biases of our institutions and modes of thought prevent us from striking a balance between social or public production and consumption and that which is wholly privately oriented. Accordingly he sees us drowning in our private opulence while we are starved for social goods. Although Galbraith's argument is not extended to the point of completely condemning all private sector undertakings, the general outline of his criticisms can be pushed that far.

The rebuttal offered by the National Association of Manufacturers is also a classic piece, which argues against the growing "centralism" of our economy and pleads for a return to a more decentralized economy.

This then is the general outline of an argument that lies just below the surface of many perplexing issues confronting America. While, as is hinted above, we have evaded the issues, more or less, for the last fifteen years, Americans must soon resolve this question.

The Theory of Social Balance

John Kenneth Galbraith

The final problem of the productive society is what it produces. This manifests itself in an implacable tendency to provide an opulent supply of some things and a niggardly yield of others. This disparity carries to the point where it is a cause of social discomfort and social unhealth. The line which divides our area of wealth from our area of poverty is roughly that which divides privately produced and marketed goods and services from publicly rendered services. Our wealth in the first is not only in startling contrast with the meagerness of the latter, but our wealth in privately produced goods is, to a marked degree, the cause of crisis in the supply of public services. For we have failed to see the importance, indeed the urgent need, of maintaining a balance between the two.

PRIVATE ABUNDANCE, PUBLIC POVERTY

This disparity between our flow of private and public goods and services is no matter of subjective judgment. On the contrary, it is the source of the most extensive comment which only stops short of the direct contrast being made here. In the years following World War II, the papers of any major city—those of New York were an excellent example—told daily of the shortages and shortcomings in the elementary municipal and metropolitan services. The schools were old and overcrowded. The police force was under strength and underpaid. The parks and playgrounds were insufficient. Streets and empty lots were filthy, and the sanitation staff was underequipped and in need of men. Access to the city by those who work there was uncertain and painful

From John K. Galbraith, The Affluent Society *(Boston: Houghton Mifflin Co., 1958). Copyright © 1958 by John Kenneth Galbraith. Reprinted by permission of the publisher, Houghton Mifflin Company and John Kenneth Galbraith.*

and becoming more so. Internal transportation was overcrowded, unhealthful, and dirty. So was the air. Parking on the streets had to be prohibited, and there was no space elsewhere. These deficiencies were not in new and novel services but in old and established ones. Cities have long swept their streets, helped their people move around, educated them, kept order, and provided horse rails for vehicles which sought to pause. That their residents should have a nontoxic supply of air suggests no revolutionary dalliance with socialism.

The discussion of this public poverty competed, on the whole successfully, with the stories of ever-increasing opulence in privately produced goods. The Gross National Product was rising. So were retail sales. So was personal income. Labor productivity had also advanced. The automobiles that could not be parked were being produced at an expanded rate. The children, though without schools, subject in the playgrounds to the affectionate interest of adults with odd tastes, and disposed to increasingly imaginative forms of delinquency, were admirably equipped with television sets. We had difficulty finding storage space for the great surpluses of food despite a national disposition to obesity. Food was grown and packaged under private auspices. The care and refreshment of the mind, in contrast with the stomach, was principally in the public domain. Our colleges and universities were severely overcrowded and underprovided, and the same was true of the mental hospitals.

The contrast was and remains evident not alone to those who read. The family which takes its mauve and cerise, air-conditioned, power-steered, and power-braked automobile out for a tour passes through cities that are badly paved, made hideous by litter, blighted buildings, billboards, and posts for wires that should long since have been put underground. They pass on into a countryside that has been rendered largely invisible by commercial art. (The goods which the latter advertise have an absolute priority in our value system. Such aesthetic considerations as a view of the countryside accordingly come second. On such matters we are consistent.) They picnic on exquisitely packaged food from a portable ice-box by a polluted stream and go on to spend the night at a park which is a menace to public health and morals. Just before dozing off on an air mattress, beneath a nylon tent, amid the stench of decaying refuse, they may reflect vaguely on the curious unevenness of their blessings. Is this, indeed, the American genius?

NATURE OF SOCIAL IMBALANCE

In the production of goods within the private economy it has long been recognized that a tolerably close relationship must be maintained between the production of various kinds of products. The output of steel and oil and machine tools is related to the production of automobiles. Investment in transportation must keep abreast of the output of goods to be transported. The supply of power must be abreast of the growth of industries requiring it. The existence of these relationships—coefficients to the economist—has made possible the construction of the input-output table which shows how changes in the production in one industry will increase or diminish the demands on other industries. To this table, and more especially to its ingenious author, Professor Wassily Leontief, the world is indebted for one of its most important of modern insights into economic relationships. If expansion in one part of the economy were not matched by the requisite expansion in other parts—were the need for balance not respected—then bottlenecks and shortages, speculative hoarding of scarce supplies, and sharply increasing costs would ensue. Fortunately in peacetime the market system operates easily and effectively to maintain this balance, and this, together with the existence of stocks and some flexibility in the coefficients as a result of substitution, insures that no serious difficulties will arise. We are reminded of the existence of the problem only by noticing how serious it is for those countries—Poland or, in a somewhat different form, India—which seek to solve the problem by planned measures and with a much smaller supply of resources.

Just as there must be balance in what a community produces, so there must also be balance in what the community consumes. An increase in the use of one product creates, ineluctably, a requirement for others. If we are to consume more automobiles, we must have more gasoline. There must be more insurance as well as more space on which to operate them. Beyond a certain point more and better food appears to mean increased need for medical services. This is the certain result of the increased consumption of tobacco and alcohol. More vacations require more hotels and more fishing rods. And so forth. With rare exceptions—shortages of doctors are an exception which suggests the rule—this balance is also maintained quite effortlessly so far as goods for private sale and consumption are concerned. The price system plus a rounded condition of opulence is again the agency.

NEED FOR PRIVATE-PUBLIC BALANCE

However, the relationships we are here discussing are not confined to the private economy. They operate comprehensively over the whole span of private and public services. As surely as an increase in the output of automobiles puts new demands on the steel industry so, also, it places new demands on public services. Similarly, every increase in the consumption of private goods will normally mean some facilitating or protective step by the state. In all cases if these services are not forthcoming, the consequences will be in some degree ill. It will be convenient to have a term which suggests a satisfactory relationship between the supply of privately produced goods and services and those of the state, and we may call it social balance.

The problem of social balance is ubiquitous, and frequently it is obtrusive. As noted, an increase in the consumption of automobiles requires a facilitating supply of streets, highways, traffic control, and parking space. The protective services of the police and the highway patrols must also be available, as must those of the hospitals. Although the need for balance here is extraordinarily clear, our use of privately produced vehicles has, on occasion, got far out of line with the supply of the related public services. The result has been hideous road congestion, an annual massacre of impressive proportions, and chronic colitis in the cities. As on the ground, so also in the air. Planes collide with disquieting consequences for those within when the public provision for air traffic control fails to keep pace with private use of the airways.

But the auto and the airplane, versus the space to use them, are merely an exceptionally visible example of a requirement that is pervasive. The more goods people procure, the more packages they discard and the more trash that must be carried away. If the appropriate sanitation services are not provided, the counterpart of increasing opulence will be deepening filth. The greater the wealth the thicker will be the dirt. This indubitably describes a tendency of our time. As more goods are produced and owned, the greater are the opportunities for fraud and the more property that must be protected. If the provision[s] of public law enforcement services do not keep pace, the counterpart of increased well-being will, we may be certain, be increased crime.

The city of Los Angeles, in modern times, is a near-classic study in the problem of social balance. Magnificently efficient factories and oil refineries, a lavish supply of automobiles, a vast consumption of handsomely packaged products, coupled with the absence of a municipal trash collection service which forced the use of home incinerators, made the air nearly unbreathable for an appreciable part of each year. Air pollution could be controlled only by a complex and highly developed set of public services—by better knowledge stemming from more research, better policing, a municipal trash collection service, and possibly the assertion of the priority of clean air over the production of goods. These were long in coming. The agony of a city without usable air was the result.

POSITIVE CASE FOR SOCIAL BALANCE

The case for social balance has, so far, been put negatively. Failure to keep public services in minimal relation to private production and use of goods is a cause of social disorder or impairs economic performance. The matter may now be put affirmatively. By failing to exploit the opportunity to expand public production we are missing opportunities for enjoyment which otherwise we might have had. Presumably a community can be as well rewarded by buying better schools or better parks as by buying bigger automobiles. By concentrating on the latter rather than the former it is failing to maximize its satisfactions. As with schools in the community, so with public services over the country at large. It is scarcely sensible that we should satisfy our wants in private goods with reckless abundance, while in the case of public goods, on the evidence of the eye, we practice extreme self-denial. So, far from systematically exploiting the opportunities to derive use and pleasure from these services, we do not supply what would keep us out of trouble.

The conventional wisdom holds that the community, large or small, makes a decision as to how much it will devote to its public services. This decision is arrived at by democratic process. Subject to the imperfections and uncertainties of democracy, people decide how much of their private income and goods they will surrender in order to have public srevices of which they are in greater need. Thus there is a balance, however rough, in the enjoyments to be had from private goods and services and those rendered by public authority.

THE DEPENDENCE EFFECT

It will be obvious, however, that this view depends on the notion of independently determined consumer wants. In such a world one could with some reason defend the doctrine that the consumer, as a voter, makes an independent choice between public and private goods. But given the dependence effect—given that consumer wants are created by the process by which they are satisfied—the consumer makes no such choice. He is subject to the forces of advertising and emulation by which production creates its own demand. Advertising operates exclusively, and emulation mainly, on behalf of privately produced goods and services. Since management and emulative effects operate on behalf of private production, public services will have an inherent tendency to lag behind. Automobile demand which is expensively synthesized will inevitably have a much larger claim on income than parks or public health or even roads where no such influence operates. The engines of mass communication, in their highest state of development, assail the eyes and ears of the community on behalf of more beer but not of more schools. Even in the conventional wisdom it will scarcely be contended that this leads to an equal choice between the two.

So much for the influences which operate on the decision between public and private production. The calm decision between public and private consumption pictured by the conventional wisdom is, in fact, a remarkable example of the error which arises from viewing social behavior out of context. The inherent tendency will always be for public services to fall behind private production. We have here the first of the causes of social imbalance.

Social balance is also the victim of two further features of our society—the truce on inequality and the tendency to inflation. Since these are now part of our context, their effect comes quickly into view.

With rare exceptions such as the post office, public services do not carry a price ticket to be paid for by the individual user. By their nature they must, ordinarily, be available to all. As a result, when they are improved or new services are initiated, there is the ancient and troublesome question of who is to pay. This, in turn, provokes to life the collateral but irrelevant debate over inequality. As with the use of taxation as an instrument of fiscal policy, the truce on inequality is broken. Liberals are obliged to argue that the services be paid for by progressive taxation which will reduce inequality. Committed as they are to the urgency of goods they must oppose sales and excise taxes. Conservatives rally to the defense of inequality—although without ever quite committing themselves in such uncouth terms—and oppose the use of income taxes. They, in effect, oppose the expenditure not on the merits of the service but on the demerits of the tax system. Since the debate over inequality cannot be resolved, the money is frequently not appropriated and the service not performed. It is a casualty of the economic goals of both liberals and conservatives for both of whom the questions of social balance are subordinate to those of production and, when it is evoked, of inequality.

SOCIAL IMBALANCE AND INFLATION

Finally, social imbalance is the natural offspring of persistent inflation. Inflation by its nature strikes different individuals and groups with highly discriminatory effect. The most nearly unrelieved victims, apart from those living on pensions or other fixed provision for personal security, are those who work for the state. In the private economy the firm which sells goods has, in general, an immediate accommodation to the inflationary movement. Its price increases are the inflation. The incomes of its owners and proprietors are automatically accommodated to the upward movement. To the extent that wage increases are part of the inflationary process, this is also true of organized industrial workers. Even unorganized white collar workers are in a milieu where prices and incomes are moving up. The adaptation of their incomes, if less rapid than that of the industrial workers, is still reasonably prompt.

The position of the public employee is at the other extreme. His pay scales are highly formalized, and traditionally they have been subject to revision only at lengthy intervals. In states and localities inflation does not automatically bring added revenues to pay higher salaries and incomes. Pay revision for all public workers is subject to the temptation to wait and see if the inflation isn't coming to an end. There will be some fear—this seems to have been more of a factor in England than in the United States—that advances in public wages will set a bad example for private employers and unions.

Inflation means that employment is pressing on the labor supply and that private wage and salary incomes are rising. Thus the opportunities for moving from public to private employment are especially favorable. Public employment, moreover, once had as a principal attraction a high measure of social security. Industrial workers were subject to the formidable threat of unemployment during depression. Public employees were comparatively secure, and this security was worth an adverse salary differential. But with improving economic security in general this advantage has diminished. Private employment thus has come to provide better protection against inflation and little worse protection against other hazards. Though the dedicated may stay in public posts, the alert go.

The deterioration of the public services in the years of inflation has not gone unremarked. However, there has been a strong tendency to regard it as an adventitious misfortune—something which, like a nasty shower at a picnic, happened to blight a generally good time. Salaries were allowed to lag, which was a pity. This is a very inadequate view. Discrimination against the public services is an organic feature of inflation. Nothing so weakens government as persistent inflation. The public administration[s] of France for many years, of Italy until recent times, and of other European and numerous South American countries have been deeply sapped and eroded by the effects of long-continued inflation. Social imbalance reflects itself in inability to enforce laws, including significantly those which protect and advance basic social justice, and in failure to maintain and improve essential services. One outgrowth of the resulting imbalance has been frustration and pervasive discontent. Over much of the world there is a rough and not entirely accidental correlation between the strength of indigenous communist parties or the frequency of revolutions and the persistence of inflation.

POSTWAR ATTACK ON PUBLIC SERVICES

A feature of the years immediately following World War II was a remarkable attack on the notion of expanding and improving public services. During the depression years such services had been elaborated and improved partly in order to fill some small part of the vacuum left by the shrinkage of private production. During the war years the role of government was vastly expanded. After that came the reaction. Much of it, unquestionably, was motivated by a desire to rehabilitate the prestige of private production and therewith of producers. No doubt some who joined the attack hoped, at least tacitly, that it might be possible to sidestep the truce on taxation vis-à-vis equality by having less taxation of all kinds. For a time the notion that our public services had somehow become inflated and excessive was all but axiomatic. Even liberal politicians did not seriously protest. They found it necessary to aver that they were in favor of public economy too.

In this discussion a certain mystique was attributed to the satisfaction of privately supplied wants. A community decision to have a new school means that the individual surrenders the necessary amount, willy-nilly, in his taxes. But if he is left with that income, he is a free man. He can decide between a better car or a television set. This was advanced with some solemnity as an argument for the TV set. The difficulty is that this argument leaves the community with no way of preferring the school. All private wants, where the individual can choose, are inherently superior to all public desires which must be paid for by taxation and with an inevitable component of compulsion.

The cost of public services was also held to be a desolating burden on private production, although this was at a time when the private production was burgeoning. Urgent warnings were issued of the unfavorable effects of taxation on investment—"I don't know of a surer way of killing off the incentive to invest than by imposing taxes which are regarded by people as punitive." This was at a time when the inflationary effect of a very high level of investment was causing concern. The same individuals who were warning about the inimical effects of taxes were strongly advocating a monetary policy designed to reduce investment. However, an understanding of our economic discourse requires an appreciation of one of its basic rules: men of high position are allowed, by a special act of grace, to accommodate their reasoning to the answer they need. Logic is only required in those of lesser rank.

Finally it was argued, with no little vigor, that expanding government posed a grave threat to individual liberties. "Where distinction and rank is achieved almost exclusively by becoming a civil servant of the state . . . it is too much to expect that many will long prefer freedom to security."

With time this attack on public services has somewhat subsided. The disorder associated with social imbalance has become visible even if the need for balance between private and public services is still imperfectly appreciated.

Freedom also seemed to be surviving. Perhaps it was realized that all organized activity requires concessions by the individual to the group. This is true of the policeman who joins the police force, the teacher who gets a job at the high school, and the executive who makes his way up the hierarchy of duPont. If there are differences between public and private organization, they are of kind rather than of degree. As this is written the pendulum has in fact swung back. Our liberties are now menaced by the conformity exacted by the large corporation and its impulse to create, for its own purposes, the organization man. This danger we may also survive.

Nonetheless, the postwar onslaught on the public services left a lasting imprint. To suggest that we canvass our public wants to see where happiness can be improved by more and better services has a sharply radical tone. Even public services to avoid disorder must be defended. By contrast the man who devises a nostrum for a nonexistent need and then successfully promotes both remains one of nature's noblemen.

The "Primrose Path" of Centralism

National Association of Manufacturers

In little more than 100 years the United States has developed from a primarily agricultural economy into the world's leading industrial nation. Our standard of living is higher than that of any other country. We are the recognized leaders of the free world. And the outlook is for further growth and a continuing improvement in our living standards.

Much depends, however, on the relationship between the government and the economy. Historically, we have in the main adhered to the principles of a free enterprise economy. The action of prices in the free market has determined the goods and services that were produced, allocated resources among industries, adjusted consumption to supply, and distributed the product among the members of society. Individual ambition has been regarded as the most universal, reliable, and powerful of human motives, and each individual has enjoyed freedom of action to satisfy his wants and to make voluntary decisions concerning his economic problems as he deemed best. It has generally been held that the aggregate of such decisions would result in wiser solutions of the economic problems of our society than would decisions imposed by an outside agency.

Yet, among those calling themselves "liberals" today, there is articulate support of the "outside agency" approach, and the agency which they consider most competent, and to be primarily relied upon, to solve all problems on almost all subjects is the federal government. In this writing, the doctrine of extreme reliance on the federal government is called "centralism. . . ."

From The "Primrose Path" of Centralism, *Government Economy Committee, New York, National Association of Manufacturers, 1960. Reprinted by permission.*

The broad national purpose in establishing the form of government under which we have lived since 1789 was never better stated than in the Preamble to the Constitution:

We the people of the United States, in order to form a more perfect union, establish justice, insure domestic tranquility, provide for the common defense, promote the general welfare, and secure the blessings of liberty to ourselves and our posterity, do ordain and establish this Constitution for the United States of America.

The people, the states, and the United States were thus recognized as collaborators in this organization of a new political and social order. They were made jointly responsible for successful achievement of the national purpose here proclaimed and each party to the compact had its own sphere of performance. Certain powers, with accompanying responsibilities, were delegated to the United States, to be exercised by the Congress, and with conscious effort to limit the authority and scope of the central government, those powers, with their accompanying responsibilities, which were not delegated by the Constitution to the United States, nor prohibited by it to the states, were reserved to the states respectively, or to the people.

The intention was to establish a balance between the powers, responsibilities, and rights of central and state governments, respectively. While a completely static balance was never visualized, it was expected that insistence by the states and by the federal government upon their respective constitutional rights and responsibilities would be a check on too great concentration of power at either point. [Recently, however,] the states have not been as jealous of their constitutional prerogatives, nor as aggressive in asserting them, as they were more than a century ago. Two important reasons for this political lassitude are evident.

The first is that during the first half of the 20th century the two most devastating wars in the world's history occurred. Our participation in these wars involved an expansion of the federal administrative and fiscal structure which could not be reduced immediately, after either event, to the pre-war level. This sheer quantitative enlargement of the federal government could have been dealt with in time, however, by insistent state pressure for restoration of better balance in their favor.

The second reason for relative state inaction has been more serious and more insidious. It was the emergence, in the depression of the 1930's, of a political and economic philosophy which, since then, has been increasingly claimed as the criterion of good public policy by a number of academicians, politicians, and other opinion makers, who in turn have convinced a good many citizens.

The advocates and adherents of this doctrine called it "liberalism." The term is as completely inappropriate to its objectives as is the use of the term "democracy" by Communist dictatorships. The current use is, in fact, a perversion of the 19th-century meaning of the word. "Liberalism" then meant the liberating of individuals from the restrictions and controls of government. The word to describe the aims and objectives of present-day self-styled "liberals" is "centralism." That is, instead of advocating and promoting the liberation of persons from the burdens and controls of government, "centralism" advocates more, not less, control and regimentation of persons and business. . . . Centralism has thus provided the rationalized basis for the steady expansion of the size, power, and cost of the federal government. But it has eroded the sense of responsibility of the states and diminished their zeal to fulfill their constitutional destiny as sovereign members of a union of states. It has caused the people to forget that they are the residual repository of sovereignty under the Constitution.

Centralism provides grants and loans to persons and to states and their political subdivisions. It participates in the support of non-federal governmental functions and of private economic activities. Instead of creating an economic climate which would help citizens and communities by motivating them to help themselves, centralism makes use of distress and natural state-by-state differences to spread and strengthen federal power. . . .

Centralism recognizes no effective limitations on federal powers, which means that while this doctrine is operative and persuasive in the formulation of public policy, the road is open for unrestricted federal expansion. As centralism strengthens, state sovereignty diminishes. Unless a popular reaction against centralism is generated and made manifest, there is no natural stopping place short of a monolithic, completely authoritarian state.

CONSEQUENCES OF CENTRALISM

Even without further expansion, the doctrine of centralism has resulted in a federal government structure too big for competent management, too powerful for the best relationship between the people and their government, and too grasping of both resources and responsibilities to permit the fullest flowering and independence of the private economy. Some of the salient evidence of this indictment is summarized herewith.

1. Diversion of Attention and Effort from the Truly National Tasks. The most serious consequence of centralism is one which has received little attention. Apparently overlooked, or at least disregarded, in the hastening course of centralist headway is a factor vital to the defense and survival of the nation. This is the diversion of the time and energy of federal officials—the Executive and the Congress—into so many byways of purpose that efficient discharge of those duties and functions which *only* the federal government can carry out [has] suffered. . . .

2. Excessive Cost of Centralism. A second serious consequence of over-loading federal officials with matters that belong elsewhere is the heavy cost which such a policy has imposed on the people. It is axiomatic that the most expensive way to get anything done is for the federal government to do it. There are various reasons for this result:

First, the full cost of federal undertakings is often not set out in the beginning. Popular acceptance is more easily obtained by underestimates of cost, by small initial appropriations and expenditures which get the project under way without too much objection. Once the commitment has been made, the cost estimates go up and up, the time schedule for completion is extended, and after it is too late the people discover that the programs and projects which seemed at first to be good bargains are anything but that.

Illustrations of this "foot-in-the-door" technique abound. The drive for federal aid to education is a current case in point. The proponents of this raid on the Treasury have clearly in mind the objective of large permanent federal grants and the initial programming of small grants for limited periods is their camouflage for the ultimate goal.

Second, Washington must operate by remote control, which is seldom highly efficient. Supervision must filter down through various bureaucratic layers which delay and impede decision making. Federal appropriations for various programs tend to be more lavish than would be provided if financial responsibility were located closer to the job to be done.

Third, wage and hour requirements, which are based on standards prevailing in metropolitan areas, increase materially the cost of federally-aided construction projects for small communities. The people will discover how deeply this two-edged sword cuts if they allow themselves to be drawn into any scheme for general federal aid to school construction.

Fourth, the people tend to be more tolerant of large federal appropriations and more unconcerned about excessive costs because of the persistent illusion that federal money is "free money." However painfully aware they may be in general of the heavy federal tax burden, the penalty of excessive cost of specific programs is seldom brought home to them. The real impact is concealed by the lack of connection, in the Congressional procedures, between spending and taxing legislation. In city councils and state legislatures, this connection is more clearly and quickly identified. . . .

3. Retention of Restrictive, Punitive Tax Rates. The cost involved in supporting government programs so unlimited as to deal with any and every problem or difficulty that may affect individuals or communities naturally becomes a justification for the retention or imposition of excessive tax rates. . . .

4. *Expansion of Federal Power Through Grants, Loans, or Subsidies.* The objective of centralism is expansion of federal power and control. The underlying rationalization of this objective is a conviction that the federal government should lead and support the people. This necessarily implies a distrust of state and local governments, and a belief that citizens are too dilatory in action and deficient in grasp to face the issues which centralist planners deem important.

The depression of the 1930's left a framework of fiscal relationships between the federal government and the states, and the government and the people, which provided an ideal opportunity for the centralists. Various federal grant, loan, and subsidy programs established in that period as rescue operations to meet economic emergencies faced by the states and the people offered ready-made patterns and specific tools for centralist purposes. Where the major emphasis of these original programs was relief, a shift of focus was apparent in their extension and in the introduction of new aid programs. The new theme was "the general public interest." A persuasive but mechanistic justification accompanied this. It was that these federal programs were needed and undertaken "to stimulate initiation" by states, communities, or individuals of certain activities deemed desirable.

From its beginning, centralism expansion faced potential resistance by the states against federal invasion of governmental areas presumably reserved to them by the Constitution. But it was forestalled by a purposeful use of the aid pattern already established. The states, in effect, were "bribed" to withhold resistance, and successive extensions of centralism were "bought" with the federal funds or credit extended. Aid programs now cover a wide range of purposes, many of which cannot be demonstrated as matters of federal concern except under a centralist interpretation of national government for promoting the public welfare. Cases of genuine need for stimulative leadership through federal aid were few, even in the beginning, in contrast to those drummed up by pressures to impose a federal pattern and to advance centralist objectives. Instead of a temporary device to be terminated once the initial impetus to action had been given, the various forms of federal aid have become permanent. They have been steadily extended into new areas. Their cost has continually increased. "Stimulation" has thus invariably become support. And support necessarily becomes control. . . .

5. *The Dominance of Minority Groups.* Centralism thrives on the principle of "divide and rule," which means in the present connection an immoderate encouragement of minority groups. The purpose of legislative action at any governmental level is to deal with matters deemed to require attention from

the standpoint of the general public interest. The active supporters or opponents of specific legislative proposals before a city council, a state legislature, or the national Congress ordinarily number many fewer than the entire group that would be affected by particular legislative measures. However, the privilege of any individual or group to present their views to government is protected by the constitutional right of petition. . . .

Logrolling among minority groups, even when their respective objectives may be in conflict, is a profitable undertaking for those concerned because it virtually always leads to more federal spending on all of the projects involved. Examples abound of this sacrifice of the general public interest to specific minority commitments. Thus, the costly agricultural subsidy program needs Congressional support from the urban districts, where the projects of slum clearance and urban renewal need the help of farm state votes.

Furthermore, excessive devotion to particular minority interests often defeats the broader interests of the taxpaying majority. To cite agriculture again— the support program costs the residents of all cities and of most states more than any benefit which they may get in return. Also, in the field of grants-in-aid, for example, an "equalization" program of federal aid for school construction or teachers' salaries would cost the citizens of many communities, as taxpayers, more than the amount they may get back in grants.

6. Demotion of the States as Sovereign Entities. The ultimate expression of centralism is the monolithic, authoritarian state, which brooks no impediment to total power. One of Hitler's first acts in his march toward dictatorship was abolition of most of the powers, duties, and functions of the several German states. The proponents of centralism would reduce the American states to the status of provinces. They deride "states' rights" as an obsolete shibboleth and are openly scornful of the states' capacity to discharge their responsibilities. They disregard the fact that while there is in this country no intentional design to dictatorship, the influence of centralism, if not abated, will lead to a vesting of total power somewhere—whether the lodgment might be with the Congress or with a "strong man" in the executive branch, or with the army. . . .

7. Business Competition with Taxpaying Citizens. As a further means of expanding federal control and domination, centralism presses for extension of government controlled and operated public power and credit enterprises, the operations of which never yield a net income for general purposes equal to that which could be realized in private hands. It has long been recognized that control of the sources of energy by government assures domination of the energy users. Conservation of natural resources has served as a means, and a cloak, for this key invasion of the private economy. Popular support has been obtained by favoring service-users at the expense of taxpayers. Furthermore:

a. Federal ownership and operation of public power facilities undermines the state and local tax base by exemption of federally owned plant[s] and equipment from the local tax rolls. In the few cases where payments are made "in lieu" of taxes, these are no more than token amounts by comparison with the local tax revenues that are collected from comparable privately owned property;

b. The income base for federal taxation is depleted;

c. The funds for government business enterprises are provided by appropriations, or by Treasury advances at interest rates below the cost of borrowed funds. The terms of repayment to the treasury, where provided for, are unrealistically long;

d. The lack of a profit motive as a spur to efficient management is paralleled, in the case of government enterprises, by the absence of an obligation to conserve the capital. If a government enterprise impairs its capital by incurring losses in operation, this impairment is made good by another appropriation or a Treasury loan at an interest rate below cost.

BRINGING GOVERNMENT BACK HOME

The . . . security for the nation and for the individual citizens in this dangerously critical period in world affairs depends upon and requires that the national responsibility be limited to the truly national tasks. All services and functions pertaining to the economic progress and welfare of the people except those which can be performed only by the federal government should be handled by a lesser jurisdiction if they are properly governmental in character, or left to private initiative. This conclusion is diametrically opposed to the thesis of centralism, which seeks to achieve security and economic progress through continued expansion of federal authority. The battle line is thus clearly drawn. Under centralism there is no logical stopping place in the extension of federal power and control short of a monolithic, authoritarian state. The attack must be directed to reversal of this trend by bringing government back home. . . .

CENTRALISM AND ECONOMIC GROWTH

Growth means an increased output of goods and services by the private economy. In order to achieve greater output, there must be a constant flow of investment into more and better capital equipment and into the discovery and development of new and better products. In a free, competitive, private enterprise society, economic growth is, indeed, "the business of the businessman."

Although centralists express belief in and reliance on the private enterprise system as the source of prosperity and economic progress, nevertheless, at the same time, their doctrine calls for more spending by government. . . . The need of the nation is growth of the economy, not growth of the government. The two are far from synonymous, but rather, in a fundamental sense, inimical to each other. Government growth competes with and impedes economic growth. . . . What government takes leaves less for use of the private economy. The bigger government becomes and the more it spends, the greater is the diversion of resources from private decisions, uses, and goals to public planning and purposes. This is a fundamental fact in the division of the economic pie— increased federal spending leaves less for the private economy. . . .

There is an ironic difference in the effect of government policies on capital formation in Communist and private capitalist systems. In the Soviet Union, where economic growth results from forced capital accumulation—sometimes even by expropriation—Russia's all-powerful government gives first priority to the creation and use of capital. Here in the United States, our government itself has erected the greatest barrier to the formation and application of capital.

The most serious domestic impediment to capital formation is excessive tax rates, especially on middle and higher bracket incomes.

THE CONFLICT BETWEEN AUTHORITY AND FREEDOM

Centralism is also a matter of serious concern to the people as a threat to the preservation of balance between authority and freedom. It has often been said that government means total authority within whatever bounds its jurisdiction extends. There can be no partial acceptance of government's will, no option to the citizens to obey or disobey. The wider the scope of government's operations, the larger the area within which the individual has no choice but to obey, and the smaller the area within which he is free of government restraint or compulsion. We need enough government to assure a peaceful, orderly community at home and to provide for security against foreign aggression; but we dare not have so much government that personal liberties are imperiled and the economic basis of individual self-support is destroyed through excesses of expenditure, taxation, and regulation.

This dilemma is real. As stated so clearly by Woodrow Wilson fifty years ago—"The history of liberty is the history of the limitation of governmental power, not the increase of it."

The insistence of centralists that government must do more and more for more people ignores the menace to freedom that is involved in such a policy. Expanding government beneficence means expanding government authority, which in turn means more regimentation both of the beneficiaries and of those on whom the increasing costs are levied. The centralism program of doing more and more for the people rests not on concern, but on distrust. It holds that they will not face up to their problems and that only a super-government can support and guide the nation. Centralism, under a cloak of humanitarianism, is really contemptuous of the ability of the people to think for themselves, to handle their own affairs, and to solve their own problems. . . .

Our job, as citizens of a republic and disciples of the creed of individual worth and freedom, is to challenge the premises of this doctrine [of centralism] and to take the initiative by attacking its vulnerable points. We should constantly drive home the gravity of the conflict between centralism and personal freedom. We should emphasize the conflict between government growth and economic growth by demonstrating that the people can have more from now on, including recognition of individual human dignity and preservation of hard-won personal freedoms, under an economic system of free, private enterprise with a minimum of government control and intervention, and with moderate tax rates, than they can possibly have under punitive tax rates and a political and economic system of government direction, dole, and domination.

QUESTIONS FOR DISCUSSION

1. *What is "social balance"?*
2. *Why does Galbraith think we have failed to attain balance?*
3. *Is there too much "centralism"?*
4. *Could we avoid "centralism" even if we wanted to?*

The Performance of the National Economy

PART FOUR

What Is the New Economics?

By now, the "new economics" is not really very new. More than thirty years have elapsed since John Maynard Keynes published his *General Theory of Employment, Interest, and Money* and laid the foundation for the "new economics." As economic theories go, that is a respectable age indeed. Nevertheless, the "new economics" is new in the sense of applying its tools and methods of analysis to public policy. As this writer attempts to show in one of the following selections, it has only been in recent years that a large measure of public and political acceptance has been obtained for Keynesian analysis. That article, it should be pointed out, was written a few years ago, when most economists were wildly (for economists) celebrating the apparent victory of Keynesian ideas in government policy-making. It was before the political, social, and economic crunch of the Vietnam War and before the presidential election of 1968. The "victory" of Keynesian ideas may no longer seem so secure as it once was, although as one conservative economist, not noted for his thorough admiration of Keynes, has observed, "We are all Keynesians."

The name, "new economics," is in some ways unfortunate since it tends to confuse and deceive people about the origins and biases of the prevailing theory. It is not "new" in the sense that it is a sharp break with traditional capitalist economics. It does not oppose private property, the business system, or the use of the market in resource allocation and price determination. Contrary to vaguely popular mythology, the "new economics" is not socialism or welfare statism.

More than anything else, the "new economics" is new in its perspective of how a capitalist economy operates. It does not impose new goals upon the economic system—only new means to obtain old goals. At this level of generalization, virtually all economists and most thoughtful politicians are to some degree Keynesians; however, when one proceeds to examine the advocacy of particular policies, it is evident that there is still much controversy and division over what type of actual policy this theoretical analysis justifies.

In the first of the following articles, Robert Lekachman discusses the breakdown of the old economic theories in the 1930's and the theoretical basis for Keynes's readjustment of these theories. The second article examines the gradual acceptance of Keynesian ideas and the gradual application of these concepts to the actual formation of American public policy. These two articles are essentially pro-Keynesian; that is, they view the adoption of the new analysis both as a step forward and as an almost irrevocable action. The last article by Milton Friedman, an economic advisor both to Barry Goldwater in 1964 and to President Nixon, illustrates much less conviction about the desirability of the "new economics." It charges that deterioration rather than improvement in the economy has been the actual result of the Kennedy–Johnson new economic years.

The General Theory

Robert Lekachman

Three decades after its appearance, *The General Theory* remains a difficult, technical treatise even for specialists. It is full of subtleties of exposition, some necessary, some the consequence of obscure thought, and some apparently designed to infuriate members of his own profession. But it was also a book with a powerful central message. This was a blast at the assumption that there were mechanisms of economic adjustment in capitalist societies which automatically produced conditions of full employment of men and resources. No doubt Keynes exaggerated the uniformity of this opinion among economists, but he was broadly accurate in his judgment that most if not all economists still retained, Great Depression or no Great Depression, a sturdy confidence in the ability of competitive markets to expand employment and production if labor accepted lower wages and businessmen accepted lower prices. Flexible prices and flexible wages were still the best answer that the conventional wisdom of the profession could offer the community.

The thrust of economic analysis is toward the explanation of large numbers of events by a very few abstract principles. When the principles and the events diverge, when existing theories of market equilibrium ill accord with the persistence of unemployment and the gloomy outlook for its alleviation, economists, like labor leaders, may grow discontented. But they will cling to their existing principles until superior principles are invented, for economics is a subject in which bad theory is preferable to no theory at all. Economists like Pigou and Robertson were not blissfully happy with doctrines that preached equilibrium at full employment. In the absence of better theories, they patched up the existing doctrines. Keynes's task, then, was twofold: destruction of bad old doctrine and creation of good new doctrine.

The older theory which Keynes attacked was founded on an old generalization, the nineteenth-century French economist Jean-Baptiste Say's Law of Markets. Often summarized in the aphorism . . . , "Supply creates its own demand," Say's Law affirmed the impossibility of general overproduction of goods, or general "glut," in Say's word. Equally impossible therefore was general unemployment. Say's reasoning was nearly as concise and simple as his conclusion. Was it not obvious that men produced goods only in order to enjoy the consumption of other goods? Capitalists invested in order to consume their profits in the enjoyment of life. Workers labored in order to consume their wages in acquiring the means of subsistence for themselves and their families. The more that businessmen spent on hiring labor and purchasing raw materials, the larger would be the incomes generated and the capacity of their recipients to purchase goods. Every increase in production soon justified itself by a matching increase in demand. Double production and infallibly you double sales. Indeed, the only limit was the amount of resources and the number of employable workers available. The version of Say's Law which Keynes quoted appeared in John Stuart Mill's 1848 *Principles of Political Economy:*

What constitutes the means of payment for commodities is simply commodities. Each person's means of paying for the productions of other people consist of those which he himself possesses. All sellers are inevitably, and by the meaning of the word, buyers. Could we suddenly double the productive powers of the country, we should double the supply of commodities in every market; but we should, by the same stroke, double the purchasing power. Everybody would bring a double demand as well as supply; everybody would be able to buy twice as much, because every one would have twice as much to offer in exchange. . . .

Keynes conceded that few of his own contemporaries stated this doctrine as plainly as Mill and Marshall, but, said Keynes, "Contemporary thought is still deeply steeped in the notion that if people did not spend their money in one way they will spend it in another." Although it was true that post-World War I economists were unable to express such opinions "consistently" in the face of the "facts of experience," these same economists failed miserably in not revising their theories and adjusting their remedies.

Such judgments dictated Keynes's initial strategy. It was to demolish the "postulates of classical economics." In Keynes's opinion the grand conclusion to which Say's Law led inexorably was the existence of some wage rate at which, in each circumstance, full employment was feasible. One by one Keynes identified and either accepted as harmless or rejected as mistaken the "postulates" which supported this conclusion. It is well worth following his reasoning.

The first of the classical postulates reads in Keynes's version, "The wage is equal to the marginal product of labour." In nontechnical language this amounts to the proposition that wages tend to equal the value of the product for which the worker is responsible, after taking other costs into account.

The second postulate is somewhat more complex in statement and meaning: "The utility of the wage when a given volume of labour is employed is equal to the marginal disutility of that amount of employment." This sentence compresses several vital assumptions, many of them with roots deep in the history of economic ideas. Five at least are important:

1. Work is painful and never undertaken for its own sake.

2. Additional work becomes more painful hour by hour.

3. Wages are pleasant because those who receive them can use them to command pleasurable objects and services.

4. Nevertheless, additional wages yield less pleasure, dollar by dollar, than their predecessors because they gratify tastes of diminishing urgency, for individuals buy items of greater pleasure with their initial dollars of income.

5. Therefore, any worker will offer his services to an employer only in the anticipation that the pleasure he receives from the wages which are the reward of his effort exceeds the pain which the additional labor causes. Hence, in a competitive labor market, workers cease to labor just before the point where additional pleasures match additional pains.

Orthodox economic theory thus imputed to the laborer the maximizing, rational, calculating tendencies upon which economic theory has habitually based its explanations of human behavior.

There was a most important corollary of this doctrine: the implication that any individual worker had it in his own power to find or to increase his own employment. All he needed to do was revise his psychic computation of pleasure and pain so as to work more hours at existing wage rates, work the same number of hours at lower wages, or, if unemployed, accept a job offer at a wage rate which previously he had deemed unacceptable. The moral for individual workers and the leaders of their unions was inescapable—the partially or completely unemployed could remedy their situation at any time; all they had to do was accept lower wage rates.

From this inference flowed another. All unemployment was either frictional or voluntary. Where unemployment was frictional, workers who were seasonally idle or between jobs could confidently anticipate re-employment as the season changed or as new jobs became available. All other unemployment had to be interpreted as the voluntary preference of the unemployed. Much as an economist might justify on humane or historical grounds the refusal of a worker to accept a reduction in his standard of life, the economist could not grant him an economic justification.

This notion that unemployment for any length of time was never involuntary was deeply ingrained. Prime Minister Harold Wilson has recalled that the late Lord Beveridge, a pioneer student and advocate of social reform, himself failed to grasp the possibility that unemployment might really be beyond the control or influence of the unemployed. In Wilson's words, "I remember his face, very puzzled, one day after he had visited a camp for unemployed men. He said he couldn't understand why decent, able-bodied men like the ones we had seen *could* be out of work. He didn't want to face the real problem. He wanted to think in terms of frictional unemployment."

However, in teasing and unpleasant fact, involuntary unemployment *did* exist. Any observer at all in touch with the social reality of the 1930s knew that quite frequently wages and employment had contracted simultaneously. Hence, as a theorist Keynes badly needed an appropriate definition of involuntary unemployment, one which could serve as a license for its existence. Not the simplest grouping of words in the English language, Keynes's definition went like this: "Men are involuntarily unemployed if, in the event of a small rise in the price of wage-goods relatively to the money-wage, both the aggregate supply of labour willing to work for the current money-wage and the aggregate demand for it at that wage would be greater than the existing volume of employment."

The definition was a summary of a mental experiment. Suppose, Keynes directed his reader, that the cost of living went up and nothing happened to the wages paid to workers. Then the average worker's *real* wage—the collection of goods he could actually purchase with his money income—must decline. Now, according to the reasoning characteristic of classical theory, the response of laborers to declines in their real income was a withholding of a portion of their labor. But was it really sensible to assume that this theoretical reaction also occurred in life? Did workers leave their jobs or work fewer hours every time the price of food and clothing went up? Of course not.

What actually happened was something quite different. Higher prices of "wage-goods" (consumer goods) implied higher profits and a more encouraging sales outlook for the sellers of the standard items that entered into the worker's budget. These sellers tended to hire more labor as the business outlook brightened. And—this was the point of Keynes's analysis—the laborers were perfectly willing to accept new employment even though their *real wage* was lower than it would have been before the cost of living rose. Under the circumstances it could scarcely have been plainer that if ordinary workers were willing to accept jobs at wages *lower* than the previous level of remuneration, then they surely would have been willing to work at the higher real wages of the past. Hence they must have been involuntarily unemployed. If their employers had only felt it worth their while to offer additional employment at lower money and real wages, they would have found willing workers. Thus, economists who were so stubbornly confident that individual employers and individual employees between them determined the level of employment were simply completely mistaken. Often enough nothing an unemployed man or woman could do was capable of having the slightest impact on his own job prospects.

This demonstration served Keynes only as a beginning. Once the presence and theoretical possibility of involuntary unemployment were granted, the harder tasks remained. What was the explanation of the size of involuntary unemployment? What occasioned fluctuations in unemployment? It was precisely at this juncture, as Keynes argued his case, that something vital was missing from the corpus of orthodox economics—nothing less than a theory of aggregate demand. The highest distinction of *The General Theory* was not the explanation of involuntary unemployment; it was the construction of this missing piece of economic apparatus.

Once the theory is stated, the error of conventional economic policy is really grasped. It becomes plain that the wage- and price-cutting which were approved pre-Keynesian specifics illegitimately leaped from the specific to the general. Any businessman can see that a reduction in his own costs—other things being equal—expands his profits and encourages him to increase his output. The heart of the matter is the failure of other things to remain equal when *all* businessmen reduce wages and costs. When wages in general fall, then the demand for all varieties of consumer goods and services inevitably falls in tune with the declining incomes of workers. At best, then, the demand for goods must fall in much the same proportion as wages. In the aggregate the demand for goods depends upon the incomes which, again in the aggregate, their potential purchasers earn. *One* employer can benefit from a reduction of his workers' wages. *All* employers cannot benefit by a general reduction of wages. To believe otherwise is to commit the logical fallacy of composition.

Hence the new Keynesian theory of economic activity was on the one hand an explanation of how the total *supply* of goods and services emerged from the decisions of hordes of individual businessmen, and on the other hand an account of how the total *demand* for goods and services evolved from the spending and saving choices of millions of individual consumers. As Keynes told his new story, events commence with the actions of businessmen. He assumed from the outset that it is individual businessmen or entrepreneurs who provide employment and pay incomes—wages to workers, salaries to executives, interest to bankers, rent to landlords. Entrepreneurs expect to sell the goods which result from the combination of the agents of production at prices which equal at a minimum the sums paid out in the process of producing them—including a normal profit. It follows that when the situation is stable (that is, when aggregate equilibrium is attained), the *aggregate* amount of income and employment which *all* entrepreneurs will offer just matches the volume of the sales which they anticipate making.*

When will entrepreneurs wish to expand the employment they offer, the incomes they provide, and the output they produce? The answer was related by Keynes to the notion of an aggregate *demand* function, which is the other half of the picture. Suppose that *in fact* when entrepreneurs offer a certain amount of employment and produce a certain volume of output, the *actual* demand for the goods they offer for sale exceeds their expectations. Accordingly, most businessmen discover that their stocks (or inventories) of goods are running short. At this point, if they are retailers or wholesalers, they increase their orders to manufacturers; if they are manufacturers, they increase their production. The aggregate demand function measures the volume of sales which corresponds to each possible level of income and output.

The actual level of employment, then, must be "given by the point of intersection between the aggregate demand function and the aggregate supply function; for it is at this point that the entrepreneurs' expectations of profits will be maximised." The contrast with Say's Law was now complete. Say's Law blithely assumed that every time businessmen expanded supply, demand simply followed in its train. The beneficent process halted only when full employment of men and resources called a halt to expansion. Keynes's alternative doctrine contained a very different moral. In the Keynesian universe, equilibrium could be reached at *any* level of employment and income between zero and full employment. Moreover, no theoretical reason existed for saying that one level of employment was more likely to occur than any other level of employment. On the possible scale of values, full employment was simply one possibility among many. It followed that at each and every level of employment other than full employment, involuntary unemployment was more than possible; it was unavoidable. What determined the level of employment was *not* the wage bargain negotiated between laborers and their employers. No matter

* Keynes defined the aggregate supply price of the output of a given amount of employment as "the expectation of proceeds which will just make it worth the while of the entrepreneurs to give that employment" (*The General Theory of Employment, Interest, and Money,* New York, Harcourt, Brace, 1936, p. 24).

how humble the former were, they could not expand their own employment. What determined employment was something quite different. It was the level of aggregate demand for the goods and services of the entire economy. . . .

Keynes had simultaneously assaulted orthodoxy, substituted a dazzlingly novel theory of employment and income, and supplemented that doctrine with a whole series of public policies. In the course of his operations, he attacked many of the shibboleths which economists venerated in common with ordinary citizens. As Adam Smith had asked long ago, was the prudence of the careful head of a family an adequate or even an acceptable model for the conduct of a great nation? Not at all. In time of depression, governments which raised taxes or reduced public spending simply threw their constituents out of work and failed even to balance the government's own budget. The reduced income of ordinary citizens infallibly diminished the tax collections of the governments which had mistakenly initiated the train of events.

Was the rate of interest the reward of the thrifty and the measure of the efficiency of the entrepreneur? No, it was not. Fundamentally, it was a price paid to speculators in exchange for the surrender of their command over cash, the most liquid of all resources. Interest rates fluctuated according to the liquidity preferences of this morally neutral group. The thrifty and the enterprising had little to do with the matter.

Was individual thrift at least still a virtue? Not during times of economic adversity. At such times the citizen who indulged himself by spending his income also benefited his fellows in society by increasing aggregate demand and employment. Blessed are the extravagant, for theirs shall be full employment. Thrift was a virtue only in time of economic boom.

Were not the debts incurred in the course of financing public works a "burden" upon future generations, as General Eisenhower has always believed? How could houses, schools, and roads be a burden on the very people who benefited from them? And even if the public funds were used frivolously, public debt was as much an asset to those who held it as a liability to the taxpayers who contributed to the interest payments.

The dragon Keynes rode out to slay was the formidable Puritan ethic which has always condemned spending, applauded saving, and considered the accumulation of riches as the occasion for stewardship, not luxurious expenditure. No doubt the ethic had its uses when capital was scarce, saving vital to economic expansion, and employment full. Elsewhere Keynes himself had eloquently sketched the benefits of high savings in a period like 1870–1914. During a war saving became virtuous indeed. But in advanced economies afflicted with persistent tendencies toward economic sluggishness and high unemployment, thrift impeded economic growth. Not the least of Keynes's successes was the weakening of the identification between virtue and thrift.

From Analysis to Public Policy

Robert B. Carson

More than two decades have passed since President Truman signed into law the Employment Act of 1946. At the time of its passage, the act evoked enthusiastic acclamation from American economists as the "Magna Carta of government planning for full employment," and over the years the statute has received appropriate notice in basic economics texts and occasional legislative and journalistic reference. However, like other documents which receive considerable lip service as important historical benchmarks, the real significance of the Employment Act of 1946 is not widely understood. As a result, there is little contemporary appreciation of the truly revolutionary importance of this enactment. To be sure, the revolutionary character of Public Law 340 was not altogether evident in 1946. When first proposed the year before, it had produced a sharp Congressional debate which ranged mostly over the philosophic implications of its wording; however, a modified version passed both houses of the 79th Congress by overwhelming bipartisan majorities and was quickly signed by the President on February 20, 1946. The act was generically akin to countless other statutes born out of the desperation of the depression and the exigencies of war. Its language was direct but scarcely startling:

> The Congress hereby declares that it is the continuing policy and responsibility of the Federal Government to use all practicable means consistent with its needs and obligations and other essential considerations of national policy, with the assistance and cooperation of industry, agriculture, labor, and State and local governments, to coordinate and utilize all its plans, functions, and resources for the purpose of creating and maintaining in a manner calculated to foster and promote free competitive enterprise and the general welfare, conditions under which there will be afforded useful employment opportunities, including self-employment, for those willing, and seeking, to work, and to promote maximum employment, production, and purchasing power.

Looking deeper than the low-keyed legislative jargon and what seemed to be a quite reasonable statement of goals, the Employment Act of 1946 proclaimed the official ending of a long esteemed but recently tarnished economic ideal. Quite simply it pronounced *laissez faire* dead. Now the market mechanism was to be regularly supplemented by government intervention aimed at keeping a stable level of economic performance. In this mixture of market plus

From Robert B. Carson, "Changes in Federal Fiscal Policy and Public Attitudes Since the Employment Act of 1946" in The Social Studies, *vol. LVIII, no. 7, December 1967.* Reprinted by permission of The Social Studies.

government, the Federal Government was to bear the ultimate responsibility for maintaining high levels of employment as well as maximizing economic freedom. To these goals specifically stated in the Employment Act, two others were implicitly added—maintenance of stable prices and a reasonable rate of economic growth.

The pronouncement of the passing of *laissez faire* was not especially startling since it was widely understood among most economists and laymen that that particular patient had contracted a fatal malady some time after October, 1929 and had expired almost unnoticed during World War II. The revolutionary impact of the Employment Act of 1946, then, lay neither in its proclaimed goals nor in its doctrinaire assertion that the Federal Government should intervene in the economy. The revolution was in what was to follow, and it was chiefly a revolution in modes of thought.

The acceptance of Federal intervention, like the earlier expansion of Federal regulative power during the progressive era, had been a pragmatic development, "a product of the intellectual ferment of the times." The thirties had seen the economic intervention of government in ways never before attempted or, for that matter, not generally considered desirable. The wartime emergency, with wage, price, and output controls, accounted for the continued expansion of Federal economic authority. While the last vestiges of the older orthodoxy were being destroyed, no theoretical replacement had yet been accepted in its place. The Employment Act of 1946, in stating that the provisional expansion of government's economic role was to be permanent policy, demanded the adoption of a politically viable economic theory which could both rationalize the development of Federal economic authority and could construct theoretical guidelines for the implementation of economic policy. To the end of developing policy guidelines, the act had created a three-man Council of Economic Advisers to advise the President and report to a Joint Economic Committee of the Congress. The Council was "responsible for analyzing and interpreting current and prospective economic developments and trends and for developing and recommending economic policies that will promote the goals of 'maximum employment, production, and purchasing power.'" Over the next twenty years, in a quiet but nonetheless coherent manner, through the workings of the Council, through the endeavors of academic economists, and through the actual expansion of Federal economic authority, the earlier pragmatic rationale for Federal economic management was replaced by a new, systematic economic philosophy. American economic thought, at both the private and political levels, was gradually expunged of old ideas and a "new economics," a new orthodoxy, was introduced. This change, which was immediately presaged by the passage of the Employment Act of 1946, must be counted as a not inconsiderable intellectual revolution.

Revolutions in thought are usually difficult to document. Ideas spring forth in obscure ways and their acceptance, if they are accepted at all, is conditioned by countless influences. There is, however, no controversy over the origin of what was to be the "new economics." As a system or a theory it appeared almost full-blown a decade before the passage of the Employment Act of 1946 with the publication of John Maynard Keynes's *General Theory of Employment, Interest, and Money*. Keynesian ideas received immediate and wide acceptance among American academic economists. Joseph Schumpeter, Harvard's Austrian economist whose great stature was to be obscured by Keynes, observed:

> The success of the *General Theory* was instantaneous and as we know, sustained. Unfavorable reviews, of which there were many, only helped. A Keynesian school formed itself. . . . Nor is this all. Beyond the pale of orthodox Keynesians there is a broad fringe of sympathizers, and beyond this again there are many who have absorbed, in one form or another, readily or grudgingly, some spirit or some individual items of Keynesian analysis. There are but two analogous cases in the whole history of economics—the Physiocrats and the Marxists.

Within the context of the depression Keynes's ideas had had a special relevance to academic economists who had seen most of the old theories of the market, money, and savings and investment smashed. Although hardly presented for a layman's understanding, Keynes's approach was direct enough: First, insufficiency of demand for goods and services is the cause for cyclical business declines. Second, this insufficiency of demand will create underemployment of resources. Third, there is, in the capitalist system, no automatic or "natural" tendency for an underemployed economy to rebound. Fourth, the primary culprit in the cyclical downturn of an economy is the activity of investors, since it is through changes in investment outlays that changes in total demand for goods and services are mostly effected.

Keynes's approach explicitly led to the position that the artificial maintenance through government of conditions which would sustain high levels of demand, especially investment demand, was essential if the economy was to be kept on an even keel. In regard to policy, the Keynesian theories were understood to justify the broad use of both monetary and fiscal policy for stabilization purposes. As to specific fiscal alternatives this meant the use of increased government spending and tax reductions, with likely budget deficits, when effective demand showed signs of falling or when there was substantial unemployment.

By 1945, a number of American economists, particularly Alvin Hansen and Paul Samuelson, fearing the return of depressionary conditions after the conclusion of the war, were advocating clearly Keynesian ideas for sustaining the war boom. The passage of the Employment Act of 1946, while admittedly a positive achievement, seemed to many of the more ardent Keynesian advocates to do too little in the way of specific policy action. However, it should be noted that in many cases their advocacy of greater fiscal and monetary action to control and stimulate the economy exceeded Keynes's own policy proposals.

Meanwhile, the theoretical implications of Keynesian policies were not yet widely understood and, within the existing American political environment, were frankly unacceptable.

It soon became apparent, however, that inflation, rather than depression, was the immediate post-war devil to be dealt with. Keynesians were quick to point out that Keynes was not simply a "Depression Economist." One of his leading American supporters, Seymour Harris, argued that when "underlying conditions required the change, he could turn off the expansion spigot which served him so well in the *General Theory* and turn on the contraction spigot." In such an instance, the counter-deflationary actions of stabilizing fiscal policies were merely reversed by closing off the rising demand through higher taxes and reduced spending, while presumably the monetary authorities were tightening credit.

In 1948, Paul Samuelson's *Economics—An Introductory Analysis* was published, and the teaching of introductory economics in American colleges would never be the same again. Samuelson attempted to synthesize the new Keynesian approach and the older classical theories as a rationalization for what was now known as "the mixed economy." Samuelson's chapters on Business Cycles, Monetary Policy, and Fiscal Policy were clearly Keynesian. They assumed, with little equivocation, that a capitalist economy could only be expected to work under some degree of general economic management of aggregate demand for goods and services and that government was the operator of the spigot which turned on or off this demand for goods. Through six editions, Samuelson has sold well over one million copies.

The academic honeymoon with Keynesian economics and innovations on Keynesian theory was underway, and, from all evidence, it has mellowed into a sublimely happy marriage. Walter Heller, chairman of the Council of Economic Advisers from 1961 to 1965, has stated that Keynesian economics is accepted by "80 to 90 percent of the nation's economists."

The understanding and acceptance of the new economic theories among political leaders was slower than among the economics fraternity. The bogeyman of government economic intervention became less frightening to most political leaders of both parties, in the post-war years, and the *President's Economic Reports* under both Democratic and Republican administrations accepted the position that the Government had "the capacity to moderate economic fluctuations." However, commitment and rationalization of policy along sophisticated Keynesian lines were gradual at best.

President Truman showed some inclination to experiment with Keynesian concepts, but Congressional action was not always complementary. In 1948, in the face of sharply rising prices, Congress reduced taxes despite modest administration protests. As the recession of 1949–50 appeared, Truman was able to maintain high levels of Government expenditures, thus, within Keynesian analysis, making up for diminished private sector demand. However, Truman was not at all convinced that such policies, when they created large fiscal deficits, were entirely desirable. His speeches and his writings often showed an older, traditional belief in the virtues of balanced budgets. The outbreak of the Korean War in 1950 and the partial war-footing of the economy soon destroyed Truman's qualms about deficits. With the Federal debt growing as the war spending increased, it became essential to raise taxes to hedge against inflationary pressures. While this fiscal action, introduced by the President and approved by Congress in 1951, was good "Keynesianism," too much can be read into the tax hike. For most Congressmen the tax increase was understood and justified not as stabilization policy but as a measure to halt Government war deficits and to "democratically" share "the burden of the war."

Under Eisenhower, "fiscal integrity" and "balanced budgets" were important watchwords in the political rhetoric. However, five of the eight years of that administration registered deficits, and experience soon dictated that "balance" and "fiscal integrity" were not to be calculated annually. Academic economists doubtless felt some accomplishment and vindication when the President finally began to talk of "cyclically balanced budgets" and "fiscal flexibility." The Administration's attitude to the recession of 1953, the inflationary pressures of 1957, and the 1958 recession remained a tolerant "wait and see" at the outset of distress; but, as conditions worsened, it responded with the approved counter-cyclical policies. However, the effectiveness of Government deficits as a cushioning device was sorely tested in 1959 as a $12.5 billion deficit was run up without the economy's rebounding from the recession.

Under both Truman and Eisenhower, some headway had been made in rationalizing a "stabilizing fiscal policy." While deficits and too active fiscal intervention were usually publicly abhorred by Government leaders, conventional wisdom dictated, in the face of severe fluctuations, eventual counter-cyclical action. Yet, as the economy sagged during the closing years of the fifties, the economics seminar rooms of American universities buzzed with talk condemning this line of policy as inadequate and proposing fiscal and monetary policies which would be aimed not at mere stabilization but at growth.

The election of John F. Kennedy in 1960 was an important watershed in the political and public acceptance of the "new economics." The questions of inadequate economic growth had been raised by Kennedy himself in the campaign. Moreover, the new President seemed to have greater appreciation for the intricacies of economic theory than any of his predecessors. Many leading American economists, such as John K. Galbraith, Samuelson, Seymour Harris, and Walter Heller, all unabashed Keynesians, began to filter into key advisory and administrative posts. In the past, the Council of Economic Advisers had played a modest role in policy creation, but under Dr. Walter Heller's leadership the CEA began to enjoy much broader prestige and influence in official Washington. While the Truman and Eisenhower administrations had from time to time accepted elements of the "new economics," the Kennedy government frankly attempted to wed policy actions with Keynesian theory. Not only did this have the effect of urging greater economic understanding upon the Congress, through the Joint Congressional Economic Committee, and upon many Federal agencies, but it filtered through the press to the people.

The new administration early announced its major economic concern to be the lagging growth rate. In the spring of 1962, it obtained a $2½ billion reduction in business taxes through investment tax credits and liberalized depreciation. On June 11, 1962, in his Yale University speech, Kennedy hinted that more was to come as he attacked American "economic mythology," particularly those myths which opposed Federal deficits as inflationary. Without reservations or apologies, Kennedy argued that deficits which spur investment and consumption would eliminate the problems of lagging growth and unemployment. The speech was the keynote to an "expansionist" approach to fiscal policy which pushed beyond mere economic stabilization.

On January 24, 1963, Kennedy sent to Congress a message requesting a general reduction in personal and corporate income taxes. In an address to the Committee on Economic Development, he pointed out that this proposal was not counter-cyclical but aimed at the long-run problem of inadequate growth. By the spring of 1964 the tax cut was put in effect after considerable political pressuring of the Congress by the new Johnson Administration. By the summer of 1965, an excise tax cut had also been passed by Congress.

The proof of the pudding is in the eating, and the new public policy indeed seemed quite palatable. In 1964, GNP grew by more than $40 billion, and in the next year, it grew about $50 billion more, with prices staying quite stable. The effect of the expansionist fiscal policy was not lost on business or the American people. Heller frankly admitted that the primary policy emphasis was shifting from the earlier concern with consumption stimulus to investment stimulus. According to Heller, this was "not a matter of trying to 'be kind to business.' It grows out of a conviction that to achieve the growth rate we need, . . . we must *deepen* capital . . . . And, side by side with that, we need to *widen* capital . . . ." That is to say, the expansionist fiscal policy was aimed at plant modernization and plant expansion. Meanwhile, in 1964 and 1965, American business reported sharp rises in profits. Clearly, a new kind of economic policy, built upon Keynesian techniques and nearly two decades of trial and error, had been created. The business community, which not long ago had seen little difference between Marxists and Keynesians, offered few complaints.

In January, 1965, shortly after President Johnson's overwhelming defeat of Senator Goldwater, the President's Council of Economic Advisers acclaimed the victory of the new economic creed, almost as if the election had been a popular referendum on its utility. With straight faces, the Council reported:

The role of the Federal Government changed in the New Deal of the 1930's and in World War II. The Government accepted responsibility for assuring a minimum of economic well-being for most individuals, for many special groups, industries, and agriculture. It undertook the task of stabilizing the economy against the destructive power of the business cycle. . . . After years of ideological controversy, we have grown used to the new relationship among Government, householder, business, labor and agriculture. The tired slogans that made constructive discourse difficult have lost their meaning for most Americans.

It has become abundantly clear that our society wants neither to turn backward the clock of history nor to discuss our present problems in a partisan spirit.

While cynics and administration critics might argue over the rightness of the new orthodoxy and protest the suggestion that all Americans opposed discussion of economic matters in a "partisan spirit," few observers of contemporary America would dispute the assertion that private and public attitudes toward government's expanded role in the economy showed a startling degree of single-minded acceptance. To be sure, some older ideas, which had once been held in universal admiration, were slow to die. The argument that government deficits were not simply inflationary but could spur economic growth was probably the most difficult "new truth" to accept. And while acceptance of this idea has been slow, at least opposition to it has diminished. Looking back on what had been largely his handiwork and what it had accomplished in changing American economic attitudes and developing new economic concepts, Dr. Heller said:

> There is today a much broader consensus on economic policy. On the one hand, conservatives have come to accept a much more active monetary and fiscal policy. . . . Liberals, in turn, are coming to a steadily wider understanding and acceptance of the high priority that has to be given investment. . . . And all of this has led to a much closer relationship, a much closer partnership of government and business.

By late 1965, increased military spending for the Viet Nam war, coupled with the expansionist fiscal policy and "Great Society" spending, had begun to generate some uneasiness over potential inflationary pressures. However, when the Federal Reserve acted to restrict credit expansion in December with a hike in discount rates on Reserve loans to banks, the Johnson Administration separated itself from the monetary authorities' actions. In the ensuing public discussion, it was apparent that the Administration, large segments of business, and even some of the banking community saw no need for alarm about the economy, and considerable support for the expansionist fiscal policies was voiced. Moreover, a widely held public and private position argued that counter-cyclical monetary actions were at best only moderately effective while, if the need arose, the more direct and effective fiscal devices could be used to heal any inflationary wounds.

The January, 1966 *Council of Economic Advisers' Report* still held to the line that inflation was no threat and "the economy has achieved the best balance of overall demand and productive capacity in nearly a decade." As prices mounted in the first quarter of 1966 (with a .6 percent rise in February alone), the expansionist Kennedy–Johnson policy drew more criticism. Congressional Republicans began to snipe at "the guns and butter" fiscal philosophy of the Johnson Administration, calling for either a tax hike or a slowdown in government spending. *The Wall Street Journal,* never certain of academic economists anyway, called the CEA Report a "political document" aimed at whitewashing the Administration. However, by March, unemployment was down to 3.5 percent, the lowest figure since 1954.

Put in proper perspective most of the criticisms leveled at the expansionist fiscal policies were matters of degree only. As Edwin Dale of *The New York Times* observed: "All of us agreed on one thing: we want the expansion to continue and to avoid a recession. Those who favor applying the brakes do so, in complete good faith, on the ground that this will prolong, not shorten, the expansion." Criticisms of the expansionist fiscal policies did not have the old partisan tenor. Keynesian economics and its policy implications were not on trial. *Time* magazine, hardly noted as a liberal publication, observed:

If the nation has economic problems, they are problems of high employment, high growth and high hopes. As the United States enters its sixth straight year of economic expansion, its economic strategists confess rather cheerily that they have just about reached the outer limits of economic knowledge. They have proved that they can prod, goad and inspire a rich and free nation to climb to nearly full employment and unprecedented prosperity. The job of maintaining expansion without inflation will require not only their present skills but new ones as well. Perhaps the United States needs another, more modern Keynes to grapple with the growing pains, a specialist in keeping economics at a healthy high. But even if he comes along, he will have to build on what he learned from John Maynard Keynes.

Meanwhile, public concern over the expansionist policies and the spectre of inflation appeared to be slight. The Viet Nam war did provide some distraction from these matters, but it should not be implied that the lack of public response to the debate necessarily implied ignorance or apathy. From several decades of experience, it had become accepted that in the expanded armory of governmental economic weapons some device of Keynesian imprint could be found sooner or later to deal with any problem. Once-obscure arguments about "excess demand," "inadequate demand," or "multiplier" and "accelerator effects" enjoyed considerable popular understanding. Some indication of public concern for earlier unintelligible discussions of economic policy is evidenced in the fact that the *Economic Report of the President* is annually a best seller, with sales in excess of 50,000 copies—at $1.25 each. Of course, the acceptance of the "new economics" was not total, but those whom most academic economists would hasten to label "economic cranks" had been driven to the very margins of political influence by 1967.

From a forced faith in pragmatic government intervention in the economy in the thirties and forties, a systematic theoretic framework for public policy had emerged. The new economic orthodoxy had been refined and accepted by American political leadership and supported by the people within two decades. Whether or not the "new economics" will prove as long lived as the old orthodoxy, struck down officially by the Employment Act of 1946, remains to be seen.

After the New Economics

Milton Friedman

The Nixon Administration will confront major economic problems in three areas: inflation, balance of payments, and the government budget. In each area, there is a stark contrast between John F. Kennedy's inheritance from the Eisenhower Administration and Richard M. Nixon's inheritance from the Kennedy–Johnson Administration. In each area, the New Economics has managed in eight years to turn a comfortable, easy situation into a near-crisis, to squander assets and multiply liabilities.

INFLATION

Kennedy. Consumer prices rose at the average rate of 1.4 percent per year from 1952 to 1960. More important, the price rise had been slowing down. A burst of inflationary pressure in 1956 and 1957 was surmounted and replaced by essential price stability. As a result, widespread fears of inflation were converted into expectations of price stability.

From Newsweek, *December 9, 1968. Copyright Newsweek, Inc., 1968. Reprinted by permission of* Newsweek.

Nixon. The consumer-price index is currently rising at a rate of 5 percent per year. The creeping inflation that started in 1964 has turned into a trot. Expectations of substantial further inflation are nearly universal.

The New Economists argue that Eisenhower bought price stability at the cost of heavy unemployment. Yet unemployment during the Eisenhower years was only fractionally higher than during the Kennedy–Johnson years: 4.87 percent vs. 4.85 percent. The time pattern was different: unemployment was higher at the end of the Eisenhower years than at the beginning, when the Korean War boom was in full blast; unemployment was higher at the beginning of the Kennedy–Johnson years than at the end when the Vietnam War is in full blast.

BALANCE OF PAYMENTS

Kennedy. The balance of payments deteriorated somewhat in the final three years of the Eisenhower Administration. The gold stock declined roughly $5 billion and there was a minor run on gold in 1960. *But,* the gold stock was still a healthy $18 billion, sales of goods and services abroad exceeded purchases by $4 billion, this trade surplus was growing rapidly, and, most important, there were no controls on exchange transactions, no concealed devaluation, no financial gimmicks to make the figures look better.

Nixon. Eight successive years of substantial deficits in the balance of payments have reduced the gold stock from $18 billion to less than $11 billion. An "interest equalization tax" on purchases of foreign securities was levied in 1964 as a "temporary" measure—a concealed devaluation of the capital dollar that is still with us. Direct controls were imposed on foreign lending by commercial banks and on foreign investment by businesses—first on a "voluntary," then on a compulsory basis. Ingenuity has run wild in creating financial gimmicks to hide the true situation—beginning with the so-called Roosa bonds (which some of us dubbed subrosa bills). And withal, the surplus on trade account has essentially disappeared for the first time in many years. The recent improvement in published figures simply reflects a shift of capital funds in reaction to the disturbances in France and the invasion of Czechoslovakia.

The New Economists leave Mr. Nixon scant reserves; even worse, they leave him a mess of controls and a set of cosmetic measures that must be eliminated before he can even guess the real size of the problem.

THE GOVERNMENT BUDGET

Kennedy. In 1960, the Federal government spent $94.7 billion and took in $98.3 billion—a cash surplus of $3.6 billion. Expenditures were 32 percent higher than in the final year of the Truman Administration, receipts 38 percent higher.

Nixon. In the first six months of 1968, the Johnson Administration spent almost as much as the Eisenhower Administration in all twelve months of 1960: $92.1 billion compared with $94.7 billion; but took in much less, $86.4 billion compared with $98.3 billion. Despite the 10 percent surtax and the reduction in expenditures legislated by Congress, the budget continues in deficit, and spending continues to grow.

And this is not all. Many programs have been started on a small scale but call for large increases in expenditures in later years. It will be a major achievement just to keep spending from growing at a rapid pace.

Many a New Economist may well have secretly sighed in relief when the election results were in. What a mess to have to straighten out! What a legacy to leave the opposition!

QUESTIONS FOR DISCUSSION

1. *What specifically did Keynes's* General Theory *attack in the orthodox economic theories of the 1930's?*
2. *According to Keynes, what accounted for unemployment? What were the remedies?*
3. *How do you account for the basic suppositions of conventional theory having gone unchallenged for so very long? Why were they challenged in the 1930's?*
4. *What were the goals, in theory at least, of the Employment Act of 1946?*
5. *Why did the idea of "balanced budgets" hold such a hallowed place in American economic ideology?*
6. *Do you agree with the statement "We are all Keynesians"? Why or why not?*
7. *Do you think that Friedman's attack on the new economics is justified? Has its performance been as bad as he suggests?*

Should the Federal
Government Deficit Spend?

Probably no issue has divided academic economists from the
vast majority of American citizens as severely as the question of federal
deficit spending. As a rule, businessmen and ordinary consumers have
tended to view the functions of government spending and tax collection as they see their own income and expenditures, and they have
subscribed to Mr. Micawber's admonition: "Annual income twenty
pounds, annual expenditure nineteen, nineteen and six; result,
happiness. Annual income twenty pounds, annual expenditure twenty
pounds, ought and six; result, misery."

On the other hand, the economics profession, now about entirely
Keynesian in its outlook, does not see government fiscal operations in
this light. Instead, economists argue that it is the federal government's
function to manage the economy, and this means using government
spending and taxing functions to manipulate either desired higher
levels of economic activity or desired counterinflationary actions. The
federal deficit is deemphasized in favor of a more flexible use of
government fiscal policy.

The ideological clash between the economists and ordinary
citizens has recently diminished somewhat in intensity. In large
measure this is because the academic economists have gained their
way and have introduced clearly Keynesian economic concepts into the
actual policy-making of the federal government. Also, Americans have
lived with a large debt for such a very long time, and this time has
been one of generally high prosperity, that the anxiety which debt
expansion earlier created among people is no longer so great. However,
the debt remains quite large and tends to increase annually, even
though it has recently lagged well behind the expansion of our GNP.

The following articles represent two views which may be taken
toward the debt. The late Senator Byrd of Virginia outlines his op-

position to federal deficits very much as an ordinary citizen might, comparing the federal debt with the problem one might expect to develop over personal indebtedness. Meanwhile, Delbert Snider offers a fairly conventional Keynesian analysis, clearly opposing the traditional attitudes toward government debt.

The Evils of Deficit Spending

Senator Harry F. Byrd

As I see it, balancing the budget without resorting to legerdemain or unsound bookkeeping methods is certainly in the category of our number one problems.

Beginning with 1792, the first fiscal year of our Federal Government, and through 1916, Federal deficits were casual and usually paid off in succeeding years. In this 124-year period there were 43 deficit years and 81 surplus years. As late as July 1, 1914, the interest-bearing debt was less than $1 billion.

In Andrew Jackson's administration the public debt was paid off in toto, an achievement in which President Jackson expressed great pride.

It can be said for this first 124 years in the life of our Republic we were on a pay-as-you-go basis. In that period I think it can be accurately said that we laid the foundation for our strength today as the greatest nation in all the world.

It is disturbing these days to hear some economists argue the budget should not be balanced and that we should not begin to pay off the debt because, they allege, it will adversely affect business conditions. Have we yielded so far to the blandishments of Federal subsidies and Government support that we have forgotten our nation is great because of individual effort as contrasted to state paternalism? Here are some of the evils of deficit spending:

The debt today is the old debt incurred by this generation, but tomorrow it will be [a] debt on our children and grandchildren, and it will be for them to pay, both the interest and the principal.

It is possible and in fact probable that before this astronomical debt is paid off, if it ever is, the interest charge will exceed the principal.

Protracted deficit spending means cheapening the dollar. Cheapened money is inflation. Inflation is a dangerous game. It robs creditors, it steals pensions,

From a speech by Senator Harry F. Byrd, reprinted in the Congressional Record, *vol. 101, part 4, 84th Congress, 1st session, May 4, 1955.*

wages, and fixed income. Once started, it is exceedingly difficult to control. This inflation has been partially checked but the value of the dollar dropped slightly again in the past year. It would not take much to start up this dangerous inflation again.

Public debt is not like private debt. If private debt is not paid off, it can be ended by liquidation, but if public debt is not paid off with taxes, liquidation takes the form of disastrous inflation or national repudiation. Either is destructive of our form of government.

Today the interest on the Federal debt takes more than 10 percent of our total Federal tax revenue. Without the tremendous cost of this debt our annual tax bill could be reduced 10 percent across the board.

Proposals have been advocated changing our budgetary system. There are two which recur with persistency, and I want to warn you of them.

First, there is the proposal for a cash budget. Those who advocate the cash budget are suggesting that the Government pay its routine bills with savings of the citizens who have entrusted protection of their old age and unemployment to the guardianship of the Federal Government. These trust funds were established from premiums paid by participants in social security, unemployment insurance, bank deposit insurance programs, etc. Not a cent of these funds belongs to the Government.

Second, some are advocating a capital budget which means that so-called capital expenditures should not be considered as current expenditures in the budget.

Those who advocate the so-called capital budget must start out with the fallacious assumption that the Government has never made a bona fide profit on any Government operation.

They must assume that debt contracted by a Federal agency is not a debt of the Federal Government and a burden on all of the taxpayers.

I am an old-fashioned person who believes that a debt is a debt just as much in the atomic age as it was in the horse and buggy days.

A capital budget must assume that Government manufacturing plants, such as atomic energy installations, are in commercial production for a profit, and that Government stockpiles are longtime investments for profit instead of precautions against emergencies when they would be completely expendable with no financial return.

Likewise, it must assume that the agriculture surplus program is primarily a long range investment deal instead of a prop for annual farm income to be used when needed on a year-by-year basis.

While the vastness and complexity of the Federal Government of the United States necessarily makes budgeting difficult, the so-called conventional budget currently in use offers the best approach to orderly financing with fullest disclosure.

What is needed for a better fiscal system is fuller disclosure of Federal expenditures and responsibility for them—not less, as inevitably would be the case with so-called cash and capital budgets.

With full disclosure of the Federal expenditure situation, the American people then would have an opportunity to decide whether they wanted to recapture control and bring the rate of spending into balance with the rate of taxing and thus reduce the tremendous Federal debt burden we are now bearing.

At home we can get along without Federal usurpation of individual, local, and state responsibilities, and we can get along without hotels, furs, rum, clothing, fertilizer, or other things.

The Bible says if thine eye offend thee pluck it out. I say if the Federal Government should not engage in such activities, we should first stop new invasions and then gradually, if not abruptly, eliminate the old intrusions. When we do these things we shall balance the budget, for lower taxes and reduced debt. There will be no further need for trick budgets and debt-ceiling evasions and hiding taxes. The Government will be honest in itself, and honest with the people.

Myth: Sound Finance Requires the Government to Balance Its Budget

Delbert A. Snider

The roots of the balanced-budget myth lie deep in the consciousness of the American people, and the myth is therefore one of the most difficult to get people to discuss unemotionally and without prejudice. The idea that everyone, including the government, should seek to live within his means, and that failure to do this is irresponsible or even immoral behavior has long been closely associated with such accepted virtues as thrift, honesty, hard work, self-denial, and other Puritan concepts of moral conduct.

A great many people—probably an overwhelming majority in our country—are deeply committed to these ideas. The commitment is not simply of a "Sunday School" variety, of concern only on special occasions. It is rather something that concerns the individual and family in daily living. How many of us are able to escape the worry and anxiety of "money matters"? Very few. And what is nearly always the cause of our anxiety? Why, of course,

From Delbert A. Snider, Economic Myth and Reality, © *1965. Reprinted by permission of Prentice-Hall, Inc., Englewood Cliffs, New Jersey.*

it is the tendency or temptation for us to live beyond our means. Millions of American families *do* live beyond their means, at least on occasion, but only a minority of these are indifferent to the virtues of thrift and self-restraint. Most of us *worry* about our budget. Countless sleepless nights, late evening "family councils" on the household budget, agonizing decisions as to whether to replace the old car, and so on—these are the symptoms of our money worries.

Few persons think this is silly—and rightly so, in the writer's opinion. The prudent family must concern itself with money matters and seriously try to avoid getting into financial trouble. This of course does not mean that a prudent family never spends more than its income. There is nothing wrong with borrowing to purchase a home, or to provide a college education for the children, or to obtain medical attention, or, for that matter, to purchase furniture or a car, *provided* there are reasonably good prospects for eventually paying off the loan. In other words, an unbalanced household budget is perfectly all right so long as it is eventually balanced after debts have been discharged.

A balanced budget—or, preferably, one showing a surplus—makes a great deal of sense in the long run for most individuals and families, whereas persistent failure to balance one's budget is almost certain to lead to financial disaster.

Starting with these eminently sensible precepts of sound personal finance, how can the economist so blithely shift his position when it comes to discussing sound governmental finance? Is not government subject to the same rules of prudent behavior as the individual household?

First, of course, we should take care to mention that there *are* rules of prudence by which government should be guided in its financial affairs. *But*—and here's the rub—*they are not necessarily the same rules which apply to individuals and families.* However homey and reasonable it may seem to regard government as a "big family," it simply isn't one. It requires only a little thought to see why. One could easily draw a long list of the innumerable respects in which government operates on an altogether different basis from the individual family. To mention only a few of the most striking differences:

1. A family derives most of its income from the sale of its labor or property; the government's income comes overwhelmingly from compulsory payments to it by taxpayers.

2. A family spends its money on goods and services for its own, private use; government spends its money on goods and services for *public* use.

3. A family may get itself into a financial hole by spending more than its income and be forced into bankruptcy; an established government need never go bankrupt in the same sense, for it always has the power to obtain more revenue through additional taxes—a power denied private individuals.

4. A family must plan its financial affairs on the basis of its limited lifetime; government continues indefinitely into the future. (In this respect, government is more like a business corporation.)

These are not just superficial differences; they are basic, and place government on a separate plane from individuals and families. Granted, you may say—but how can these differences justify different rules of financial prudence?

An example will show how. If you were asked when it would be most unwise for a family to spend more than its income, no doubt you would say: whenever the family is already heavily in debt, or whenever its income is decreasing or is expected to decrease because of unemployment or illness. Under such circumstances, the prudent family either wields the budget axe and cuts back on its expenses, or else it makes a determined effort to raise its income (through the wife's working, or the breadwinner's "moonlighting," for instance).

Should not government respond in the same fashion under comparable circumstances?—For so state the traditional tenets of "sound" government finance. Thus during the early years of the Great Depression from 1930 to 1933, for example, when the government's revenue fell sharply, the cry was for "economy" in government. Both President Hoover and candidate, later President, Franklin Roosevelt proposed budget reduction as the proper course of action to meet the economic crisis.

We now know that this prescription could not have been more incorrect. Whereas it is only common sense for a *family* to cut back on expenses when its income falls off, it is utter nonsense for *government* to do so in a similar situation. To understand the general problem, one must first find the answer to the question, "Why did the federal government's tax income fall in the early years of the Great Depression—from over $4,000 million in 1930 to less than $2,000 million in 1932, or by more than 50 percent?" It was *not* because the government deliberately sought to reduce its income; tax rates were *not* lowered. *The decrease in tax collections was caused solely by a decline in the national economy's production and income.* During the first three years of the Great Depression, the gross national product of the United States fell by over 40 percent! Inasmuch as the amount of revenue that taxes yield depends upon the level of incomes and production on which the taxes are levied, it is small wonder the government's income fell so drastically during this period.

In other words, a deficit in the government's budget is not always a case of too much government spending. It may also be caused by a *too-low level* of national production and employment. The distinction we make between these two causes of budget deficits is not mere mumbo-jumbo, for the remedy to the problem is exactly opposite in the two cases.

Unlike a family, the government, if it sought to balance its budget when its tax receipts were reduced because of a depression, would most likely find itself *increasing* its budget imbalance. Here is a startling reversal of the rules we are familiar with in our personal living, which no doubt accounts for the difficulty we have in understanding the workings of the federal budget. Actually there is no mystery involved; it is just a question of the basic difference between a family and government discussed previously.

When an individual family cuts back on expenses, there is no reason for it to expect this action to boomerang and cause its income to fall too. But the government *has* to expect such a boomerang effect under similar circumstances. The reason is simple: if the government cut back on expenses or increased tax rates during a depression, the nation's production and income—the source of tax revenue—would further decline. Suppose the government tried to make up for a $10 billion loss in tax revenue—due to a decrease in the economy's production and income—by cutting government expenditure $10 billion while holding tax rates the same. The effort would in all probability fail, for reduced government spending in turn would mean a *still greater reduction* in national production and income and therefore in the source of tax revenue.

But why, the reader might ask, should reduced government spending cause national production and income to fall? The first reason is simply that government spending on goods and services is *part* of the country's production and income. In recent years, the purchases on all levels of government—federal, state, and local—has amounted to about 20 percent of the gross national product. The federal government's purchases alone currently amount to over 10 percent of the gross national product. Therefore if the government reduces its spending it directly reduces the nation's income. Nor is this the end of the story. If the government spends $10 billion less, individuals and businesses will not receive the $10 billion for goods and services they would have otherwise sold to the government. Now that private incomes are less, private spending will be less than before. Hence, other people will find their incomes reduced because of reduced *private* spending, and they in turn will tend to cut back on *their* spending. In other words, the effects of the reduced government purchases are multiplied as they spread throughout the economy. (Economists call this the "multiplier" effect.)

A policy of reduc[ed] government spending (or increased tax rates) during a recession does not therefore help restore balance in the government's budget; but it does have the very important—and very unfortunate—consequence of pushing the economy deeper into recession by further contracting income and employment in the economy as a whole. Even if the policy were to succeed in balancing the budget, the price paid to achieve it would be unreasonably high.

This conclusion was borne out by our experience of a few years ago. During 1958 the American economy fell into a serious recession—the third since the end of the war. Normal increases in national production ground to a halt and unemployment rose to 6.8 percent of the civilian labor force. As we would now expect under such circumstances, tax revenue of all government units responded to the recession, falling by over $5 billion between 1957 and 1958. Consequently the federal government, which had a small budget *surplus* in 1957, incurred a *deficit* in 1958 that grew, as tax receipts continued decreasing, to a peacetime high of over $12 billion in 1959.

In a deliberate effort to eliminate this large budget deficit, the federal government adopted a policy of reducing its spending between 1959 and 1960. The goal was achieved immediately and the budget showed a small surplus in 1960. But the "success" was short-lived, for in 1961 a budget deficit developed again. More important, even the temporary budget success was achieved at the expense of a severe blow to the national economy, which was painfully struggling to emerge from the recession when the depressive effect of reduced government spending slapped it back down. Unemployment, which had declined after the 1958 peak of 6.8 percent, began to climb again in 1960. By the end of the year it was back to 6.8 percent.

In short, that government "economy" is incorrect policy in a period of recession has been demonstrated both theoretically and practically. What, then, *is* sensible policy in a recession? The answer has already been suggested by previous comments, but let us state it explicitly. The proper policy in such periods is *to develop a deliberate budget deficit,* either by increasing government spending or by decreasing tax rates, or both.

This no doubt strikes many people as a startling statement, one that seems to offend common sense and contradict all the rules of financial prudence. But we have already seen that during a recession the probability is strong that the government will automatically incur a budget deficit because of decreased tax receipts. The proper response to this situation is to *add* deliberately to the deficit by spending more or taxing less—even though a family which acted in such an irresponsible fashion would surely be heading for trouble!

The government, as we have seen, is not a family. What the government does affects the whole economy, including, ultimately, itself. Even if our only concern were to restore balance to a budget thrown out of kilter by a recession-induced decrease in tax income, it would still make more sense to follow a policy of increased spending or reduced taxes than vice-versa. When we consider that a second goal is to help bring the national economy back to prosperity and full employment, the case for such a policy becomes overwhelmingly strong.

The case for consciously creating a deficit to balance the budget in a period of recession surely sounds like the least reasonable proposal to many people. How can the government expect to *reduce* a budget deficit by taking measures that *increase* it? The answer is: because of the "boomerang" effect we spoke of earlier, but a boomerang working this time against the recession.

As stated earlier, an increase in government spending tends to raise the nation's level of production and income. A decrease in tax rates brings about the same results. When households and businesses are left with greater disposable incomes because of reduced tax liabilities, their spending on goods and services ordinarily increases. Idle resources are put to work to satisfy the additional demand. As production and income rise, the revenue yielded to the government by taxes increases. Total tax *receipts* may thus easily rise above their previous level even though tax *rates* are lower.

Nor is this all. As the national economy approaches full production and employment, the government may decrease its spending or increase tax rates without causing production and income in the economy to fall. Indeed, as we shall see in a moment, such policy may be highly desirable for reasons other than its effect on the government's budget.

In short, a deliberate policy of creating (or adding to) a budget deficit in periods of recession may be the most sensible way of finally balancing the budget. But this is not all, for in the process of equalizing tax receipts and government spending, the economy is put back on its feet. Indeed, this latter result is probably much more important than merely achieving a balanced budget. The vast majority of economists would argue that even if the fiscal policy just advocated did not completely eliminate the budget deficit, it would still be justified by its desirable effect on national production and employment. If a choice has to be made between government budget deficits and full employment in the economy, economists would generally opt for full employment; for the unfavorable consequences of unemployment are real and indisputable, whereas the unfavorable consequences of budget deficits are highly exaggerated and often more imaginary than real.

We have demonstrated that a consciously created budget deficit in periods of economic recession is wise and proper governmental policy. A word of warning is now in order, lest this prescription be misconstrued. We have not said budget deficits are *always* desirable, as some have accused economists of saying. In fact, economists recommend the conscious creation of budget *surpluses* under certain circumstances. What are these circumstances? The exact opposite of the circumstances calling for budget deficits—namely, when the economy is experiencing or threatened with *inflation*.

Again we are confronted with the apparent paradox that wise government policy is frequently the reverse of wise family policy. A family may be justified in spending more than its income when its income is on the rise and can be expected to continue to increase in the future. A prudent government, on the other hand, will seek most carefully to *avoid* spending more than its tax revenue when the national economy is booming. Indeed, if government tax income is rapidly rising because of a rapid increase in production and employment in the economy, at some point it becomes prudent to allow—or if necessary, to force—total tax receipts to exceed government spending. This can be accomplished either by restraining government spending or by increasing tax rates.

What is that critical point at which such a policy becomes desirable? When inflation becomes a threat. . . . Inflation is caused by an excess of total spending in the economy. Since government purchases are a significant part of total spending, a reduction in its purchases naturally reduces total spending. Alternatively, the government can force a cutback in private spending by raising tax rates and thus decreasing the disposable income of households and businesses.

Total spending becomes "excessive" and threatens to cause inflation when the economy's output of goods and services is unable to keep up with the demand for goods and services. But this ordinarily will not happen if there is widespread unemployment in the economy, for then production can easily be increased by putting idle men and resources to work. Inflation can become a serious problem only if the economy is already at, or closely approaching, full employment and capacity output—this is why government deficits can ordinarily be used to combat unemployment without fear of causing inflation. But once the economy reaches a state of full employment, a continuation of government deficits might very easily cause prices to rise. In this case, balancing the budget or creating a budget surplus will help prevent inflation. And if the government does not go too far in reducing total spending in the economy, inflation can be stopped without reducing production and employment in the economy.

REALITY: Reasonable fiscal policy requires flexibility in government spending and tax policies, including the conscious creation of budget deficits during periods of slack in the economy, and of budget surpluses during periods of threatened inflation. Only rarely does a balanced government budget constitute truly "sound" finance.

QUESTIONS FOR DISCUSSION

1. *Senator Byrd seems to suggest that, in the past, efforts to hold down the national debt were the basis for the economic and social growth of America. By implication, he is also suggesting that the great growth of the federal debt in recent times has weakened the nation. Do you agree or disagree? Why?*

2. *How does Snider feel about the charge that the debt must necessarily be passed on to our children or our grandchildren? What do you think?*

3. *What is your view toward Snider's argument that deficits should be seen as a means of managing the economy rather than as an accountant's measure of economic stability?*

4. *Is the national debt really like personal debt? Why or why not?*

Can We Find Jobs for All?

Since the Employment Act of 1946, the federal government has been committed by law to a policy of maintaining high levels of employment. The act, as is to be expected of such general legislation, does not prescribe the particular path for obtaining this end; but, as noted earlier, the general policies of the new economics have been accepted by most economists and politicians as the proper means to this goal. During most of the last half of the 1960's these policies seemed to have been successful in dealing with the traditional problem in a capitalist economy of maintaining high and stable levels of employment. By mid-1969, unemployment was hovering around 4 percent of the work force. While this figure may still have seemed high, meaning approximately 2.5 to 3.0 million men, unemployment was as high as 25 percent in 1933 and even 6 to 7 percent in 1961. However, by the close of 1969, the unemployment problem was reappearing as jobless rates again rose.

The problem of maintaining high levels of employment in the future has two dimensions. Since we have come to understand that employment is dependent upon levels of income, we first must recognize that the maintenance of adequate demand is essential. In recent years this Keynesian axiom has been qualified somewhat by evidence that technological and structural changes in the economy may make some unemployment less responsive to higher levels of aggregate demand. Regardless of the level to which demand is raised, the presently unemployed coal miner in West Virginia is likely to remain unemployed. There simply are no jobs now, or likely in the future, for a man with his skills in his area. Attempts at solving the unemployment difficulties of such workers through raising demand will be only partially successful. A few may find jobs but the cost borne by the whole nation may be price inflation, since the economy is really near full employment even though there may be millions who are unemployed. These would-be workers are presently a "technological surplus."

The contours of the unemployment problem for the future are then quite different from what they were in the 1930's. The policy implications of the current employment problem are examined in the first of the following articles by Dr. Walter W. Heller, former chairman of President Kennedy's and President Johnson's Council of Economic Advisers. Heller's article is, at first glance, dated. It was written before the tax-cut legislation of 1964 and before the economy took off in its long expansion between 1964 and 1969. But, as unemployment now emerges as a serious problem, Heller's analysis is again relevant and has more than merely historical significance. The issues outlined in the early 1960's are still at the center of debate for the 1970's. The unemployment problem has not been resolved, and the tax-cut controversy may yet rage again. The second article, by Seymour L. Wolfbein, attempts to identify and categorize the membership of what we call the structurally unemployed.

Unemployment: Lack of Demand, Structural, or Technological?

Walter W. Heller

Mr. Chairman and Members of the Committee, we are pleased to have an opportunity to participate in these hearings on Employment and Manpower. The employment problem is not only of the greatest importance to the country and at the center of government economic policy, but is of particular interest to an agency operating, as the Council does, under the mandate of the Employment Act of 1946.

Recent discussions may have generated an impression of greater disagreement among the Nation's economists about the origins and solutions of the employment problem than actually exists. For in fact, the great majority of those who have studied the matter carefully would agree with the Administration's view that our excessive unemployment today cannot be traced to a single cause nor eliminated by a single cure. Rather, it has a mixture of causes which must be dealt with by a mixture—an amalgam—of cures.

From the statement of Walter W. Heller, chairman, accompanied by Gardiner Ackley and John P. Lewis, members of the Council of Economic Advisers, before the Subcommittee on Employment and Manpower of the Senate Committee on Labor and Public Welfare, October 28, 1963.

One problem, and a central one, is that total expenditures in the economy—total demand for goods and services—are not sufficient to generate an adequate total number of jobs. We can, for convenience, call this kind of unemployment "demand-shortage" unemployment. In our view, demand-shortage unemployment can and must be attacked by vigorous policies—principally tax reduction—to raise the total demand for goods and services.

Another problem is that the characteristics of our available workers—their locations, skills, education, training, race, sex, age, and so on—do not fully match the characteristics employers are seeking in filling the jobs that are available (or that would be available at full employment). In a dynamic, changing economy there is always some of this mismatching, and we call the unemployment that results from it "frictional." But when the pockets of such unemployment become large and stubborn—especially when they impose chronic burdens on particular disadvantaged groups and regions—we speak of the unemployment problem as "structural."

This type of unemployment is also a serious problem, which requires major policy actions to overcome its corrosive effects. Structural problems are not new. And the available evidence does not show that the proportion of our total unemployment problem that we label "structural" has increased significantly, nor that its character has materially changed. But this in no way diminishes the need for attacking these structural problems with vigorous policies—principally education, training and retraining, and special regional programs—to match the supply of labor skills more closely to the changing demand for labor skills.

Along with demand-shortage and structural unemployment, one also hears a great deal about the problem of "technological unemployment"—of men being put out of work by machines and, more particularly, by the process which has come to be called "automation." This is, indeed, a serious and continuing problem. But two points should be emphasized at the outset.

First, "technological unemployment" is not a third form of unemployment, separate from the other two. Rather, it expresses itself through these other forms. Technological change causes obsolescence of skills and therefore produces some of the mismatching between available workers and jobs that we call "structural" unemployment. Moreover, by raising output per worker, technological change is one of the principal sources of growth in our *potential* total output or GNP—which, if not matched by corresponding growth in *actual* GNP, opens a gap in demand and thereby causes demand-shortage unemployment.

Second, those who maintain that the economy now faces a problem of "technological unemployment" that is somehow new, and more formidable than in the past, implicitly assert that the rate of technological change has recently speeded up. Unless this is the case, the problem is not new—it has always been with us and has not proved to be a long-run problem for the economy as a whole. The continuing process of rapid technological change, which has constituted the very core of the American economy's strength and progressiveness for at least 150 years, has always put particular workers and businesses out of jobs and required particular adjustments that have been difficult and sometimes painful. It poses a new general problem for the economy only if technological change becomes so rapid that the demand adjustments and labor market adjustments it requires cannot be accomplished by the economic processes of the past. . . .

These, then—demand-shortage elements, structural elements, and a possible aggravation of both by accelerated technological change—are the principal ingredients of the unemployment problem your Committee is examining. It would be unwise and imprudent to ignore any of these ingredients either in diagnosing the problem or in prescribing remedies.

The primary attack on high unemployment must be through fiscal measures to speed the growth of total demand and thereby to create new job opportunities. But this need not—indeed, must not—impede a simultaneous attack on our stubborn structural problems. The two approaches are not merely complementary; they are mutually reinforcing. On the one hand, training and other programs to facilitate labor mobility can ease and speed the process by which demand-stimulated increases in output are translated into increases in employment. On the other, since structural maladjustments tend to flourish in slack markets, a vigorous expansion in demand helps cut structural problems down to size. . . .

UNEMPLOYMENT AND TAX REDUCTION

The American economy has been plagued with persistently excessive unemployment for 6 years. The unemployment rate has been 5 percent or more for 71 consecutive months. Since 1957, it has averaged 6 percent. Even in the face of annual advances of about $30 billion in GNP (annual rate), unemployment has not been diminishing. Thus, although GNP rose from $556.8 billion in the third quarter of 1962 to $588.5 billion in the third quarter of 1963, the unemployment rate remained the same in both quarters. And even with a prospective increase of $100 billion in the GNP rate from early 1961 to early 1964 (a rise of 20 percent in current dollars and about 15 percent in constant dollars), the unemployment rate will have come down only about $1\frac{1}{2}$ percentage points in that 3-year period.

The persistence of this high level of unemployment is sometimes cited as evidence of structural difficulties which will blunt the effect of the proposed $11 billion tax cut now being considered by the Senate Finance Committee and make it difficult to reach the interim full-employment goal of 4-percent unemployment, let alone our ultimate goals beyond the 4-percent level. The structural problem will be examined in some detail later in this statement.

But here, several points should be noted to indicate why the road to 4-percent unemployment is clearly open to demand-powered measures:

1. The pre-1957 postwar performance of the U.S. economy gives ample evidence of its ability to achieve 4 percent and even lower levels of unemployment without excessive strain.

2. The availability of 1.1 million excess unemployed workers (even by the modest 4-percent criterion and not counting the labor force dropouts resulting from slack job opportunities) and of substantial excess capacity (even after large gains, the average operating rate in manufacturing is running at only 87 percent of capacity) demonstrates that we are still suffering from a serious shortage of consumer and investment demand.

3. There are virtually no signs of economic tension, of the barriers that would divert the force of demand stimulus away from higher output, more jobs, and higher incomes into higher prices—there are no visible bottlenecks in the economy, wage rate increases have been the most moderate in the postwar period, and the record of price stability in recent years has been outstanding.

In reference to the first point, the unemployment rates in the first postwar decade deserve a further word. In the period of vigorous business activity in 1947 and 1948, unemployment averaged 3.8 percent of the labor force. After the recession of 1949 and the recovery of 1950, the rate was relatively stable from early 1951 to late 1953, averaging 3.1 percent. Since that time, the rate has drifted upward. In the period of stable unemployment from mid-1955 to late 1957, unemployment averaged 4.3 percent, an increase of more than one-third above the 1951–53 period. In the first half of 1960, unemployment averaged 5.3 percent, nearly one-fourth above the 1955–57 level. Following the recession and recovery of 1960–61, the rate fluctuated within a narrow range averaging 5.6 percent in 1962 and 1963 to date, a little higher than early 1960. Looking at the 1947–57 period, the average unemployment rate was below 4 percent in each of the following years: 1947, 1948, 1951, 1952, and 1953, and below $4\frac{1}{2}$ percent in 1955, 1956, and 1957.

When one looks behind these figures to get a grasp of the economic conditions that produced them, the most notable difference between the pre-1957 and post-1957 periods is found in the strength of market demand. In the first postwar decade, markets were strong. Backlogs of consumer demand had to be worked off. The demands of the Korean conflict had to be met. Outmoded plants and equipment had to be replaced or modernized, and capacity had to be enlarged. Deficiencies in housing, office facilities, and public works had to be made up.

But 1957 marked a watershed. In the ensuing period, demand has slack-ened at a time when our labor force growth has been accelerating in response to the postwar jump in the birth rate. Business-fixed investment dropped off from 10–11 percent of the GNP to only 9 percent—indeed, the level of such investment in 1962 barely struggled back to its level in 1956, while GNP was rising by nearly one-fifth (both in constant prices).

Thus, the clearest and most striking change since 1957 is the weakening of demand. So the clearest and most urgent need today is to remove the over-burden of taxation which is retarding the growth in demand to full employment levels. Income tax rates enacted to finance war and fight inflation—though reduced in 1954—are still so high that they would yield a large surplus of revenues over expenditures if we were at full employment today. They are, in short, repressing demand and incentives in an economy operating well short of its capacity.

To avoid misunderstanding, it is important to stress that any employment program would be unbalanced and incomplete without determined measures (a) to upgrade and adapt the skills and education of the labor force to the more exacting demands of our advancing technology and (b) to facilitate the flow of workers from job to job, industry to industry, and place to place. Nevertheless, our principal reliance for a return to the 4-percent-or-better levels of unemployment we took for granted in the early postwar period must be on measures to boost demand for the products of American industry and agriculture.

The amount of the increase in total demand which would be necessary to reduce unemployment to the 4-percent interim-target level can be approxi-mated in several ways. We have made direct estimates of the relationship between unemployment rates and output levels; and we have independently estimated the potential GNP that the economy could produce at 4-percent unem-ployment. Both of these approaches yield consistent estimates of the output and demand requirements associated with 4-percent unemployment at a given time. Except for small differences reflecting cyclical variations in productivity and erratic fluctuations in labor force participation rates, these estimates of potential output (in constant prices) are very closely approximated by a $3\frac{1}{2}$-percent trend line passing through actual GNP in mid-1955. The several methods of computing potential GNP were reviewed in some detail in our *Annual Reports* both for 1962 and 1963, and are analyzed more fully in a recent paper by one of the Council's consultants. Although estimates of this kind cannot be precise—and efforts to improve and update them as new data come in must continue—the careful cross-checking by different methods provides confidence in their general order of magnitude.

These estimates show that the gap between actual GNP and the potential GNP at 4-percent unemployment has been substantial in every year since 1957. In both 1962 and 1963, it has approximated $30 billion.

Our analysis thus suggests that total demand for goods and services would have had to average some $30 billion higher than it was in each of these past 2 years for unemployment to average 4 percent. The basic purpose of the tax cut is to close that $30 billion gap—and to realize the benefits to employment, growth, and our international competitive position that will flow from this advance.

To be sure, by the time the full effects of the proposed two-stage tax cut will be reflected in demand and output, the economy's potential will have grown considerably, and total demand growth will therefore have to be considerably more than $30 billion. But when the tax cut lifts the expanding level of private demand in the United States economy by the extra $30 billion (in terms of 1963 GNP and price levels) that can confidently be expected, it will have achieved its basic purpose. Had this increase been effective during the past 6 years, it would have eliminated our persistent slack and allowed our unemployment rate to average 4 percent.

The process by which an $11.1 billion tax cut can add as much as $30 billion to total demand has been frequently described and needs only to be summarized briefly here.

If the new proposed personal income tax rates were in full effect today, disposable after-tax incomes of consumers would be approximately $8.8 billion higher than they are, at present levels of pretax incomes. In addition, if the lower corporate tax rates were now in effect, after-tax profits would be about $2.3 billion higher. Based on past dividend practice, one can assume that corporate dividends received by individuals (after deducting personal income taxes on such dividends) would then be more than $1 billion higher, giving a total increment of consumer after-tax incomes—at present levels of production—of about $10 billion.

Since consumer spending on current output has remained close to 93 percent of disposable income in each of the past dozen years, one can safely project that consumer spending would rise by about 93 percent of the rise in disposable incomes, or by over $9 billion.

But this is far from the end of the matter. The higher production of consumer goods to meet this extra spending would mean extra employment, higher payrolls, higher profits, and higher farm and professional and service incomes. This added purchasing power would generate still further increases in spending and incomes in an endless, but rapidly diminishing, chain. The initial rise of $9 billion, plus this extra consumption spending and extra output of consumer goods, would add over $18 billion to our annual GNP—not just once, but year-in and year-out, since this is a permanent, not a one-shot, tax cut. We can summarize this continuing process by saying that a "multiplier" of approximately 2 has been applied to the direct increment of consumption spending.

But that is not the end of the matter either. For the higher volume of sales, the higher productivity associated with fuller use of existing capacity, and the lower tax rates on corporate profits also provided by the tax bill would increase after-tax profits, and especially the rate of expected after-tax profit on investment in new facilities. Adding to this the financial incentives embodied in last year's tax changes, which are yet to have their full effect, one can expect a substantial induced rise in business plant and equipment spending, and a rise in the rate of inventory investment. Further, higher consumer incomes will stimulate extra residential construction; and the higher revenues that State and local governments will receive under existing tax rates will prompt a rise in their investments in schools, roads, and urban facilities. The exact amount of each of these increases is hard to estimate with precision. But it is reasonable to estimate their sum as in the range of $5 to $7 billion. This extra spending would also be subject to a multiplier of 2 as incomes rose and consumer spending increased. Thus there would be a further expansion of $10 to $14 billion in GNP to add to the $18 billion or so from the consumption factor alone. The total addition to GNP would match rather closely the estimated $30 billion gap.

THE PERSISTENT PROBLEMS OF STRUCTURAL UNEMPLOYMENT

The tax cut would thus increase demand to levels consistent with a 4-percent rate of unemployment. It would ease our most pressing unemployment problems. But no one can assume that our worries about unemployment would then be over. Some of its most distressing and inequitable aspects would remain.

To be sure, tax-reduction will create new jobs in every community across the Nation and expand employment in every industry. The overwhelming majority of American families will benefit directly from the income tax cuts that will accrue to 50 million tax-paying individuals and 600,000 tax-paying corporations. Their direct rise in after-tax income will soon be translated, through the marketplace, into stronger markets for all kinds of goods and services and a quickening of the business pulse in all communities. With average working hours already at a high level, this added demand and activity will in large part be translated, in turn, into additional jobs, and income for the unemployed. Thus, the non-taxpaying minority will, in a very real sense, be the greatest beneficiaries of the tax program.

Experience . . . clearly shows (1) that the unemployment rate will decline for every major category of workers and (2) that the sharpest declines will occur where the incidence of unemployment is the highest: among teenagers, the Negroes, the less-skilled, the blue-collar groups generally.

But even so, the unemployment rates of many groups will still be intolerably high. Back in 1957, for instance, when the average unemployment rate was just over 4 percent for the whole economy, the rates were much higher for many disadvantaged groups and regions—e.g., 10.8 percent for teenagers, 8.0 percent for nonwhites, 9.4 percent for unskilled manual workers, and 11.5 percent for workers in Wilkes-Barre–Hazleton, Pennsylvania.

These *high specific unemployment rates, which persist even when the general rate falls to an acceptable level,* are the essence of the problem of structural unemployment. Even a fully successful tax cut cannot solve problems like these by itself. They require a more direct attack.

To reduce the abnormally high and stubborn unemployment rate for Negroes requires a major improvement in their education and training and an attack on racial discrimination. To reduce the persistent high rate for the unskilled and the uneducated groups demands measures to help them acquire skills and knowledge. To reduce excessive unemployment associated with declining industries and technological advance requires retraining and relocation. To reduce high unemployment in distressed areas of Pennsylvania, Michigan, Minnesota, and elsewhere calls for special measures to rebuild the economic base of those communities and assist their workers.

Both the Administration and the Congress have recognized that these measures must be taken concurrently with measures to expand aggregate demand. Coal miners in Harlan County are structurally unemployed *now,* and so are Negro and Puerto Rican youths in New York City. Yet, programs to reduce structural unemployment will run into severe limits *in the absence of an adequate growth of demand,* i.e., in the absence of rapid expansion of total job opportunities. Such expansion is needed to assure that retrained and upgraded workers, for example, *will* find jobs at the end of the training period and *will not* do so at the expense of job opportunities for other unemployed workers. As structural programs create new and upgraded skills, they will in some cases fit the participants for jobs that had previously gone begging. But for the most part, the needed jobs must be created by expansion of total demand.

Quite apart from the human significance of structural unemployment, it also has great economic importance. For only as we reduce structural and frictional unemployment can we achieve the higher levels of total output which would be associated with unemployment rates below our 4-percent interim target. The Council emphasized this point in its 1963 *Annual Report* (p. 42), as follows:

> Success in a combined policy of strengthening demand and adapting manpower supplies to evolving needs would enable us to achieve an interim objective of 4-percent unemployment and permit us to push beyond it in a setting of reasonable price stability. Bottlenecks in skilled labor, middle-level manpower, and professional personnel [now] tend to become acute as unemployment approaches 4 percent. The result is to retard growth and generate wage-price pressures at particular points in the economy. As we widen or break these bottlenecks by intensified and flexible

educational, training, and retraining efforts, our employment sights will steadily rise.

Every worker needlessly unemployed represents a human cost which offends the sensibilities of a civilized society. But each worker needlessly unemployed also represents a waste of potential goods and services, which even an affluent society can ill afford. More intensive measures to attack structural unemployment are necessary to reduce the unemployment rate not merely to 4 percent, but beyond. . . .

Who Are the Structurally Unemployed?

Seymour L. Wolfbein

Side by side with the forces of economic growth—in fact, inextricably bound up with them—have been and are significant alterations in the very structure of the demand for and supply of workers. Five major developments have assumed major roles in the employment–unemployment problems of the United States in recent years. They have in a significant manner exacerbated the demand-shortage nature of the unemployment problem by making it more difficult to achieve the desired level of aggregate demand and by making that level higher than it would have to be if these changes were not present. By the same token, the prognosis for dealing effectively and satisfactorily with these structural problems is poor without increasing economic growth. And to complete the circle, dealing effectively with structural problems makes it that much easier and more likely that desired levels of economic growth will be achieved.

MANPOWER PROFILE OF THE 1960s

In terms of sheer numbers and kinds of people involved in the labor force, the 1960s represent an enormous change in structure from the 1950s.

From Employment, Unemployment, and Public Policy, *by Seymour L. Wolfbein. Copyright* © *1965 by Random House, Inc. Reprinted by permission of the publisher.*

The number of new young workers (fourteen to twenty-four years of age) in 1970 is expected to be 6,000,000 higher than the figure for 1960—*fifteen* times the net increase in number of workers of this age group which took place during the 1950s. The tidal wave of population which swept over the elementary and high school grades and reached the colleges has already begun to move into the labor force, and will have a growing impact upon the labor force in the immediate future. How sharply the demographic situation has been altered is illustrated also by another age group—those thirty-five to forty-four years of age. Here the numbers in the population and in the labor force will actually fall between 1960 and 1970. In part, this consequence is to be traced to the decline in birth rates during the depression of the 1930s.

There is still another significant change in the composition of the labor supply during the 1960s. For more than fifteen years after the end of World War II, a considerable majority of new entrants into the labor force were women—the consequence, in good part, of the existence of plentiful job opportunities for them, especially of the part-time variety. As a result, about two thirds of the labor-force increase in the postwar period was represented by women. From 1965 on, however, the sex ratio of labor-force entries will change, and men are expected to account for about half of the new worker supply between that year and 1970 and an even higher proportion after that. The entry into the labor force of large numbers of men born immediately after World War II and the corresponding anticipated tapering off in increase in participation of adult women are expected to bring about this reverse.

Thus, in terms of numbers, age, and sex the labor supply of the 1960s is turning out to be dramatically different from that of the 1950s. The fact that the manpower profile is different from what it was before does not necessarily constitute a problem. The factors that make for problems are: (1) the huge upturn in numbers comes face to face with a less-than-needed growth in demand and production; (2) the fact that a changing age distribution, with emphasis on the younger worker, comes at a time when other structural changes are operating to constrict sharply the pathways to entry into the working world by the young—especially the 30 percent likely to be school dropouts; and (3) the fact that men will be making up a bigger proportion of the labor supply when the strong probability is that employment in industries with predominantly male working forces—e.g., manufacturing, mining, and farming—will continue to decline relative to the total.

THE SHIFT TO SERVICE- AND WHITE-COLLAR
EMPLOYMENT

The less than satisfactory growth in some industrial sectors is part of a major structural change which has seen the service-producing industries (trade, finance, transportation, personal services, government) overtake the goods-producing industries (manufacturing, mining, construction, agriculture) in 1950. Just after World War I, about two thirds of all wage and salary jobs were in the goods-producing sector. Today, about three fifths of all wage and salary jobs are in the service-producing sector of the economy. For the period 1960–75, the service-producing industries are expected to provide three times as many job opportunities per year as the goods-producing sectors.

Side by side with these changes in the industrial composition of the labor force have been corresponding shifts in the occupational structure away from the blue-collar, manual trades to the white-collar, service fields. White-collar jobs (professional, technical, managerial, clerical, sales) became the single largest occupational grouping in 1957. They have been widening their lead ever since, and are expected to go on doing so through 1975. For example, if relatively high levels of growth are maintained, official government projections call for an increase in employment of 22,000,000 in the interval 1960–75. The great majority of these new jobs, about two thirds, is expected to be in the white-collar category. No increase is expected in the unskilled job category—reducing even further the proportion of total employment that is unskilled, which now stands at only about 5 percent.

Within this context, another shift has taken place in recent years which has caused considerable concern and is significantly related to the unemployment problem. In the critical seven years 1957–63, for example, when the unemployment rate remained consistently and perseveringly above the 5 percent mark, the great majority of new jobs were generated *not* in the private sector of the economy, but in the "not-for-profit" sectors, including government and nonprofit institutions. Actually, the fastest growing has been and is employment at the state and local levels. Between 1957 and 1963, about 40 percent of the net increase in nonfarm jobs in this country took place in the states and various local government jurisdictions. In 1964, one out of every eight nonfarm workers was a state or local government employee. The strictly private sector accounted for only about one fifth of the net job increase during the 1957–63 period, as the following shows:

TABLE 1

NET INCREASE IN NONFARM JOBS

	Number in Millions	Percent
Federal employment	.2	5
State and local employment	1.7	39
Employment owing to federal, state, and local government procurement	.8	19
Employment by nonprofit institutions	.7	16
Employment generated by private demand	.9	21
Total	4.3	100

These statistics bear on the relationship of structural changes to the demand-shortage problem, and emphasize the importance of measures to spur the demand for goods and services produced by the private sector.

One industrial group merits special mention. Since the end of World War II, agricultural employment has declined by an average of 200,000 a year, in substantial part among farmers and their families. These events have produced at least three problems of major concern: (1) the displacement of very large numbers of persons from their jobs; (2) the disappearance of what was once an important area of job opportunities for new workers; and (3) the underemployment and underutilization of manpower on marginal farms.

GEOGRAPHIC SHIFTS IN INDUSTRY

The occupational and industrial changes reviewed so far also have brought about and in some cases reflected the substantial change that has occurred in the map of employment opportunities in the United States. Behind the geographic shifts is a very complex mixture of events ranging from the changing size and composition of defense activities (including, in turn, a range of events varying from the provision of large numbers of jobs through granting of defense contracts in some states and areas to the closing of military installations in others) to the opening of new markets associated with population shifts, the depletion of natural resources, and changing technologies.

This complex mixture of events has brought about a very uneven distribution of employment growth. In the post-World War II period, employment has increased at double the national average in such states as California, Texas, and Florida, and at only half the national average in such states as Massachusetts, New York, and Illinois. Furthermore, actual declines in employment have occurred in Rhode Island and West Virginia. As a result, substantial unemployment has persisted in many sectors of rural America, in major regions such as Appalachia, and in large-population, urban, industrial centers such as San Diego. The geographic concentration of joblessness and poverty dictates an area or regional approach to programs for dealing with these problems.

TECHNOLOGICAL CHANGE

For the past several years, there has been a debate in the United States over the rate and character of recent technological change. The key questions are whether it has been accelerating and whether it is different in kind from what has been experienced throughout the life of man, from the time of the introduction of fire and the wheel to the innovations which produced what is called the Industrial Revolution. Much of the case for the view that recent technological change is different in kind rests upon the evidence of great changes in technological hardware, the manpower concentrations in this area (more engineers and scientists are now employed in the United States than were employed in the whole history of mankind up to now), the development of new sources of power and fuel, and of basically new conceptions of processes of production.

Fire, the wheel, and the Industrial Revolution were major structural changes in technology. They led to social, economic, and political transformations. The point has been made that current and projected changes revolving around automation contain the potentialities for similar transformations in the life of man and his society. To those who see such changes as changes in degree rather than kind, Norbert Wiener offers the contrary view. "It is very well," he writes, "for the classical economist to assure us suavely that these changes are purely changes in degree, and that changes in degree do not vitiate historic parallels. The difference between a medicinal dose of strychnine and a fatal one is also only one of degree." Agreement does prevail, however, that technological change, whether it be called "automation" or "cybernation" or "increased output per manhour" or "reduced manhour requirements per unit of production," means a decrease in the amount of manpower needed to generate a given volume of production.

On the basis of the productivity trends which have prevailed during the post-World War II period, and therefore not assuming any accelerated changes in this field, an average of about 2,330,000 jobs a year will be affected by technological change. For the 1960s, this represents about 24,000,000 jobs which will be altered or eliminated under the impact of changing technology. This total is often added to the estimated 12,500,000 net increase in the labor force scheduled for the decade, to give a grand total of about 36,500,000 jobs needed during the 1960s to take care of labor force growth and technological change alone.

Another way of representing the situation to show the importance of economic growth is to say that during the 1960s enough of an increase in demand for goods and services will be needed to generate enough of an increase in output which, in turn, will provide enough new jobs to afford employment opportunities for 36,500,000 persons—the number representing the net increase in the labor force and the people affected by technological change. The experience of the early 1960s strongly supports these estimates. For example, the 1963 increase in productivity for the economy as a whole (2.75 percent) represented the equivalent of about 2,000,000 jobs. In other words, at 1963 levels of productivity, 1962's GNP could have been produced with 2,000,000 fewer workers.

The interrelatedness among the structural changes discussed is underscored by the strong association between productivity and technological change and, for example, the occupational and industrial changes described. All the available evidence shows that the goods-producing industries have experienced more rapid and extensive technological changes up to now, and therefore have had their employment growth affected to a much larger extent than the service industries. By the same token, the changing occupational structure has reflected the fact that technology is restricting job opportunities in the unskilled fields while emphasizing occupational needs in the professional and technical fields.

Already across the threshold and coming along fast are completely new dimensions to electronic computers; instrumentation and automatic controls, especially in optics, metallurgy, and nuclear engineering; hitching computers to machine tools (numerical control devices); advancing communication technology, e.g., data transmission as an adjunct of data processing and closed-circuit TV systems; new automatic machinery for presswork, packaging, harvesting on the farm; mechanization of materials handling, e.g., pneumatic conveyors for moving granular materials by air pressure; transportation technology, e.g., unitized railroad coal trains, supersonic transports, supercharged diesel engines, automated ships; and completely new materials, e.g., plastic pipe, new synthetics in leather. All these are concrete, specific examples of the new technology in being.

Many of these developments will generate employment growth, as they have already. For example, employment in the electronics industry has gone up by more than 200,000—about one third—in the period 1958–62; during the same period employment in the production of semiconductors doubled. Similarly, thousands of jobs have been created in the computer constellation—programers, systems analysts, console operators, tape librarians. Service centers, business services allied to computers, have been established. Again, employment in the instrument and related products industry rose by 49 percent between 1950 and 1963, about 4½ times the employment growth in manufacturing as a whole during that period.

Nevertheless, the data also continue to emphasize the fact that a prime thrust of technological change is reduction in manpower requirements. From 1957–62, no industry division in this country with an increase in productivity of as much as 2.5 percent a year was able to have a big enough countervailing upturn in the demand for its production to avoid an employment decline. The only industries with an employment increase in 1957–62 were construction, trade, finance, and service—all with productivity increases of less than 2.5 percent per year.

RISING EDUCATIONAL REQUIREMENTS

Table 2 shows the results of a recent survey of the educational background of persons in various occupational fields. There is an enormous spread over the range of occupations, from little more than an elementary school education among the unskilled to more than a baccalaureate among professional personnel. In March 1964, the median school grade completed by all workers was 12.2; the average worker in the United States already had a little more than a high school education.

TABLE 2

EDUCATIONAL ATTAINMENT BY MAJOR OCCUPATION, MARCH 1964

Occupation	Average Years of Education
Professional, technical	16.3
Proprietors, managerial	12.5
Clerical	12.5
Sales	12.5
Skilled	11.5
Service (other than domestic service)	11.1
Semiskilled	10.5
Unskilled	9.3
Farmers, farm managers	8.8
Domestic service	8.8
Farm laborers	8.5

SOURCE: Bureau of Labor Statistics.

The rise in educational attainment has been steady and persistent during the past generation as a more educated group of young Americans has moved into the labor force and a less educated older generation exited through death and retirement. The biggest change has come at the high school level. In 1940, about one third of all workers had a high school education or better; by 1964 the corresponding proportion was over 55 percent.

Every official projection of occupational trends shows above-average growth in fields where the educational prerequisites for employment are high and below-average growth where they are low. These expectations are in line with the occupational, industrial, and productivity trends already described. Yet, more than 3,000,000 workers are still classified as "functional illiterates," i.e., they have not gone beyond the fourth grade. More important, the Office of Education estimates that fully 30 percent of the tidal wave of new workers will enter the labor force without a high school diploma. What this may mean is indicated by the fact that currently 40 percent of the unemployed never went beyond grade school, and 67 percent are high school dropouts.

QUESTIONS FOR DISCUSSION

1. *What are the causes of our present unemployment?*
2. *When we talk of "full employment," what do we mean?*
3. *What does Heller mean by "technological unemployment"?*
4. *How should we deal with structural unemployment?*
5. *Why has there been a shift from blue-collar to white-collar jobs?*
6. *What are some important recent geographic shifts in industry and employment?*

Can We Hold the
Line Against Inflation?

A second charge to the federal government under the Employment Act of 1946 was the maintenance of price stability. Overall, the performance of prices since the end of World War II has been good, showing only a little more than a 2.5 percent average increase per year. For the period 1958 to 1965 inclusive, prices rose only a little more than 1 percent a year. However, since the expansion of the Vietnam War, inflation has reappeared as a serious problem. The reason is fairly clear. The increase in government spending at a time of very nearly full employment, plus the continued expansion of private sector demand, has produced a classical case of excess-demand inflation. Until recently this type of inflation has not been very fashionable in the discussions of economists who, during the late fifties and early sixties, were fairly single-minded in asserting that most of our inflationary problems were "cost-push," the result of market frictions caused either by excessive union power or by the "administering" of prices by oligopolistic industries.

Inflation, whether the cause is demand-pull or cost-push, remains a very threatening idea to most Americans. Citizens of all economic pursuits are fairly agreed in its condemnation, for inflation erodes capital values, interferes with financial decision-making, and penalizes fixed income groups. Despite the fact that many economists will argue that a little bit of "creeping" inflation may be good if it produces expansion of employment, the reality of inflation is likely to be more feared by people than the often abstract threat of unemployment.

The potential trade-off between policies aimed at raising levels of employment and inflation is examined in detail in the following articles.

The second article examines the Johnson Administration's proposal to deal with wage-price movement through an "economic guidepost" policy, which connects wage increases directly to productivity gains. Whereas the text-book explanation of the monetary authorities' power over price increases is usually lodged in their control over interest rates, which in turn, theory argues, is the determinant of credit availability, the third article reports a somewhat different analysis and suggests a different monetary approach, that of "Chicago school" theorist, Milton Friedman.

Inflation and/or Unemployment

Federal Reserve Bank of Philadelphia

Milton Berle once said that inflation means "your money won't buy as much as it would have during the Depression when you didn't have any."

The comedian included the remark in one of his rapid-fire monologues, hoping it would get a laugh. Actually this old chestnut contains a good deal of wisdom as well as wit for it helps explain the public attitude about inflation that prevailed during much of the 1940's and 1950's.

Prices rose rapidly after the Depression but average incomes and profits increased considerably faster. As a result, many individuals and businessmen were far better off financially—in spite of inflation.

We don't mean to say that people liked inflation—most of them certainly did not—but with an ever improving standard of living to take some of the sting out of rising prices, the majority of Americans appeared willing to tolerate some degree of inflation as a sort of necessary evil. At least they felt it was better than high unemployment. The source of this attitude goes back at least 30 years.

THE SCARS OF UNEMPLOYMENT

One day in October 1929 the stock market crashed, signaling the start of the worst Depression this country has ever known. During the next decade

From an educational bulletin with the same title published by the Federal Reserve Bank of Philadelphia, 1968.

unemployment blanketed the Nation like a chilling fog, reaching into every town and street and touching virtually every family.

Unlike moderate inflation, which may hold a deceptive although temporary charm, unemployment brings obvious and often immediate suffering. Economic privation is only part of it. Also important is the frustration that festers in healthy, willing workers during periods of enforced idleness. When one remembers that up to 25 percent of the labor force was jobless during the Depression it is not surprising that the unemployment of the period inflicted a deep wound on the Nation's psyche.

The wound healed but a permanent scar remained. Even when the economy was booming during and after World War II, unemployment still was the number one economic danger in the minds of many. Sensitive to this national neurosis, Congress passed the Employment Act of 1946. The Act was not particularly specific but its implication was clear. Any Administration in power had the responsibility to minimize unemployment; if it failed it must face retribution on election day. This is as true now as it was in 1946 and those who shape the Government's economic policy know it full well.

THE NEW SENSITIVITY TO INFLATION

While unemployment retains its power to stir public resentment, a subtle but important change seems to have occurred in the Nation's attitude toward inflation. Within recent years, the American people apparently have developed a greater distaste for rising prices and are no longer as willing to tolerate the consequences of inflation as they were in the 1940's and 1950's.

There is ample evidence of this new attitude. It can be found in the press where the latest reports on prices have moved from the financial section to the front page. Housewives became so incensed about rising prices during the autumn of 1966 that they turned out to picket food stores all across the country. Inflation was one of the crucial issues in the 1966 elections and was said to have played a large part in their outcome.

INFLATION HURTS MORE PEOPLE IN MORE WAYS

Undoubtedly growing dissatisfaction with inflation has numerous causes. Many of them are closely related to fundamental changes which have occurred in the past decade or two, changes that mean more people are hurt in more ways by inflation. This section explains how inflation affects certain groups and attempts to show that they have become either more important and influential, or more susceptible to the pain of inflation.

Fixed Incomes. Each time the cost-of-living index ratchets upward another notch it robs the market baskets of those who live on pensions, insurance proceeds and other fixed incomes. In recent years the number of people retired on such incomes has swelled dramatically and thus a larger proportion of the population is especially vulnerable to inflation. The importance of these senior households is even greater than their numbers indicate because they have the spare time and often the inclination to exert more political influence than their hard-working sons and daughters.

Lagging Wages. In a sizable number of job categories long-run wage increases tend to lag behind increases in consumer prices. Many of these jobs are found in teaching, government and the service industries. The fact that these are among the fastest growing of all occupations means a larger percentage of workers is likely to suffer particular pain from inflation.

Eroded Investment. Inflation reduces the value of financial assets such as savings accounts, bonds, pension plans and insurance policies. These investments have a constant face value, and rising prices mean the dollars a person gets back will buy less than the ones he put in. Inflation, therefore, tends to shift purchasing power from these investors, who are essentially lenders, to borrowers.

The notion once was popular that lenders were usually rich and borrowers often poor. If this idea ever were true, it is no longer valid in these affluent times. Surveys show that every income grouping of individuals—even the lowest—now has more financial assets than indebtedness. Put another way, every income group is a net lender, on the average, and thereby stands to lose purchasing power through inflation. Who are the "poor" debtors who stand to gain? All levels of government rank high among them.

It would be disastrous if inflation caused a reduction in the amount of money saved and invested in new or expanded factories, offices, farms and stores. This process is the mainspring of economic growth and, because of modern technology, requires huge amounts of extra funds every year.

Distorted Business Decisions. One of the most important, but least understood, ways inflation disrupts the economy is through its effect on business decisions. Inflation increases the value of inventories on hand which creates more profit when the goods, or products made from them, are sold. These are strictly windfall profits but they are easily confused with the returns from regular operations.

Inflation also undermines depreciation accounting. Depreciation is a method of accumulating money to replace a building or machine when it is no longer useful. The amount set aside usually is based on the original purchase price. This sum obviously is inadequate if inflation raises the replacement cost during the time the item is in use. Depreciation is a legitimate expense of doing business and, as such, is deducted from income before profits are figured. If depreciation is understated—because of inflation—it follows that profits must be overstated. Estimates indicate that from 1940 to 1952 business profits were twice as large as they would have been if inflation were fully accounted for.

When reported profits are larger than true profits, taxes paid on profits are higher than they should be. More important, perhaps, the businessman often is deluded into thinking that his company is more profitable than it really is. With visions of artificially sweetened profits dancing in his head, he may decide to expand his operations more than the real potential warrants. If this happens to enough firms at the same time it can jet-propel the economy into an unsound boom which usually leads to a serious slowdown in business spending or even to a recession.

A DANGEROUS PASSAGE

Policymakers now face a dilemma much like the one Ulysses found when he had to sail through a narrow strait where a man-eating monster dwelt on one side and a huge whirlpool boiled on the other. To bring the situation up to date just change the names of the two hazards from the mythological Scylla and Charybdis to inflation and unemployment. If the "helmsmen" of the economy veer too far to avoid the monster of inflation they run the risk of plunging into the whirlpool of increasing unemployment, and vice versa.

Before we discuss some of the courses that might be plotted to avoid or at least minimize these twin perils, it is well to provide some background on the history and causes of inflation.

OLD AS MONEY

One of the first recorded inflations began about 3000 B.C. when Egypt adopted a unit of value known as the Skat which depreciated slowly until it was worth nothing. Alexander the Great set off a major inflation when he conquered Persia and carried away its treasure. This infusion of new wealth halved the value of all the gold and silver in the civilized world. Beginning with Nero, the Roman Emperors inflated money so extensively that their entire currency system collapsed and the Empire had to resort to barter for a time.

The Black Death of A.D. 1348 killed one third of all workers in Europe and production of goods and services fell drastically. The money supply was not particularly affected and survivors bid prices sky high on whatever was produced. Several centuries later the plunder of Aztec and Inca gold swelled the amount of money circulating in Spain and caused prices to soar.

Serious inflations occurred in Europe and Asia after both World War I and World War II. The classic inflation of modern times, however, probably was the one that convulsed Germany from 1921 to 1923. It illustrates well the incredible things that can happen if inflation is permitted to run unchecked.

In the three years prior to December 1923 German wholesale prices rose more than a trillion times. Inflation accelerated so fast that many restaurant patrons paid in advance because if they waited until they finished eating the price of their meal might double. Beneficiaries seldom bothered to collect on life insurance policies because the proceeds often were worth less than the current price of a stamp to notify the company. All the mortgages in Germany in 1913, then worth about 10 billion in dollars, could have been paid off with one American cent in 1923.

When the German inflation finally was stopped by shutting down the money presses, production was at a standstill and millions of hard-working Germans, the backbone of the nation, found their savings, property and influence virtually wiped out. This as much as any other factor paved the way for the rise of Hitler.

What caused such a titanic and tragic inflation? Essentially a misunderstanding. The Germans continued to print money at a furious rate in what they thought was an attempt to keep up with rising prices. In actual fact, however, it was this continuing cascade of new money that caused prices to rise.

UNITED STATES INFLATION

Happily this country has never endured anything that even remotely approaches the German experience. The United States has, however, had a number of serious inflations.

. . . Four major inflations [occurred] after the War of 1812, the Civil War, World War I and World War II. The relationship to war is no accident. All major American inflations were the legacies of wars, which were financed to a large extent by creating huge quantities of new money.

History amply demonstrates that inflation occurs when there is a significant increase in the amount of money in circulation relative to the production of goods and services. In effect, purchasers flush with money are able to bid up the prices of the goods and services that are offered for sale.

This process is often called DEMAND PULL inflation, because purchasers have the money, or demand, to pull up prices.

Economists have isolated another kind of inflationary virus. They call it COST PUSH inflation. Workers, particularly those affiliated with strong unions, sometimes gain larger wage increases than the growth in their efficiency justifies. This raises the cost of labor to a producer and he often tries to pass the higher cost along by increasing the price of whatever he sells.

Demand pull and cost push inflations are closely related. It seems safe to say that, although one type may start first, both often operate at the same time and each one tends to aggravate the other.

POSSIBLE COURSES BETWEEN THE MONSTER
AND THE WHIRLPOOL

One of the fundamental ways to combat inflation is to slow the economy and take some of the steam out of it. But this action, by its very nature, also may increase unemployment. Conversely, the basic method to reduce unemployment is to speed up the economy, a process which, if carried too far, tends to increase inflation.

Tight Money. The Federal Reserve tries to curb rising prices by slowing the rate at which new money is created, making it more expensive and more difficult to borrow. The idea is to slow the growth in spending with borrowed money which, in turn, should help to bring total spending more in line with the near-capacity production of goods and services.

There is little question that a tight monetary policy, if applied with enough vigor, could slow or even stop inflation. But in order to do this the Federal Reserve might have to make money so expensive and difficult to borrow that the economy would slow beyond the danger point where unemployment begins to increase.

Very tight money also has an uneven impact throughout the economy. It tends, for example, to hit housing and some small businesses particularly hard.

In short, tight money is an effective and valuable instrument in controlling inflation, but it works best when used together with some of the other available tools. The same can be said about an easy money policy when the primary objective is to cut unemployment.

Reduced Federal Spending. What happens when the Government spends less, but doesn't reduce taxes? For one thing there is less demand pull on the prices of goods and services. Indeed, reduced Government spending could be a highly effective weapon in the fight against inflation.

But another thing happens when the Government cuts its spending. All sorts of private interests who sell to, or take from the Government may suffer financial losses, if not genuine hardship, and there is nothing like a pain in the pocketbook to inspire an irate letter or a vindictive ballot. The country's foreign commitments in peace and war are other built-in props holding up the Federal budget. For these and other reasons, Federal expenditures have declined only four times in the past 20 years.

Apparently, reduced Federal spending, which could be one of the most effective of all anti-inflation measures, also is one of the most difficult to implement. Looking for a bright side, this implies that it is highly unlikely that Government outlays could be cut far and fast enough to bring on a full-fledged recession. But the next measure, if improvidently used, might do just that.

Increased Taxes. If the Government raises taxes and does not spend more than it otherwise would, the pull of overall demand should contribute less to inflation.

The idea of a general tax increase was discussed throughout 1966. Consumer prices rose about 3 percent during the year and the need for some action, in addition to tight money, was widely recognized. The fact that a tax increase was discussed for such a long time points up some of its defects as a means to curtail inflation. Higher taxes are politically unpopular and Congress is naturally hesitant to act until the need is abundantly clear—particularly if an election is approaching.

Delays only make the job of restraining prices without increasing unemployment more difficult, for they permit the inflationary process to gain momentum. Rising prices lead unions to demand higher wages, which increases prices still more, and the vicious circle turns faster and faster. As inflation gains momentum more powerful measures are required to slow it and the danger of "overkilling" inflation and bringing on unemployment is that much greater.

AIMING AT COST PUSH INFLATION

Guidelines. President Johnson undoubtedly had the inflation-unemployment dilemma in mind when he proposed guidelines for wages and prices. He asked labor not to seek wage increases in excess of 3.2 percent a year which was the long-term average increase in worker productivity for the Nation as a whole. In theory at least, increased productivity then would absorb the impact of higher wages and companies would be under little pressure to raise prices. Indeed, the President also asked business specifically to refrain from price increases.

The guideline program met with some success but it also received much criticism, ranging from the technical (should a broad average be applied uniformly to many diverse industries?) to the philosophical (should labor and business be asked to do less than their best in performing their basic economic functions; that is, to seek the highest wages and profits?).

Criticism, however, should not obscure the fact that the guidelines were an important experiment and continuing efforts to find new ways to solve the inflation-unemployment dilemma should be encouraged.

Break Up Monopoly Power. Cost push inflation thrives when unions and corporations are able to exert some degree of monopoly power. It seems to follow, then, that one way to check this kind of inflation is to reduce monopoly power wherever it exists. This would include breaking up industrywide unions and more vigorous antitrust action against corporations.

But these drastic policies could change the basic structure of the American economy and there would be no telling whether the new structure would work as well in all ways as the existing one. Chances are it wouldn't, according to many experts. Sweeping changes in antitrust policy, therefore, usually are ruled out as too upsetting and politically unfeasible to be used solely as a means to combat cost push inflation.

Direct Controls. Both wages and prices were controlled by the Federal Government during World War II and, for a time in the Korean War. Direct controls are being proposed again but they have serious disadvantages which may make them undesirable or impractical except in wartime. Wage-price controls are like a lid placed on a boiling pot. They may keep prices from boiling over for a while, but they do little if anything to moderate the source of the heat. Pressure continues to build and when the lid is finally removed, prices burst out just as they did in the latter 1940's and the 1950's.

Direct controls also require a huge and expensive bureaucracy to administer because, without adequate enforcement, they have all the containing power of a lid made of Swiss cheese.

Furthermore, controls over prices and wages require that the American public surrender some of its economic freedom to the Government. It seems doubtful that many citizens, when faced with additional restrictions of this nature, would stand for direct controls except as a matter of win-the-war patriotism.

CONCLUSION

During much of its history this country operated on the principle that the Federal Government should not attempt to influence the business cycle. Then, in the 1930's, persistent and pervasive unemployment brought demands that the Government do something to create jobs. For the next 30 years public policy emphasized high-level employment, sometimes to the jeopardy of stable prices.

In the past few years the Nation's willingness to tolerate inflation has lessened appreciably while the old abhorrence of unemployment remains. This creates a serious dilemma for policymakers because actions intended to avoid one of these economic perils may bring on the other.

It is impossible to eliminate inflation and unemployment at the same time so the objective becomes holding both to a practical minimum. But how?

The key words in the prescription for action are *promptness* and *precision.* In economics, as in medicine, the sooner a drug is administered, the smaller the dosage usually required and the less danger there is of undesirable side effects. The dosage, of course, should be measured out in quantities precisely suited to the seriousness of the malady and to the patient's overall strength and recuperative powers.

Numerous recommendations have been made to improve the promptness and precision of Federal economic policy. Among them are improved statistics on the performance of the economy. More timely and more accurate information should improve the decision-making process in the Nation's economic high command.

Both President Kennedy and President Johnson requested authority from Congress to make small tax changes at their own discretion. This would greatly accelerate the lengthy procedure now required to enact new tax legislation and would permit smaller, more frequent changes to offset relatively minor changes in business conditions. As yet Congress has been unwilling to delegate this authority to the Chief Executive.

It is often suggested that the use of the various fiscal and monetary tools should be better coordinated. Basically this means directing the Government's powers to spend and tax as well as monetary policy toward the same economic objectives at the same time. This approach could provide more flexibility and might help to maximize the advantages of each weapon while minimizing the undesirable reactions to it.

In spite of the results of the guideline program there is little question that the Government should continue its efforts to find better ways to influence the course of the economy when it is in the public interest. After all this is the age of research and modern R & D techniques could be used in economic policy just as profitably as in science and industry.

Investigation and experimentation might be concentrated in at least three general areas: (1) improvement of existing economic tools and better coordination in their use; (2) reduction of artificial obstructions which inhibit the workings of the market or price system; (3) development of new, previously untried economic tools.

When a helmsman must navigate a difficult and dangerous course he needs the very best instruments he can get.

How Shall We Deal with the Wage-Price Spiral?

Council of Economic Advisers

The magnitude of the stakes involved in moving promptly toward restoration of reasonable price stability is abundantly clear. It is equally evident that the steps taken to achieve this objective must not impair our other essential goals: maintaining high employment; preserving the effectiveness of free markets in allocating productive resources; and encouraging efficiency and minimizing waste.

The various policies available to improve price stability must be evaluated in the light of all these goals.

DIRECT CONTROLS

The most obvious—and least desirable—way of attempting to stabilize prices is to impose mandatory controls on prices and wages. While such controls may be necessary under conditions of an all-out war, it would be folly to consider them as a solution to the inflationary pressures that accompany high employment under any other circumstance. They distort resource allocation; they require reliance on either necessarily clumsy and arbitrary rules or the inevitably imperfect decisions of Government officials; they offer countless temptations to evasion or violation; they require a vast administrative apparatus. All these reasons make them repugnant. Although such controls may be unfortunately popular when they are not in effect, the appeal quickly disappears once people live under them.

FISCAL AND MONETARY MEASURES

Fiscal and monetary policy always plays a central role in price stabilization efforts. When over-all demand threatens to outrun supply, restrictive fiscal and monetary measures can reduce the growth of demand to keep it in line with the growth of productive capacity.

Once a wage-price spiral has developed—from whatever source—a sufficiently restrictive fiscal and monetary policy can stop it, but only at the cost of creating a rather wide margin of underutilization of resources. It is possible

From "Annual Report of the Council of Economic Advisers, 1968," Economic Report of the President *(Washington, D.C.: United States Government Printing Office, 1968).*

for a spiral to slow down gradually without a retreat from high employment. But the existence of the spiral makes it particularly important to use fiscal and monetary restraints to minimize the risk of upsurges in demand which would give the spiral new momentum.

Most economists believe that the rate of price increase would be significantly lower than it now is if we had attained the present level of unemployment more gradually. Nevertheless, few would disagree that, at the present level of resource utilization, prices would in any event rise somewhat faster than in the early 1960's. Clearly, we cannot afford to attempt to achieve price stability by returning to the unemployment conditions of those years. Equally clearly, we need to find other policies which will serve to reduce the rate of price increase that occurs at high levels of employment.

IMPROVING MARKET EFFICIENCY

In its 1967 Report, the Council discussed at some length the possible contributions to price stability of programs to upgrade labor skills—especially of the disadvantaged groups—and to bring about a closer match between the capacities of the labor force and the needs of a changing economy. It also discussed efforts to strengthen competition, break bottlenecks, and raise the rate of productivity gains—especially in sectors where the productivity trend is now low.

Over time, these and similar measures should gradually reduce inflationary bias and thus permit the economy to achieve higher levels of utilization and lower rates of unemployment without increasing pressures on the price level. Such programs are highly important for many reasons. They offer substantial benefits over the long run and are an essential part of our efforts to combine price stability with full employment.

INCOMES POLICIES

In seeking still further ways to reconcile high employment with reasonable price stability, the governments of most industrial countries have concluded that it is necessary to develop specific policies aimed at the tendency, under conditions of high employment, for money incomes to rise faster than production—so-called "incomes policies."

These policies seek to induce industry, labor, and possibly other groups to avoid the irresponsible and self-defeating use of market power when the demand for their products or services increases temporarily. It is recognized that shifts in relative prices or wages should occur to bring about a needed reallocation of resources. But incomes policies encourage business and labor not to take full advantage of every opportunity to charge what the traffic will bear—in their own longer run interest and in the general interest of the economy.

The Council's Guideposts. The Council's well-known "guideposts," first presented in January 1962, represent a form of incomes policy for the United States. The guideposts do not merely appeal for general restraint, but in addition try to provide guidance to individual unions and firms as to the specific behavior of wages and prices which would be consistent with general price stability as well as with efficient allocation of resources.

The genesis, objectives, and principles of the guideposts were reviewed in detail in the Council's 1967 Report, and need not here be elaborated. In general, the wage guidepost calls for increases in hourly compensation to be limited to the trend rate of productivity growth for the economy as a whole. The price guidepost calls for prices to remain stable in industries in which the trend gain in productivity approximates the average rate for the economy; it points to price declines where productivity gains exceed this average; and it recognizes the need for prices to be increased as required where the improvement is lower than average.

The Council recognizes that many sellers of commodities and services have little or no discretion over the prices they can charge. In these cases, however, the workings of competitive markets may be expected to yield results similar to those prescribed by the guideposts, so long as the general movement of wages and prices is consistent with the guideposts. It is also recognized that many wages are not set by collective bargaining. But, in an environment of general price stability, these wages may be expected to move in line with the productivity guidepost, especially since many nonunion wages are tied more or less automatically to union wages.

There are, of course, many commodities whose price movements are not directly determined by the domestic wage level or by discretionary decisions of firms with market power. Imports and farm products are the most important examples. But imports, though significant in some industries, do not have a major direct impact on the general trend of costs and prices. And farm prices show no marked long-term trend, although they display wide short-term fluctuations. To be sure, such fluctuations can cause a temporary bulge in the average level of consumer prices. But that bulge would not necessarily become permanent if labor unions recognized the nature of the situation and avoided seeking immediate long-term compensatory increases.

Thus, if the guideposts were essentially observed by those firms and unions that possess discretion with respect to prices and wages, the inflationary bias inherent in a high-employment economy should be largely overcome.

Economic Validity of the Guidepost Logic. In their simplest form, the guideposts rest on three basic propositions:

1. While changes in wage rates in any particular year reflect special conditions in specific segments of the labor market, they tend to be broadly similar throughout the economy. Existing wage differentials largely reflect a whole set of institutional factors and basic differences in skill requirements or other attributes of the job, and it is reasonable that they should change rather slowly.

2. Price changes in any industry or sector are strongly influenced by unit labor costs and also reflect the influence of the value of capital used per unit of output and the prices of materials and services purchased from other industries. For the economy as a whole, the influence of purchased materials and services essentially cancels out, so that prices depend largely on wages and returns to capital—profits, interest, and depreciation. If prices move in proportion to unit labor costs, the relative shares of wages and returns to capital will remain constant. Moreover, since the capital employed per unit of output shows little trend in most sectors, the rate of return on capital will remain stable.

3. Simple arithmetic requires that, for the average of unit labor costs in the entire economy to be stable, it is necessary that the average change in hourly compensation match, as a percentage, the average change in output per man-hour in the entire economy; and, for the average of prices to be stable, the movements of prices should conform to the movements of unit labor costs.

In defending the first two of these propositions, the Council has frequently asserted not only that they reflect the ways in which wages and prices "ought" to behave, but that they basically reflect the way in which wages and prices tend, in the long run, to behave under free-market conditions. Data have recently become available which provide additional evidence that, in fact, they do behave in such a manner. . . .

This analysis thus supports the guidepost conclusions that price stability can be achieved and maintained only to the extent: (1) that increases in hourly compensation generally conform to the average economy-wide improvement of output per man-hour; and (2) that changes in prices in individual sectors generally conform to changes in unit labor costs in those sectors.

The former requirement was clearly violated beginning in 1965, and there have been notable exceptions to the second requirement in a few major industries throughout the 1960's. The crucial problem for 1968 and the years ahead is to find means to achieve both requirements without sacrificing other essential objectives.

Meaningful progress toward the restoration of price stability will not be easy to achieve in 1968. The policy choices must be assessed in the light of current and prospective pressures on prices and wages.

The basic forces working on wages and prices this year will be similar in many ways to those at work in 1967. Unemployment and capacity utilization will show relatively little change.

In the areas not directly affected by the market power of unions and business, the available evidence does not point to a significant net reduction in price pressures. Farm prices are likely to rise a little instead of declining as they did in 1967. Strong demand pressures will continue to pull wages up rapidly in several areas, including engineering, scientific, and technical occupations; State and local governments; and medical and hospital services—though in some markets supplies may begin to catch up with demands, with a consequent reduction in wage pressures. Moreover, the 14-percent increase in the minimum wage in 1968 will have an even greater impact than did the 1967 increases, which mainly restored the minimum wage to a more typical relationship with the average wage level in the economy.

Responsible Private Decisions. Major union settlements in 1967 provided wage and benefit increases averaging about 5½ percent a year over the life of the contracts, while average hourly compensation in the entire private economy increased by 6 percent. (These two figures are not strictly comparable. Average compensation reflects new and continuing contracts in organized sectors as well as all compensation in nonunion areas; it also reflects changes in employers' contributions for social insurance. Moreover, it is influenced by shifts in the composition of the labor force.)

If new collective bargaining settlements reached in 1968 should again average 5½ percent, the rise in average hourly compensation for the economy as a whole would be appreciably larger than in 1967. One reason is that the second- and third-year provisions of contracts negotiated in 1966 and 1967 will provide larger increases, on the average, in 1968, than were inherited in 1967 from similar provisions of earlier contracts.

Despite the favorable prospect that productivity gains in 1968 should exceed those of 1967, the pressure of rising unit labor costs on prices would continue to be strong in 1968, on the assumption of a 5½-percent average for new union settlements. And stronger demand conditions will make it easier for cost increases to be passed on in prices. Thus, there would be no prospect of any slowing down in the rate of increase of consumer prices.

In fact, several prominent settlements last year substantially exceeded 6 percent a year, and some unions have already taken this figure as their target to meet or beat in negotiations during 1968. If new union settlements were to average even higher in 1968 than in 1967, a clear acceleration of price increases would be likely in 1968.

Such an acceleration in 1968—or even a continuance of the 1967 rate of price increase—would have a major impact on the prospects for prices in 1969 and even 1970. It would push the ultimate restoration of reasonable stability farther into the future. And as the momentum of the spiral became built into attitudes, expectations, and practices of business, labor, and consumers, the restoration of stability would not merely be pushed farther into the future but would become progressively more difficult to achieve.

On the other hand, if the rise of prices slows down in 1968, there is the clear possibility of restoring reasonable price stability in subsequent years. Hence, every effort must be made to slow down the rate of price increase in 1968. This surely can only be achieved if the average of new union settlements is appreciably lower than the 5½-percent average of 1967 and if business firms avoid any widening of their gross margins over direct costs and indeed absorb cost increases to the extent feasible. A decisive slowing down from the recent rate of price advance could then take place in 1968. This would be the first step toward our target of essential stability of prices.

The Government will continue in 1968 to urge both business and labor to exercise the utmost restraint in their decisions. Such restraint will demand some immediate sacrifices. The rewards of such restraint lie in the assurance of continued high employment, a steady rise in real compensation, and healthy expansion of markets, sales, and profits. These gains may be less immediately perceptible than the costs—but no less certain and far greater in the end.

Productivity Principle. In calling for restraint in wage and price decisions, the Council recognizes that, in 1968, as in 1967, it would clearly be inappropriate to set the trend of productivity as a numerical target for wage increases. In the face of the 3-percent increase of consumer prices that occurred during 1967, it would be patently unrealistic to expect labor to accept increases in money wages which would represent essentially no improvement in real hourly income.

Nevertheless, despite the justification for compensation increases in excess of the productivity trend, such increases are inevitably inflationary. As the Council stated in its 1967 Report:

The only valid and noninflationary standard for wage advances is the productivity principle. If price stability is eventually to be restored and maintained in a high-employment U.S. economy, wage settlements must once again conform to that standard.

In the discussion above, the Council has outlined the pattern of price and wage decisions required in 1968 to begin progress toward the target of price stability. That target cannot be achieved in 1968. It will be achieved only when wage settlements once more conform to the productivity standard, and only when business engages in responsible price-making, which means that prices in each industry should conform to the trend of unit costs, with no widening of margins.

The discussion . . . should make clear that the task of reconciling price stability with high employment will require sustained efforts of public policy on many fronts. The full resources of the Government should be enlisted to deal effectively with structural problems that impede economic efficiency and contribute to inflation.

The machinery of Government policymaking and administration should be adapted to keep the objective of over-all price stability clearly in focus, and to give it a high priority in the formulation and administration of Government programs throughout the entire range of Federal activities. . . .

Friedmanism

Milton Viorst

Half-jocularly, Milton Friedman says that his favorite country in the world is Japan, because he's such a tall man there. Friedman admits unhappily to being just 5 feet 3, but adds that when he was an undergraduate he measured at least 5 feet 4½. He's been squashed down since then, he says.

But if Milton Friedman has been squashed down in height, that's surely about all. In economics, he is certainly the most irrepressible, outspoken, audacious, provocative and inventive thinker in the United States—and even at 5 feet 3, he may stand taller than all his colleagues in the profession. When the Nobel Prize is next awarded for economics, it is regarded as even money that Milton Friedman will win it. [He didn't. It went to Paul Samuelson instead.]

Nonetheless, it's hard to get responsible people, whether in academia or in government, to acknowledge that they've been influenced by Friedman. He is disturbing, if only because of his contempt for the conventional economic wisdom. He is too aggressive in challenging the premises themselves of long-standing economic policy. He's just too damned radical. And, in many circles, the fact that he was tied up with Barry Goldwater during the 1964 campaign doesn't recommend him either.

Still, there is no doubt that at Harvard and M.I.T., where he is considered a heretic, to say nothing of the University of Chicago, where he is the chief luminary of the "Chicago school" of economics, his ideas have had an enormous impact. Meanwhile, down in Washington, the people who make policy have begun to realize that there might be a lot of good sense in what Milton Friedman's been saying.

Currently, the doctrines known as Friedmanism are engaged in a major assault upon the Federal Reserve System, the high church of economic orthodoxy.

From The New York Times Magazine, *January 25, 1970,* © *1970 by The New York Times Company. Reprinted by permission of the publisher and author.*

The Fed is the issuing authority for the nation's money. It is empowered to regulate the supply of money in circulation—usually defined as actual currency, plus checking-account balances—through such devices as the sale and purchase of Government bonds, the setting of reserve requirements for banks, or even the actual printing of bills. It also exercises certain leverage over the use of this money by influencing the interest rate at which most credit flows.

The Fed's goal is to contribute to economic stability, normally by "leaning against the wind," a wind which may be inflationary in some cases and deflationary in others. Friedmanism shares this goal but contends that the Fed has been going after it backwards.

Friedman argues that the Fed has blundered by tinkering with interest rates to stabilize the economy. Instead, the Fed should concentrate on regulating the quantity of money itself and let interest rates fall where they may. Friedman says the Fed's preoccupation with interest rates is not useless merely; it is positively harmful. In fact, he goes a step further by arguing that not only interest rates but Federal fiscal policy itself—that is, Federal spending and taxation—have a negligible impact on economic stability.

This rather extreme view—which holds that taxes, spending and interest rates do not compare in importance with the size of the money supply—has been designated, chiefly by its disgruntled opponents, as Friedman's "Only money matters" doctrine.

Friedman seized upon this doctrine in the course of preparing, with Dr. Anna Schwartz, the book called *A Monetary History of the United States,* now recognized as a classic in the literature of economics. From the data he accumulated, he made the observation that economic instability over the past century has been the consequence principally of abrupt fluctuations in the money supply. During the Great Depression of the nineteen-thirties, for example, the Federal Reserve Board allowed the quantity of money in circulation to shrink by more than a third, with disastrous results. From these observations, Friedman concluded that the Fed should aim to keep the money supply stable—or have it increase (via a fixed rule laid down by Congress) at a steady percentage to keep up with economic growth.

Milton Friedman's reputation as a provocateur waxes by the moment as this doctrine makes headway in the corridors of power, particularly in the Fed, which changes chairmen this week. But because Friedman, at 57, is the reigning "monetarist" in the United States, it should by no means be assumed that his disruptive ideas stop there. His mind ranges across the entire field of economics and spills over into politics itself. To him, virtually no concept, no institution, no personality is sacrosanct.

When he was a 21-year-old graduate student at the University of Chicago, he emerged from a couple of days in a sickbed with a corrective of the work of Prof. Arthur C. Pigou of Cambridge, one of the leading economists of the day, which was published in the eminent *Quarterly Journal of Economics.*

Ever since, he's been a gadfly, but because his capacity to nettle is matched by an indisputable scholarly brilliance, he could never quite be ignored.

Some say his most significant work is not on monetarism at all, nor on political economics, but in an abstruse book meant only for the experts called *A Theory of the Consumption Function,* which showed that consumption, in the short run, tends to remain constant despite sharp fluctuations in income. Though it may be true that Friedman is at his best in technical economics, he has not become a major public figure because of his esoteric economic theories. Rather, it is because he is willing to leave his ivory tower and, in behalf of ideas that are dear to him, come out scrapping.

He was born in Brooklyn of Jewish immigrant parents and raised in Rahway, N.J., where his father did sweatshop work that provided a marginal income for the family. When he reached college age, he won a scholarship to nearby Rutgers and came to the attention of a young economics professor named Arthur Burns, who recognized in him a superior mind. Friedman also came under the influence of a young professor named Homer Jones, who had brought with him from the University of Chicago certain ideas about how to rescue the country from the Depression through a selective return to laissez-faire economics.

Friedman, who at first specialized in math, acknowledges that it was Burns who steered him into economics, while it was Jones who had the greatest impact on his early intellectual development. Jones, he says, steered him to the graduate school at the University of Chicago.

But much as his brilliance was recognized, Friedman was far from an immediate success in the intellectual world. Leaving Chicago, he had difficulty getting a university position. Some academic mandarins maintained that he was more interested in being daring than thorough, and there was some truth to the charge. Others considered him excessively aggressive, a compensation, friends observed, for his small stature and uncomely visage. In at least one instance, and probably more, he was a victim of academic anti-Semitism.

So, from the mid-nineteen-thirties to the end of World War II, Friedman held a variety of Government jobs, and for a time it appeared he would end up a Government statistician. Thanks to Arthur Burns, he was given a staff appointment at the National Bureau of Economic Research, where he worked full-time at scholarship from 1936 to 1940.

But apart from one year on a campus, during which he was the subject of a bitter intrafaculty fight, it was not until 1945 that he got his first teaching post, at the University of Minnesota; and only the following year that he was invited to return, with faculty status, to the University of Chicago. Apart from various visiting professorships, it is there that he has remained since.

Because he has championed economic freedom in an age when the left has put its faith in Government intercession—whether of the Marxian or the

Keynesian variety—Milton Friedman has inevitably been considered a "right-wing" economist, an impression seemingly confirmed by his association with Goldwater in 1964.

But if the term "right-wing" implies an inordinate sympathy for the vested interests of society, along with a high degree of indulgence for existing social institutions, then nothing could be further from the truth. Friedman is no Chamber of Commerce economist, and surely no Bircher. Whatever the classical foundations of his thinking, he professes ideas that are warmly social and espouses programs that are, within the framework of our time, genuinely radical. Friedman may not be a pure egalitarian, but he has no tolerance for a system of government that proclaims programs to help the poor but winds up with a structure that enriches the rich. . . .

At the heart of the Friedman principles, then, is a deep cynicism about the processes of government, founded largely on the judgment that men are essentially incompetent or venal, if not both. In a way, the feeling goes back to Montesquieu and Jefferson during the Enlightenment, and to Lord Acton in the last century.

But if Montesquieu, Jefferson and Acton feared political tyranny, Friedman's preoccupation is chiefly with economic tyranny. He simply does not believe that a governmental system can be devised which will not be taken over by vested economic interests and exploited for the preservation and enhancement of their own wealth. He concludes, then, that individual opportunity is best served when the power of government is least.

Despite the favor he has found among many conservatives and right-wingers, Friedman has sometimes contemplated characterizing himself as a "philosophical anarchist." The term, however, is probably too strong. It is enough to say that he would organize his society on the basis of individual economic freedom, curbed by government only to the degree necessary to keep markets free, competition open and innocent bystanders unharmed.

This essentially anti-Government approach appealed strongly to Goldwater in 1964 and in the course of several meetings together he borrowed heavily from Friedman without ever accepting the Friedmanite cosmology *in toto*. Four years later Richard Nixon, though more conventional in his economic thinking, also turned occasionally to Friedman for ideas. If the press has tended to exaggerate Friedman's personal influence on both men, neither of whom he saw very often, Friedman himself makes no apologies for voting Republican and giving advice to one or the other. However different his social objectives may be from theirs, he reasons that they are more likely than liberal Democrats to build a system that approximates his ideals.

Most of Friedman's formulations on the political economy were laid out earlier in this decade in a book called *Capitalism and Freedom* (known by the wags as *Capitalism and Friedman*). Many members of the economics community regard it as a shameless political tract, unworthy of a scholar. But Friedman, while acknowledging it as a popular and not an academic work, is extremely proud of it. He has named his summer home "Capitaf" in its honor. He is pleased that it is collateral reading in economics at many colleges and that, in paperback, it sells tens of thousands of copies every year.

Many of the ideas Friedman conveys in platform talks and in the column he now writes every third week for *Newsweek* first appeared in *Capitalism and Freedom*. Taken as a whole, it unfurls the Friedmanite cosmology. Examined in parts, it provides interesting and useful hypotheses for solving some of the country's most puzzling politico-economic problems.

Friedman's prescription for maintaining the economy vigorously competitive, thereby striking at privilege and serving the consumer, is an odd mélange of ideas previously heard from both left and right. He would abolish protective tariffs (left), oil subsidies and quotas (left), and farm-price supports (right). He would abolish corporate income taxes (right), but he would require corporations to attribute all their earnings to stockholders, who would be taxed on them at the regular rather than the capital-gains rate (left), and he would discourage amassing of great reserves as a temptation to gobbling up other companies.

He would deprive the regulatory agencies of their rate-setting powers (right), without impairing safety regulations (left), in order to encourage more price competition within such industries as securities, airlines and railroads, and he would open radio and television licenses to public bidding (left). He would repeal such codes as would require auto manufacturers to install seat belts, on the grounds that individual purchasers can make that decision (right), but he would retain such requirements as the installation of antipollution devices, on the grounds that these devices protect the rights of third parties (left).

Friedman acknowledges that in the case of natural monopolies, such as the telephone system, there is no ideal means of maintaining competition. But so great is his distrust of bureaucrats that he concludes that, in preference to a public corporation or a regulated industry, it is better to take a chance with private monopoly.

His formula for dealing with poverty is, perhaps, even more daring—though it is the one that the Government, under President Nixon, has come closest to adopting. Friedman, once asked what he thought was the best way to help the poor, replied, "Give them money." To implement this simple idea, he devised the now celebrated plan for a negative income tax, which would put money into the hands of the poor without their having to pass through a labyrinthine welfare apparatus.

But as Friedman sees it, the negative income tax would change little, unless accompanied by other basic reforms. What he proposes is to do away with the bureaucracy not only of welfare but of the war on poverty, urban renewal, Medicare, minimum wage and even Social Security itself. The Social Security system, cornerstone of the New Deal's program for social justice, particularly irritates him. Financed by a "regressive" system of taxation, it takes from the poor at a much more onerous rate than from the rich, yet rewards the rich more generously than the poor.

Similarly, Friedman says that Federal housing programs—which bulldoze away the homes of the poor while subsidizing mortgages on the homes of the rich—are basically discriminatory and unjust. As for the minimum wage, Friedman figures that it rigs the market place in favor of the upper echelons of the labor force, and drives the old and the young, whose market value is below the legal minimum, completely out of work.

Friedman is frank to admit that he does not, in principle, approve of a system that takes money from some citizens to give it to others, whether the beneficiaries are rich or poor. He feels it is an impingement on freedom and, if he had his way, the poor would be supported by private volunteer charity.

But he acknowledges that reliance on charity would be impractical, if not inhumane, and, as he sees it, the negative income tax is the best alternative. As long as it provides the poor with a livable income, while presenting them with built-in incentives to work, their buying power would assure them an adequate diet, decent medical care and suitable housing. Furthermore, he says, freed of oppressive bureaucracies, they could make their own spending decisions and, having an impact on the law of supply and demand, influence the market place to meet their needs.

Education, too, Friedman would open to the competition of the market. Like most Americans, he observes that the quality of the public schools has declined disastrously in our time, even though billions in new funds have been spent upon them.

The chief victim of this inferiority in educational opportunity, he points out, is not the rich but the poor. "Let a poor family in a slum have a gifted child," he says, "and let it set a high value on his schooling. . . . The 'good' public schools are in the high-income neighborhoods. The family might be willing to spend something in addition to what it pays in taxes to get better schooling for its child. But it can hardly afford simultaneously to move to the expensive neighborhood. . . . Our present school system, far from equalizing opportunity, very likely does just the opposite."

What Friedman wants to do is to break the virtual monopoly of the educational bureaucracy over mass schooling in the United States. To achieve this end, Friedman would grant for each school-age child a "voucher" good for a certain sum of money, preferably equal to the average per capita cost of public education. A family would then be empowered to present this voucher either at the nearest public school or at the private school of its choice, where it would serve as full or partial tuition payment. Such a system, he says, would at once encourage competent educators to build a network of private schools, which would then compete for students against the public schools—giving both a positive incentive to maintain a high level of quality.

The Government's role in this plan would be to enforce certain minimum standards, perhaps including a prohibition of racial discrimination. Otherwise, it would leave the private schools free to cater (be "responsive") to the needs and peculiarities of their student bodies.

It goes without saying that the Keynes-oriented economists of our day— and that probably includes a substantial majority—do not share Milton Friedman's faith in the competitive market, or his distrust of the processes of government. Many see even his advocacy of a fixed rule for governing the money supply, leaving to fallible men a bare minimum of discretion, as proceeding directly from ideology rather than from scholarly analysis.

"Sure, Milton has forced us to tighten up and see things in a more balanced way," said Arthur Okun, a Keynesian and former chairman of the President's Council of Economic Advisers. "But he doesn't see things in a balanced way himself. You can't buy and sell everything on the market, like honesty and racial equality. Under Milton's system, why not wives? Why not votes? Milton talks as if it's a perfect—or perfectible—marketplace, where everyone has perfect information and perfect understanding when he makes his marketplace decisions. But I think Milton's world is only a caricature."

Paul Samuelson of M.I.T. says that Friedman mixes up sequence with causation and that in his desire to be a "big swinger" on the economic stage he engages in "intellectual tightrope walking." Nonetheless, there is more than enough hard logic in Friedman's arguments to keep the Keynesians from dismissing them as hokum. And there is even some factual evidence—as in the recent successful readjustment of European exchange rates on the open market—that at least a few of his positions on economic freedom are correct.

As for Friedman's money doctrine, what the generation of economists nurtured on the teachings of Lord Keynes seemed to have forgotten is that Keynes himself had recognized a major function in the money supply. This was obscured by the lessons Keynes taught about the role of government fiscal policy in maintaining economic stability.

Friedman never claimed that he invented the money doctrine, but he did reintroduce it to the general body of economic thought, in a fashion so scholarly and persuasive that it could scarcely be ignored. Samuelson has injected more and more of Friedmanesque monetary theory into successive editions of his basic economics textbook—in use in most colleges—while denying vigorously that Friedman has had anything to do with it. Samuelson, often looked upon as Friedman's principal rival for America's first Nobel Prize for economics, now readily admits that "money matters," but in common with other Keynesians he dismisses as nonsense the Friedman doctrine that "*only* money matters."

Now two of the seven members of the Fed's board of governors have aligned themselves publicly with the principles, if not with the details, of Friedman's teachings, and there is indication that perhaps one or two more have become private converts. In Congress, the prestigious Joint Economic Committee has recommended that the Fed shift to essentially Friedmanite policies, and within the President's Council of Economic Advisers, Chairman Paul McCracken has confessed to being "Friedmanesque," if not a full-fledged Friedmanite. It is now being said that opinion at the Fed is so closely divided that future policies will be determined by the incoming chairman, Arthur Burns—who was Milton Friedman's first teacher of economics at Rutgers and is now one of his most intimate friends.

Already, the Fed has conceded the existence of Friedman, if only by beginning to publish periodic figures on the nation's money supply. One of the Federal Reserve System's 12 semi-autonomous regional banks, the St. Louis branch, has been virtually captured by Friedmanism, and researchers there have done much to substantiate the essence of Friedmanite doctrine. (The research director in St. Louis is none other than Friedman's other Rutgers mentor, Homer Jones.)

But William McChesney Martin, Jr., the Fed's chairman since 1951, is an ex-stockbroker, not a professional economist, and, according to most careful observers of the Fed, he barely perceived what Friedman was trying to convey. Besides, the members of the Fed, taken as a whole, could scarcely help but react to a message that was so clearly directed against them. In his *Monetary History*, published in 1963, Friedman designates the Federal Reserve System as the villain bungling the nation into economic disruptions. If Friedmanism has quietly infiltrated the Fed, Friedman himself has found no reason to change that judgment on the basis of Federal Reserve policy since.

In bringing this judgment up to date, Friedman cites the Fed's much-disputed decision to stuff a large quantity of money into the economy just after Congress, as an anti-inflationary fiscal move, passed the surtax in 1968. What followed was a vast new surge of inflation, which even many non-Friedmanites blame on the Fed.

Then, in the middle of last year, the Fed decided to reduce the rate of increase in the money supply to zero. Again and again, Friedman has argued that this policy is so drastic that it will lead directly to an economic recession. The full impact of this policy, he said, would take about six months to be felt—which makes him believe that a recession is now imminent. Friedman acknowledges a rather remote chance that he is mistaken, since economics is a science based on probability rather than mathematical certainty. But he is prepared, as are his antagonists, to consider the recession which he predicts as a fundamental test of Friedmanite doctrines.

So persuaded is Friedman of the institutional incompetence of the Fed that if he *really* had his way, he says, he would abolish it altogether. In its place, he would have Congress legislate a fixed annual rate of increase in the money supply, somewhere around 4 percent. At the moment, he says, economists still do not know enough about the processes of the economic system to justify constant intercession, and a fixed rule could hardly be worse, and would probably be better, than the Fed's tinkering.

Arthur Burns, in testifying before the Senate Banking Committee prior to his confirmation last December, gave the first public clue on the position he takes on Friedmanism. To no one's surprise, Burns revealed himself to be far more conventional in his views than Friedman himself. He regards a reduction in Federal spending and a balanced budget as fundamental to halting inflation. He considers it important to have the Government's anti-inflationary posture appear "credible" to the business community. He does not dismiss interest rates as a significant factor in economic stability.

But Burns conceded that he saw more than a little truth in Friedman's recession forecast, and he said his "impulse" was to follow Friedman—though not with the rigid Friedmanite formula—in maintaining a relatively constant but gradually increasing supply of money in circulation. Thus it became quite clear that, after William McChesney Martin goes at the end of this week, Milton Friedman will have won a victory (though hardly an unconditional surrender), and the Fed will never again be quite so casual about whether or not "money matters." . . .

QUESTIONS FOR DISCUSSION

1. *Why are Americans so sensitive to inflation?*
2. *What are the economic and social effects of inflation?*
3. *In terms of dealing with our most recent inflationary experience, what policy would you propose? Why?*
4. *Why are "direct controls" on prices and wages "undesirable"?*
5. *Does the Council of Economic Advisers' "guidepost" policy seem to be an effective anti-inflationary approach?*
6. *What are the advantages and disadvantages of linking wage increases to productivity?*
7. *How does Friedman's money theory run counter to monetary and fiscal policy of the past few years? How do you respond to his approach?*

Can We Have Continued
Economic Prosperity?

Until comparatively recent times, the prospect for periodic economic collapse in the American economy was every bit as real as the long-term upward thrust in output and productivity. As a rule, through the nineteenth and into the early twentieth centuries, the economy would simply "go bust" every eight to twelve years. Although the prevailing economic theory of the time made little or no effort to explain such cyclical behavior, it was an accepted fact of life. Since World War II, the national economy has suffered no exceptionally deep or sustained downward shifts. To talk about depressions, or the Great Depression, is to many people rather like discussing the passenger pigeon. Not very many people have even seen one and most people believe they are extinct anyway.

To state flatly that we are permanently rid of serious periodic downswings in the economy because of our new uses of public policy is nevertheless a difficult proclamation for any economist to make. Many recall the stories of some of their predecessors who looked at the Great Bull Market of 1929 and saw nothing but continued expansion.

Even if we are depression-proof, we are not ipso facto assured of "continued economic prosperity." The last half of the 1950's were without serious depression, but they exhibited a disappointingly slow rate of economic growth leaving us with serious unemployment problems and lagging increases in real income. During the Kennedy and most of the Johnson administration, debate on the question of how to maintain an adequate rate of growth held central position among economic issues; and a variety of public policy devices to spur growth, from tax cuts to cajoling businessmen to invest, were tried out with apparent success.

No one seriously opposes the goal of maintaining stable economic growth. Along with high levels of employment and stable prices, it is part of the "trinity" of modern economic policy making. The means to this end are not at all agreed upon and there are still important differences in emphasis among economists.

In the following section, two views toward sustaining economic prosperity are examined. The first article, by Walter W. Heller, chairman of the Council of Economic Advisers to President Kennedy and President Johnson, represents the outlook of a man largely responsible for national economic policy over most of the past decade. His is the "new economics." He is confident about the future capacity of the nation to deal with all economic problems if it builds upon what it has learned from the flexible and innovative use of monetary and fiscal policy of the past decade. The second article is by Arthur F. Burns, economic adviser to President Eisenhower and President Nixon, and recently appointed chairman of the Federal Reserve Board. Here the tone is more cautious and the emphasis on a more methodical and conservative approach to government policy. Yet the last "news item" suggests that beyond the difference in tone and the labels of "conservative" or "new economist," there is virtually no difference between most economists or politicians on the ends of public policy, and, maybe, only little difference over the means.

Policy and Promise for the Future

Walter W. Heller

To keep our economic perspective, we need to look beyond the temporary period of economic turbulence during and after Vietnam. Given the experience of the sixties and the advances yet to come, we can confidently count on economic expansion a much higher proportion of the time in the future than in the past. We will have far fewer ups and downs than we did in the 1949–1960 period when we had four recessions. This is not to say that we are about to enter a new era of perpetual prosperity. The "new economics" provides no money-back guarantee against occasional slowdowns or even

Reprinted by permission of the publishers from Walter W. Heller, New Dimensions of Political Economy *(Cambridge, Mass.: Harvard University Press, 1966). Copyright 1966 by the President and Fellows of Harvard College.*

recessions. As President Johnson has put it, "In principle, public measures can head off recessions before they start. Unforeseen events and mistakes of public or private policy will nonetheless occur. Recessions may be upon us before we recognize their warning signs."

Yet we have good reason to expect the U.S. economy to advance more steadily and, on the average, more rapidly than either its long-run real growth rate of about 3 percent or its postwar rate of $3\frac{1}{2}$ to 4 percent. Growth in real GNP potential should average between 4 to $4\frac{1}{2}$ percent in the coming decade. And with reasonably good management of our prosperity actual growth should not fall much below the growth in potential.

The core of such management will be the skilled deployment of the $7 to $8 billion a year of added Federal revenues automatically generated by normal economic growth. An average advance in GNP of just over 4 percent in real terms, and between $5\frac{1}{2}$ and 6 percent in current prices, will add about $9 billion to the flow of Federal cash receipts each year at existing tax rates. Of this amount, between 1\frac{1}{2}$ and $2 billion will be absorbed by the automatic annual growth in social security benefit payments. This will leave something over $7 billion of new revenue each year—a rise of nearly $40 billion between 1966 and 1971—to rear its ugly head as fiscal drag or, properly managed, its lovely head in the form of recurring fiscal dividends.

Except in times of excess demand . . . dividends must be declared to be realized. If allowed to turn into fiscal drag they will disappear in economic slack and retarded growth. The choices among alternative forms of dividends may not be easy. Yet they are essentially pleasant choices aimed not at the lesser evil but at the greater good. For they enable us to finance vital new or expanded Federal programs, including a helping hand to the social security system; to provide well-timed tax cuts; and to make more generous transfers of funds to hard-pressed state and local governments. Just to list these choices is to make clear that although they are in part economic—because some combinations will deliver more growth and stability than others—the proper mix will depend even more on the country's social and political priorities.

The demands of Vietnam and of anti-inflationary policy, together with the inescapable growth in certain civilian expenditures, may preempt the dividends for the immediate future. On the other hand, it is quite possible that the need and opportunity to declare such dividends may reappear sooner than we think.

The remarkable power of our Federal revenue system is such that, if defense spending were to level off at the rate programmed in the fiscal 1967 budget (which, alas, it won't), a potential fiscal drag of some $12 billion would develop by fiscal 1969, and would reach nearly $20 billion by fiscal 1970 (before allowing for increases in nondefense spending other than programmed increases in personal transfers and interest payments). We would still be fighting a war overseas, and yet have to take deliberately expansionary fiscal steps to maintain the health of our economy at home. If we did not, having shown that we can have both guns and butter in 1966, we could find ourselves risking both war and recession in 1968. Our great strength is that our economy is capable of so much. Our weakness would be a failure to make full use of this capability.

The size of the immediate fiscal feast once Vietnam ends will depend in part on our budgetary target at high employment. If money rates come down readily and private investment demand is strong, first claim on our rising revenues would be to hold some of them as a high-employment surplus for debt retirement. But if money rates prove to be stubborn, or if business investment and housing demands—with or without easy money—do not rise to the occasion, a balanced budget at high employment might again be the appropriate target.

Given this target, and leaving aside the extra post-Vietnam dividends, we need to refer to past experience to see how much of the $7 billion-plus a year might be claimed by "normal" growth in Federal civilian expenditures. These expenditures—which are net of defense and space spending and the trust fund outlays already allowed for—rose by an average of less than $2½ billion annually between the fiscal years 1955 and 1966. This pace suggests that we will have ample leeway not only to step up the tempo of our Great Society programs but to share some of the revenue bounty with Federal taxpayers and state-local treasuries. How should these prospective fiscal dividends be apportioned among the competing claimants to realize the full promise of modern economic policy?

THE SOURCES AND USES OF GROWTH

If the U.S. economy of the future will be, not recession-proof, but at least recession-repellent—as I believe it will—we can and should focus more and more of our future economic policy attention on growth, on its sources, its costs, and its uses.

I am not unmindful that the economic growth we measure is not everything. There is more to economic life than goods and services, and more to life than economic life. Justice, freedom, valor, leisure, and wit are not counted in the national product—not because they are unimportant parts of the good life, but because they cannot be measured—the markets for justice and valor are too thin to yield reliable price quotations.

Also I am keenly aware that Galbraith's "penultimate western man, stalled in the ultimate traffic jam and slowly succumbing to carbon monoxide," will hardly be enchanted "to hear from the last survivor that in the preceding year Gross National Product went up by a record amount."

The picture of a mindless and heartless process of growth that Galbraith puts before us is, I am sure, part of an effort to get us to put our minds and hearts to redirecting its fruits toward uses of high purpose and quality. This is all well and good. I would only add that unless we first put our backs to it we will have no fruits to redirect.

So future fiscal dividends must be declared with an eye not just to the uses but to the *sources* of growth. In the past few years part of our rise to the top of the growth ladder has been accomplished by losing the GNP, or production, gap. With the economy operating at or near its potential, our realized growth in the future will depend chiefly on the rate of increase in that potential. We can no longer pad the figure, so to speak, by taking up economic slack.

Rising productivity will be the key. In part, this will require continued measures to maintain high levels of private investment in plant and equipment. In part, also, it calls for measures to improve efficiency and hence productivity by adjustments—many of them politically painful—in our policies for transportation, manpower allocation, agriculture, and the like. Advances on these microeconomic fronts are long overdue.

But beyond this—and especially if balance-of-payments considerations bar the use of easy money as a growth stimulant, or if further fiscal and monetary encouragements were to add but little to the sustainable rate of private investment—the search for faster growth of our productive capacity will lead us ever more directly to wellsprings that only government can provide through its investment in education, research, and physical resources. When we add to this the Federal government's responsibility for overcoming some of the *ravages* of economic growth, and its commitment to those *uses* of growth that will raise the quality of life, Federal expenditures become a top claimant on the fiscal dividends in our future. . . .

The promise of modern economic policy, managed with an eye to maintaining prosperity, subduing inflation, and raising the quality of life, is indeed great. And although we have made no startling conceptual breakthroughs in economics in recent years, we *have*, more effectively than ever before, harnessed the existing economics—the economics that has been taught in the nation's college classrooms for some twenty years—to the purposes of prosperity, stability, and growth. As we have seen, we cannot relax our efforts to increase the technical efficiency of economic policy. But it is also clear that its promise will not be fulfilled unless we couple with improved techniques of economic management a determination to convert good economics and a great prosperity into a good life and a great society.

Pathways to Stable Prosperity

Arthur F. Burns

In recent decades . . . the business cycle has no longer run a free course. Taking seriously its new responsibility, the federal government has used extensively its monetary, fiscal, and regulatory powers to promote a stable prosperity. Its contracyclical efforts have not always been well timed or appropriate to the need, but by and large they have proved constructive. So too, on their more limited plane, have the efforts of the business community to control inventories. Meanwhile, a favorable conjuncture of structural changes in the economy, many of which were entirely unconnected with planning for stability, has facilitated the task of the managers of national prosperity.

The employment structure of our country has become transformed in recent decades, and the trend has been preponderantly in a stabilizing direction. Manufacturing, mining, construction work, freight transportation—these are the cyclically volatile industries; but their relative importance as providers of jobs has for some years been declining, while that of the more stable service industries has been increasing. In addition, the proportion of people who work as managers, engineers, scientists, accountants, secretaries, salesmen, or are otherwise engaged in occupations that have something of an overhead character has been rising rapidly, while the proportion of "blue collar" workers—whose jobs are typically much less steady—has been falling. These changes in the industrial and occupational structure have served to blunt the impact of cyclical declines of industrial production on the lives of working people.

Other developments in our economy have helped to stabilize private incomes by creating a buffer between the fluctuations of production and the flow of income to individuals. During each of the recessions of the postwar period, the government has offset automatically and to a significant degree the decline in the flow of income from production, first, by collecting much less in taxes from corporations and individuals, second, by increasing unemployment insurance and other social security payments. Corporations, in turn, have reacted to the decline in their profits by reducing their savings rather than the flow of dividends or pensions to individuals. Such automatic stabilizers have long been a feature of the American economy, but they have become much more powerful in our generation as a result of the vast expansion of government, the increased role of the income tax in public revenues, the shift of income tax collection to a pay-as-you-go basis, the growth of unemployment insurance and other programs of social security, the growing frequency and scale of private pensions, the spread of business corporations, and their increasing pursuit of stable dividend policies.

From Arthur F. Burns, The Management of Prosperity *(Pittsburgh: Carnegie Press, 1966). Reprinted by permission of the publisher.*

In short, several major developments—the more active role of government in promoting stable prosperity, more efficient control of inventories by the business community, and structural changes in the economy—have combined to moderate the business cycle. More than twenty-five years have already elapsed since we last had a severe economic decline. Over thirty years have elapsed since we last experienced a financial panic. Since 1937 we have had six recessions, the longest of which lasted only 13 months. Since 1945 we have experienced five recessions, but even the severest of these was less intense than the average pre-war decline. This sequence of relatively mild and brief contractions marks a break with the long past. Moreover, while contractions have become shorter and milder, expansions have tended to become longer. The duration of the four expansions between 1945 and 1960 averaged 36 months, in contrast to an average duration of 26 months for the ten expansions from 1900 to 1937. And the current expansion, which has already lasted longer than any of its peacetime predecessors of which we have a definite record, is still running strong.

In view of this record of achievement, the business cycle has lost much of its terror. Most businessmen, government officials, trade union leaders, and other influential citizens now take it for granted that the course of the economy will be shaped in large part by governmental policy and that the more serious mistakes of the past can and will be avoided. Certainly, no administration nowadays would tolerate destruction of one-third of the nation's money supply during a period of declining economic activity. Yet that is precisely what our government permitted to happen between the fall of 1929 and the spring of 1933. Nor is any administration soon likely to raise taxes all around at a time of heavy unemployment, which is what the Congress kept ordering from 1932 to 1936. We have learned to avoid such blunders of policy, and we have become more mindful of the need to pursue economic objectives in ways that take account of the state of confidence.

Recent progress in moderating the business cycle has stirred the wholesome hope that we may do still better in the future. Unhappily, it has also given rise to the view, which is spreading among businessmen as well as intellectuals, that the business cycle has already been mastered. This view has been encouraged by the durability of the current economic expansion, by the role of the government in prolonging it, and especially by the success of the recent tax reductions which were undertaken to reinforce expansion rather than to counteract any recession. On all sides we hear that a "new economics" has been born, that the federal government is now able, by adjusting taxes or its own rate of spending, to keep the aggregate demand for goods and services closely adjusted to what our economy can produce at full employment, and that the government has finally resolved to manage prosperity in this fashion.

The "new economics," or the new fiscal theory which is its essence, undoubtedly provides a useful framework for economic thinking about some of the problems that surround our national prosperity. It would be unwise, however, to permit this theory or any other to lull us into the belief that prosperity is assured by the government. The new fiscal theory might help to reduce mistakes in governmental policy, but it surely cannot prevent mistakes.

Before the new theory can be applied, forecasts must be made of the nation's capacity to produce and of what actual production would be in the absence of fresh governmental actions. Economic forecasting, however, is still a rudimentary art. Indeed, even our knowledge of the present is quite imperfect, as the revised estimates of national income that the Department of Commerce published earlier this year have helped to remind us. Experience indicates that the best of experts not infrequently make serious mistakes when they attempt to predict the gross national product more than six months ahead. Needless to say, the forecasts required by the new fiscal theory are vastly more difficult. It is also well to bear in mind that the new theory disregards the structure, as distinguished from the level, of both taxes and expenditures, and that it equates—except for a technical factor involving savings—the stimulative power of tax reduction to that of increased governmental spending. Since the theory proceeds on a highly abstract plane, as theories generally do, it cannot of itself provide much practical guidance on ways of nourishing the main source of our national prosperity—which is still, as it has always been, the hopefulness, skill, and energy of the American people.

Moreover, fiscal policy does not encompass all of governmental action. Important though fiscal policy is, it must still be fitted in with other matters of large governmental concern—that is, policies involving gold, the labor market, corporate mergers, education, defense, foreign trade, and so on. These policies too have their influence on the state of confidence and prosperity. Indeed, the effectiveness of a particular fiscal policy will always depend on what other policies have been recently pursued or are currently being pursued. An expansionist fiscal policy, for example, may come to naught if credit is simultaneously being restricted. Or to give a historical example, the proposal that President Roosevelt made in early 1937 to enlarge the membership of the Supreme Court would have caused little stir outside of legal and academic circles had it been made by President Hoover in early 1929. As it was, this proposal followed a mass of legislation that deeply disturbed the business community, and it came at a time when a wave of sit-down strikes posed a threat to property rights. In these circumstances, it was widely feared that the Supreme Court proposal was a step toward abridgment of constitutional safeguards of private property. I doubt if any fiscal policy that was plausible at the time could have prevented the collapse that occurred in business confidence and investment.

As these remarks suggest, it is unrealistic to expect the "new economics" to protect government officials from making mistakes in their efforts to manage prosperity. In fact, by helping to bend governmental policy toward inflation, the new fiscal theory will at times promote mistakes, just as the older theory of balanced budgets did by bending governmental policy at times toward deflation. To be sure, the new theory requires that the government should reduce spending or increase taxes, if aggregate demand keeps growing faster than productive capacity once full employment has been achieved. In actual life, however, inflationary pressures do not wait until this point is reached. They usually emerge much earlier—that is, when the presence of a gap between productive capacity and actual production still requires, according to the theory, an expansionist fiscal policy. The theoretical system of the "new economics" cannot deal with this early type of inflation because it falls outside the system. Hence, the adherents of the theory are forced to resort to improvisation—which may be guidelines for wages and prices today, and something else tomorrow. The steel price episode of April 1962 should suffice to remind us that here too is a source of possible misadventures.

I need not labor further the point that the "new economics" provides no assurance of continuing prosperity. Nor does the history of our times, to say nothing of the long past, provide any such assurance. What history discloses is a succession of business cycles no two of which have ever been alike. The business cycle of experience is a highly variable phenomenon. If the current expansion in economic activity has been exceptionally long, it has also been less vigorous than some of its predecessors. Long though the current expansion has been, another two years will need to elapse before it can match the one that spanned World War II. Protracted expansions have been fairly common abroad, but recessions have nevertheless occurred. Japan is now in the throes of a recession while Italy is recovering from one. And in our own country, the economy is no longer displaying the balance that characterized the earlier stages of expansion. Signs of strain, such as normally occur during the upswing of the business cycle, have been multiplying, and it is only prudent to recognize them.

One of our great economic assets in the past few years has been the comparative absence of an inflationary psychology. With our wholesale price level steady, while other industrial nations were practicing inflation, we were able to increase our export surplus and thereby check the deterioration in the balance of payments. We were also able to avoid inventory speculation, over-building of industrial facilities, or a cost-price squeeze in critical manufacturing industries. Now, however, with economic exuberance quickening, the precious asset of general price stability may be going to waste. Of late, consumers have not only been spending liberally their rising incomes, but also borrowing at an increasing rate. Business firms have been borrowing heavily to enlarge their capital expenditures, which are growing at a pace that is adding to inflationary pressures and threatening a later imbalance between industrial capacity and production. State and local governments too have been sharing in the mood of prosperity by increasing both their spending and their debts. For a while, in order to facilitate Congressional acceptance of a massive tax reduction, the federal government stabilized its spending. That period lasted about eighteen months and is already at an end. A new upsurge of federal spending has gotten under way, with welfare and other civilian programs expanding rapidly at the very time that the war in Vietnam is becoming a larger burden on our material and financial resources. Under the circumstances, cost and price pressures are increasing. An inflationary psychology is again becoming a force in the market place, and this may lead to economic trouble.

To be sure, in view of the substantial progress toward economic stability that our nation has made in this generation, it would be reasonable to assume that future recessions will be milder on the average than they were before the 1940's. But if we assume more than that, our hopes may mislead our practical judgment. The forces that generate business cycles are still with us. Economic trends can shift with little or no notice. The structure of our economy, which has been changing on balance in a stabilizing direction, need not continue to do that. Military expenditures, for example, which necessarily depend on international developments, could become a larger source of instability. Our economy is not insulated against political or financial shocks from abroad. The machinery of governmental policy-making sometimes moves slowly, and the policies themselves may be inadequate or inappropriate. Rather than cling to delusions about perpetual prosperity, let us do what we can as a people, first, to prevent overheating of the economy in the immediate future, second, to strengthen our defenses against future recessions. . . .

Of course, a shift to a less liberal monetary and fiscal policy also involves risks. There is always a chance that the shift will be handled clumsily and a recession brought on in the process. Moreover, we still have too much unemployment, and the government is rightly committed to a policy of reducing it. But this objective can be pursued by dealing more vigorously with the structural causes of unemployment, rather than continuing to press expansion with monetary and fiscal tools. The theory that aggregate demand is still deficient has lost much of the plausibility that it had during earlier stages of our economic expansion. After all, the aggregate demand for labor includes the unfilled jobs as well as those that are being manned, just as the aggregate supply of labor includes the unemployed workers as well as those who have jobs. In pursuing a full employment policy, the managers of prosperity have developed the habit of comparing actual production with fragile estimates of potential output. These comparisons may mislead us. The vital relationship is between the aggregate demand for labor and the aggregate supply of labor—or, what comes to the same thing, between the number of vacant jobs and the number of the unemployed. Unfortunately, since our government has not yet taken the trouble to gather the facts, we cannot be certain what the relationship is currently between job vacancies and unemployment. We do know, however, from records on help-wanted advertising and of jobs registered with public employment offices, that job vacancies have of late been increasing rapidly, so that more attention to labor market policies can surely prove effective in reducing unemployment.

It is important, moreover, to lay plans so that a policy of full employment may be pursued in the future with less danger of inflation. For this purpose, carefully compiled and comprehensive statistics on job vacancies are essential. When the amount of unemployment is larger than the number of job vacancies at existing wages, the aggregate demand for labor is clearly insufficient to provide employment for everyone who is able, willing, and seeking to work. At such a time, a deficiency of aggregate demand exists, and a governmental policy that relies on monetary and fiscal devices to expand demand is, in principle, suited to the nation's needs. On the other hand, when the number of vacant jobs is equal to or larger than the number of the unemployed, there is no deficiency of aggregate demand. A government that is seriously concerned about inflation will not seek to expand aggregate demand at such a time, but will instead concentrate its efforts on securing better matching of the men and women who seek work with the jobs that need to be filled. By equipping ourselves in the future with the information needed to determine whether, when, or to what degree aggregate demand is deficient, we should be able to pursue the objective of full employment with less danger of causing serious inflation.

In considering the future, it is also important to keep in mind, as President Johnson wisely observed in his Economic Report of last January, that "a time of prosperity with no recession in sight is the time to plan our defenses against future dips in business activity." Re-establishment of equilibrium in the balance of payments, or better still the achievement of a moderate surplus for a year or two, would contribute to this objective. In the first place, it would give more room for manoeuvre to our monetary authorities, which they will need in the event of recession. Second, a stronger balance of payments, provided we achieve it with a minimum of protectionist devices, would enable our country to exercise more effective leadership in reforming the international monetary system to facilitate the future growth of the world economy on which our own fortunes heavily depend.

We also need to strengthen the unemployment insurance system, which aids the economy by maintaining the flow of income to individuals at the very times when income derived from production is depressed. By extending coverage to some of the millions who are still denied this protection, a larger part of the loss during recessions can be offset. This objective will be further served by providing for a more or less automatic extension of benefits during periods of abnormally large unemployment. In 1958 and again in 1961, when unemployment rose on account of the recession in business activity, the Congress passed legislation to extend temporarily the duration of benefits. In each instance, however, the supplementary benefits became available only after recovery started.

We can be quite sure that the Congress will not sit idly by when the next recession strikes. But unless the Congress acts in the near future, there is a risk that the supplementary benefits will once again come too late to serve as an effective brake on the forces of recession.

The case for stand-by legislation that would provide for extended duration of unemployment insurance at a fairly early stage of recessions is a compelling one. However, to derive maximum practical benefit from this reform, other changes in the unemployment insurance system are also required. If we permit a larger flow of benefit payments to the unemployed but do nothing else, more marginal workers will be tempted to join the labor force and some of the unemployed will tend to proceed more leisurely in searching for new jobs, thus nullifying, at least in part, the stabilizing effects of the liberalized unemployment benefits. To avoid such frustrations, the liberalization of unemployment insurance needs to be accompanied by stiffer eligibility requirements, so that seasonal and intermittent workers, who are already a heavy drain on the insurance system, may largely be kept out. The administration of insurance benefits also needs to be stiffened, so that anyone who loses his job because of misconduct, or who quits without good cause, or who refuses to take a suitable job, is in fact—not merely nominally, as is now the case in numerous localities—excluded from benefits.

In laying plans for better management of prosperity in the future, it would also be desirable to seek legislation permitting fairly prompt tax reduction if the economy needed stimulation. To achieve this objective, economists have frequently proposed that the Congress pass stand-by legislation that would empower the President to put into effect a temporary reduction of the personal income tax, within limits specified by statute, once a recession started or threatened. In 1962 President Kennedy actually recommended such a law. He knew, of course, that the Congress is accustomed to guarding jealously its power over the public purse and that delegation of any significant part of its taxing power to the President was out of the question for the present. He hoped, however, that discussion would be stimulated and that some future Congress would look more favorably on the proposal. As events turned out, the Congress did not even consider the proposal. In view of this experience, and yet feeling a need for stronger anti-recession planning, President Johnson cautiously suggested in this year's Economic Report that "the Congress could reinforce confidence that jobs and markets will be sustained by insuring that its procedures will permit rapid action on temporary income tax cuts if recession threatens." However, the President did not indicate what the procedures might be or whether the temporary tax reduction should be confined to the personal income tax. . . .

I can think of no policy that is better designed to stimulate the long-term growth of the economy than a general rule of year-by-year reductions of tax rates. That, in effect, is what Japan has done in the post-war period, and the policy has worked remarkably well in that country. That is also what we ourselves have begun to do, although our future course has recently become clouded by the renewed upsurge of federal spending. At present, as I have sought to emphasize, the economy does not need any additional fiscal stimulus; but that happy condition will not continue indefinitely. To enable our economy to flourish and advance as it both can and should, further reductions of income tax rates will be needed. In another two years or so, if the budget is again nearly in balance, the federal government should be able to embark prudently on a systematic program of annual tax reductions. In order to do that, detailed legislative plans will have to be worked out earlier, and it is not too soon to begin.

The Congress has shown a willingness to pass tax legislation that is to take effect in a series of steps. This principle can be usefully extended. Thus, legislation might provide lower tax rates over the range of both personal and corporate incomes, the reductions proceeding annually over a period of, say, five years. The legislation, however, should permit some flexibility, and one way of doing this that may be acceptable to the Congress would be to stipulate that the reduction specified for a given fiscal year will not go into effect if the President decides that the national interest would be better served without it. In that event, however, the President should be required to inform the Congress of his decision, as well as the reasons for it, several weeks before the start of the new fiscal year, so that the Congress might have the opportunity, if it so chose, of overriding the presidential decision.

Tax legislation along these lines would serve to strengthen economic incentives throughout the economic community and therefore encourage enterprise, innovation, and investment. By applying a moderate but steady stimulus to the economy, it would provide some protection against both recession and inadequate growth. By giving the President a limited discretionary authority, it would provide some protection against inflation. By committing the nation to a moderately expansionist fiscal policy, it would facilitate a more active use of general credit restraints when they are needed to protect the balance of payments. Of course, economic circumstances of a future time may require stronger fiscal measures, whether to combat recession or to combat inflation or to offset credit restraints undertaken for international reasons. On an abstract plane, such needs could be met by broadening the range of presidential discretion. But I very much doubt whether the Congress or the nation will be willing to go beyond the minimum of delegated authority that I have suggested. And, in any event, the Congress can still act on whatever tax measures it may at any particular time deem suited to the nation's needs.

A long-term tax policy such as I have sketched would also help to keep in check the growth of federal expenditures. If a five-year federal tax program is desirable, so too are five-year budgets. Much too often new governmental programs have a low initial cost, but eventually grow far beyond what the

Congress contemplated at the time of their adoption. Better control over federal expenditures would be achieved if probable costs were projected for several years, so that the Congress and the nation at large could judge more realistically the magnitude of the new undertakings together with the old. The need for prudence in federal spending is all the greater because of the pressing needs at the state and local level. Large cities across the nation are struggling with problems arising out of traffic congestion, air and water pollution, slums, and inadequate police protection. And the pressure is strong in small as well as large communities for more or better schools, roads, sanitary provisions, and welfare facilities. Lower federal tax rates would make it easier for state and local governments to finance their growing needs, and there would thus be less reason for the federal government to concern itself with activities that can usually be managed better on a decentralized basis.

The true test of any economic system is whether it betters human life. That is more than a matter of production, or prices, or employment. It involves also the freedom and the security of the individual. By and large, the American economy has met well the test of human betterment in our generation. We have preserved the essentials of economic and political freedom in a revolutionary age, when many other nations have lost or destroyed their freedom. Our economy has continued to grow in size and efficiency. The fruits of industry have been widely distributed among our people, so that poverty—as our parents once understood this condition—has been nearly eliminated in our country. We have made great strides in moderating the business cycle. Our future can be still better if we remain constantly alert to governmental economic policies, seek to improve them by being receptive to new economic ideas, and yet remain mindful of the teachings of experience about the vital importance of free markets, adequate economic incentives, and prudent management.

Humphrey, Nixon Agree on
Economic Ends, Differ on Means

H. Erich Heinemann

A broad national consensus has developed in the United States since the end of World War II on the basic goals of economic policy. This is the salient fact to emerge from a careful examination of the positions of the two major candidates on how they propose to guide the fantastic productive machine that is the United States economy—a machine currently turning out goods and services at a rate of close to $900 billion a year, or about $2.5 billion every day.

Hubert H. Humphrey and Richard M. Nixon are in fundamental agreement that full employment and stable prices would be the primary goals of their Administrations. But they differ sharply on some—but by no means all—of the means that should be used to achieve those aims.

An Administration headed by Vice President Humphrey would, to quote his term, take an "activist" line. The Democratic candidate would use the full weight of the Government's power to tax and spend, to pump money into the economic bloodstream or pull it out, as well as the prestige of the White House to influence crucial wage-and-price decisions in order to keep the economy growing close to its long-range potential.

Conversations with the men who would be Mr. Humphrey's key economic advisers give the strong impression that of the twin goals of national policy, full employment—which translated to laymen's terms means a high rate of over-all economic growth—would get by far the greater emphasis than the ending of inflation.

Mr. Nixon, on the other hand, while equally committed to growth in jobs and income, would seek to improve the performance of the economy by managing it less from Washington.

"There would be far less Federal involvement in the economy," Mr. Nixon stated, "than is currently going on in the Administration of which Mr. Humphrey is an integral part. Our country has basically a healthy economy," he added, "and I believe we will need fewer artificial restraints if we avoid an overdose of artificial Government stimulants."

Mr. Nixon has expressed this philosophy clearly in his statements calling for limits on Government regulation of the securities markets, and for an end to the mandatory restrictions on foreign investments imposed by President Johnson last January.

From The New York Times, *October 27, 1968.* © *1968 by The New York Times Company. Reprinted by permission.*

The free and healthy operation of the market, Mr. Nixon said, rather than Government controls, is of the "utmost importance."

In large measure, the divergence between the candidates is no more than should be expected from looking at their teams of advisers. The hard core of the Humphrey economic team has been recruited from among the more liberal alumni of the Kennedy and Johnson Administrations, and naturally they can be expected to try to continue in the same tradition.

Walter W. Heller, chairman of President Kennedy's Council of Economic Advisers, is the intellectual leader of a small and compact group whose chief members are Joseph A. Pechman, a Brookings Institution economist who has long been a power behind the scenes in Washington, and Charles Schultze, former director of the Bureau of the Budget, who is also at Brookings now.

Robert R. Nathan, a consulting economist and vice chairman of Americans for Democratic Action, is working practically full time as an unpaid staff co-ordinator for the entire Humphrey economic brain trust.

Mr. Nixon's advisers, by contrast, are a far less homogeneous, if far more conservative, group. They range from, on the right, Alan Greenspan, a New York economist who is working full time on the campaign, to Paul W. McCracken, a University of Michigan economics professor and former member of President Eisenhower's Council of Economic Advisers, who tends to be slightly left of center.

Mr. Nixon's devotion to the goal of reducing the Government's role in the economy cannot be questioned. But at the same time, there should be no illusion—and Mr. Nixon does not intend to suggest it—that under the Republicans the economy would be simply left to fend for itself.

Not long ago, in an important but little-noticed address, Arthur F. Burns, a Columbia University economist who was chairman of President Eisenhower's Council of Economic Advisers and who would be likely, whether in Washington or not, to play a key role in a Government headed by Mr. Nixon, spelled out what would probably be the economic philosophy of an incoming Republican Administration.

"When there is a sizable gap between the nation's actual output and its potential output at full employment," he said, "and when it seems unlikely that the private economy will soon close the gap, the Federal Government should increase its own spending or reduce taxes, but in either event make credit cheaper and more readily available."

Mr. Humphrey's advisers would have no quarrel with this formulation. Indeed, they have high respect for Mr. Burns as a practitioner of political economics.

Their argument is that a Humphrey Administration would use the tools of economic policy—the control of taxation and spending, the balancing or unbalancing of the Federal budget and the control over money and credit—more aggressively and skillfully than would the Republicans.

But the differences in economic policy are not simply those of degree. In line with his activist approach, Mr. Humphrey would ask for, or employ, several tools of economic management that Mr. Nixon rejects.

"I have suggested," Mr. Humphrey said, "that we should either (1) give the President stand-by authority to make temporary changes in personal income tax rates subject always to Congressional veto, or (2) convince Congress to install new procedures to insure quick action on Presidential proposals to activate agreed changes in tax rates."

Nixon Rejects Idea. Mr. Nixon says simply that "this is not a solution."

For his part, Mr. Humphrey is also a strong advocate of developing a mechanism for cooperative action by labor, business and Government to slow "firmly" the price-wage spiral. "My task force on inflation," the Vice President said, "recommended the establishment of an annual conference on price-wage policy composed of labor and business leaders, to hammer out a set of principles for responsible wage and price behavior."

This, of course, is simply the wage-price guidepost concept developed under President Kennedy, with the added wrinkle that the standard for wage increases (originally set at 3.2 percent in line with the long-term trend in growth of productivity) should be established by business and labor, rather than be imposed by Government.

Decision Transfers. Mr. Nixon charges that "wage-price guidelines tend to transfer too many economic decisions away from the free-enterprise system, and into the hands of the Washington planners. Moreover," he adds, "their use deals only with symptoms of the inflation problem rather than basic cures."

Over the longer run, the Republican candidate proposes a four-point fiscal strategy to deal with the growth in Federal revenues that can be expected from a growing economy:

Part of this money will be used for tax credits to stimulate the private sector to meet pressing social needs.

Some will be used for high priority Federal programs.

Some will be used for "grants to state and local governments in areas where tax credits cannot be expected to do the job."

Part of the dividend [that is, the increase in tax revenues] can also be used for outright reductions in tax rates.

Spending Restraint Backed. In his statement to *The New York Times,* Mr. Nixon is not explicit on the long-range approach that he plans to achieve price stability. His advisers, however, make plain that their strategy will be to reduce significantly the rate of increase (though not the actual total) of Federal Government spending.

Mr. Nixon says that "while I acknowledge that tax cuts and defense [spending] increases could coincide and pinch the domestic budget, I plan to avoid that situation. We will need money to meet the urban crisis, though my own emphasis on greater involvement for the private sector and local and state governments will be less costly—and much more effective—than the massive Federal spending favored by my opponent."

A Different View. Some of Mr. Nixon's advisers, however, foresee a much more severe squeeze on spending for domestic social programs than the candidate's statement implies. They argue that tax credits for individuals and private business—to encourage a wide range of social goals including slum housing, pollution control, an urban teacher corps, plus many others—[are] essential if urban decay is to be dealt with effectively.

As for the trade-off that many economists believe exists between inflation and unemployment—namely, that falling unemployment can be had only at the cost of higher prices—Mr. Nixon rejects this choice as "a false alternative."

"Either option [price stability, full employment]," he asserts, "is unacceptable when the other does not accompany it. A Nixon Administration will strive to attain both goals, concurrently. I firmly believe this can be done."

Mr. Humphrey is equally adamant in his unwillingness to accept higher unemployment as the price of an end to inflation. "I do not believe," he said, "that it is either necessary or desirable to sacrifice full employment to maintain reasonable price stability."

"A 5 percent unemployment rate," he added, "would mean the loss of $30 billion a year in the output of goods and services, as well as disastrous unemployment rates among youth, Negroes and the unskilled."

QUESTIONS FOR DISCUSSION

1. *How would you evaluate Heller's program for maintaining economic prosperity?*
2. *In what ways do Heller and Burns agree? In what ways do they disagree?*
3. *How do you respond to the question: "Are we depression-proof?"*
4. *Do you agree with Heinemann that there is really very little economic difference between the major political parties?*

What If Peace Breaks Out?

Just as recent American political and social history cannot be understood apart from an examination of the crucible of Vietnam, the functioning of the contemporary national economy is similarly intricately tied to the war. An appreciation of the formation and implementation of recent fiscal and monetary policy and the direction of price, output, and employment movements requires the admission that things have not been quite "normal" since the escalation of the Vietnam War in about the middle of 1965. Whatever the tortured political and moral arguments over the "rightness" of the war, the economic estimate of its effect at home must be negative. War and threats of war are, of course, nothing new in recent American history. Since 1941, the United States has spent over $1 trillion (that's a one with twelve zeros after it) on defense expenditures. Wars in the past have even had a certain stimulating effect upon a lagging economy as in the cases of World Wars I and II and the Korean conflict. However, the Vietnam build-up came not at a time of economic decline but during a boom that was already nearly three years old. The additional expenditures required for war, amounting annually to between $35 and $50 billion, created considerable economic problems.

As we know from our study of Keynesian analysis, the creation of additional aggregate demand (say from this additional government war expenditure of $35 to $50 billion) at a time of nearly full employment will create an inflationary push. The problem from the government's point of view can only be resolved by taking offsetting actions, such as increasing taxation or using a tight money policy to hold down private sector expansion, or lowering government spending in other areas, or some combination of these policies. All these policies were tried in varying degrees as the solid business boom of the mid-1960's began to tail off into a fleshy inflationary expansion. Unemployment fell to all-time lows but prices edged forward and income taxes were hiked. Aggregate output grew but the prosperity was not shared by all industries as credit restriction had differential market effects. The federal government was able to obtain appropriations for the war effort but only after reducing its domestic spending, reducing the effectiveness of its social welfare programs. This impact on domestic programs and the war's effect on the nation's balance of international payments are noted later in the readings.

The Vietnam War did not end the long boom of the 1960's but it did wrench the structure of the national economy. The following articles discuss this wrenching effect. The first article, by the Committee for Economic Development, tends to see the effect as quite temporary and easily overcome by the proper reconversion program when the war ends. The second article is more critical of the economy's performance, raising questions about our ability and our willingness to rebound from the effect of the war. Both articles, however, agree that the Vietnam War cannot be ignored in a contemporary study of how the national economy functions.

Problems of Transition from War to Peace

Committee for Economic Development

There will be no shortage of valuable uses for the resources set free by a reduction of defense spending. However, there may be a problem of activating these new claims on resources at a rate parallel to the rate of their release. It is important that the new claims come into the market fast enough to absorb the released resources without recession and unemployment, but not so fast as to stimulate inflationary forces.

THE GENERAL PROBLEMS

The main difficulty stems from inability to foresee when the decline of defense spending will begin and how fast it will proceed. This creates the

From *Committee for Economic Development,* The National Economy and the Vietnam War (New York: *Committee for Economic Development, 1968*).

danger that the necessary responses will be initiated too late and will operate too slowly to prevent a dip in the economy during a period of transition. Moreover, the policy requirements will be quite different if the economy is then experiencing inflation than if it is in the doldrums. Therefore, we cannot prescribe a blueprint and time schedule of economic actions to be taken. Flexibility will be necessary but this should not inhibit advance planning.

In some respects, maintaining a high level of employment in the face of a substantial decline in military spending is likely to be more difficult than achieving the same result when there are contractive forces in the private economy. The postwar transition will involve a bigger and more sudden shift in the composition of output, and more transfer of workers among locations and industries. Therefore, a higher pressure of demand for labor, with more job vacancies, may be needed to keep unemployment at a low level.

The problem of effecting a smooth transition will be easier if the decline is spread evenly over the two-year period, or if most of it comes in the latter part, than if most of it occurs in the first year or six months. From this standpoint the decline of the defense expenditures may be misleading. As was seen during the build-up period, the economic impact came before government expenditures increased, as defense contractors received orders and began work before payments were made. Similarly on the way down, government expenditures are likely to decline more slowly than the work done by contractors. Also, there may be quick and important although indirect effects as businesses try to cut down their inventories and release workers. Unless stimulating measures are ready to be taken promptly, even the leveling out of government defense spending and the anticipation of a decline are likely to cause businesses to try to cut down their inventories, and this may be the channel through which the first strong impact will be felt.

As we have suggested, the cutback of defense spending may be nearly as large, relative to the GNP, as after the Korean War. At that time two-thirds of the decline in government defense spending came in the first year. We are unable to measure the post-Korean War decline in the inventories of defense producers, but if we combine defense spending and total inventory investment, all of the decline came in five quarters, from the second quarter of 1953 to the third quarter of 1954, and 60 percent of the decline came in the first two quarters. It seems to us only prudent to be prepared for the possibility that the impact of the post-Vietnam letdown will come early and will be concentrated in a short period.

It may turn out that even with advance preparation the direct effects of government action to sustain the economy will not be felt during most of the period when defense-connected production is declining. There are probably few steps, if any, that the government can take which will have a significant direct effect on aggregate demand for output within a period of six months from the date of the decision. But still the indirect, psychological effects can be prompt and important. General recognition that the government is prepared with strong measures to support total demand and will take them promptly, even though their direct effect may be delayed, will help to prevent a cutback in private spending, especially in private inventory investment, in anticipation of a period of economic slack.

To make clear its intention to support total demand, it would be helpful for the government to review and bring up to date a shelf of public programs deferred because of the war. Readiness to put these programs into effect will improve confidence in our ability to support total demand if necessary. Local governments could follow suit with respect to projects that have been postponed because of high interest rates.

Prompt reduction of wartime tax increases and monetary expansion are the flexible and adjustable means for sustaining aggregate demand in the face of an unpredictable but possibly rapid release of labor and product from the military effort. Federal spending cannot serve this function equally well, because the decision-making process is too slow and is properly dominated by considerations other than the support of aggregate demand. Therefore, we do not propose a "crash" program of federal spending when the war ends. We repeat, however, that the government should have a shelf of expenditure requirements deferred because of the war, and should be prepared to reinstate programs previously deferred. This is especially important now when the prospect includes a possibility—the end of the Vietnam War—which would permit a significant change in the level of nondefense spending. Such studies would enable the government to make expenditure decisions more quickly when the change in military requirements comes. However, these decisions should be made in terms of the value and efficiency of particular programs, and through the normal Administration and congressional processes. . . .

THE MORE SPECIFIC PROBLEMS OF ADJUSTMENT

Reduction in Armed Forces. In the middle of 1968 there are expected to be about 3.5 million persons in the armed forces, as compared with about 2.7 million at the middle of 1965. Probably a good guess is that after the war the armed forces would revert to a level around 2.7 million. This would mean, in time, an increase in the civilian labor force of about 800,000. However, this would not occur all at once, not only because the decline of the armed forces will occur over some period, such as two years, but also because perhaps a third of the men released will go to school before entering the labor force.

The addition to the civilian labor force resulting from the decline of the armed forces will be heavily concentrated in the category of males aged 20 to 24. Relative to the existing size of even this specific category, about

5 million in 1966, the addition is not large. However, this is a category in which the rate of unemployment is already higher than the rate for the labor force as a whole—4.6 percent compared to 3.5 percent in January 1968. Therefore, the reduction of the armed forces may tilt the composition of the labor force in a direction which adds to the unemployment problem. This problem will be not only, and probably not mainly, a "veterans'" problem. The veterans will probably be better qualified for employment than the average of their age group, as a result of experience and training in the armed forces as well as of education obtained after discharge under the provisions of the G.I. Bill. They will get special attention from the Employment Service. Many of them will have re-employment rights; about half of the recently separated veterans had such rights. The Defense Department is experimenting with a program to provide training in civilian jobs for military personnel within one to six months of their discharge. This program seems very promising and should be generalized if the present tests confirm that promise.

Private Employment Attributable to Vietnam War. According to a recent study, in the fiscal year 1967 about 1 million persons were in private employment attributable to the Vietnam War. This was about 1.7 percent of total private employment. The number would presumably be higher in fiscal 1969, but the rates would probably not exceed 2 percent of total private employment. If generally high employment is maintained, with total nonwar demand for labor rising to absorb the workers released from war production as well as the growth in the civilian labor force, there will be no decline of employment in an industry where the release from war production and the rise of nonwar employment are both average. Even where there is a heavier involvement in the war, and some net decline of employment in the change-over, there may be no serious problem for workers, because voluntary retirements and quits will permit a substantial reduction in force in the period of a year or two without requiring layoffs and involuntary unemployment.

Thus, if there are problems they are likely to arise where industries have substantially more than the average proportion of their employment attributable to the Vietnam War, located in markets where they account for a large part of total employment, or using skills that are highly specialized to their industry. These industries can be readily identified. According to the study cited above, in fiscal 1967 there were seven industries in which employment attributable to the Vietnam War accounted for 5 percent or more of total employment. While employment attributable to the war will be higher in fiscal 1969, it seems unlikely that there would be a significant problem of adjustment for any industry not included on this list, although this does not rule out the possibility of difficulty for isolated firms in other industries. . . .

As might be expected, the critical industries are ordnance and aircraft. They have about one-fourth of the private employment attributable to the Vietnam War, and such employment accounts for a large part of their total employment.

Most employment in ordnance production is in localities where ordnance employment is a small part of total employment. There are no large or even medium-sized labor markets that are heavily dependent upon ordnance employment. Moreover, the industry does not use highly specialized skills which are valueless in other industries. While it seems unlikely that the industry could avoid a significant decline in employment after the war, most of the employees released from the industry should find other employment opportunities in their present localities.

The situation of the aircraft industry is rather different. A large part of aircraft employment is in localities where aircraft employment is a large part of total employment, and some localities of substantial size are heavily dependent upon the aircraft industry. In 1966, three areas which accounted for almost 40 percent of total employment in the industry were importantly involved. . . .

Undoubtedly the degree of dependence in these areas on aircraft industry employment will be higher in 1968. Moreover, the industry employs a large number of people, including engineers, whose skills would be much less valuable in other industries. On the other hand, the aircraft industry is relatively much less involved in production for the Vietnam War than is the ordnance industry. It has the prospect of a large and growing market for civilian aircraft as well as for an increase in other government purchases for the continuing defense program and for the space program, which have been held back during the war. Beyond this, the industry has the managerial and technical capability to engage in a variety of activities other than aircraft production, and it is exploring the new markets which its capability could serve. Thus a cutback in aircraft employment is not certain, despite the high proportion of its output which now goes for the war. It would be unrealistic to think that there will be major difficulties for the firms and workers in the industry.

LOCAL RESPONSIBILITIES

The prospect of transitional difficulties in these and possibly other industries does not necessarily call for a new federal program to deal with them. Both the responsibility and the capacity for meeting the problem are primarily with the firms and workers directly involved and with the communities in which they are located. The local communities are not in the condition of the classic chronically depressed area, where the productive facilities are obsolete, the workers old, unadaptable, or unskilled, and the community services run down. If a community needs to attract new industries, nothing but the local community can offer the decisive attractions. We emphasize this point because businesses, communities, and workers should not interpret discussion of federal measures for adjustment to mean that the federal government is going to make the adjustment for them.

Attention must be called to one area in which advance preparation for the absorption of workers can be most helpful. Numerous estimates have suggested that the demand for construction, and therefore for construction workers, would rise substantially in a fully employed economy after the Vietnam War. It will be very important for a smooth transition and for improving the opportunities of men now consigned to casual or unskilled employment to increase the supply of construction workers. This will require removal of union restrictions on entry, abolition of racial discrimination, and enlarged training and apprenticeship programs, which might in part be provided by the Defense Department for service men nearing release from the armed forces.

Where there is reason to suspect that the local community is vulnerable to a cutback of the defense program, it is a responsibility of the community leadership, public and private, to verify as well as it can whether this is probably the case. For example, the state of Connecticut's Department of Labor has estimated that only 40,000 of its 500,000 manufacturing jobs are in Vietnam-related defense industries. Where preliminary investigation suggests that there may be a problem, an organization of the public and private leadership should be created, if it does not already exist, to prepare for it. In most cases the first step would be an evaluation of the conditions in the community which would affect the possibility of expanding existing industries and of attracting new industry if that should prove necessary and desirable. The techniques for making such an evaluation are now well known. . . .

On the basis of such study, the community can decide tentatively whether in the event of a serious cutback its strategy will be to try to expand existing industry or attract new industry, and if so how, or whether it should adjust to a lower level of employment and activity. The second alternative is always accepted reluctantly, but it is sometimes the better one, and if so that should be known early.

Where the Department of Defense is itself a major employer and owner of facilities its cooperation in timing the release of workers and property can contribute much to the smoothness of the transition. The Department's performance in this regard has, we believe, been good. Moreover, in such cases the Department, through its Office of Economic Adjustment, can be an invaluable source to the local community of advice derived from experience in other areas. Also the Office can provide information about the services available from other federal agencies and arrange contacts with them.

Where the Department of Defense is not the direct employer it is still possible for a community affected by defense cutbacks to find out the full range of government aids that are available to it. The Economic Development Administration of the Department of Commerce is the central source of such information. As termination begins, its capability of making such information known, especially its field offices, should be strengthened.

Existing programs can be helpful in the postwar transition. It should be noted that none of these programs was in existence at the end of World War II except the Employment Service. The country is far better equipped to deal with the transition than it has ever been before. The main kinds of Federal assistance a community may be able to obtain are:

1. The assistance of the United States Employment Service in informing workers of available jobs, including a special program for registering and classifying workers involved in mass layoffs.

2. Training programs initiated by the Department of Labor to adapt workers to available jobs.

3. In areas of substantial unemployment, or where substantial unemployment is expected to result from a defense cutback:

(a) Financial assistance for economic planning,

(b) Loans to businesses unable to raise funds privately,

(c) Advances for public works planning,

(d) Loans to permit the advance acquisition of land for public works,

(e) Grants for public works,

(f) Preferential treatment in disposal of surplus federal property,

(g) Loans to local development corporations.

4. Loans for small businesses.

5. Grants to assist comprehensive urban development planning programs.

We would not expect most of these programs to be called upon in most cases of community adjustment. Mainly the programs are designed to deal with problems that would persist for a long time, so that even rather slow-moving measures may yet make a contribution.

The activity which could be most helpful in speeding up the normal process of adjustment is the United States Employment Service. Improvement of the Employment Service has been badly needed for a long time.

We conclude from this review of the probable size and character of the readjustment which may follow termination of a Vietnam War of the present size, and from our review of the adjustment programs now available, that no crisis effort will be called for. Since companies, communities, and individuals most likely to be affected have adequate guidelines to follow if they take the initiative to undertake planning, we urge that they exercise such initiative. Aids from government exist, although some temporary expansion may be needed as defense cutbacks occur. In our opinion, these observations are not complacent but realistic. They take into account what we have learned from earlier studies and experience.

The transition problems we have been discussing would be greatly eased, of course, if the recommendations . . . for immediate fiscal restraint are implemented.

Can the Freedom Budget Solve Our Problems?

Horst Brand

Those who believe that the American economy can provide the means both to fight the war in Vietnam and wage massive attack on poverty at home must also believe that economic resources can be shifted from private to public purposes, without affecting privileged positions and vested interests and possibly without jeopardizing the very sources which under American capitalism generate growth. For such a shift would, at the least, require heavy increases in taxation, which would weaken private investment and consumption and strengthen the public nondefense sector. They also must read into available unemployment statistics the view that the utilization of manpower is running below optimum levels, and must infer that enough "slack" exists to permit, given the "will," a more energetic attack on domestic problems.

President Johnson's timidity in requesting even a puny surtax which would have reduced personal income by 1 percent, and the stubborn refusal by Congress to enact the request when it was finally made, dispose of the first assumption as being simply apolitical. The second assumption is weakened by the record-low jobless rate among adult males (the chief repository of knowledge and skills), large numbers of whom have been absorbed either by the military or in defense and closely linked capital-goods industries—and who are thus unavailable for tasks of social reconstruction.

Those, on the other hand, who insist that it is the war in Vietnam which prevents effective dealing with problems at home are guilty of either or both of two errors: One, they imply that the end of the Vietnam War will free the resources necessary to wage peace at home, which may be the case but does not follow with compelling logic: the end of the Korean War was suc-

From Horst Brand, "Vietnam and the U.S. Economy," Dissent, March–April 1968.

ceeded by recession in the economy and virtual stagnation (even the threat of regression) in social legislation. Two, they read into the "war" on poverty a promise of acceleration which was never made, and they ignore the fact that until sometime early last year, the means devoted to antipoverty programs continued to increase at about the same stingy rate that had obtained prior to the escalation of the Vietnam conflict. The expansion of the defense sector has itself contributed to yielding revenue required to sustain domestic programs: between the second quarter of 1965—just prior to escalation—and the third quarter of 1967, military expenditures rose by 49 percent, and their rise represented one-fifth of the increase in the national product over the $2\frac{1}{4}$-year period. Government sources estimate that about one-fourth of defense spending returns as tax revenue.

Both camps proceed from a common assumption, i.e., that growth of the American economy can be taken for granted (this I shall not argue), and that gains in federal revenue generated by growth can more or less freely be allocated among armaments, social purposes, and private consumption via tax cuts. Thus the disposal of the "fiscal dividend" has come to be seen as the key to the elimination of social ills. Institutional change appears no longer to be a prerequisite for that. Indeed, the structure of the economy and society which generates the dividend can be, perhaps must be, left untouched—it is the goose that lays the golden eggs.

No doubt, I have oversimplified the grouping of existing points of view on current economic possibilities of dealing with social problems. A third point of view has been espoused by Seymour Melman, who attacks military priorities as part of a "policy system" which he altogether rejects. He proposes an alternative policy system, structured so as to emphasize social priorities on a worldwide scale. My sympathies are close to Melman, but his "policy systems" are a technocratic construct lacking a social content on which political pressures could operate.

Here, my concern will be briefly to contrast the Freedom Budget, which is broadly representative of current left-of-center thinking (and to which I allude in the first paragraph of this article), with the actual tendencies in the disposition of the fiscal dividend.

Sponsored as it was by persons of divergent views, the Freedom Budget necessarily represents a consensus. Its objectives are readily reconcilable with a Democratic party platform. Since, however, representatives of labor as well as socialists are prominently associated with the Freedom Budget, it strikes the critical reader by its studied political neutrality: poverty, inadequate health, education, and welfare services, and other evils are documented in some detail, but their *causes* are nowhere identified in terms of the social and economic institutions which breed them. Hence, no institutional reforms are proposed by the Budget. The Federal Budget—"the main instrument of national economic policy"—is the only mechanism which would deal with the "priorities" set forth in the Freedom Budget. Its authors know, of course, that allocations in the Federal Budget are the result of political pressures; the Federal Budget reflects these pressures, and is not in itself an agent of institutional change or social planning.

The authors of the Freedom Budget eschew, however, all suggestions of either. Nor do they propose any *shift* in financial resources within the Federal Budget to provide funds for larger social programs. They would rather draw (presumably by way of taxation whose rate structure would remain unchanged) on the annual *increment* in the national product, "the economic growth dividend," which is expected to amount, cumulatively, to $2.3–$2.4 trillion over the 1965–75 decade. The authors declare that "even those who are already affluent or wealthy would not be penalized in any way in order to accomplish [the] great priority purposes" of the Freedom Budget, and while there are occasional references to inequality in the distribution of income, no proposals to eliminate it are made. In any case, the references are not functional elements of the exposition.

By insisting that major social ills can be eliminated without disturbing the traditional balance between private and public sector, the Freedom Budget avoids the question of whether that "balance" does not itself engender or perpetuate those ills. Yet, it would not be hard to show, for example, that corporate control over prices and capital investment vitiates wage policies favoring low-income earners, crimps funds for adequate pensions for all, cuts into manpower and material resources required for public services, and virtually precludes rational regional and intraregional planning. Maybe it *is* true that poverty can be eliminated without interfering with the existing private-public balance, but the Freedom Budget cites no historical example which demonstrates that it has been done. Relatively decent working conditions in the factories came about because trade union struggles changed the "balance" between labor and industry and helped incorporate the changed balance in law. Analogously, major extensions of the "welfare state" in the United States are much more likely to develop through organized struggle (whatever the form) than by asking for crumbs off the tables of the affluent and assuring them at the same time that they need not fear for their privileges.

In the absence of a shift in the relationship of political forces, the dominant interests of the American body politic have first call on the fiscal dividend (which is what the Freedom Budget's "economic growth dividend" is all about)—and in fact they do and did, with the explicit support of the Johnson and predecessor Administrations. The tax cuts made in 1964, worth $19 billion to individuals and corporations, were and remain exemplary of the use of the dividend: the cuts were meant not only to stimulate the business sector but to enlarge its share of economic activity as against the government sector. That was at the time the clear mandate of Chairman Mills of the House Ways and Means Committee, endorsed by Presidents Kennedy and Johnson. According to Secretary of the Treasury Fowler, President Kennedy "rebutted any notion that rising federal revenue in the years ahead means that federal outlays should rise in proportion to such revenue increase. . . . [He asserted that] as the economy climbs toward full employment, a substantial part of the revenue increases must go toward eliminating the deficit."

President Johnson spoke in a similar vein when he signed the 1964 tax reduction into law, and Fowler has cited numerous examples of Johnson's continued fiscal conservatism—a conservatism that is not merely opportune but real enough to anyone who compares Johnson's talk of Great Society programs with recent cutbacks in social welfare programs—programs which had been skimpy to begin with. Furthermore, says Fowler, "the first item on the President's post-Vietnam agenda" is the possibility and priority of tax reduction—not any step-up in antipoverty programs.

That part of the increment in federal revenue which has not been, or is not to be, absorbed by tax cuts has been and is predominantly applied to past, present, and future wars. Between fiscal 1962—the first in nine years when a Democratic Administration had full control of the purse strings—and fiscal 1968 . . . federal tax revenues will have totaled, cumulatively, an estimated $700 billion, and deficits (which are additions to the public debt) about $44 billion. Of the available $744 billion, 80 percent or $593 billion were spent on defense, space, international affairs, interest on public debt (incurred mainly for war financing), and veterans' benefits. The share of all domestic programs comprised 20 percent or $150 billion—which included many expenditures that cannot be regarded as social welfare measures.

If we look only at the *increment* in tax revenue and in the deficit—$47 billion between 1962 and 1968—the relative share of domestic programs is 28 percent or $13 billion. This is the sum which became available for new or expanded domestic or civilian programs. Over the same period, the increment in the total national product will have amounted to about $250 billion. Thus one nickel out of every dollar of the economic growth dividend of the past six years will have flowed into such programs—a relationship that may or may not change in the years ahead, but that cannot be altogether ignored when appraising the prospects of even so modest a proposal as the Freedom Budget.

If government policy thus aims at the deliberate strengthening of the private sector by means of tax reductions (when these are feasible), and if defense spending continues high or rises further, then the very availability of the fiscal dividend on the scale envisioned by the Freedom Budget is in question.

It is of more immediate political importance here, however, that the Johnson Administration has brought disrepute to the New Economics, which teaches that government expenditures should exceed tax revenues by an amount roughly in proportion to the magnitude of those resources which the private sector fails to absorb. Unwilling to intensify conservative opposition to its domestic programs or to heighten the controversy over an unpopular war, the Johnson Administration only belatedly asked for . . . a tax boost. It has had to finance the war by enormous deficits. These deficits have, on the one hand, failed to reduce unemployment significantly below 4 percent—an outcome predicted by many economists who have viewed much of present unemployment as stemming from the changing skill structure of the economy, rather than from inadequate final demand.

On the other hand, the deficits have added to the strong upward pressure on prices which stepped-up war production has engendered. Not only have price rises prevented real incomes from advancing (at the end of 1967, real weekly take-home pay of a worker with a family was all of 50¢ higher than the year before); they also raise the costs of public services, thus further straining the fiscal capacity of sub-federal jurisdictions and intensifying the inadequacy of such services. Moreover, the large federal deficits, financed as they have been in capital markets already heavily drawn on by business and state and local units, have been a major cause of increases in interest rates.

The Federal Reserve, frequently the scapegoat of easy-money advocates, has gingerly avoided attracting criticism. It has done what it could and under its charter must do to facilitate government finance. Not monetary policy but a politically cowardly fiscal policy has lifted interest rates to levels where they have throttled the flow of capital into residential construction. In consequence, home and apartment vacancy rates have declined close to early postwar lows, and the incipient housing shortage has made the country's ghettos even more airtight than they already were.

To liberals and leftists, deficits may seem a painless way of helping to finance desirable social programs and of obtaining full employment. To Chairman Mills and his like, however, deficits do not merely serve as a pretext to compel cutbacks in domestic programs. Mills, after all, represents a society in which "balancing the books" is inherently virtuous, and a government deficit defines a social disequilibrium, signaling a possible shift in the relationships of power in favor of the state.

According to Chairman Mills, the threatening disequilibrium must be restored not only by tax increases—on the contrary; tax increases unaccompanied by "real and significant expenditure reductions and firmer controls would have a serious long-range impact upon the direction of our economy. I fear it would mean bigger and bigger government with a smaller and smaller range of freedom of activity for the private sector. I do not intend to be a party to this kind of program" (*New York Times,* November 21, 1967).

This is not ideological phraseology but articulation of a conservative position. Yet, the validity of this position seems hardly more questionable than that of those left-of-center liberals who view the fiscal dividend as a politically neutral instrument which obviates institutional change as the means of rooting out social ills.

The conservative stance chooses to ignore the sustaining force of government spending and of fiscal policy in the economy. The left-of-center position, welcoming the greater role of government, generally remains silent, at least in its programmatic statements, about the frequently observed effects of some kinds of large-scale government expenditures in aggravating the evils which social programs are expected to remedy. Examples include agricultural price supports, which have contributed to capital intensity on farms, and thus to the exodus of the rural poor to urban slums; or the highway and urban renewal programs, which in many instances have tended to worsen the condition of the urban poor.

Finally, defense programs, far in excess of demonstrably rational requirements, typify the tendency of modern capitalism to apply its rich pool of technology and talent to unproductive and outright destructive purposes. Over the long term, this tendency deprives the forces of social reconstruction of needed moral and physical resources.

The Freedom Budget, thoughtful in estimating required funds for a wide variety of social improvements which would account for somewhat more than two-fifths of projected 1975 federal outlays, abdicates responsibility ("makes no attempt at independent judgment") in regard to the other three-fifths that are to be devoted to defense, space, and international programs. Its assumptions about these programs involve a gain of $23 billion between fiscal 1967 and fiscal 1975 when the war in Vietnam is likely to have ended. Since the assumptions are only implicit, they cannot be debated, but it should be noted that few qualified observers share them.

"Many careful projections of defense expenditures show a basic stability for the coming decade," writes Murray Weidenbaum, who is an outstanding expert in the field (in *Prospects for Reallocating Public Resources,* American Enterprise Institute, page 56). Whether or not such projections are more "realistic" than those of the Freedom Budget, on the surface they strengthen the Freedom Budget's case that resources for the elimination of poverty and other ills are ample. Its unrationalized defense-space projections do, however, underline its excessive concern with not upsetting the "traditional balance between federal actions and other public and private actions." Yet if this "balance" results in ever larger defense-space outlays, it implies a political line-up not dissimilar to the one prevailing at present—one that is hostile to making the resources available on which the realization of the Freedom Budget's objectives depends.

The political implications of a large, powerful defense-space complex cannot be discussed here. Its economic importance as an autonomous source of economic "growth" is now such as to make even partial reconversion, were that contemplated, quite difficult. This is shown by an examination of the direct effects of defense spending on employment. In mid-1965, 9 percent of total payroll employment was directly attributable to defense spending; by mid-1967 the ratio had risen to more than 10 percent. Of the 3.2-million rise in total employment over these two years, roughly one-third was due to the Vietnam build-up. Considering the indirect effects of expanding defense employment, there can be no question that the boom of the past two years had its source in that build-up; according to calculations by Daniel Suits of the University of Michigan, the unemployment rate would exceed 7 percent but for Vietnam. Only about 5 percent of all jobs in private industry (or close to 3 million) are currently directly generated by defense, but in industries where value added and capital investment are highest, the relevant proportions are considerably greater. In manufacturing, nearly 11 percent of employment is defense-generated, while in services, the proportion is less than 3 percent.

Defense activities employ relatively large numbers of skilled and semi-skilled workers, and relatively small numbers of unskilled and service workers. Numbering 1.9 million in 1967, the semiskilled and skilled represented 16 percent of all workers in their occupations, or 44 percent of total defense employment (but only 32 percent of *total* industry employment). Such workers have experienced the sharpest job gains due to Vietnam. For many, the end of Vietnam will raise major problems of re-employment, arising in part from the slowdown in the economy, in part from the difficulty of transferring skills.

There is no backlog today of urgent consumer needs or of capital invest-ment requirements. And in a society that of necessity must seek to expand job and investment opportunities in services, the men and women made unem-ployed by the end of the Vietnam War will offer experience in goods-production work or in war-oriented research and design. We must remember that we are speaking only of the end of the Vietnam conflict, which would present difficulties, although not insuperable ones.

The American economy would not, however, be able to cope with dis-armament on any larger scale; it remains dependent, as a matter of indisputable fact, on heavy defense expenditures, and it possesses at present neither the "flexibility" nor the institutional means to abandon any significant portion of its military-industrial apparatus. Comparisons with the aftermath of World War II would be sorely misleading. So would comparisons with other industrial countries, many of which are beginning to face problems of structural unemploy-ment and insufficient investment outlets with which the United States has had to grapple since the mid-fifties.

There has never been much doubt on the part of the Left about the productive power of capitalism—leftists were the first to note and analyze it. A major preoccupation of the Left, however, has traditionally been the distribu-tion of wealth and income, and its relationship to politics. With steady economic growth, high levels of employment, and an annual fiscal dividend being evi-dently assured, that preoccupation seems to have become outmoded.

But it turns out that employment remains contingent in good measure upon continued spending on armaments and on a rising level of private consumption, and that the conservative forces which base themselves on such an economy thus become major claimants to the fiscal dividend. Hence, we cannot count on its automatic availability. Social advance remains a painful struggle in the realm of politics. It must indeed concern itself with broadening the base of the welfare state; but its strategic objective must be to change the institutional alignments which lie at the root of social evils—including that greatest of evils, war.

QUESTIONS FOR DISCUSSION

1. *What are some of the basic adjustment problems which the ending of the Vietnam War poses for the national economy?*
2. *How would the Committee for Economic Development solve these problems?*
3. *What is meant by the "Freedom Budget"?*
4. *How does Brand see the "transition" after Vietnam?*
5. *Which analysis do you feel more adequately describes the problems that peace poses for the national economy?*

America and the World

PART FIVE

How Can We Solve
Our Gold Problem?

The "balance of payments" is an accounting procedure to measure international transactions between one country and the rest of the world, reflecting the movement of goods, services, loans, gifts, and gold. Until quite recently, gold has served as the balancing item in this system of international accounts with gold being paid by nations with deficits in their other accounts to creditor nations. Beginning in 1958, the United States began to suffer a persistent and worsening drain on its gold stock and creditors began to demand payment on accounts in gold. Between 1958 and 1966, the United States gold stock fell from $23 billion to less than $10 billion. A number of factors have been pointed to as villains in this "gold drain," among them are: (1) a comparatively rising volume of foreign imports over United States exports (although the USA has still a trade surplus), (2) increased outward flow of private capital investment overseas, (3) United States government grants and loans overseas, and (4) military expenditures abroad.

Of special importance to the growing problem were private capital outflows and military spending. Partially successful attempts were made by the government to induce businesses to curtail their profitable overseas investment; but, as the Vietnam War grew hotter through 1966 and 1967, overseas military spending grew rapidly, accelerating the payments problem and putting great pressure on the United States' gold stock. Meanwhile, trouble was increased by the steadily deteriorating import-export balance of the United States. In 1964, the United States had a $7.8 billion cushion of exports over imports. By 1968 this had fallen to less than $1.5 billion, and some economists were talking about a trade deficit within a few years, especially if the inflationary pressure within the country was not soon halted. This, of course, meant, as long as an international gold exchange standard was maintained, an end to United States international liquidity and, given the dominance of the United States in world trade, an end to world liquidity.

By 1968, the problem had reached its peak and a series of international conferences were called by monetary authorities. The following articles explore the agreements finally made to deal with the problem. They represent differing points of view. The first sees more crises for America. The second one holds a more optimistic view. Both see the solution attempted in 1968 as only temporary, with the problem of international payments sure to rise again.

The Sieve of Gold

Michael Hudson

It may seem strange that the huge power of America should be thwarted by a crisis over the depletion of gold, a primitive human fetish. But however irrational the financial power of gold may appear, it is less irrational than the power of paper. Paper currency depends upon faith in the stability of its value, and hence faith in the economic strength and wisdom of the country that issues it. Gold, of course, requires no such faith. The movement out of paper into gold is a protective measure on the part of people who are experiencing a loss of faith in the purchasing power of the paper.

Until 1968 Europe had, in an important respect, borne the major cost of supporting world confidence that America's overseas military expenditures would not impair the value of America's currency. Europe did this by holding onto the dollars thrown off by these expenditures rather than cashing them in for United States gold. The Europeans had protested since 1964 against absorbing these dollars, and finally, with the gold crisis, they drew the line against continuing thus to finance United States military policy. America was left to pay the costs itself, but they were beyond its means. And at that point it became clear that the United States could not continue its current rate of overseas military spending—much less increase it—without bringing on a complete collapse of confidence in its currency.

From Ramparts, *May 1968. Copyright Ramparts Magazine, Inc., 1968. By permission of the Editors.*

The breaking point of America's financial power has long been near and would soon have been reached even if there had not been a war in Vietnam. The tension between our military and economic power abroad and our living standards at home was too great to have been sustained indefinitely.

This tension was withstood through seventeen years of deficits only because the United States entered the postwar years riding on a tremendous cushion of gold. This cushion was one of the major factors permitting the spectacular expansion and consolidation of worldwide American interests after the Second World War. Throughout the crucial years for the development of United States Cold War policies, we had a hoard of gold so huge that balance-of-payments deficits were of no concern to us at all.

The rapid growth in American gold holdings began in January 1934. At that time the United States gold stock stood at $7.4 billion, an amount equal to 35 percent of world monetary gold reserves. By 1938 the gold stock had increased to $12.7 billion, or 55 percent of world reserves. This inflow was not the result of "normal" economic conditions, however, nor was it the result of any trade surplus. Rather, it resulted from the fact that European individuals and corporations, recognizing the threat posed by Hitler, transferred their funds into United States securities, a transfer which was accompanied by an outflow of gold from European central banks to the United States. Most of the additions to the United States gold stock during this period came from Britain, France and the Netherlands.

So extraordinary was this inflow that at the time the United States government acted to "sterilize" it so as to avoid its inflationary potential. This sterilization was done by adding the new gold to the Treasury's own account rather than to that of the Federal Reserve System, so that it would not tend to swell the reserves of the banking system. By this action, Europe's gold was financially segregated from that gold earned earlier by the United States in its "normal" international transactions—though it all belonged to the United States regardless of accounting procedures.

This gold inflow continued through 1939–40 as Europe became more and more dependent on America for its supply of armaments following Hitler's invasions of Czechoslovakia and Austria. And though America did grant its allies lend-lease credits after its entry into the war in 1941, Europe continued to lose gold.

By year-end 1945, the United States government possessed 59 percent of world monetary gold reserves: $20.1 billion in gold (including United States Treasury and Federal Reserve accounts and disregarding gold shipped to America by other governments merely for safekeeping). In the dissipation of this gold during the Cold War years, the United States was not so much living off its savings as squandering the inheritance left by the demise of prewar European power.

Peace returned. But the specter of Europe's post-World War I hyper-inflation and economic crises afforded the United States a warning of the political instability which might repeat itself should an impoverished Europe be left to reconstruct its devastated economy with only its own meager resources. Clearly, the United States was the only nation at that time capable of filling Europe's reconstruction needs. But just as clearly, under the gold standard—according to which balance-of-payments deficits were settled in gold bullion—the massive infusion of American goods needed for reconstruction would have the effect of utterly depleting Europe's monetary reserves, thus also creating a massive inflation. This would have had obvious political repercussions in view of the strength of Europe's Communist parties, especially in France, Italy and Greece.

It was to avoid such a monetary crisis and still supply Europe with adequate reconstruction resources that the United States took the lead in 1944 in forming the International Monetary Fund (IMF) and the International Bank for Reconstruction and Development (IBRD), or World Bank.

Their establishment was marked by a controversy highly political in nature. At the meetings, held at Bretton Woods, Britain put forth John Maynard Keynes' plan to create an international unit-of-account, an international paper money—not unlike the Special Drawing Rights which are now being established at United States insistence. This plan called for the creation of "paper gold" for Europe to use in settlement of its balance-of-payments deficits with the United States and other suppliers of reconstruction materials. This paper credit would have been accepted by the United States (and other surplus nations) in lieu of gold. At the end of the reconstruction process, according to this plan, the United States would be left with international reserves comprising both gold and paper credits, while Europe would be left with virtually no growth or loss in its net reserves, but with a massive accumulation of real capital and a viable economic base. Through this stratagem, therefore, Europe could have retained what meager gold stocks it still possessed, meanwhile financing its reconstruction with a heavy importation of American goods (much as today, America is asking to finance its domestic and overseas expenditures with European credits).

But America summarily rejected this proposal, not only because of what it believed to be an inflationary potential for the United States economy, but also because it felt little desire to accumulate the "paper gold" certificates which Keynes proposed. For if this paper credit were to be counted in its own reserves, the United States recognized, it would entail the same inflationary potential as gold itself. (Again, much the same attitude has been taken by Europe in recent years, insisting that United States payments deficits are "exporting" America's inflation to Europe.) And if this "paper gold" could not be counted as bona fide reserves, then this would be the equivalent of merely giving away American goods. America did not at this time conceive of the day in which it would itself be desirous of obtaining such credit.

The United States advocated a literal "fund," made up of gold and foreign currencies, whose resources would be lent to deficit nations to help them meet their balance-of-payments deficits. Because it was apparent that the United States dollar would in fact be the major currency in demand—since the United States would be the major exporter of reconstruction goods—it was agreed that the United States should supply the largest single share of the capital for the IMF-IBRD institutions: 22 percent.

Because voting power was based on the share invested and an 80 percent majority was required to pass any proposal, the United States was the only country possessing a veto. And because any country that needed to borrow more than its quota—established by the IMF on the basis of share invested—was required to give assurances that it was taking "corrective measures," i.e., the Adjustment Process, the United States was in a position to block any loan or policy proposal if it did not approve of the character of the proposed correctives.

This locked in European—and later Latin American, African and Asian—development policies with United States world strategy. For example, the United States used its power to put pressure on Castro when he sought an IMF-IBRD development and stabilization loan before turning to Soviet aid: "Castro could obtain aid, but only by acquiescing in terms (credit restraint and a balanced budget) that would prevent him from carrying through the social revolution by denying him the use of the tool of deficit financing for handling industrialization and agrarian reform, and by imposing economic controls that would be very apt to stir popular unrest against his government. The stabilization conditions, in other words, were basically designed to preserve the Cuban status quo, allowing only a few fringe reforms to be put into operation" (*New York Times,* April 22, 1959).

Even the World Bank's massive reconstruction loans and the IMF's balance-of-payments stabilization loans proved inadequate to meet the financial needs of European recovery. During 1946–47, in fact, France alone lost 60 percent of its gold and foreign exchange reserves, while those of Sweden fell 75 percent. Meanwhile, the United States continued to accumulate gold; its gold stock increased from $20.1 billion in 1945 to $24.8 billion in 1949, an all-time high.

This huge inflow, far from constituting an unmixed blessing to the United States, became a matter of the most urgent concern. Not only did the continuing transfer of gold to the United States threaten to reduce the vitality of the nation's export markets, the Commerce Department noted, but it also threatened to bring about domestic inflation—much in the same manner as the prewar inflow of European gold would have done had it not been "sterilized." It was because of these potential problems that the United States adopted policies designed to *repatriate* Europe's gold through foreign aid, trade, lending and investment policies. As a result, the United States gold stock declined by $6.7 billion during 1950–62, while that of what was to become the European Common Market rose by some $9.7 billion, reaching $11.5 billion by the end of 1962.

America's balance-of-payments deficits were welcomed abroad during the 1950's. And they aided the United States economy at home by helping to restrain potential inflationary pressures. European economic activity thrived, and with it the demand for United States exports grew. In addition, European prosperity paid the political dividend of laying to rest whatever fears of widespread economic depression and left-wing political ascendency may have been left over from 1945. Europe was firmly in the Western bloc.

THE TABLES TURN

By year-end 1962, however, the "dollar gap" had become transformed into a "dollar glut." The Common Market's gold reserves had risen to $11.5 billion, while its additional $6.7 billion in liquid claims upon the dollar represented an amount which, if converted into gold, would have reduced United States gold stocks by 42.5 percent. Furthermore, United States deficits were beginning to impose serious economic strains upon European economies, especially those of Germany, France and Holland. It was at this time that Europe's central bankers concluded that the time had come for equality in treatment with the United States, and they began to insist that the United States feel itself bound by the same economic constraints, the same Adjustment Process, to which European nations had subjected themselves in periods of deficit.

The United States recognized that its long string of deficits had enabled it to obtain over $1 billion a year more in foreign goods and services than it supplied. And so, although President Kennedy agreed in 1963 to take steps to reduce America's payments deficit, the United States—much as any debtor—was somewhat reluctant to relinquish its privileged status. Joined by its sister-in-deficit, Britain, the United States proposed a reform of the IMF which was designed to make being in debt easier.

The basic aims of United States financial policy at this time were twofold. The first was to minimize the actual outflow of United States gold in settlement of deficits. In effect this meant obtaining credit in one form or another, either by borrowing from the IMF or by inducing other nations not to cash dollars in for gold.

To achieve the second aim, the operations of the now disbanded Gold Pool were crucial, dating from its formation in 1961. By backing the value of the dollar at $35 per ounce of gold, the Pool encouraged individuals and governments to hold onto their dollars.

In the IMF at this time our proposals were limited merely to expansion of its reserves, which would enable the United States and Britain to finance their payments deficits by borrowing from the IMF. But in view of the sustained run of United States deficits since 1950 (save for a small surplus in 1957), the Common Market nations were adamant in their opposition to increasing international reserves for the purpose of enabling the United States to run its deficits unchecked.

In addition, the Common Market economists were already complaining about America's growing investment in European industry. They correlated this investment outflow with America's payments deficit and concluded that the United States was obtaining a cost-free takeover. For while private United States investment funds were buying out European enterprises with dollars, the payments were turned over to central banks which refrained from cashing the dollars in for United States gold on the grounds that this would disrupt world financial conditions.

Thus at the IMF's 1963 meetings, the German representative stated that: "I should like to warn against the conclusion that, as if by some purely technical reform, one could solve in an automatic or painless way the adjustment problems which are due either to structural distortions or to policy discrepancies between the member countries of our international system. . . .

"I want to stress that any improvements that might be thought out for our international monetary system should not be concentrated only to the question how best *to finance* balance-of-payments deficits, but also on the even more important question of how to provide sufficient incentives for *curing* them."

During 1964 Europe became even more reluctant to finance the United States deficit. At that year's IMF meetings, Italy joined in calling for " 'multilateral surveillance' of the means of financing balance-of-payments disequilibria." France urged that "reference will have to be made to gold," in financing future balance-of-payments deficits, as "the only monetary element outside the scope of government action." (It may be noted that de Gaulle's objection of March 20, 1968, to world currency reform was virtually a restatement of the unanimous position of the Common Market in 1964.)

However, Europe's voice remained ineffective. The United States defaulted thoroughly on its intention to restore equilibrium in its balance of payments. True, it had tied foreign aid to the purchase of United States exports, so that only about 6 percent of United States aid since 1962 represented an actual balance-of-payments outflow. True, it had imposed the Interest Equalization Tax to discourage the outflow of United States funds for the purchase of foreign securities which offer higher interest premiums. True, early in 1964 President Johnson had imposed controls upon bank lending abroad and upon foreign investment, under the euphemistically entitled "President Johnson's Voluntary Balance-of-Payments Program." And true, even foreign spending by the United States military in Europe had been cut back. But these were only palliatives in view of the immense drains upon the dollar which were to be set in motion in 1965 by the Vietnam War.

The role of Vietnam in America's balance-of-payments problems posed to Europe more clearly than ever the basic question: To what degree were they willing to absorb the costs of an aggressive American Cold War over which they had no control? For as United States military spending increased, the likelihood of America settling its payments deficits decreased.

The *direct* foreign exchange cost of American military activity abroad is now running at the rate of $2.6 billion annually; according to Richard Janssen, writing in the *Wall Street Journal* (April 1, 1968), $1.5 billion of this may be chalked up to the Vietnam War. And the *indirect* cost of the Vietnam build-up is $2 billion. This figure includes the effect that intensified war production and high defense spending has on our balance of trade—a shortage of capital and skilled labor, an increased rate of inflation, special import needs and diversion of production facilities away from exports.

Thus Senator Hartke, writing in the *Saturday Evening Post* on April 22, 1967 concluded: "To put it bluntly, Vietnam has ruined any chance we might have had for attaining equilibrium in our balance of payments. . . . Until recently there was curiously little official acknowledgment that after all Vietnam is the real culprit."

Certainly Undersecretary of State Nicholas Katzenbach still gave curiously little acknowledgment nearly a year later. At a meeting in Rome on January 5, 1968 he said: "Even if Vietnam did not exist," the United States payments problem would be "about equal" to what it is now.

But regardless of the official ignorance on the part of the United States, the Europeans insisted on connecting further extension of credits with the Vietnam War. Indeed, the Italian foreign minister suggested at the Rome meeting with Mr. Katzenbach "that a prompt end to the Vietnam War would help solve the United States balance-of-payments problem."

And on March 12—just two days before all the United States gold not tied up in the 25 percent domestic legal backing for Federal Reserve notes was depleted—the connection was made in the halls of Congress, as Senate doves joined to oppose a waiver of the 25 percent "gold cover" on American currency. They recognized that if they could prevent the release of more gold for shipment overseas to settle United States payments deficits, the Administration, in order to continue the Vietnam build-up, would be forced to ask Congress for a Declaration of War.

The Senate's final vote approved the waiver by the narrow margin of 39 to 37, with Senate doves Aiken, Church, Gruening, Hatfield, McGovern and Young in dissent. (They were joined by numerous hawks who had their own reasons for wanting to exert congressional restraint over President Johnson.) But the Gold Pool, the fixed link between the dollar and gold, was not to survive even the next weekend.

DEFEAT OF THE GOLD POOL

The magnitude of America's defeat when the Gold Pool was dissolved may be indicated by the intensity with which the United States had fought to create and preserve it. After all, the Gold Pool had been formed in 1961 to maintain the dollar "as good as gold"—namely at $35 an ounce. It was during the Kennedy-Nixon campaign of 1960, in response to a speculative flurry which pushed the price up to $41 an ounce, that the United States took the lead in "pooling" its gold reserves with those of Britain, the six Common Market nations and Switzerland. The result was a $31 billion gold fund, the stated purpose of which was to supply gold at $35 per ounce to anyone who wished to buy it on the London gold market, thus maintaining a stable price.

But from that moment in the early 1960's when foreign short-term dollar claims came to exceed the United States gold stock, the dollar has no longer been "as good as gold." This was not emphasized until 1966, however, when the United States began to exert strong pressure upon European governments not to cash in their dollars for gold, virtually a diplomatic refusal to redeem the dollar with gold. For seven years the Pool succeeded in maintaining the price of gold on the London market, although overseas markets continued to reflect higher prices. But as the position of the dollar deteriorated further, bringing sterling down in its path, it became impossible to maintain the orderly market which the Pool was formed to insure.

The Pool's collapse on March 4, 1968, came at the end of a series of events that began in June 1967. France withdrew, refusing to suffer any further gold losses as the penalty for America's overseas military expenditures and expanding foreign investments. In order to preserve the Pool, the United States picked up France's 9 percent share, thus increasing its gold contribution to 59 percent of the net Pool sales. In order not to spur gold speculation, France obligingly remained silent about its withdrawal.

Gold losses by the Pool's active member nations proceeded at a moderate rate. But havoc ensued when the pound sterling was devalued on November 18, 1967. Gold Pool sales amounted to nearly $800 million during the last two weeks of November alone. Nor was the furor mitigated when France—which no longer felt compelled to remain silent about its withdrawal—revealed that it had indeed terminated active membership in June. This announcement was taken in some quarters to indicate that France had joined Russia and South Africa in anticipating a higher price for gold.

In an attempt to stem the ensuing movement out of paper into gold, the Gold Pool nations—without France—met in Frankfurt on November 27, 1967. At the conclusion of this meeting they announced their determination to continue meeting any and all demands for gold at $35 an ounce. This statement temporarily dampened speculative activity.

Meanwhile, however, continuing pressures on the dollar worked to undermine the Pool's activities. Not only did the United States hesitate to take corrective measures—to increase its income taxes, reduce its budget deficit and slow the rate of domestic inflation—but increasing talk of a further build-up of forces in Vietnam clearly implied that an even more rapid deterioration in the United States balance of payments would be in the offing. The Tet offensive of the National Liberation Front, followed by North Korea's seizure of the *Pueblo,* strengthened this speculation.

By early March 1968, the death of the Gold Pool was imminent. In effect, the sources feeding it had dried up. Italy also had as much as withdrawn. With the money it received for the gold it gave the Pool to sell on the market, it had turned around and bought more gold to replenish its own stocks. Belgium, seeing Italy's gold stock rise rather than decline, was balking at further contributions. The Bank of England's ability to meet further gold sales out of its own reserves was virtually exhausted. And by the close of trading on Thursday, March 14, the United States—because of the necessity to maintain a 25 percent legal gold cover for its Federal Reserve notes—was unable to supply the Pool with enough gold to meet another day's sales. In response to the growing panic, the London gold market was closed, and three days later the seven active Gold Pool nations, meeting in Washington, announced that the Gold Pool had disbanded.

Among the new financial arrangements brought about by the demise of the Pool was the "two-tiered price system," which the United States had proposed in November 1967, but which was rejected by the other Pool members as unstable. One price is set for official sales between governments, which will continue to be transacted at $35 an ounce. The other price applies to all non-governmental traders in gold, and will be allowed to change from day to day just as does the price of copper, zinc and other metals—thereby satisfying South Africa's and Russia's demand for a higher gold price. This proposal effectively revalues the price of gold, while simultaneously enabling the United States to maintain its commitment to buy and sell gold at $35 an ounce to settle official intergovernmental transactions.

One of the first responses to the new two-tiered pricing system came from the oil-producing nations. Through their joint cartel, they requested an immediate increase of the royalties and taxes due from United States and British petroleum companies in proportion to the decline of these currencies vis-à-vis gold. This was an early sign that the two-price system represented a disequilibrium which meets many of the essential conditions of actual devaluation of the dollar.

While the two-price system will stop the drain of United States gold through the Gold Pool into the open market, it does not prevent governments from cashing in their dollars for gold at the rate of $35 an ounce. For the time being, however, there seems to be an agreement among the major holders of dollars that no such demands will be made on the United States gold stock.

At the same time, the "Special Drawing Rights" created by the IMF will provide an alternative to either demanding gold or holding dollars. The SDRs are essentially a new kind of international money, created by international agreement, that may be used like gold to settle payments accounts. The SDRs would be allotted in proportion to each nation's contribution to the IMF, so the United States would receive more than a fifth of the $5 billion worth proposed to be created over a period of five years—probably starting in early 1969. It might seem that this provides us with a painless way to incur deficits, yet avoid the Adjustment Process. And indeed this was what the United States had in mind when we first proposed the SDRs some time before the gold crisis. . . .

GOLD AND THE COLD WAR

America's desire to see gold eliminated from the world monetary system is understandable. It had used gold as a lever with which to exercise world power, not only to purchase foreign businesses, but also to finance its overseas Cold War operations. Gold, America perceived, was power; as long as gold was the basis of the world monetary system, power followed it. Therefore, when its gold stockpile was depleted, America naturally wanted to transform the monetary system in such a way as to phase gold out, thereby preventing any other nation from using the power it provides—especially in view of the fact that the major potential gold bloc nations are the Soviet Union, South Africa and France.

If the United States has lost the lever of gold in world financial influence, it has obtained a not unsubstantial lever in the very size of its international debt. In this, its position is not unlike that of Germany in the late 1920's when the German government used its indebtedness as a tool with which to exact "restraint" among its creditors, holding up the alternative of a monetary collapse.

This threat of a worldwide financial collapse explains the high degree to which Europe has accommodated the United States. Europe is considerably more dependent upon the smooth functioning of international finance than is the United States; foreign trade represents about 25 percent of the Common

Market's combined national income, compared to only 4 percent for the United States. Disruption of Europe's foreign trade would result in severe dislocations of its economic life, causing massive unemployment of its capital and labor resources.

Because of his efforts to avoid this situation, Charles de Gaulle has been made into the whipping boy of the greater part of the American press. According to popular opinion in the United States, it is he who is threatening the stability of world finance. De Gaulle, however, has only joined the already established Common Market position of 1963 and '64 that it is the United States that produced chaos by the public demonstration that it has finally, by its own mismanagement, *spent* its power in the world. Faced with the decision of whether or not to enter the Vietnam War—when it was already overextended in its foreign accounts—the United States chose to dissipate its world power and render obsolete the exchange standard upon which rested the edifice of the world's postwar monetary order, rather than adjust its activities to its new limitations. In advocating a return to the pre-World War II gold standard— under which *all* international deficits had to be settled with gold—General de Gaulle was only calling for the United States to pay the price of its Cold War posture, a price figured in the very gold which had been the crux of America's world power and which came to this country as a result of Europe's political and financial crises preceding and during World War II.

De Gaulle's appeal to the "universal and impartial" character of gold is seen as a threat by this country—and this is an accurate perception, for the impartial logic of gold has negated the imperatives of American power. As early as April 1963, Professor Terence McCarthy saw clearly that we could not evade this logic. In *A Strategy for American Security,* he wrote: "The claim is made that the enormous annual expenditure on armaments and the military establishment in this country is vitally essential to the maintenance of America's world position. It is nearer the truth to say that without a shot being fired, without United States armies once engaging the enemy, her world position is being frittered away, irretrievably, by America's tacit repudiation of the basic value of her currency."

Death of the Gold Standard

Abba P. Lerner

High financiers rarely exchange bankers' gray for the more flamboyant hues of revolution. Yet the seemingly conservative decision of the leading Central Banks and the International Monetary Fund (IMF) to continue trading gold with each other at $35 an ounce, taken at a conference in Washington last March 17, was actually a revolutionary act: In a fit of absent-mindedness, they finally liberated the world from the last remnants of the Gold Standard, replacing it with what is in reality a Dollar Standard.

Although the conference concentrated on stopping the *sale* of gold by the monetary authorities to profiteering speculators at $35 an ounce, the important aspect of the new policy is that it prohibits the monetary authorities from *purchasing* free market gold. Thus monetary gold (what is held by the authorities) and non-monetary gold (held by all others) have become two different noncompeting commodities. Hopefully, the monetary authorities will not inadvertently restore the Gold Standard by resuming purchases when the free market price falls to $35, or by being seduced with an offer of gold at a "below market" price of $35.

So long as this does not happen, the approximately 40,000 tons of monetary gold (comprising $40 billion out of the $72 billion of international liquidity) play only the ceremonial role of counters or "chips" representing dollars. A millon dollars, now represented by a ton of monetary gold, could just as well be represented by a symbolic microgram of the metal.

The essence of the Gold Standard is the guarantee of governments to buy or sell gold for their currency in unlimited amounts at an established price (with a small "service charge"). Under the new arrangement this guarantee is replaced by a prohibition. The agreement of the governments to trade their monetary gold only among themselves and the IMF means that their currencies can now be used to buy or sell anything at all except monetary gold.

For its proper functioning a true Gold Standard requires a perfect flexibility of wages and prices in response to supply and demand. If there were such flexibility, the Gold Standard could serve as a single monetary system for the whole world. While the fairly stable size of the total world gold stock would preclude severe general price inflations or deflations, relative price inflations and deflations between different countries would automatically cure any balance of payments problems. Every country with an unfavorable balance of payments would lose gold to those countries with favorable balances in the process of covering its deficit. This would lower demand and prices in

Reprinted with permission from New Leader *of July 8, 1968. Copyright* © *American Labor Conference on International Affairs, Inc.*

the deficit countries and raise them in the surplus countries, stimulating exports from the one and discouraging exports from the other. The deficits and surpluses would automatically disappear.

But we do not have the required price and wage flexibility to make the system work. The surplus countries hoard vast quantities of gold to check price inflation, while in the deficit countries attempts to check the gold outflow produce economic depression rather than price deflation.

Depression would eventually also cure the deficit by equalizing imports and exports, but not without exacting a great toll in unemployment and overall reduction of spending. Understandable unwillingness to suffer so much depression led to the abandonment of the Gold Standard for domestic purposes.

For international payments, however, gold continued in use. The supply was often inadequate—that is, insufficient to maintain prosperity at the current price level—so substitutes were developed, such as British pounds sterling and United States dollars, to provide additional international liquidity. Now Special Drawing Rights (SDRs) are to be created for this purpose.

But even reasonably adequate overall levels of international liquidity do not solve balance of payments problems. Deficit countries are unable or unwilling to engineer sufficient depression to eliminate their deficits. Surplus countries are unable to expand enough, and unwilling to inflate enough, to eliminate their surpluses. This is why we have problems like the one that has caused so much excitement in recent months—the United States balance of payments deficit.

The deficit stems from the United States' spending more abroad (on imports, foreign investment, foreign aid and overseas military outlays) than the foreign exchange it is earning by its exports, and covering the difference by paying out dollars. These dollars were a welcome—indeed a lifesaving—supplement to gold in providing additional international liquidity, but for various reasons some holders cashed them in for gold. The consequent outflow of much of the United States gold stock led to a speculative splurge in gold purchasing based on the expectation that the monetary authorities—essentially the United States Treasury—would be panicked into raising the price of gold above the established $35 an ounce, perhaps doubling it or possibly even increasing it to a nice round $100.

Claims that the price of gold is unnaturally low regardless of these recent developments—that other prices have risen greatly since gold was pegged at $35 an ounce in 1934—strike me as unjustifiable. After all, at the present price the supply of gold from new production in recent years has been more than double the demand for industrial uses (including jewelry). Only the expectation that the United States might soon be paying a higher price has created a demand for gold among speculators larger than the new production of gold mines, so that there was an actual decline in monetary gold from $43 to $40 billion. But the March 17 separation of monetary gold from free market gold, if maintained, puts an end to this expectation and will lead to a sharp fall in the free market price of gold—at least to the level where industrial demand will absorb the whole of current new production. The recent South African offer to sell gold to the Central Banks at $35 an ounce is, in effect, a last ditch attempt to keep the price of gold from falling on the free market by not unloading additional quantities there.

The price of gold will fall much below even this level when the hoarded gold is unloaded by disappointed speculators, and of course much lower still if and when the Central Banks realize that the ceremonial role of monetary gold can be played just as well by a symbolic microgram of the metal (or even by purely fictional gold) and decide to release for industrial purposes the 40,000 tons they are keeping off the market. (This amounts to about three times the estimated total of privately owned gold hoards throughout the world, some 70 times the annual industrial use, or almost half the total quantity of gold ever mined.) It is clear that the monetary authorities, by holding these vast amounts of gold, have been maintaining an unnaturally high, rather than an unnaturally low, support for gold.

Yet despite such supplements as dollars, pounds sterling and other currencies, there has been what looks like an overall insufficiency of international liquidity. Surplus countries have not had a balance of payments favorable enough to induce them to get rid of surplus international liquidity by discouraging exports or encouraging imports, and thereby dissolve the deficits of other countries. Deficit countries have not corrected their own problems internally because, with fixed exchange rates and the absence of price flexibility, the only cure for a permanent deficit is a permanent depression, which they rightly regard as worse than the disease. Consequently, the deficits have become chronic.

But the insufficiency visible here is not really a shortage of liquidity or international *money*. The void here is for the continued financing of countries that cannot correct their deficits.

Indeed, the failure of all attempts to set up a world monetary authority capable of serving the international economy in the way a national monetary authority serves a national economy is due to the unwillingness of surplus nations to accept permanent flows of IOUs from chronically deficit nations in exchange for real goods and services. What is called for in this circumstance is not Special Drawing Rights, which can only provide additional international liquidity to cover temporary gaps between a country's payments and receipts, but "Chronic Deficits Rights" ("CDRs"). Precisely this kind of provision was made for the adjustment of exchange rates in the event of chronic foreign deficits—then called "Fundamental Disequilibrium"—when the IMF was formed in 1944. But false patriotism, fear of competition, and bureaucratic conservatism have prevented these adjustments from ever being carried out.

It should be apparent by now that the price of gold is not the solution to the balance of payments problem. A rise in the dollar price of gold would be matched by an equivalent rise in the price of gold in other currencies, thus canceling its impact. While international liquidity would be increased (providing, incidentally, a handsome reward to gold producers and speculators), the concept of CDRs would not have been made more attractive. And the basic problem, the United States balance of payments deficit, would remain unsolved.

A deficit in a country's balance of payments is fundamentally *a shortage of foreign currency at the current price*. In the absence of the necessary flexibility to correct the situation by a painless wage and price deflation, the natural cure for a shortage of any commodity is a rise in its price. This eliminates the shortage by reducing the amount of the commodity that is demanded and increasing the amount supplied. But in the United States the natural cure is seen as a shameful devaluation of the dollar in terms of other currencies (and confused with a devaluation in terms of gold—a rise in the dollar price of gold). The cure is therefore rejected and the deficit becomes chronic, calling for unlimited CDRs.

Just as raising or lowering the price of gold would not help end the deficit, though, neither does the divorcing of international money from free market gold, as long as the rates of exchange remain fixed. The chronic deficit continues until the gold, other reserves, credits, SDRs and the hypothetical CDRs are all exhausted. The devaluation of the deficit country's currency in terms of other currencies can then no longer be prevented.

Devaluation is more easily accepted in the impure form of taxes on particular imports and on certain expenditures abroad, together with subsidies on some exports. Like outright currency devaluation, albeit less efficiently, these taxes and subsidies redistribute expenditure from outside to inside the deficit countries.* The danger is that protectionist measures taken by one country invite retaliatory restrictions on freedom of trade by other countries, thus canceling any impact on balances of payments. A perfect example of this was the announcement in Paris on June 26 that import quotas would be imposed on foreign goods and export subsidies granted for French goods. The United States immediately announced that countervailing American duties would be introduced to offset the French moves.

---

* This "impure" devaluation is inefficient in two ways. First, most taxes are easily avoided (and subsidies misused) by changing the form of the expenditure. Second, to the degree that taxes are not avoided (and the subsidies not perverted), they do not concentrate the redistribution where there is the least difference between internal and external prices and therefore the least interference with the gains in economic efficiency arising from the international division of labor. If great care is taken to adjust the taxes and subsidies so as to minimize the interference with efficiency, this approach develops into an even tax on all imports and a subsidy, equal to the tax, on all exports. The "impurity" is thus completely removed and the result is distinguished only in name from a devaluation of the currency of the same magnitude as the taxes and subsidies.

The greater danger for the United States is that if all other methods fail to reduce its balance of payments deficit, the government might take the desperate step of engineering a domestic depression. It could well be that this is exactly what was promised by the United States to get the Central Banks to agree to the March 17 arrangement. The words "engineering a depression" would not be used, of course, but rather some phrase like "putting our house in order." . . .

The sensible solution to the United States' (and all other countries') balance of payments problems has been made much easier by the March 17 isolation of monetary gold from the free market. As we have noted, the present trouble is due to the rigidification of exchange rates through national pride and bureaucratic arteriosclerosis. The Central Banks are now in a position to adjust monetary exchange rates to meet changing conditions, as the IMF attempted to do when it was established in 1944. The banks need merely provide surplus countries with such stocks of international liquidity that they would willingly let them decline by importing more, exporting less, or more openly raising their relative exchange rates so that the deficit countries automatically find their currencies devalued.

Additional international liquidity can be provided in two ways. The banks can raise the nominal price of the ceremonial monetary gold they hold—without paying tribute to gold producers, hoarders or speculators. Alternatively, they can create new international money without reference to gold—by issuing new SDRs, for example. In either case, what is important is not the quantity of international liquidity itself but the induced flexibility of the exchange rates. This flexibility is the only solution to balance of payments problems that avoids depression.

But even if the Central Banks should not reach such an agreement—and it does not seem very likely that they will—all is not lost. The United States then can and should unilaterally declare the following measures in effect, which would achieve all the important objectives:

1. No more gold will ever be bought by the United States for monetary purposes.

2. Except for a single symbolic ingot, the currently held United States gold stocks will be sold for industrial uses at whatever price they bring.

3. The United States will endeavor to keep the purchasing power of the dollar constant in terms of a specified index-number of American exports, rather than in terms of gold or other currencies.

4. In the event of a fall in the dollar's purchasing power (i.e., a rise in prices according to the index), the United States government will fully compensate all holders of dollars, or dollar securities guaranteed by the United States, for the loss.

As a result of these measures the price of gold would almost certainly collapse. Gold would lose all its usefulness as international money, and there would be a great increase in the dollar demand for international liquidity. The Dollar Standard would then completely replace the Gold Standard in form as well as in substance, differing from it only in the greater availability of dollars—since it is easier for almost all countries to earn dollars than to produce gold, and there are so many more products that can be sold for dollars (to the United States or to other countries that have obtained dollars in return for *their* products).

The United States balance of payments would be solved for a long time, the deficit being covered (or indeed turned into a surplus) by the export of dollars to provide other countries with international liquidity. But the change to the Dollar Standard would not reduce the foreign deficits of these other countries. There would be the same rigidity of exchange rates as under the Gold Standard, and for the same reasons. In fact, it would worsen the balance of payments of those countries that felt the need to import dollars for the purpose of filling the gap in international liquidity left by the demonetization of gold.

There would, of course, be outcries of bad faith—wholly unjustified, I feel. The obligation of the United States is not to gold producers or speculators but to those who have been cajoled or bullied into holding dollars, and they would be fully protected by the purchasing power guarantee. The United States would also be accused of swindling the rest of the world by getting useful goods and services in exchange for pieces of paper—dollars or dollar securities. The resentment would probably not be much reduced by pointing out that this is the same business—namely, providing international liquidity—carried on for so long by South Africa, except that we would be providing it not in the form of gold metal but in the much more convenient form of dollar bills and securities. And a reminder that all acquisitions of dollars would be perfectly voluntary, or a proposal to turn the profits over to universally accepted charities and other good causes, might simply increase the resentment.

This means that the Dollar Standard could not be a permanent solution. Growing resentment would ultimately lead countries to liberate themselves from the dollar by letting the value of their currencies rise and fall in relation to it. They would then discover that international liquidity is largely unnecessary if chronic deficits are cured by exchange rate adjustments. The surplus dollars could be cashed in for United States products for consumption or investment.

The final step in this progression, and the real boon to everyone, would be the ultimate creation of a system of flexible exchange rates pegged to supply and demand rather than to the dollar. Besides dispelling the fears of chronic deficits and relieving countries of the need for dollar reserves, this system would remove many of the temptations to restrict mutually beneficial foreign trade and capital movements. All countries would be free to manage their monetary and fiscal policies for domestic prosperity, stability and growth.

1. *Is gold just a fetish?*
2. *What is "paper gold"? Does it really solve the gold problem?*
3. *Is gold really our problem or is something else to blame for our international financial difficulties?*
4. *Do you agree or disagree that our foreign policy is a root cause of our balance of payments difficulties?*
5. *What possible problems for the United States and the world do you see in Lerner's proposal to abandon both a dollar and a gold standard? What benefits?*

What Should Be America's Role Toward Developing Nations?

From the close of World War II until comparatively recently, the focus of American economic attention overseas has been on the problem of developing economies. The discovery of the underdeveloped nations, or "Third World," was prompted by a number of events. First, the ending of the old European colonialism, its structure shaken by war and threatened by the rise of political nationalism among the colonies, compelled the developed world to shed its traditional myopia toward the poor two-thirds of the earth's population. Second, the formation of the United Nations with its real and promised elevation of the poor nations to levels of international political importance created an actual political power for this third world. But, lying behind these developments and of greater importance were the developing contours of the cold war—the vision of the whole world divided into ideological camps of "Western Democracies" and Soviet Communism. At any rate, the effect of these forces was to commit the United States gradually to an international economic policy of providing foreign aid for development.

Between 1945 and 1968, the United States provided about $115 billion in foreign aid. Of this, a little more than a third went to European nations, largely under the Marshall Plan and other postwar rehabilitation programs, and the remainder went to the developing economies of Asia, Latin America, and Africa. Typically, not all American aid went for actual economic development, but much was military support, understood to be essential within the requirements of the developing Cold War. Indeed, only about two-thirds of American aid went for "economic development."

By the late 1960's, the foreign aid program of the United States, at least that portion of it aimed at developing economies, seemed to be in trouble. Although actual foreign aid appropriations had grown from under $2 billion in 1959 to over $4 billion in 1967, disappointment and criticism of aid programs was general among the people, the Congress, and economists. Programs were attacked from a number of different points. They had failed to create real economic development. They had not bought us dependable friends. They had not provided social stability for recipient nations. Moreover, a war in Vietnam, which many somehow saw as a failure of our aid programs and our foreign policy toward developing nations, and a worsening balance of payments problem had moved the United States by 1970 toward the unmistakable direction of cutting back its aid programs.

The first of the following articles by Robert L. Heilbroner, although admitting the possibility of failure, argues that we must provide economic aid to avoid even greater failure. Heilbroner holds that it is the developed world's duty to help the poor. Paul Baran, a respected Marxist economist, argues in the second article that imperialism clearly dominates our actions toward developing nations, and that altruism is not a serious consideration.

The Challenge to the West

Robert L. Heilbroner

It is one thing to encourage public approval for economic development as a kind of international charity, and another to see in it an agency of deliberate sacrifice, whether of today's generation in the name of tomorrow's, or of tomorrow's in the name of today's. So too it is one thing to engage America in the world-wide struggle for development on the assumption that a successful Great Ascent will strengthen the forces of democracy and capitalism, and another to ask it to engage itself in a struggle whose successful end-result is apt to be a growth of political authoritarianism and economic collectivism.

Of course, one hopes for an attack on the problem of world poverty which will combine the dedication and the willingness to undertake monumental tasks of the revolutionist with the tolerance and open-mindedness of the humanist. One hopes for a program of development which will judiciously temper the need for sacrifice with a compassion for those who must make the sacrifice.

From "The Challenge to the West" in The Great Ascent *by Robert L. Heilbroner. Copyright © 1963 by Robert L. Heilbroner. Reprinted by permission of Harper & Row, Publishers, and William Morris Agency, Inc.*

But what if such combinations are not available? What if the inherent obstacles of waging a campaign against stagnant social orders naturally bring to the fore revolutionaries of narrow minds and cruel appetites? What if tolerance and open-mindedness prove to be qualities incompatible with the iron discipline needed for a rapid escape from the pit? What then?

There are no easy answers to such grinding questions. The harsh prospects and problems of development sweep away the satisfying identification of self-interest with altruism and leave in its place only the unsatisfying necessity to choose the lesser among inescapable evils. And what is true for our private moral determination is no less true for our public decisions as a nation. There are no responses on the part of our government which will make of development a benign process whose outcome naturally accords with American ideals and institutions. On the contrary, the realization forced upon us by economic development is that our power to shape the context of the future is much less than it has been in the past. Economic development, with its immense drive and its dangerous proclivities, places us in a defensive position in which our freedom of maneuver is necessarily limited.

It is not, of course, totally gone. Limited intervention in the future, as in the past, may enable us to bolster friendly but shaky governments or to unseat inimical and shaky regimes. But the presence of the Russian and Chinese counterforce makes it unlikely that military action can exert more than a marginal restraint on revolution in the more distant underdeveloped world, while in Latin America anti-American sentiments may make even of diplomatic intervention a risky and possibly disastrous course of action. The probabilities are great that we shall have to stand more or less impotently by while the dynamics of development work their troubled way, "surrounding" us in Asia, Africa, and South America with governments whose policies and programs point in a general direction counter to that which we ourselves desire.

THE THREAT OF ISOLATIONISM

If active intervention to repress the revolutionary tendency of development is apt to be largely denied to us, another possibility remains. It is not inconceivable that the untoward drift of world affairs will give rise to powerful voices urging a Western—and, in particular, American—disengagement from the underdeveloped world, a curtailment of aid, a turning away from active participation in or support for the Great Ascent.

It is an uncertain question as to how far the Western economies *can* sever their connections with the raw material producers of the backward continents. There is no question at all, however, that such a course would make things incalculably worse for the West. All the adverse trends latent within the underdeveloped lands would be vastly accelerated were America to turn its back on development. If we cannot easily divert or contain the revolutionary consequences of development despite generous assistance, we certainly cannot prevent them by refusing aid. The revolutions will take place whether we offer money or not; and if the immediate pace of advance would be slowed down, were we to turn aside, the wrath and disorder of the development revolution would only be increased. To some extent Russia can supply the materials we would refuse. Unquestionably, she would be the immense beneficiary of world sentiment and political orientation. In the international arena, isolationism would spell the decline of American world influence—an influence which . . . can still be exercised to some advantage.

Even more self-defeating would be the moral effect of isolation at home. After all, the Western nations are an immense reservoir of wealth in an impoverished world. In America we have enormous surpluses of food which embarrass us while the world's belly aches from emptiness. We have excess capacity in many industries while in the backward lands the pace of progress creeps for lack of machines and materials of every kind. We have skills and talents which go begging or are frittered away in second-rate employments while the underdeveloped continents cry out for expertise of every kind. We throw on the junk heap vehicles which would furnish invaluable transportation to a world which still totes much of its burdens on its backs; we discard outmoded wardrobes which would clothe men and women who have never known what it was like to have an unused garment; we spend in night clubs a sum which would cover the national budgets of a dozen pinched nations. Not to use this abundance for the betterment of mankind would be evidence of a moral decay as destructive of the West as any number of external revolutions.

And then there is a final thought. The political prospect of an isolated America—even an isolated West—is not a reassuring one. A beleaguered fortress of privilege, its doors closed and its walls manned, does not tend to nurture wise and tolerant government. To live in fear of the developing world, to count its successes as our defeats, to feel the rush of the history-making process into the vacuum of the East and South as a threatening current, could well encourage the ugliest political possibilities in the West. Isolationism might free us from the need to deal with extremist governments abroad, but it is likely to do so at the price of having to deal with them at home.

SELECTIVE SUPPORT

A much more positive and appealing program would throw us into the struggle for development on a selective basis. That is, it would urge us to concentrate our assistance on those nations which stand a chance of struggling up the mountain of development without resort to totally collectivist, extreme left-wing measures. Mexico, Argentina, Brazil, and India have often been proposed as the main objects for such a concentrated program of assistance.

There is a good deal of justification for channeling our money where the pay-off possibilities are greatest, not only because the successful developers offer the greatest chance for spending that money usefully, but also because they offer us the best chance to keep our *own* morale high. To a certain extent the realities of the development process do in fact result in such a concentration of aid. Yet there are difficulties in the way of adopting this as an "official" policy. For even with the most successful noncommunist developers the outlook is not all propitious. India's fate hangs in the balance, and after Nehru's death it is entirely possible that the nation will fly apart into linguistic fragments and that development along Western lines will go into the discard. Brazil is still racked by revolutionary sentiment in the north. Argentina has recently shown the revolutionary potential that lurks beneath a seemingly firm government. Mexico gives more promise of stability, but we have caught a glimpse of the disturbing possibilities inherent in its proletariat.

And even if all goes for the best in these nations, it will not be easy, or perhaps even possible, to keep aid restricted to them without accelerating an unwanted trend in other nations. What will happen to Pakistan if it is short-changed in comparison with India? Can we help Argentina and not Chile, Colombia, Venezuela? And if them, can we ignore Peru and Bolivia? Is it feasible to assist Nigeria but not Ghana? The pressures of political reality almost inevitably impose a diffusion of a would-be concentration of aid. Certainly, it makes sense to bend our first efforts where they are most likely to succeed. But it is doubtful if we can do so to the exclusion of other countries. If we are to have any foreign aid program, it will have to include, to some degree, a wide variety of nations—the less successful developers along with the more successful, the less friendly along with the more friendly.

THE PREMISES OF POLITICAL POLICY

What can we do, then, to live with the revolutionary trend of economic development?

It must be clear that the first essential is not a change in policy so much as a change in point of view. We must lift ourselves out of our accustomed American frame of reference and catapult ourselves across a distance wider than the oceans that separate us from the continents in which the struggle for development is taking place. . . . We must learn to see the Great Ascent as it is, and not as we would like it to be.

From such an altered point of view comes the realization that we can only exert an influence over the direction of economic development, if we use our power in consonance with the drift of events and not against it. In a word, if we are to modify the general direction of the Great Ascent, we can only do so by accepting the need for political authoritarianism and economic collectivism during the early stages of development of many nations. To put the matter in its bluntest terms, *we must forge a foreign policy which begins with the explicit premise that democratic capitalism, as a model for economic and political organization, is unlikely to exert its influence beyond the borders of the West, at least within our lifetimes.*

It need hardly be said that the official articulation of such a premise would present extraordinary difficulties—practical as well as ideological. At home it would expose an administration to the grave political risks of expounding an unpopular and "defeatist" world view to an electorate which has hitherto been led to believe that the Western system had every prospect of expanding— not by force but by force of example. Abroad it would destroy at one blow the simple guideline that automatically equates our national interest with economically "liberal" governments and opposes it to economically collectivist ones.

Ironically, however, such a "defeatist" view is apt to be the most effective means we have to protect our own institutions and to maintain some area of effective influence. For it asks us to recognize that by supporting governments which, for whatever reason, do not accelerate development to the utmost we may be only laying the groundwork for eventual revolutions of uncontrollable tendencies, while in helping governments of unpalatable authoritarian and collectivist hues we may be in fact preventing the rise of something worse. To be sure, this does not mean that tyrannous governments are by virtue of their very repressions the ones which America must support. The infinitely difficult discrimination which a realistic premise for policy enjoins is the need to distinguish between mere oppression and oppressive but purposeful discipline, between static dictatorship and dictatorial development. Very often both will be visible. In that event we shall have to guard against the easy temptation to confuse the rights of property with the rights of man, and thereby to rationalize our support for conservative regimes and our opposition to radical ones.

Above all, an effective policy requires a change in the official attitude of America toward "socialism" in the underdeveloped world. We have already noted that very few, even among the most radical development elites, wish to be pulled into the existing communist orbit. But under the cumulative pressures of the Great Ascent, noncommunist governments may well be forced into that camp unless they receive the strongest possible encouragement—and not merely a grudging acquiescence—in finding independent solutions along indigenous socialist lines.

Our executive and planning staffs have already come a considerable distance toward recognizing the necessity for political authority and economic planning as preconditions for rapid development. But there still remains a long way to go. A long and deep educational process will be needed if enlightened executive policies are to receive legislative support. And then, too, it is not easy to communicate with the leaders of the underdeveloped world so long as powerful private voices continue to give lip service to the pieties and polemics of free private enterprise and democracy in a situation in which all too frequently both are not only totally inapplicable, but would spell chaos or even retrogression. When, for instance, the leadership elites of the backward nations read an editorial in the *New York Times* lamenting the rise of socialism in Egypt and urging that "it is necessary for us in the West to prove that our democratic free enterprise system is better than any variation of socialism," these leaders feel that important interests in America are willing to consign them to a slower rate of economic growth and a lesser portion of economic justice in defense of their own well-padded system of economic privilege. And insofar as these American interests are suggesting that capitalism rather than socialism should be the main vehicle of development, the leaders of the under-developed nations are right.

Thus one consequence of a new view of the realistic possibilities before the majority of the developing countries must be that strategic groups in America learn to speak a new language abroad—certainly not the dogmatics of Marxism-Leninism, but the language of planning, of controls, of social and economic justice. If America wishes to make its counsels heard among the revolutionary elites, its spokesmen must speak the words that answer their questions.

THE INTERNATIONALIZATION OF FOREIGN AID

The initial premise of Western foreign policy toward economic develop-ment must thus be an acceptance of its revolutionary potentials. Yet it is clear that, even with the best of intentions and most audacious of political leadership, the United States must not expect too much. A rich and privileged nation in a poor and underprivileged world cannot avoid becoming the target of hostilities and frustrations. An anti-Western, anti-American attitude is likely to color the general foreign outlook of most developing nations, regardless of our ability to soften their animosity by a new show of understanding for their internal problems.

This is bound to place America in the difficult position of seeking to extend assistance to nations which are not only authoritarian and collectivist but which are more or less actively anti-American. If we accept this, too, as part of the price of development, then a subsidiary aspect of American policy must be the creation of avenues for assisting development without incurring unacceptable conflicts of immediate interest. That is, we must find ways of speeding development without placing ourselves in the impossible position of directly extending help to nations which are publicly unsympathetic or even unfriendly in their relations with our government.

There is only one way in which this difficult objective can be achieved. More and more of the development effort must be handled by international agencies. The support of development must be placed as much as possible outside the arena of domestic politics.

This is not an aim which can be accomplished overnight. The organizational means for an effective handling of aid on an international basis do not now exist. The present international agencies have not excelled in their administration of aid, erring sometimes on the side of laxness, sometimes (and especially in the case of the World Bank) on the side of overstrictness. To advocate the immediate wholesale transfer of assistance to the United Nations, or even to some new *ad hoc* body of Western nations, would probably result in a considerable diminution of congressional appropriations and would thus be bitterly opposed by the present recipient nations.

Nevertheless it is necessary to think and plan ahead. The tensions and disruptions of the developing world are by no means apt to diminish. . . . If we project the likely revolutionary drift of affairs in the underdeveloped world and consider the problem of assisting governments whose political complexion may well become increasingly distasteful, it is necessary to consider how conflicts of interest can be diluted and buffered, and how aid to development can be continued when it is no longer a "popular" object of public support.

Against this impending possibility there seems to be no adequate response but the internationalization of assistance on a considerably larger scale than that of today. The depoliticizing of foreign aid has already begun with respect to certain aspects of development: health, technical assistance, agricultural research, etc. The World Health Organization, the Technical Assistance Board, the Food and Agriculture Organization already make decisions and administer programs, many of which would be extremely difficult to carry out as "American" projects. Such a transfer of administrative responsibility to international groups, whether under the aegis of the UN or of other agencies, will certainly not remove the conflicts of interest which are inherent in the process of aiding revolutionary governments, but it may well prove to be the best means of holding these conflicts within manageable proportions. This is not, of course, incompatible with the maintenance of direct bilateral aid wherever this continues to offer the smoothest and most fruitful working relationship.

REFORM AT HOME

The gradual internationalization of aid may succeed, to some extent, in diluting the hostility which the Great Ascent is likely to stir up at home. It will not, however, affect the hostility which development will surely stir up in the emerging countries themselves. Against this powerful animus, the United States has but one effective response. It must demonstrate to the leaders of the underdeveloped nations that we too have our profound problems, albeit of a different sort, and that we are capable of as much political courage at home as we do not hesitate to ask abroad.

This forces the consideration of a delicate but central problem—that development today is largely a "colored" problem, and that it is taking place in a world which is still dominated by nations many of which regard the colored races as inferior to the white. Here the Western powers, and in particular the United States, must candidly assess their own attitudes. It is an ugly word, but the United States today is a racist nation—not, to be sure, at the center of official government, but emphatically and openly in some of its state governments, and pervasively and silently in the attitudes and actions of the majority of its white population.

And whereas the official policy of the Federal Government is against racial discrimination, its willingness to take risks and fight battles on behalf of this policy has not, to date, been remarkable for its bravery. To the colored nations of the world, what is visible in our country is a scale of values which does not inhibit our government from using force to oppose an alien political philosophy but which plucks at its sleeve with a thousand cautions when the internal racial question is raised. On the face of it, racial equality is not an aim for which the United States Government is prepared to run outstanding political risks, an aim which is preached loudly but practiced softly. Until this great flaw is remedied, or at least made the target of courageous and unremitting effort, it will not be easy for America—and to a somewhat lesser degree, for the West at large—to parade as the political ideal on which the black, yellow, and brown nations of the underdeveloped world should model themselves.

There is here an issue still larger than that of racial injustice in itself. It is the issue of demonstrating to the emergent leaders of the world that the United States is still the bearer and the guardian of the ideals of freedom in whose name it was founded. For it is well to recognize that freedom is not the banner under which the West marches, in the eyes of many who see it from the South and East. Those who find the leaders of the underdeveloped world ungrateful or unperceptive for failing to recognize the West as the "champion of freedom" might reflect that Nehru wrote his great book in a British jail, that most of the leaders of the Indonesian Republic were at one time political prisoners of the Dutch, that the original leaders of the Algerian revolution were shamefully betrayed and incarcerated by the French while traveling on a "safe passage," that Guatemala was subverted by American power following its first revolution, that the nations of Africa won their independence against Belgian, French, and British resistance and still struggle against Portuguese colonialism. Country by country, it has been almost without exception the nations of the "freedom-loving" West which have opposed and fought the independence of the new nation-states. If the communists have Korea, Tibet, Hungary, and the Baltic states on their conscience, we have enough on ours.

Hence the task confronting the Western nations is not to maintain but to regain their historic identification with freedom—to win it anew in the eyes of the world. To some extent this can be done by the exercise of a wise, realistic, and generous foreign policy. But to a much more important degree it will have to be done at home. It is idle to pretend that the West can be an effective model for the immediate economic and political development of the backward world. What we must hope and work for is to make it a model for their long-term evolution. The West and America can offer, in the living examples of their societies, meanings of freedom which can exert their powerful attractions for the future: a genuine solicitude for the right of the dissenting individual, a greater concern for the disprivileged individual than for the privileged one, an encouragement of personal life goals that go beyond the mere accumulation of consumer goods. The West may yet be a lodestar for the global revolution which is now only in its incipient stages, but it will hardly succeed in inspiring the world's imagination unless it first succeeds in inspiring its own.

THE CHOICE BEFORE AMERICA

Thus the price of leadership in world economic development comes home to us as a domestic political challenge—perhaps in the end as the supreme domestic political challenge.

It may be that the challenge will be too great. It may be deemed political suicide to speak of problems of development in blunt terms, to force a consideration of unpleasant alternatives and moral dilemmas, to encourage governments whose political and economic structures are alien and even antipathetic to ours. It may appear impractical to urge an internationalization of foreign aid; impolitic to engage in an uncompromising campaign for racial equality; unnecessary to press forward on a hundred difficult fronts of domestic reform. In other words, the actions which are open to us may be open only in theory, in the abstract, and not in hard fact. In that case, if the argument [set forth here] is valid, we must be prepared to bear the consequences of inaction, which is to say, the probable slow loss of prestige and leadership to the communist world.

Whether or not the United States and the West will be capable of risking the heroic course needed to maintain a working influence on the historic transformation of our day is difficult to say. The gulf between conditions in the underdeveloped world and our own is so great that what appears from their point of view as a cautious and conservative program for us to follow appears to us as a daring and radical one. Without question the measures needed to gird the United States against the future—much less to establish its moral leadership in a revolutionary world—will strain to the hilt the adaptability of our social order, both at its centers of power and among the electorates whom it entertains and diverts and semieducates. No one can confront this impending test with an easy assurance as to its outcome.

What is certain is that the price of economic development will not be borne by the developing world alone. Its stresses and strains will have to be faced as well in the advanced countries. Ahead lies a long gantlet through which rich and poor, favored and disfavored alike, must pass; and in that period of trial it is less likely that the poor will falter who have their lives at stake than the rich who may fear for their way of life.

Yet if the Great Ascent is slow, cruel, even fearsome, it is also irresistible, stirring, grandiose. It is an avenue of history which, however difficult, leads from an eternity of dark suffering toward the possibility of light and life. That it will surely usher in a period of disorder, readjustment, even temporary defeat is as true for the fortunate few as for the unfortunate many, but it is also possible to see such a period as prelude to a more distant era in which, for the first time, the potentialities of the entire human race may be explored. Thus if the trial is very great, so is the ultimate prospect. In the end it must be this prospect on which we fix our eyes and hopes if we too are to make our Great Ascent.

A Marxian View

Paul A. Baran

Aroused by the staggering irrationality and oppressiveness of their social and economic order, weary of the continuous exploitation by their foreign and domestic masters, the peoples of the underdeveloped countries have begun to manifest a mounting determination to overthrow a social and political system that is perpetuating their squalor, misery, and stagnation. . . .

What is decisive is that economic development in underdeveloped countries is profoundly inimical to the dominant interests in the advanced capitalist countries. Supplying many important raw materials to the industrialized countries, providing their corporations with vast profits and investment outlets, the backward world has always represented the indispensable hinterland of the highly developed capitalist West. Thus the ruling class in the United States (and elsewhere) is bitterly opposed to the industrialization of the so-called

From Paul A. Baran, The Political Economy of Growth (New York: Monthly Review Press, 1957). Copyright © 1957 by Monthly Review, Inc. Reprinted by permission of Monthly Review Press.

"source countries" and to the emergence of integrated processing economies in the colonial and semi-colonial areas. This opposition appears regardless of the nature of the regime in the underdeveloped country that seeks to reduce the foreign grip on its economy and to provide for a measure of independent development. Whether it is a democratically elected government in Venezuela, in Guatemala, or in British Guiana, an indigenous popular movement (as in Kenya, in the Philippines, or in Indo-China), a nationalist administration (as in Iran, Egypt, or Argentina) that undertakes to oppose the foreign domination of its country—all leverages of diplomatic intrigue, economic pressure, and political subversion are set into motion to overthrow the recalcitrant national government and to replace it with politicians who are willing to serve the interests of the capitalist countries.

The resistance of imperialist powers to economic and social development in colonial and dependent territories becomes even more desperate when the popular aspirations to national and social liberation express themselves in a revolutionary movement that, internationally connected and supported, threatens to overthrow the entire economic and social order of capitalism and imperialism. Under such circumstances, the resistance hardens into a counter-revolutionary alliance of all imperialist countries (and their reliable retainers) and assumes the form of a systematic crusade against national and social revolutions.

The requirements of this crusade have molded decisively the attitude toward the development of underdeveloped countries prevailing at the present time in the Western world. As the Prussian Junkers presented the continuation of serfdom on their estates as indispensable for the defense of Christianity against the onslaught of liberal godlessness, so the drive of the Western ruling classes to maintain the economic, social, and political *status quo* in underdeveloped countries is proclaimed as the defense of democracy and freedom. As the Prussian Junkers' interest in high tariffs on grains was announced to be dictated solely by their deep concern with the preservation of German food supplies under conditions of war, so the anxiety of dominant Western corporations to safeguard their investments abroad and to remain assured of the accustomed flow of raw materials from the backward world is publicized as patriotic solicitude for the "free world's" supply of indispensable strategic materials.

The arsenal of "united action" against the independent development of underdeveloped countries comprises an entire gamut of political and ideological stratagems. There are in the first place the widely broadcast statements of Western statesmen that appear to *favor* economic development in the underdeveloped world. Indeed, much is being made at the present time of the advanced countries' aid and support for the economic advancement of the backward areas. This advancement is conceived of as a slow, gradual improvement of the living standards of the native populations, and it is expected to *lessen* popular pressure for industrialization, to *weaken* the movement for economic and social progress. However, this scheme of "bribing" the peoples of the underdeveloped countries to refrain from overthrowing the existing system and from entering the road to rapid economic growth is beset by a host of insuperable contradictions. The logic of economic growth is such that a slow and gradual improvement of living standards in little-developed countries is an extremely difficult if not altogether impossible project. Whatever small increases in national output might be attained with the help of such Western investment and charity as may be forthcoming are swamped by the rapid growth of the population, by the corruption of the local governments, by squandering of resources by the underdeveloped countries' ruling classes, and by profit withdrawals on the part of foreign investors.

For, where far-reaching structural changes in the economy are required if the economic development of a country is to shift into high gear and is to outstrip the growth of population, where technological indivisibilities render growth dependent on large investments and long-run planning, where tradition-bound patterns of thought and work obstruct the introduction of new methods and means of production—then only a sweeping reorganization of society, only an all-out mobilization of all its creative potentialities, can move the economy off dead center. . . . The mere notions of "development" and "growth" suggest a transition to something that is new from something that is old, that has outlived itself. It can only be achieved through a determined struggle against the conservative, retrograde forces, through a change in the social, political, and economic structure of a backward, stagnant society. Since a social organization, however inadequate, never disappears by itself, since a ruling class, however parasitic, never yields power unless compelled to do so by overwhelming pressure, development and progress can only be attained if all the energies and abilities of a people that was politically, socially, and economically disfranchised under the old system are thrown into battle against the fortresses of the *ancien régime.*

But the crusade against national and social revolutions conducted at the present time by the Western powers relies upon a mobilization of altogether different social strata. It cements an international entente of precisely those social groups and economic interests that are, and are bound to be, bitterly antagonistic to genuine economic and social progress, and it subordinates considerations of economic development to the purpose of strengthening this alliance. It provides economic and military aid to regimes in underdeveloped countries that are manifestly inimical to economic development, and it maintains in power governments that would have been otherwise swept aside by the popular drive for a more rational and more progressive economic and social order.

It is as part of the same effort to bribe the peoples of the underdeveloped countries while avoiding the appearance of old-fashioned imperialism that political independence has been recently granted to a number of dependent nations and that native politicians have been allowed to rise to high offices. There is hardly any need to stress that such independence and autonomy are little more than sham as long as the countries in question remain economic appendages of the advanced capitalist countries and as long as their governments depend for survival on the pleasure of their foreign patrons.

What is more, the attainment of political independence by colonial peoples yields results under the conditions of imperialism that are frequently quite different from those hoped for by these peoples themselves. Their newly won political independence often precipitates merely a change in their Western masters, with the younger, more enterprising, more resourceful imperialist power seizing the controls that have slipped out of the hands of the old, now weakened imperialist countries. Thus where it is politically no longer possible to operate through the medium of the old-fashioned and compromised colonial administrations and to impose its control merely by means of economic infiltration, American imperialism sponsors (or tolerates) political independence of colonial countries, becoming subsequently the dominant power in the newly "liberated" regions. Both methods of expansion of American influence can be studied in Africa, Southeast Asia, and the Near East.

QUESTIONS FOR DISCUSSION

1. *Why does Heilbroner hold that we must give aid?*
2. *What changes in attitudes at home toward foreign aid does Heilbroner see as essential?*
3. *Why might economic development aid given to a poor country by the United States actually cause us some political difficulties?*
4. *How do you evaluate Baran's charges?*

Unfinished Business at Home

PART SIX

How Great Is the
Poverty Problem?

Probably the most painful and perplexing paradox of the contemporary American economy is the existence of considerable poverty
alongside the fairly high level of affluence that is characteristic of most
Americans. Poverty, of course, is nothing new to the nation. Throughout much of our history, poverty has been the rule for many, probably
most, Americans. As we know, the "American dream" has always been
based on the desire to escape impoverishment, and the ideal of "better-
ing oneself" is supposedly the guiding force behind individual economic affairs. By the early 1960's, when Americans "officially" discovered poverty again, many citizens had taken for granted that the
dream was working for almost everyone in America. The discovery
that between 20 and 40 percent of the population was "poor" (depending upon the income definition of poverty applied), and that
very little or no progress was being made by these "poor" to escape
their economic plight, evoked great national concern. The recognition
of the depth and breadth of this poverty is reported in the following
reprint of the 1964 Council of Economic Advisers Report, a document
that was the basis for action under President Johnson's proclaimed
War on Poverty.

Since the early 1960's thoughts on the problem of poverty have
greatly matured. Many economists and a sizable body of sociologists
now contend that the original statement of the problem was overdrawn
or tended to misconceive the real meaning of poverty. An extreme
example of some statements of this type can be seen in John B.
Parrish's article, although his view is by no means widely held among
the economics profession. However, by the beginning of the 1970's, an
observer is struck by the fact that the initial concern for poverty has
dwindled and that very many Americans appear to have become hard-
ened to emotionally charged discussions of "poverty in an economy of
plenty." In a following section on policies for dealing with the

economically disadvantaged this point is taken up again. Perhaps this change of attitude is the result of the frustrations which the "war on poverty" encountered and reflects the general belief that recent attempts to alleviate poverty have failed. Whatever the reason, it is likely that Americans will in the future have to discover poverty again.

The Problem of Poverty in America

Council of Economic Advisers

ELIMINATING POVERTY—A NATIONAL GOAL

There will always be some Americans who are better off than others. But it need not follow that "the poor are always with us." In the United States today we can see on the horizon a society of abundance, free of much of the misery and degradation that have been the age-old fate of man. Steadily rising productivity, together with an improving network of private and social insurance and assistance, has been eroding mass poverty in America. But the process is far too slow. It is high time to redouble and to concentrate our efforts to eliminate poverty.

Poverty is costly not only to the poor but to the whole society. Its ugly by-products include ignorance, disease, delinquency, crime, irresponsibility, immorality, indifference. None of these social evils and hazards will, of course, wholly disappear with the elimination of poverty. But their severity will be markedly reduced. Poverty is no purely private or local concern. It is a social and national problem.

But the overriding objective is to improve the quality of life of individual human beings. For poverty deprives the individual not only of material comforts but of human dignity and fulfillment. Poverty is rarely a builder of character.

The poor inhabit a world scarcely recognizable, and rarely recognized, by the majority of their fellow Americans. It is a world apart, whose inhabitants are isolated from the mainstream of American life and alienated from its values. It is a world where Americans are literally concerned with day-to-day survival—a

From "Annual Report of the Council of Economic Advisers, 1964," Economic Report of the President (Washington, D.C.: United States Government Printing Office, 1964).

roof over their heads, where the next meal is coming from. It is a world where a minor illness is a major tragedy, where pride and privacy must be sacrificed to get help, where honesty can become a luxury and ambition a myth. Worst of all, the poverty of the fathers is visited upon the children.

Equality of opportunity is the American dream, and universal education our noblest pledge to realize it. But, for the children of the poor, education is a handicap race; many are too ill prepared and ill motivated at home to learn at school. And many communities lengthen the handicap by providing the worst schooling for those who need the best.

Although poverty remains a bitter reality for too many Americans, its incidence has been steadily shrinking. The fruits of general economic growth have been widely shared; individuals and families have responded to incentives and opportunities for improvement; government and private programs have raised the educational attainments, housing standards, health, and productivity of the population; private and social insurance has increasingly protected families against loss of earnings due to death, disability, illness, old age, and unemployment. Future headway against poverty will likewise require attacks on many fronts: the active promotion of a full-employment, rapid-growth economy; a continuing assault on discrimination; and a wide range of other measures to strike at specific roots of low income. As in the past, progress will require the combined efforts of all levels of government and of private individuals and groups.

All Americans will benefit from this progress. Our Nation's most precious resource is its people. We pay twice for poverty: once in the production lost in wasted human potential, again in the resources diverted to coping with poverty's social by-products. Humanity compels our action, but it is sound economics as well. . . .

A few significant features of this bleak landscape deserve emphasis in advance. Poverty occurs in many places and is endured by people in many situations; but its occurrence is nonetheless highly concentrated among those with certain characteristics. The scars of discrimination, lack of education, and broken families show up clearly from almost any viewpoint. Here are some landmarks:

One-fifth of our families and nearly one-fifth of our total population are poor.

Of the poor, 22 percent are nonwhite; and nearly one-half of all nonwhites live in poverty.

The heads of over 60 percent of all poor families have only grade school educations.

Even for those denied opportunity by discrimination, education significantly raises the chance to escape from poverty. Of all nonwhite families headed by a person with 8 years or less of schooling, 57 percent are poor. This percentage falls to 30 for high school graduates and to 18 percent for those with some college education.

But education does not remove the effects of discrimination: when non-whites are compared with whites at the same level of education, the nonwhites are poor about twice as often.

One-third of all poor families are headed by a person over 65, and almost one-half of families headed by such a person are poor.

Of the poor, 54 percent live in cities, 16 percent on farms, 30 percent as rural nonfarm residents.

Over 40 percent of all farm families are poor. More than 80 percent of nonwhite farmers live in poverty.

Less than half of the poor are in the South; yet a Southerner's chance of being poor is roughly twice that of a person living in the rest of the country.

One-quarter of poor families are headed by a woman; but nearly one-half of all families headed by a woman are poor.

When a family and its head have several characteristics frequently associated with poverty, the chances of being poor are particularly high: a family headed by a young woman who is nonwhite and has less than an eighth grade education is poor in 94 out of 100 cases. Even if she is white, the chances are 85 out of 100 that she and her children will be poor.

THE NATURE AND EXTENT OF POVERTY

Measurement of poverty is not simple, either conceptually or in practice. By the poor we mean those who are not now maintaining a decent standard of living—those whose basic needs exceed their means to satisfy them. A family's needs depend on many factors, including the size of the family, the ages of its members, the condition of their health, and their place of residence. The ability to fulfill these needs depends on current income from whatever source, past savings, ownership of a home or other assets, and ability to borrow.

Needs and Resources. There is no precise way to measure the number of families who do not have the resources to provide minimum satisfaction of their *own* particular needs. Since needs differ from family to family, an attempt to quantify the problem must begin with some concept of average need for an average or representative family. Even for such a family, society does not have a clear and unvarying concept of an acceptable minimum. By the standards of contemporary American society most of the population of the world is poor; and most Americans were poor a century ago. But for our society today a consensus on an approximate standard can be found. One such standard is suggested by a recent study, described in a publication of the Social Security Administration, which defines a "low-cost" budget for a nonfarm family of four and finds its cost in 1962 to have been $3955. The cost of what the study defined as an "economy-plan" budget was $3165. Other studies have used different market baskets, many of them costing more. On balance, they provide support for using as a boundary a family whose annual money income from all sources was $3000 (before taxes and expressed in 1962 prices). This is a weekly income of less than $60.

These budgets contemplate expenditures of one-third of the total on food, i.e., for a $3000 annual budget for a 4-person family about $5 per person per week. Of the remaining $2000, a conservative estimate for housing (rent or mortgage payments, utilities, and heat) would be another $800. This would leave only $1200—less than $25 a week—for clothing, transportation, school supplies and books, home furnishings and supplies, medical care, personal care, recreation, insurance, and everything else. Obviously it does not exaggerate the problem of poverty to regard $3000 as the boundary.

A family's ability to meet its needs depends not only on its money income but also on its income in kind, its savings, its property, and its ability to borrow. But the detailed data [of the Bureau of the Census] available for pinpointing the origins of current poverty in the United States refer to money income. Refined analysis would vary the income cut-off by family size, age, location, and other indicators of needs and costs. This has not been possible. However, a variable income cut-off was used in the sample study of poverty in 1959 conducted at the University of Michigan Survey Research Center. This study also estimates the over-all incidence of poverty at 20 percent; and its findings concerning the sources of poverty correspond closely with the results based on an analysis of Census data.

A case could be made, of course, for setting the over-all income limit either higher or lower than $3000, thereby changing the statistical measure of the size of the problem. But the analysis of the sources of poverty, and of the programs needed to cope with it, would remain substantially unchanged.

No measure of poverty as simple as the one used here, would be suitable for determining eligibility for particular benefits or participation in particular programs. Nevertheless, it provides a valid benchmark for assessing the dimensions of the task of eliminating poverty, setting the broad goals of policy, and measuring our past and future progress toward their achievement. . . .

Organizing the Attack on Poverty. In this latest phase of the Nation's effort to conquer poverty, we must marshal already developed resources, focus already expressed concerns, and back them with the full strength of an aroused public conscience.

Poverty, as has been shown, has many faces. It is found in the North and in the South; in the East and in the West; on the farm and in the city. It is found among the young and among the old, among the employed and the unemployed. Its roots are many and its causes complex. To defeat it requires a coordinated and comprehensive attack. No single program can embrace all who are poor, and no single program can strike at all the sources of today's and tomorrow's poverty.

Diverse attacks are needed, but we must not lose sight of their common target—poverty. Many programs are directed against social problems which the poor share with the non-poor—insecurity of income, depressed regional economies, inefficient and unattractive rural and urban environments, disabilities of health and age, inadequate educational opportunities, racial discrimination. These are all to the good. But we must not let poor individuals and families get lost between these programs. Programs must be sufficiently coordinated [so] that, whatever else they individually accomplish, they act together to lift the economic and social status of America's poor. And soon. For war has now been declared on poverty as such.

This coordinated attack must be adapted to local circumstances. The needs of the poor are not the same in East Kentucky and in West Harlem. Coordinated programs of community action will play a critical role in the assault on poverty. Communities will be encouraged and helped to develop individual programs aimed at the special problems of their own poor families. Individual communities thus can participate in a nationwide action, research, and demonstration program, backed by the interest and resources of State and local governments and private organizations, and the coordinated efforts of Federal agencies working in such fields as education, health, housing, welfare, and agriculture.

Conquest of poverty is well within our power. About $11 billion a year would bring all poor families up to the $3000 income level we have taken to be the minimum for a decent life. The majority of the Nation could simply tax themselves enough to provide the necessary income supplements to their less fortunate citizens. The burden—one-fifth of the annual defense budget, less than 2 percent of GNP—would certainly not be intolerable. But this "solution" would leave untouched most of the roots of poverty. Americans want to *earn* the American standard of living by their own efforts and contributions. It will be far better, even if more difficult, to equip and to permit the poor of the Nation to produce and to earn the additional $11 billion, and more. We can surely afford greater generosity in relief of distress. But the major thrust of our campaign must be against causes rather than symptoms. We can afford the cost of that campaign too.

The Nation's attack on poverty must be based on a change in national attitude. We must open our eyes and minds to the poverty in our midst. Poverty is not the inevitable fate of any man. The condition can be eradicated; and since it can be, it must be. It is time to renew our faith in the worth and capacity of all human beings; to recognize that, whatever their past history or present condition, all kinds of Americans can contribute to their country; and to allow Government to assume its responsibility for action and leadership in promoting the general welfare.

Is U.S. Really Filled with Poverty?

John B. Parrish

When future historians write the history of the 1960s, there will be no more extraordinary episode in their accounts than the rise of America's "new poverty" cult. Intellectuals from every social-science discipline, every religious denomination, every political and social institution have climbed aboard the poverty bandwagon.

This article is concerned with a few fundamental questions: How did the new cult get started? What are its claims? Does the economic evidence support the claims? Are we moving toward a new and better social order or toward social chaos?

After a decade of exploring every nook and cranny of the poverty world, the "new poverty" cult has settled on a few basic doctrines which together form a dogma that apparently must be accepted on faith. These claims may be briefly summarized as follows:

1. The economic process, which in earlier years brought affluence to a majority of Americans, recently has slowed up and apparently stopped. As a result, a large minority of Americans are "hopelessly" trapped below the poverty line.

2. The size of this poverty population is "massive," and may be increasing. Minimum estimates place the number at 30 million, maximum at nearly 80 million.

3. Despite its great size, the poverty population is hidden away—"invisible," unknown, unwanted, unaided, helpless.

4. The hard core of the "other America" is the Negro. Because of racial discrimination, he has been unable to participate in economic progress. He is frustrated, embittered, forced to live outside the affluent society of the majority.

5. The "new poverty" can only be eradicated by massive, federal social-action programs involving income maintenance, self-help, education and training, in a milieu of racial integration, the latter voluntary if possible, compulsory if necessary.

Does the evidence on diffusion of economic well-being support the "new poverty" cult? Has diffusion mysteriously slowed to a halt, leaving millions "hopelessly trapped"? Are 30 to 80 million suffering acute deprivation in today's

Reprinted from U.S. News & World Report, *September 4, 1967. Copyright 1967, U.S. News & World Report, Inc.*

America? The plain truth is there is no basis in fact for the "new poverty" thesis. The high priests of the poverty religion have been exchanging each other's misinformation. Let's look briefly at some illustrative evidence.

Diet. The diet of United States families has continued to improve steadily over time until today at least 95 percent, perhaps 96 percent or 97 percent of all families have an adequate minimum daily intake of nutrients.

Automatic Cooking Equipment. Are 20 percent, perhaps 40 percent of United States families without decent equipment with which to prepare this food intake? No. As a matter of fact, 99 percent of all United States households have automatic cooking equipment, including most of those families living in rural and urban "ghettos." The diffusion has been consistent and persistent over the last six decades.

Refrigeration. Could it be that millions of American families are experiencing dull and dreary meals because they have no way to preserve foods and beverages against spoilage? No. About 99 percent of all United States families have purchased electric or gas refrigerators. It is reasonable to assume they know how to operate them, even in the "ghettos."

Communication. Are millions of America's poor shut off from all contact with the rest of their affluent countrymen—alone, frustrated, in that "other world" of poverty isolation? At last count, the diffusion of TV sets had reached 92 percent of all United States households, providing instant access to entertainment, news, sports, cultural enrichment. Since a small percent of middle- and upper-income families who can afford TV have chosen not to buy, the percent of families having TV who want it must be around 96 or 97 percent—a diffusion achieved in just 15 years.

Medical Aid. Have the "new hopeless poor" found the doors to modern medical service "slammed shut," forcing them to rely on quack remedies, superstition, midwives, or to die alone and unattended?

In 1910, only one of every 10 American families had access to hospitals for childbirth. The diffusion since then has been spectacular and persistent for all groups, including nonwhites. By 1960, over 97 percent of all American women had their babies born in hospitals. Today it is somewhere between 98 percent and 99 percent.

The Luxury of Telephone Service. Telephone service is ordinarily not a rock-bottom consumer necessity. It is useful and convenient but not an absolute requirement, as was demonstrated during the Great Depression of the 1930s when the percent of families with telephones declined.

Yet today nearly 90 percent of all United States households have telephones. Since there are still a few pockets of unavailability, it is reasonable to conclude that close to 95 percent of all United States households in availability areas who would like this luxury actually enjoy it.

THREE POVERTY FALLACIES

The foregoing illustrative evidence raises an interesting question: *How can the "massive" group of America's "hopeless poor" buy so much with so little?* Perhaps this basic question can be put another way: How could the poverty intellectuals be so wrong? The answer is actually very simple. The intellectuals have chosen to be wrong. Most members of the "new poverty" cult are quite well-trained in statistics. Some are acknowledged experts. They know better. But, for the sake of the "new poverty" religion, they have chosen to accept three poverty fallacies.

The "new poverty" cult has built much of its case on family-income statistics. Some technical matters aside, there is nothing wrong with these statistics, per se. But there is something wrong, very much wrong, with their use. It is impossible for anyone adequately to interpret them in terms of average family economic well-being.

Poverty fallacy No. 1 got its big push from the 1964 report on "The Problem of Poverty in America" by the Council of Economic Advisers. CEA determined that households with less than $3000 annual income were in poverty. Using this income yardstick, it was determined that 20 percent of United States households containing 30 million persons were in the poverty class.

This report provided a wonderful takeoff point for poverty statisticians. With 30 million to build on, it was not difficult to find millions of additional families who should be added to the poverty population. The poverty numbers game became quite exciting. Who could count the most? Honors so far have gone to those claiming nearly 80 million. A majority of cult members have settled for a more modest 40 to 50 million.

The truth about poverty-income statistics is this: Under no reasonable assumptions does income below $3000 indicate poverty status. It may or may not, and to say otherwise is not only erroneous but absurd.

Let's take as an example a young married couple, the Smiths. They are attending college. They constitute a statistical household. Their annual income is $1500 a year. They are not being "hopelessly" shut out from the good things of life. They are, along with other American youth, enjoying a rate of access to higher education greater than the youth of any country, any time, any place. They enjoy electric lighting, refrigeration, adequate if not fancy food, and a second-hand automobile or motorcycle. They would like a new Cadillac, but will manage without one. They aren't "poor" and need no crocodile tears shed in their behalf.

At the other end of the life cycle are the Joneses. Mr. Jones has been a machinist all his life. He and Mrs. Jones had always wanted to visit the country's great national parks after the children had grown up and left. So he has opted to retire at age 60. The retirement income will come to only $2000 a year. Are they poor? The poverty cult says, "Yes," these people are suffering from deprivation. They have been "hopelessly" cast aside. Yet the truth is they have a small home paid for, a modest automobile paid for. They enjoy refrigeration, automatic cooking equipment, inside plumbing, TV, enough clothes to last for years—the accumulation of a lifetime. And now they propose to enjoy more leisure, in more comfort, for more years than similar working-class families of any country, any time. The Joneses think the Council of Economic Advisers is statistically wacky.

And take the Browns. They are in the middle years. Both Mr. and Mrs. Brown work. Their three children are in school. They have a modest new home, partially paid for, some savings, some insurance, good clothes—yes, and a paid-for refrigerator and TV set. They have a new car and six installments still outstanding. Mr. Brown becomes ill. Mrs. Brown quits work to take care of him. Their income drops to below $3000 for the year. Are they in trouble? Yes. Are they in desperate consumer poverty? Are they "hopelessly trapped"? By no means. After a tough year they will resume as members of the affluent society even by CEA's definition.

ECONOMIC WELL-BEING: CUMULATIVE

These illustrations could be multiplied many times. Cross-section household-income statistics are a very inappropriate yardstick with which to measure economic well-being, which is a longitudinal and cumulative process.

Let's return for a moment to the telephone as a luxury—or at least a semiluxury—consumer good. Now take the desperately poor on whom the doors of affluency have presumably been "slammed shut." Now take the "poorest of the poor"—those at the very rock bottom of the income scale, those desperately deprived households earning less than $500 a year. You just can't get much poorer than that.

Now observe that nearly 60 percent of these poorest of the poor had telephone service in 1965. How could this be? Why would families presumably facing the grim miseries of malnutrition order telephone service? And, if we make allowance for the availability factor and the "can afford but don't want" factor, then it is reasonable to conclude that 70 to 80 percent of America's poorest poor had telephones in 1965.

If this is the "new poverty," it is apparently not too severe. How to explain this paradox of income poverty, consumer-goods affluence? The answer is quite simple. Income data are a very bad measure of economic well-being.

The Smiths, the Joneses, the Browns, all had telephone service even though the CEA's income statistics put them in the "poverty class."

There is a second big fallacy in the "new poverty" claims, and in some respects an inexcusable one. The poverty cult measures the economic well-being of families at all income levels by determining what they can buy with their income at current retail prices. In fact, the poverty cult makes much out of the fact that because of the greed of retail merchants and the gullibility and lack of buying savvy on the part of many poor buyers, the "new poor" actually pay more for the same goods than the affluent classes. This is hogwash.

The truth is, America's low-income classes have access to a low-price consumer-goods market in which prices are a fraction of published retail prices, and in which the purchasing power of "poor" dollars is multiplied many times. This discount market yields levels of consumption far above that indicated by retail prices.

As the poor could explain to CEA and the poverty intellectuals, this market is America's enormously big resale market—the world's largest. Every year, from 25 to 65 percent of many consumer durable-goods purchases involve second- or third-hand goods moving in established trade or in informal, person-to-person channels.

Take as an example a popular consumer durable good, the electric refrigerator. In 1923, this appliance was a new item. In current dollars, it cost around $900. Its capacity was small, averaging less than 6 cubic feet. It averaged only six years of service life, or about $150 a year. There were too few produced, and service was too short for a resale market. Only the rich could afford a refrigerator.

Today a good new refrigerator can be purchased for about $300. Its capacity will average about 10 cubic feet. Service life will be around 18 years. The average replacement year currently is around 10. So the first buyer pays about $30 a year, minus trade-in. Resale value will be about $50. This will permit the second buyer to purchase eight years of the same quality of refrigeration for about $6 a year. The low-income buyer, not particular about the latest style, has expanded his purchasing power 500 percent over that of the first high-income buyer.

Today's low-income, "new poverty" buyer has purchasing power 25 times greater than that of the rich buyer of 1923. America's consumer durable-goods market is operating under a law of accelerating diffusion. America's low-income families are not being shut out. They are being pulled into affluence at an ever-increasing rate.

There is a big, hidden, tertiary consumer-goods market not measured even by retail or resale price statistics. This is the intergeneration movement of goods accumulated over time and handed down or distributed from one generation to another. In an affluent society this becomes a very large market. Sewing machines, automobiles, electric irons, kitchenware, furniture, silverware, dinnerware, bicycles, etc.—all these provide an enormous source of consumption for all income classes, including the poor.

If ignoring the durable-goods resale market is inexcusable, the failure of the poverty cult to take account of the rapid growth in low-cost or no-cost goods and services in America is well-nigh incredible. It is incredible because much of it has been brought about by the very federal agencies whose economists have been among the high priests of the poverty cult. This failure constitutes poverty fallacy No. 3.

To illustrate: Nearly 90 percent of all Negro births today are in hospitals. Yet the United States House Committee on Education and Labor in 1964 said half the Negroes in America were suffering from acute poverty, measured by income statistics. How can so many poor afford so much medical service? For two reasons: First, as already noted, the income data are faulty. But more to the point here, almost every urban community has free or very low-cost medical services for low-income families. In fact, surveys show that in some communities the lowest-income families have more medical checkups, vaccinations, chest X rays, eye examinations than some higher-income groups.

The number of low-cost food programs has been growing rapidly. For example, the national school-lunch program provided low-cost noon meals for nearly 20 million children in 1967. The food-stamp plan provided low-cost food for 1 million persons in 1966, and was scheduled to rise to 2 million in 1967. The low-cost milk plan—along with school lunch—accounted for 5 percent of total United States nonfarm fluid-milk consumption in 1966, and would have expanded even more in 1967 had not cutbacks been ordered because of Vietnam.

The total number of low-income persons reached by various food-subsidy programs came to nearly 30 million in 1966, or precisely the number of persons classified as poor in 1964 by the Council of Economic Advisers. Since many of CEA's 30 million didn't belong in the poverty classification in the first place, some questions may well be raised as to who and how many poor have been "forgotten."

If the evidence suggests the "new poverty" intellectuals have grossly exaggerated the extent of poverty in America, can we now sit back comfortably and forget the poverty claims? Unfortunately, we cannot.

SOME DISTURBING TRENDS

There are some very disturbing social trends which have accompanied the spread of affluence. Even more disturbing is the possibility that the federal antipoverty programs may be casually as well as associationally related to these developments. We may be headed not toward a great new society, but toward social chaos. Let's look briefly at six problem areas, all of them interrelated:

1. The various federal-state income-maintenance programs seem to have generated an explosion of illegitimacy in America that will have far-reaching consequences for the future. The illegitimacy rate has doubled in the last few years, until today 1 out of 12 Americans is born illegitimate. At recent rates of growth, every tenth American by the early 1970s will be born out of wedlock.

2. Related to illegitimacy is the long-run growth in households managed only by females, a large proportion subsidized by various federal-state aid programs. Today in America, 1 out of 10 households is fatherless. There is every reason to expect this to rise in the future. Among Negro families the percentage is already 1 out of 4.

3. A particularly disconcerting development over and above trends for the whole population is the upsurge in the number and proportion of unwanted and unguided Negro youth. Today 1 out of 4 Negroes is born illegitimate. In some sections of large urban areas the percentage is very much higher. If the trends of 1950–64 continue, then by 1975 about one third of all Negro youth born in the United States will be born outside normal family-life patterns. They will be arriving at the teen ages not suffering from malnutrition or abject consumer-goods poverty, but from acute social and intellectual poverty. The future consequences for the rest of the urban populations, both white and nonwhite, will be considerable.

4. Related to but not solely derived from problems 1 to 3 is the rise of juvenile delinquency. The rate has doubled in the last decade. How long can society tolerate such a rate of growth? At least in part, the steady climb of delinquency may be due not to poverty, but to an affluent society—more leisure, more spending money, fewer responsibilities, less motivation, failure of rehabilitative programs.

5. The diffusion of affluency has been accompanied not only by rising juvenile delinquency but by a rising rate of general crime. The rate rose by one third, 1960 to 1964. The law-abiding segment of the population has an ever-increasing struggle to avoid the depredations of criminals, the latter experiencing not acute deprivation but the encouragement of easy and profitable pickings of the affluent state.

6. Perhaps no problem illustrates so well the failure of the poverty intellectuals than the upward drift of youth unemployment. Very strenuous and dedicated efforts have been made by the United States Congress to do something about youth unemployment. A great diversity of programs has been attempted. Recent conditions of tight, full employment have provided a favorable labor market. Yet the "new poverty" intellectuals have only failure to show for their efforts. Youth unemployment has not retreated. For nearly 20 years it has shown a rise—slight for white youth, sharply upward for nonwhite youth.

Could it be the "new poverty" cult has been fighting the wrong war? Measured by consumer-goods yardsticks, less than 5 percent of United States households are below the poverty line, and the percentage continues to decline.

There is a war to be fought, however. There are disturbing signs of deep social problems around us, and more on the horizon. The most rapidly growing segment of the American population is the illegitimate segment. The largest proportion of this "other America" is Negro.

Who is to discipline, guide, train this growing army of unwanted, unmotivated? The ordinary family influences, so strong among earlier ethnic groups immigrating to United States cities, appear to be lacking. In fact, such influences appear to be declining and may well be disintegrating.

The churches, historically an important institution in shaping constructive life patterns, appear to have limited and perhaps declining influence.

The "new social problem" is being dumped onto the public schools and the police. But schools cannot discipline—and without discipline they cannot educate.

The police can discipline—but they cannot educate and motivate. Racial-integration efforts have created new antagonisms to add to the problems of the already overburdened schools and police.

PHONY STATISTICS: HARDLY CONVINCING

The poverty intellectuals say they are building a great new society. Perhaps they are. But phony statistics are hardly convincing proof. Perhaps they should take a second look. They may well be rushing us pell-mell toward social chaos. The dogmas of the poverty cult may not prove as effective as expected.

Efforts to force racial integration may bring about as many disruptive as constructive influences. We may well need some new institutions designed for the problems of an affluent society of the present, not the poverty society of the past.

If this conclusion is even partially correct, then we should be about the task before it is too late. It may be already too late.

QUESTIONS FOR DISCUSSION

1. *According to the Council of Economic Advisers, who is poor in America?*

2. *How do you account for each group's poverty?*
3. *Do you think the $3000 income line is an adequate definition of poverty? Why or why not?*
4. *How do you account for the fact that American concern for poverty seems to ebb and flow historically?*
5. *Do you agree or disagree with Parrish that poverty has been over-emphasized in the United States? What is your reaction to this article?*

Is the Economic
Disadvantage of Black
America a Special Problem?

One of the great recognitions made in America's exploration of
poverty problems in the 1960's and a discovery that is not likely to re-
cede into the limbo of forgotten social priorities is the special economic
problem of black Americans. While the poverty and disadvantage of
such groups as the aged, the marginal farmer, and the poorly educated
is undeniable, these groups clearly lack the social visibility and the
political cohesion that characterize the blacks in American society.
It may also be argued that for many of the whites who are statistically
poor in the United States, the feeling of real impoverishment is lacking; but, for the black American, poverty is more sharply felt because
the economic gulf between the average black and the average white and
a three-hundred-year legacy of racial discrimination are constant re-
minders of an inferior social and economic position.

The statistical picture of the black man's special disadvantage as
represented in the first article is fairly common knowledge. His family
income stands at only about 60 percent of white earnings. He is twice
as likely to be unemployed as whites, and while blacks amount to
about 10 percent of the national population, they account for more
than 20 percent of what the Department of Labor classifies as poor.
To this economic picture the second article, a U.S. Department of
Labor publication authored by Dr. Daniel P. Moynihan, now special
adviser to President Nixon, adds a grim sketch of the social anatomy
of black poverty, particularly examining the impact of poverty and
racism on family life. The Moynihan Report has received near universal condemnation from the black community for its allegedly
"racist" suggestion that black America's difficulties are "special" and
not really economic. It is reprinted below because it represents a substantial body of "official" thought on the problems of black America.

The potential for violence and disorder that is a part of the special economic case of the black American hardly needs to be pointed out here. Americans have already seen frustration and alienation boil up in bloody street riots. That black Americans are impatient in most cases and in violent opposition to the American economic and social system in others is in part the legacy of a decade or more of civil rights agitation and legislation with few real economic gains to be shown as results. A variety of solutions to the problems of black America have been advocated, from the militant's cries of "Black Power," or black control of the ghetto economy and political structure, to "Black Capitalism," an attempt to subsidize black ghetto entrepreneurs to create jobs and economic opportunity, to a call for revolution. The last two articles survey the Black Power and Black Capitalism arguments.

Social and Economic Conditions of Negroes in the United States

Bureau of Labor Statistics and Bureau of the Census

This is a statistical report about the social and economic condition of the Negro population of the United States. It shows the changes that have taken place during recent years in income, employment, education, housing, health and other major aspects of life. The report was prepared jointly by the Bureau of Labor Statistics and the Bureau of the Census.

Virtually all of the statistics are from the Census or from Federal Government studies designed and conducted by technical experts. Many of the figures have been previously published. Others are scheduled to appear soon in regularly recurring government reports. Some of the data were tabulated specially for this report.

The aim throughout has been to assemble data to be used by government agencies at all levels, and by the general public, to help develop informed judgments on how the Negro is faring in this country.

A statistical report cannot present the complete picture because it is necessarily limited to those aspects of life which can be measured. Many elements

From Bureau of Labor Statistics and Bureau of the Census, Social and Economic Conditions of Negroes in the United States, *BLS Report No. 332 and Current Population Reports, Series P-23, No. 24 (Washington, D.C.: United States Government Printing Office, 1967).*

which are crucial for a dignified life in a society of equals cannot be measured. Yet much can be learned from a careful examination of the factual evidence at hand.

The statistics provide a mixed picture. There are signs of great improvement in some sections and of deterioration in others. The data show that large numbers of Negroes are for the first time in American history entering into the middle-income bracket and into better environments in which to raise their families.

Yet others remain trapped in the poverty of the slums, their living conditions either unchanged or deteriorating.

The kaleidoscopic pattern begins to make sense only when we stop thinking of the Negro as a homogeneous, undifferentiated group and begin to think of Negroes as individuals who differ widely in their aspirations, abilities, experiences and opportunities.

Millions of Negroes have uprooted themselves in search of better jobs, greater freedom and wider horizons. Many have taken advantage of education and training programs in recent years. The fact that these opportunities exist, and that large numbers of Negroes are using them, proves that there are open avenues of upward mobility in our society. Many who were at the bottom are finding their way up the economic ladder.

The substantial improvement in the national averages for Negroes in income, employment, education, housing and other subjects covered in this report reflects the widespread nature of the social and economic gains experienced by most Negroes in recent years.

Yet, large numbers are living in areas where conditions are growing worse.

In part, the deterioration in the poorest Negro neighborhoods reflects the fact that these areas are constantly losing their most successful people to better neighborhoods, leaving behind the most impoverished. As a first home in the city, these areas also attract rural newcomers who come with the hope—as did immigrants of previous generations—of making a better living, but with few skills to equip them for urban life.

This complicated pattern of progress mixed with some retrogression makes it hazardous to generalize about the social and economic conditions of Negroes in America. The statistics show dramatic achievements; they also reveal a large remaining gap between the circumstances of whites and Negroes.

The single most important fact in the economic life of most Americans—white and Negro alike—is the great productivity of our economy. Millions of Negroes who just a few years ago had small jobs, small incomes and even smaller hopes have made considerable gains.

Although Negro family income remains low in comparison with the rest of the population, the incomes of both whites and Negroes are at an all-time high and during the last year the gap between the two groups has significantly narrowed.

Still, despite the gains, Negro family income is only 58% of white income. A majority of Negro families still live in the Southern Region where incomes are far below the national average and where employment opportunities for them are more restricted than elsewhere. Outside the South, Negroes do much better. In the Northeast Region—the median family income for Negro families is $5400—two-thirds the white median; in the North Central area, the median income of Negro families is $5900—about three-fourths the white median.

Today, over 28% of the nonwhite* families receive more than $7,000 a year—more than double the proportion with incomes that high seven years ago, as measured in constant dollars taking into account changes in prices. Outside the Southern Region, the percentage of Negro families with incomes of $7,000 or more rises to 38%.

The incidence of poverty among nonwhite families remains high, with about one out of three classified as poor. Still, just six years ago one out of two of the nonwhite families [was] poor. Last year, the number of nonwhites in poverty was reduced by 151,000 families. The majority of nonwhites who are poor work for a living and are not dependent upon welfare assistance.

Whites and Negroes have both benefited from the prosperous conditions of recent years. Continued prosperity for more than six years has brought with it increased job opportunities. Many who had been out of work have moved into jobs; others who worked only part time are now working full time or overtime; and still others who were employed at menial tasks have taken advantage of the opportunity for upgrading their skills or status.

Unemployment rates for nonwhites are still twice those of whites, but the level for both groups has dropped dramatically. For nonwhite married men, who are the chief providers in nearly three-fourths of the nonwhite homes, the unemployment rate dropped at a faster rate than for white married men during the last five years and now stands at about 3½%.

Despite the decline in the unemployment rate, nonwhite males are somewhat more likely to be "not in the labor force," that is, neither working nor looking for work.

Further, unemployment has not decreased sharply everywhere. Teenage unemployment continues very high at 26%. In one of the worst areas of Cleveland (Hough) unemployment rates from 1960 to 1965 moved downward less than 2 points—and remained at 14% in 1965. The subemployment rate, which reflects part-time work, discouraged workers, and low-paid workers, was 33% in 1966 in the "worst" areas of nine large cities.

The decline in unemployment and the rise in income reflected an expanding

---

* Data for "Negroes" were used where available; in all other cases the data are shown for "nonwhites." Statistics for "nonwhites" generally reflect the condition of Negroes.

range of well-paying jobs. The number of nonwhites in professional, white-collar and skilled jobs went up by nearly half during the past six years.

Even with this substantial progress, it should be noted that Negroes are still far less likely to be in the better jobs. For the first time, however, the number of Negroes moving into good jobs has been of sizeable proportions. Since 1960, there has been a net increase of about 250,000 nonwhite professional and managerial workers, 280,000 clerical and sales workers, 190,000 craftsmen, and 160,000 operatives in the steel, automobile, and other durable goods manufacturing industries. There was a net increase of nearly 900,000 nonwhite workers in jobs that tend to have good pay or status during the past six years. Yet, many Negroes remain behind: a nonwhite man is still about three times as likely as a white man to be in a low-paying job as a laborer or service worker.

Education has often been considered as the key to economic success in our society. Recent improvements for nonwhites in this area parallel those previously described in employment and income.

Six years ago, nonwhite young men averaged two years less schooling than white young men. Today the gap is only one-half year. Nonwhite teenage boys are completing high school and going into college in increasing proportions, and for the first time the typical nonwhite young man can be said to be a high school graduate.

Despite the gains in "years of education attained," the only data available that deal with the "level of achievement" show a major gap: Negro students test out at substantially lower levels than white youths—up to 3 years less in the twelfth grade. Further, about 43% of Negro youth are rejected for military service because of "mental" reasons, compared with an 8% rate for white youth.

One of the encouraging signs revealed by this statistical study is the very active participation of Negroes in voting and registration.

Outside of the South, almost as large a proportion of Negro as white adults voted in the 1964 Presidential election. Almost 70% of all registered Negroes voted in the 1966 Congressional election. By 1966 there were over 140 Negroes in State legislatures, almost triple the number four years earlier.

One of the somber notes sounded by this report concerns the increase in residential segregation: a survey of 12 cities in which special censuses have been taken shows increased rates of segregation in 8 cities.

But perhaps the most distressing evidence presented in this report indicates that conditions are stagnant or deteriorating in the poorest areas.

About half a million poor Negro families—10% of the total—have lived all their lives in rural areas with very limited opportunities for improvement in education, employment, housing or income.

Another 10%—half a million Negro families—have incomes below the poverty line and live in poor neighborhoods of large central cities. This tenth lives in comparatively wretched conditions—many have poor housing; a sizeable proportion are "broken families"; they are at the bottom of the job ladder; and they have the highest unemployment rates.

The unevenness of social and economic progress among Negroes can be seen most dramatically in the results of the Census that was taken in Cleveland two years ago.

Outside of the poor neighborhoods in Cleveland, Negro families made major gains between 1960 and 1965. Average incomes rose, the incidence of poverty and the number of broken families were reduced.

But in the poorest neighborhoods, all of these social indicators showed decline.

In Hough, which is one of the worst of the poor neighborhoods, the incidence of poverty increased, the proportion of broken homes increased, and the male unemployment rate was virtually unchanged. A similar study was made in various neighborhoods in South Los Angeles after the riot in Watts several years ago, and showed much the same pattern.

Despite the general improvement in the conditions of life for Negroes nationally, conditions have grown worse in places like Hough and Watts. As Negro families succeed, they tend to move out of these economically and socially depressed areas to better neighborhoods where they and their children have the opportunity to lead a better life. They leave behind increasing problems of deprivation in the heart of our largest cities.

The facts in this report thus show a mixture of sound and substantial progress, on the one hand, and large unfulfilled needs on the other. They do not warrant complacency. Neither do they justify pessimism or despair.

The Negro American Family

U.S. Department of Labor

At the heart of the deterioration of the fabric of Negro society is the deterioration of the Negro family.

It is the fundamental source of the weakness of the Negro community at the present time.

There is probably no single fact of Negro American life so little

From U.S. Department of Labor, The Negro Family: The Case for National Action (*Washington, D.C.: United States Government Printing Office, 1965*). *This document has become better known as the "Moynihan Report," after Daniel P. Moynihan, then a Labor Department official responsible for its publication.*

understood by whites. The Negro situation is commonly perceived by whites in terms of the visible manifestations of discrimination and poverty, in part because Negro protest is directed against such obstacles, and in part, no doubt, because these are facts which involve the actions and attitudes of the white community as well. It is more difficult, however, for whites to perceive the effect that three centuries of exploitation have had on the fabric of Negro society itself. Here the consequences of the historic injustices done to Negro Americans are silent and hidden from view. But here is where the true injury has occurred: unless this damage is repaired, all the effort to end discrimination and poverty and injustice will come to little.

The role of the family in shaping character and ability is so pervasive as to be easily overlooked. The family is the basic social unit of American life; it is the basic socializing unit. By and large, adult conduct in society is learned as a child.

A fundamental insight of psychoanalytic theory, for example, is that the child learns a way of looking at life in his early years through which all later experience is viewed and which profoundly shapes his adult conduct.

It may be hazarded that the reason family structure does not loom larger in public discussion of social issues is that people tend to assume that the nature of family life is about the same throughout American society. The mass media and the development of suburbia have created an image of the American family as a highly standardized phenomenon. It is therefore easy to assume that whatever it is that makes for differences among individuals or groups of individuals, it is not a different family structure.

There is much truth to this; as with any other nation, Americans are producing a recognizable family system. But that process is not completed by any means. There are still, for example, important differences in family patterns surviving from the age of the great European migration to the United States, and these variations account for notable differences in the progress and assimilation of various ethnic and religious groups. A number of immigrant groups were characterized by unusually strong family bonds; these groups have characteristically progressed more rapidly than others.

But there is one truly great discontinuity in family structure in the United States at the present time: that between the white world in general and that of the Negro American.

The white family has achieved a high degree of stability and is maintaining that stability.

By contrast, the family structure of lower-class Negroes is highly unstable, and in many urban centers is approaching complete breakdown.

There is considerable evidence that the Negro community is in fact dividing between a stable middle-class group that is steadily growing stronger and more successful, and an increasingly disorganized and disadvantaged lower-class group. There are indications, for example, that the middle-class

Negro family puts a higher premium on family stability and the conserving of family resources than does the white middle-class family. . . .

There are two points to be noted in this context.

First, the emergence and increasing visibility of a Negro middle-class may beguile the nation into supposing that the circumstances of the remainder of the Negro community are equally prosperous, whereas just the opposite is true at present, and is likely to continue so.

Second, the lumping of all Negroes together in one statistical measurement very probably conceals the extent of the disorganization among the lower-class group. If conditions are improving for one and deteriorating for the other, the resultant statistical averages might show no change. Further, the statistics on the Negro family and most other subjects treated in this paper refer only to a specific point in time. They are a vertical measure of the situation at a given moment. They do not measure the experience of individuals over time. Thus the average monthly unemployment rate for Negro males for 1964 is recorded as 9 percent. But *during* 1964, some 29 percent of Negro males were unemployed at one time or another. Similarly, for example, if 36 percent of Negro children are living in broken homes *at any specific moment,* it is likely that a far higher proportion of Negro children find themselves in that situation *at one time or another* in their lives.

NEARLY A QUARTER OF URBAN NEGRO MARRIAGES
ARE DISSOLVED

Nearly a quarter of Negro women living in cities who have ever married are divorced, separated, or are living apart from their husbands.

The rates are highest in the urban Northeast where 26 percent of Negro women ever married are either divorced, separated, or have their husbands absent.

On the urban frontier, the proportion of husbands absent is even higher. In New York City in 1960, it was 30.2 percent, *not* including divorces.

NEARLY ONE-QUARTER OF NEGRO BIRTHS ARE NOW
ILLEGITIMATE

Both white and Negro illegitimacy rates have been increasing, although from dramatically different bases. The white rate was 2 percent in 1940; it was 3.07 percent in 1963. In that period, the Negro rate went from 16.8 percent to 23.6 percent.

The number of illegitimate children per 1000 live births increased by 11 among whites in the period 1940–63, but by 68 among nonwhites. There are, of course, limits to the dependability of these statistics. There are almost certainly a considerable number of Negro children who, although technically illegitimate, are in fact the offspring of stable unions. On the other hand, it may be assumed that many births that are in fact illegitimate are recorded otherwise. Probably the two opposite effects cancel each other out.

On the urban frontier, the nonwhite illegitimacy rates are usually higher than the national average, and the increase of late has been drastic.

In the District of Columbia, the illegitimacy rate for nonwhites grew from 21.8 percent in 1950 to 29.5 percent in 1964.

A similar picture of disintegrating Negro marriages emerges from the divorce statistics. Divorces have increased of late for both whites and nonwhites, but at a much greater rate for the latter. In 1940 both groups had a divorce rate of 2.2 percent. By 1964 the white rate had risen to 3.6 percent, but the nonwhite rate had reached 5.1 percent—40 percent greater than the formerly equal white rate.

ALMOST ONE-FOURTH OF NEGRO FAMILIES ARE
HEADED BY FEMALES

As a direct result of this high rate of divorce, separation, and desertion, a very large percent of Negro families are headed by females. While the percentage of such families among whites has been dropping since 1940, it has been rising among Negroes.

The percent of nonwhite families headed by a female is more than double the percent for whites. Fatherless nonwhite families increased by a sixth between 1950 and 1960, but held constant for white families.

It has been estimated that only a minority of Negro children reach the age of 18 having lived all their lives with both their parents.

Once again, this measure of family disorganization is found to be diminishing among white families and increasing among Negro families.

THE BREAKDOWN OF THE NEGRO FAMILY HAS LED
TO A STARTLING INCREASE IN WELFARE DEPENDENCY

The majority of Negro children receive public assistance under the AFDC program at one point or another in their childhood.

At present, 14 percent of Negro children are receiving AFDC assistance, as against 2 percent of white children. Eight percent of white children receive such assistance at some time, as against 56 percent of nonwhites, according to an extrapolation based on HEW data. (Let it be noted, however, that out of a total of 1.8 million nonwhite illegitimate children in the nation in 1961,

1.3 million were *not* receiving aid under the AFDC program, although a substantial number have, or will, receive aid at some time in their lives.)

Again, the situation may be said to be worsening. The AFDC program, deriving from the long established Mothers' Aid programs, was established in 1935 principally to care for widows and orphans, although the legislation covered all children in homes deprived of parental support because one or both of their parents are absent or incapacitated.

In the beginning, the number of AFDC families in which the father was absent because of desertion was less than a third of the total. Today it is two-thirds. HEW estimates "that between two-thirds and three-fourths of the 50 percent increase from 1948 to 1955 in the number of absent-father families receiving ADC may be explained by an increase in broken homes in the population.". . .

The steady expansion of this welfare program, as of public assistance programs in general, can be taken as a measure of the steady disintegration of the Negro family structure over the past generation in the United States. . . .

What then is the problem? We feel the answer is clear enough. Three centuries of injustice have brought about deep-seated structural distortions in the life of the Negro American. At this point, the present tangle of pathology is capable of perpetuating itself without assistance from the white world. The cycle can be broken only if these distortions are set right.

In a word, a national effort towards the problems of Negro Americans must be directed towards the question of family structure. The object should be to strengthen the Negro family so as to enable it to raise and support its members as in other families. After that, how this group of Americans chooses to run its affairs, take advantage of its opportunities, or fail to do so is none of the nation's business.

The fundamental importance and urgency of restoring the Negro American family structure has been evident for some time. E. Franklin Frazier put it most succinctly in 1950:

As the result of family disorganization a large proportion of Negro children and youth have not undergone the socialization which only the family can provide. The disorganized families have failed to provide for their emotional needs and have not provided the discipline and habits which are necessary for personality development. Because the disorganized family has failed in its function as a socializing agency, it has handicapped the children in their relations to the institutions in the community. Moreover, family disorganization has been partially responsible for a large amount of juvenile delinquency and adult crime among Negroes. Since the widespread family disorganization among Negroes has resulted from the failure of the father to play the role in family life required by American society, the mitigation of this problem must await those changes

in the Negro and American society which will enable the Negro father
to play the role required of him.

Nothing was done in response to Frazier's argument. Matters were left
to take care of themselves and, as matters will, grew worse not better. The
problem is now more serious, the obstacles greater. There is, however, a profound change for the better in one respect. The President has committed the
nation to an all-out effort to eliminate poverty wherever it exists, among
whites or Negroes, and a militant, organized, and responsible Negro movement
exists to join in that effort. Such a national effort could be stated thus:

*The policy of the United States is to bring the Negro American to full
and equal sharing in the responsibilities and rewards of citizenship. To this
end, the programs of the Federal government bearing on this objective shall
be designed to have the effect, directly or indirectly, of enhancing the stability
and resources of the Negro American family.*

Black Power

Stokely Carmichael and Charles V. Hamilton

The adoption of the concept of Black Power is one of the most legitimate
and healthy developments in American politics and race relations in our time.
The concept of Black Power speaks to all the needs mentioned [here]. It is
a call for black people in this country to unite, to recognize their heritage,
to build a sense of community. It is a call for black people to begin to define
their own goals, to lead their own organizations and to support those organizations. It is a call to reject the racist institutions and values of this society.

The concept of Black Power rests on a fundamental premise: *Before
a group can enter the open society, it must first close ranks.* By this we mean
that group solidarity is necessary before a group can operate effectively from
a bargaining position of strength in a pluralistic society. Traditionally, each
new ethnic group in this society has found the route to social and political

viability through the organization of its own institutions with which to represent its needs within the larger society. Studies in voting behavior specifically, and political behavior generally, have made it clear that politically the American pot has not melted. Italians vote for Rubino over O'Brien; Irish for Murphy over Goldberg, etc. This phenomenon may seem distasteful to some, but it has been and remains today a central fact of the American political system. There are other examples of ways in which groups in the society have remembered their roots and used this effectively in the political arena. Theodore Sorensen describes the politics of foreign aid during the Kennedy Administration in his book *Kennedy:*

No powerful constituencies or interest groups backed foreign aid. The Marshall Plan at least had appealed to Americans who traced their roots to the Western European nations aided. But there were few voters who identified with India, Colombia or Tanganyika [p. 351].

The extent to which black Americas can and do "trace their roots" to Africa, to that extent will they be able to be more effective on the political scene.

A white reporter set forth this point in other terms when he made the following observation about white Mississippi's manipulation of the anti-poverty program:

The war on poverty has been predicated on the notion that there is such a thing as a community which can be defined geographically and mobilized for a collective effort to help the poor. This theory has no relationship to reality in the deep South. In every Mississippi county there are two communities. Despite all the pious platitudes of the moderates on both sides, these two communities habitually see their interests in terms of conflict rather than cooperation. Only when the Negro community can muster enough political, economic and professional strength to compete on somewhat equal terms, will Negroes believe in the possibility of true cooperation and whites accept its necessity. En route to integration, the Negro community needs to develop a greater independence—a chance to run its own affairs and not cave in whenever "the man" barks—or so it seems to me, and to most of the knowledgeable people with whom I talked in Mississippi. To OEO, this judgment may sound like black nationalism. . . .

The point is obvious: black people must lead and run their own organizations. Only black people can convey the revolutionary idea—and it is a revolutionary idea—that black people are able to do things themselves. Only they can help create in the community an aroused and continuing black consciousness that will provide the basis for political strength. In the past, white allies have often furthered white supremacy without the whites involved realizing it, or even wanting to do so. Black people must come together and do things for themselves. They must achieve self-identity and self-determination in order to have their daily needs met.

Black Power means, for example, that in Lowndes County, Alabama, a black sheriff can end police brutality. A black tax assessor and tax collector and county board of revenue can lay, collect, and channel tax monies for the building of better roads and schools serving black people. In such areas as Lowndes, where black people have a majority, they will attempt to use power to exercise control. This is what they seek: control. When black people lack a majority, Black Power means proper representation and sharing of control. It means the creation of power bases, of strength, from which black people can press to change local or nation-wide patterns of oppression—instead of from weakness.

It does not mean *merely* putting black faces into office. Black visibility is not Black Power. Most of the black politicians around the country today are not examples of Black Power. The power must be that of a community, and emanate from there. The black politicians must start from there. The black politicians must stop being representatives of "downtown" machines, whatever the cost might be in terms of lost patronage and holiday handouts.

Black Power recognizes—it must recognize—the ethnic basis of American politics as well as the power-oriented nature of American politics. Black Power therefore calls for black people to consolidate behind their own, so that they can bargain from a position of strength. But while we endorse the *procedure* of group solidarity and identity for the purpose of attaining certain goals in the body politic, this does not mean that black people should strive for the same kind of rewards (i.e., end results) obtained by the white society. The ultimate values and goals are not domination or exploitation of other groups, but rather an effective share in the total power of the society.

Nevertheless, some observers have labeled those who advocate Black Power as racists; they have said that the call for self-identification and self-determination is "racism in reverse" or "black supremacy." This is a deliberate and absurd lie. There is no analogy—by any stretch of definition or imagination— between the advocates of Black Power and white racists. Racism is not merely exclusion on the basis of race but exclusion for the purpose of subjugating or maintaining subjugation. The goal of the racists is to keep black people on the bottom, arbitrarily and dictatorially, as they have done in this country for over three hundred years. The goal of black self-determination and black self-identity—Black Power—is full participation in the decision-making processes affecting the lives of black people, and recognition of the virtues in themselves as black people. The black people of this country have not lynched whites, bombed their churches, murdered their children and manipulated laws and institutions to maintain oppression. White racists have. Congressional laws, one after the other, have not been necessary to stop black people from oppressing others and denying others the full enjoyment of their rights. White racists have made such laws necessary. The goal of Black Power is positive and functional to a free and viable society. No white racist can make this claim.

"Black Capitalism" and the Business Community

A. Wright Elliott

Before becoming too deeply immersed in the troubled waters of "black capitalism," it would be wise to dispense with rhetorical and semantic games and agree upon a definition of terms.

We must go beyond simplistic slogans and admit that what we are really talking about is *ways that blacks can legitimately acquire a larger stake in our society.* In the economic sense, this means that they must legitimately acquire and control more resources. The concept of private property, which is a major foundation of capitalism, offers no support for color prejudice or special advantage.

We are suggesting, then, that before we proceed any further, we attempt to spell out just what business is being asked to get into. Far more questions will be raised than answered; but in large part we perceive this—the posing of critical questions—as our primary task.

Let it be clear, however, that we are not in any way questioning either the presence or the severity of a critical national problem. Nor are we in any way suggesting that business should not be involved in the implementation of solutions to this and other problems that we have traditionally labeled as "social."

What we are saying is: when so many people's lives—and indeed, perhaps the very life of our society—are at stake, let us be as certain as we can that we know what we are about. . . .

From A. Wright Elliott, " 'Black Capitalism' and the Business Community" in Black Economic Development, *edited by William F. Haddad and G. Douglas Pugh,* © *1969 by The American Assembly, Columbia University. Reprinted by permission of Prentice-Hall, Inc., Englewood Cliffs, N.J.*

No one knows better than a successful American industrialist the traditional meaning and function of capitalism. But is there a change when the word "black" is inserted in front? The business community, as well as the black community, must be alerted to the fact that, even if the name of the game has been changed only slightly, the game itself will very probably be played according to a different set of rules.

A New Jersey newspaper editorial trying to explain what blacks are really seeking notes that ". . . militants are calling for black capitalism, for the creation of self-contained, self-supporting economies inside the Negro community." . . .

THE NEW GAME: AN ALTERED SET OF RULES

In order to make some sense with regard to a definition of black capitalism, we might begin by considering what has happened in the area of employment. For in this area, where the business community and the black community have already interacted for an extended period of time, we have learned a great deal that can be useful for the questions posed by ghetto entrepreneurship.

With the major push launched by the National Alliance of Businessmen, some 100,000 minority group persons were gainfully employed in industry in 1968 alone. As the tempo of hiring increased and as companies learned to build in the requisite supports necessary to effectively employ and retain disadvantaged persons, the charge of "reverse discrimination" arose more than once from members of the non-black work force.

In response to this charge, many companies have attempted to educate their employees on the "new facts of life"—namely, that special corporate efforts must be made to help the new minority workers because of the deficits, resulting from life-long discrimination, with which they enter the labor market. The case has . . . been successfully made that such special efforts are necessary . . . in order to bring employees from the hard-core up to that point where they can successfully compete, at which time the "unequal support" can be discontinued

By the same token, efforts to help blacks become successful entrepreneurs will obviously require other "special supports"—in terms of financial, managerial, and technical assistance—so that black entrepreneurs, in most instances lacking a history of business involvement and experience, may be helped to compete on equal terms.

But, if this need be done, if the rules must be altered (and we think they must), does this not have serious implications for *existing* small companies, whether owned and managed by blacks or whites, currently struggling to stay alive and healthy? How will these companies perceive these special supports?

For years, they have been told that "competition is the name of the game," that "nice guys finish last"; but now, certain new, smaller companies will be receiving special help to assist them toward eventual success in the market place. There have already been some cries of "foul" from those in established-but-marginal businesses who have never received special supports.

Has the impact of this problem really been considered? Have we learned anything, hopefully, from our minority employment efforts? Should we really move into high gear, helping minority group members establish businesses in significant numbers across the country, before we have articulated well-reasoned answers to the charges of special privilege?

We would suggest that, again, as with programs to hire the hard-core, some type of arrangement will probably have to be worked out to help balance the competitive situation between the less successful established enterprises and their new competitors. Companies employing the hard-core are finding that, in the end, it is *more productive* (i.e. profit-oriented) to demonstrate additional concern for the entire work force, in order to forestall dissension.

Moving on, let us look for a moment at the demands of many of the black separatists. What they seem to want from the major corporations is, quite simply and bluntly, capital. They want either direct loans to assist in establishing black-owned enterprises, or capital investments in ghetto facilities to establish initially white-owned enterprises which will, after a designated period of time, be divested with regard to majority ownership.

What then is corporate management really being asked to do? To (1) invest capital in a highly risky venture with a return much lower than normal if analyzed in terms of the degree of risk; (2) train black managers and employees, thereby—to judge by a wealth of empirical data—requiring a higher than normal expenditure for training and a consequent reduction in net profit in the earlier years; (3) provide continuing technical management assistance to the new corporation.

And what can the investing company expect to receive in return? Simply this: once the new corporation becomes successful and in a position to begin to generate a return on the invested risk capital, the investing company is asked to divest ownership—or at least, to relinquish a majority position.

Realistically, of course, the major corporations are not investing this capital for the *primary* purpose of capital return. What they are hoping to "buy" (and we must be totally honest about it) is a long-range social harmony, whereby twenty years from now their companies will exist in a climate as free as possible from upheaval and disruption. Or to state it positively, they will thus exist in a climate where economic integration has led to the fullest participation of all of our citizens, regardless of color, in our national prosperity.

Capitalism? Not really, not in the sense of the term as it is applied in this country today. But if a relatively small investment today serves to protect the overall economic and political system—if, in the long run, our traditional system survives as a result of this investment—then perhaps what we are talking about is little different from an investment in new plant, or new equipment, or an investment in middle-management education. That is, it can be compared to an expenditure for long-term corporate improvement.

Parenthetically, any definition of capitalism in the "purest" sense is open to question. There are numerous instances of government subsidies to the profit-making sector, for example, that make the process of definition a difficult one. In short, discarding any glib definition, is there a difference between capitalism and "black capitalism"? Are we not talking really about making the benefits of our capitalistic system more accessible to the black community, full well recognizing the concomitant benefits to the *total* society?

This would seem to suggest, then, that this form of corporate investment in the future is not only required but legitimate to the interests of the stock-holders of major corporations. It suggests something else as well: Such investments could qualify for special consideration within a broadened concept which might be called "Social Cost-Accounting."

Capital investment by business corporations can do much to overcome and rectify past inequities to the black community, partially through assisting in the development of Negro-owned and Negro-managed enterprises. Therefore, some incentive, some allowance (some "social-credit") might be allowed. As an example, we must, at the least, intensively study proposals that would provide a tax credit to corporations that establish ghetto facilities.

The remainder of this [article] will be devoted to a description of where we feel both the black community and the business community are; and more important, to some tentative suggestions as to where the two must go—together.

THE BUSINESS COMMUNITY: A HARD LOOK AT ITS ROLE

To begin, what must the business community do if it is to assist the development of black business enterprise?

First, the white business community must honestly assess the differences that exist between it and the black business community. It must admit that, with few exceptions, it is technologically far more advanced; it possesses far more capital; it currently has a much larger pool of managerial talent than is generally available in the black community.

It must recognize that there are currently relatively few people in the black community who are fully prepared to build and manage enterprises—without some assistance; and finally that this gap between black and white America must be closed, employing as high a degree of problem-solving creativity as business has ever displayed in the past.

We face a significant national problem, one that demands special solutions. Therefore, rigidity in thought, as well as in action, is virtually intolerable. This means the business community must look honestly at such concepts as "sheltered markets," which guarantee the survival of a newly-launched enterprise for a stated period of time. It means that business must invest heavily in education and training, with a different reading of the balance sheet.

An initial decision has to be made as to the particular goal a given company wishes to achieve in its relationship with the black business community. Should the company consider opening a branch operation in the ghetto staffed by minority group members? Set up an operation with the avowed purpose of turning it over to the black community as soon as indigenous staff can be trained to run the firm? Or provide managerial and technical assistance to on-going black firms, in the process of developing necessary expertise? Obviously, the problem is not simply the typical case of how the company best maximizes profits. To enter into many minority communities today is comparable, virtually, to crossing an international border. Failure to consider the impact of this move on the ghetto inhabitants is comparable, in business terms, to ignoring the marketing function completely.

And simply to give in to the most insistent minority voice (or group) on the matter of participation may be, in the end, the most costly and least productive way to proceed. The decision must take into account the needs of *both* the company and the community. In the end, a cooperative relationship between the black and white business worlds is vital if long-term results are to be productive.

Another important point must be made with regard to the white business community. It is unfortunate, but probably true, that most businessmen, when they leave the making of cars, steel, or computers in order to serve on the board of non-profit or voluntary agencies, somehow manage to leave behind at the office their hard-nosed pragmatism—to leave behind the rigorous questions as to performance and achievement that make their companies successful and viable entities.

Nothing could be worse for the black capitalism effort, in which white businessmen are needed as *businessmen*. What must be brought to bear in this task is the best of our management tools, but, even more important, the best of the proved managerial attitudes.

Much will have to be "given," regardless of the terms of giving, and there is an obvious danger that the white business community runs the risk of becoming collectively "social workers in disguise." If it lends too much managerial assistance, and for too long; if the "sheltered market" ("in-house" contracts) stays sheltered, beyond judicious limits; if capital is repeatedly lent, in spite of continued non-achievement, over too long a period of time (that is, without regard to the discipline required of profit-making) then, we may find ourselves in the process of creating merely a new state of dependency—in which the black man finds himself permanently dependent upon the business loan and the borrowed executive consultant instead of on the welfare check and the case worker. . . .

MUTUALITY: THE ULTIMATE CHALLENGE

One thing is certain, and it needs little elaboration: If black-white business interaction is to succeed, there must be trust, there must be openness, there must be a climate that makes "leveling" easy (as easy as it can ever be). The time for "playing games" is indeed over.

There must be, flowing out of this climate of trust, a spirit of accommodation, of useful compromise, of negotiation. For if we really believe in a mutuality of interest, this means each of us has something to gain, and at the same time, something very precious to lose.

Perhaps this is at the essence of what "black capitalism" truly means, for it is here that the concepts, when tested, must really work. There are products, or values, to be "sold" by both black and white alike, and at the same time, both are consumers for those products. In short, we are in the market place, where love and admiration are desirable but not crucial, where a relationship of trust can be based on mutual self-interest, on a bargaining process in which there are potential benefits for all parties. This is where we are; if we can accept it as an encounter in the market place, then we can begin; that in itself implies a commitment to try.

A final word: At the heart of what we have attempted to say is a deep awareness of both the urgency of the problem and the great opportunity that is present. The effective involvement of Negroes with the business establishment is one vital element of a national effort to resolve our most profound domestic crisis.

And yet, if only because of this urgency, there is the danger that, plugging in quickly without comprehending the complexity of the problem, we would find that we have invested heavily in time, money, and emotion, without a sufficiently meaningful return. This is not to say that we should sit back and wait for the results of further surveys and studies. To the contrary, we would agree that the ghettos have had, if anything, too many studies, and far too little action. We are suggesting, however, that as we proceed we work double time at understanding what it is that both the ghetto residents and the business community need and are asking for—so that we might determine how we can best mutually use our resources to fulfill those needs.

Of one thing we are certain: Negroes in this country must have their rightful place at last in the processes of capitalism, and reap the rewards that come with greater involvement, if we are to have a truly free and just society.

1. *How does the economic condition of black America compare with that of white America?*
2. *What special effect does the history of slavery and racism have on black people's present economic opportunity?*
3. *Is "Black Power" a potential political and economic lever for changing black America's economic situation? Why or why not?*
4. *Do you think that "Black Capitalism" is a viable alternative to a continuation of the present problems? Why or why not?*

How Shall We Deal with the Economically Disadvantaged?

On March 16, 1964, President Lyndon Johnson presented to the Congress the first massive antipoverty legislation since the New Deal administrations of Franklin Roosevelt. In defending his proposed Economic Opportunity Act, which called for an initial annual expenditure of about $1 billion for youth programs, community-action projects, rural antipoverty undertakings, and other miscellaneous programs, the President called for a "war on poverty." Looking back on these efforts, their initial enthusiasm, and their later frustration, it is difficult to make an estimate of their worth. The "war on poverty" has been criticized by some for trying to do too much, too fast, and by others for being too little, too late. Meanwhile, it must be pointed out that the massive escalation of the Vietnam War after 1965 put serious restraints upon domestic welfare and antipoverty programs which drastically reduced their effectiveness. Nevertheless, whether or not the Johnson Administration programs will ultimately be judged as successes or failures, few knowledgeable Americans will argue that this nation has solved its poverty problems.

Exactly what the next round of antipoverty activity will be is not now certain. Clearly, specific programs will have to be devised to deal with the economic and social problems of black Americans. Probably government spending for antipoverty programs, while largely federal in appropriations, will be more controlled in particular expenditures by state and local agencies. Meanwhile, the idea of placing an income floor under all Americans, which is discussed in the first two readings, has gained a great measure of bipartisan support. Both "new economists" of the Johnson Administration and conservatives of the stature of Milton Friedman, an adviser to both Senator Goldwater and President Nixon, have supported the principle of a guaranteed annual wage or a negative income tax. However, as A. Dale Tussing points out in a following article, we still have much to learn about what poverty really is, who is really poor, and exactly what effects well-meaning welfare programs have upon the lives and the democratic freedoms of the poor.

In reading the literature of antipoverty, one must be struck by the optimism that seems to permeate virtually all proposed solutions to the problem. But a reflective citizen must ask himself why, in the face of such traditional optimism, is poverty such a serious problem in America? What is it that has inhibited such a wealthy society in finding solutions? Indeed, the antipoverty question opens a Pandora's box of deep and searching philosophical debate over the organization and goals of our economic system.

The Background to the Guaranteed-Income Concept

Robert Theobald

Social critics often claim that the present need for economic and social reform stems from past failures in economic and social policy. There is, of course, much merit in this contention. It is, however, far more realistic to perceive present problems as resulting not from failures but from the extraordinary success of Western societies in fulfilling their drive for ever-greater mastery over nature and, in particular, developing the productive potential that today makes it possible to provide every individual in the rich countries with a decent standard of living while requiring a decreasing amount of toil from the vast majority of the population.

The economic history of the past two hundred years may perhaps most properly be couched—to paraphrase H. G. Wells—in terms of a race between increasing production based on ever more complex and sophisticated technology and man's cultural inventiveness in devising and gaining acceptance of new methods of distributing and using this increasing production. It is surprising, therefore, that the mainstream of economics has only recently become concerned with the problems of balancing the available production with the rights of individuals and institutions to obtain this production. Throughout the nineteenth century it was rather generally accepted by economists that production and purchasing power—effective supply and potential demand—would automatically stay in balance. This assumption, called Say's law after its originator, dominated economic analysis until the great slump of the 1930s.

Innovations in techniques of distributing rights to resources have not, therefore, been based until recent years upon theoretical analysis but rather on pragmatic adjustments to the need to be able to sell what could be produced or to obtain the labor force required for the production of quality goods. The lack of a theoretical basis for changes in techniques of distributing income inevitably led to widespread controversy about the impact and implications of each new measure designed to raise purchasing power or attract workers. Thus Ford's five-dollar day, rapid growth in consumer credit and advertising, social security, and unemployment compensation were, in the past, just as controversial as the guaranteed income is today.

The motivation of Ford in introducing the five-dollar day early in the twentieth century and thus doubling the wages of his workers is still far from clear. Some interpreters argue that his main aim was to increase the number of people who could afford to buy the cars that he was turning out in ever greater numbers. Some have concluded that he was motivated by a desire to obtain a more highly skilled and stable labor force, and some believe he wished to increase the welfare of his workers. It would certainly be unprofitable to re-evaluate Ford's motives at this point in time. It would be equally unprofitable to examine in this essay the implications of the fact that the pattern of income distribution that has resulted from Ford's initiative cannot be reasonably explained in terms of existing economic theory—and indeed destroys its validity. It is important to recognize here only that Ford did introduce a mechanism that made it possible for the wages and salaries of workers to rise in parallel with production. This mechanism has been the chief factor responsible for ensuring that American purchasing power has kept in reasonable balance with American productive power during the last fifty years—with, of course, the exception of the Great Depression.

Two major developments in methods of distributing and using production occurred in the twenties. First, widespread use of consumer credit developed—people were allowed to purchase *before* they had earned the required funds. Second, manufacturers and distributors widened the range and scope of selling activities designed to cultivate new tastes. Despite these efforts, however, potential supply was so far ahead of effective demand by 1929 that the economy collapsed.

It was the Great Depression, which followed this collapse, that led economists to become deeply concerned with the problem of maintaining purchasing power. The change in the thrust of economic analysis is generally and correctly attributed to John Maynard Keynes's book *The General Theory of Employment,*

Interest, and Money. Nevertheless, it must be noted that there is a good deal of evidence suggesting that the brute facts of the Depression forced politicians to move in the direction of increasing purchasing power before a full economic justification for this step had been found—and indeed even while a large proportion of the economics profession was still opposing this step and calling for decreases in government expenditure. Thus social security and the make-work schemes of the thirties were conceived as a response to social unrest rather than justified on economic grounds as a means of ending the recession through increasing demand.

It is also important to recognize that present developments in economic theorizing, which are generally believed to be an extension of Keynesian analysis, do not adequately reflect the spirit of Keynesian thought—as opposed to his technical conclusions. Keynes's main contribution to theory came when he proved that it was possible for unemployment to persist over long periods because effective demand would not necessarily rise as fast as potential supply. Modern economic theorists grasped this insight and set to work to devise policies that would lead to a sufficiently rapid increase in effective demand to balance increases in potential supply and thus ensure minimum unemployment. However, this is not the *only* policy proposal that can be derived from an interpretation of Keynesian analysis: society could equally well decide that it no longer wished to channel the quasi-totality of its efforts toward the goal of full employment but rather desired to seek a new social order that would allow us to take full advantage of the potential of emerging abundance and our ability to eliminate toil.

Keynes himself quite clearly hoped for the second development, arguing that

> when the accumulation of wealth is no longer of high social importance, there will be great changes in the code of morals. We shall be able to rid ourselves of many of the pseudo-moral principles which have hag-ridden us for two hundred years, by which we have exalted some of the most distasteful of human qualities into the position of the highest values. We shall be able to afford to dare to assess the money-motive at its true value. . . . All kinds of social customs and economic practices affecting the distribution of wealth and its rewards and penalties which we now maintain at all costs, however distasteful and unjust they may be in themselves . . . we shall then be free, at last, to discard.*

It is quite clear, therefore, that although present policy is justified on the basis of Keynesian analysis, Keynes would, in present conditions, reject many

* J. M. Keynes, "Economic Possibilities for Our Grandchildren," *Essays in Persuasion* (New York: Harcourt, Brace and Company, 1932), pp. 369–70.

of the policy prescriptions being advanced, for he would hold that they perpetuated the worst of the values of the industrial age.

What methods have economists proposed to ensure that potential supply and effective demand would stay in balance? The first step toward this goal, which was accomplished around the end of the Second World War in almost all Western countries, was the passage of legislation pledging the efforts of governments to ensure that supply and demand would remain in balance and thus provide jobs for all: in the United States this was accomplished by the Employment Act of 1946.

This commitment to a full employment policy through balancing supply and demand has deepened in all Western countries in the years since the Second World War. The United States has undoubtedly been the last country to understand the full implications of this policy approach, but the first five years of the sixties have marked its final acceptance. It is now generally believed, not only by economists but by the vast majority of businessmen, that it is the responsibility of the government to ensure that the economy remains in balance—that the government should aim to balance the economy rather than to balance the budget. As Meno Lovenstein points out . . . the government has now essentially taken a commitment to "guarantee the national income" by ensuring that rights to all available productive resources are distributed.

The difference between this approach to the government's responsibility and that current in the nineteenth century, when it was believed that government damaged the operation of the economy whenever it intervened, is so vast as to need no stressing. Unfortunately, economic theory has not yet re-examined all the implications of the shift in approach. For example, if the government is deeply involved in guaranteeing the national income of the whole country, and if, as is inevitable, its interventions affect the pattern of income distribution, what goals should it adopt? Another facet of this problem results from the fact that a large number of people are unable to earn their living because they are too old, too young, too mentally or physically ill. How should they be provided with incomes and what amount of resources should they receive? Economics has few, if any, answers to these and similar questions.

The problem of providing incomes to those who are too old, too young, or too sick to hold a job is already urgent and is certain to become more so in coming years because of the inevitable shifts in patterns of age distribution. This reality is already causing the emergence of a new consensus that cuts across party lines and interest groups. This consensus is based on a belief that the government has already taken an implied commitment to provide a minimum level of income to all individuals, but that the present mosaic of measures designed to ensure this result is both excessively complex and unduly costly. It is argued that it would therefore be desirable to introduce a single plan that would meet the implied commitment of government as simply and cheaply as possible through the introduction of a guaranteed income floor for all those who either cannot, or should not, earn their living through holding a job.

There should be no need to justify payments to the physically and mentally ill: they cannot work and society should surely provide for them. Some justification, however, is often felt to be required for more adequate payments to the old, for one of the most sanctified of our work myths is that older people both could and should have saved enough to provide for their old age. This is, of course, merely a cynical fiction. Those who are old today worked in an era when their income was necessarily far lower than is paid for jobs demanding a comparable level of skills and application today. They needed to spend a large proportion of their income just to cover their expenses, including the education of their children. They were therefore able to save very little, if anything, whether directly or through insurance schemes. Today's labor force, however, would not be enjoying its present level of income without their hard work and that of earlier generations who had even less to show for their toil. Any fair distribution of the nation's resources should ensure that old people be allowed to share in the wealth they created. Their labor was, in fact, wealth, and it was invested in the national economy at a time when its value was at a premium. Today this group should be collecting their "earned interest."

It will, perhaps, help to put this question in perspective if we recognize that most of those presently being paid social security benefits are receiving more than the actuarial value of their contributions: i.e., they did not pay enough money to cover the benefits they are receiving. Continuing expansion of the social security system makes it almost certain that it will not become actuarily sound at any point in the future. Thus we have already accepted, on a practical basis, that the old are entitled to a more adequate income than would be theirs on an insurance basis. The next step is to bring the logic of this position into the open and see what more needs to be done.

The question of income distribution among the young poses equally serious problems, for we have not yet been willing to accept the fact that we have extended the principle of parental support of the young far beyond the breaking point. In an agricultural or even an early industrial society, a child was wealth. After a few years of care, the child added to the family income rather than subtracted from it. In addition, the younger generation was expected to support their parents as they grew old. There was, thus, a rough balance between the economic responsibility of the parents and that of the children.

Let us contrast this with the situation today. Because of the demands of the new world in which we live, a child should be educated at least until he is twenty-one and perhaps until he is twenty-five or thirty. Despite the growing number of loans, grants, and scholarships, it is still a fundamental assumption of our society that the primary economic responsibility for the education and support of the child lies with the parent. However, the parent receives little financial return, for by the time the child leaves the educational process he is generally married and feels little obligation for the economic support of his parents. Parents should no longer be expected to underwrite the lengthy education process that the future society requires of today's and tomorrow's young people. We must recognize that the student is already "working" as relevantly as the man in the factory or the office. . . .

In the relatively near future, therefore, those who need to expand their plant to meet created demand will prefer to buy machines rather than to hire men: the machines they buy will be produced predominantly by other machines. The new machines purchased will be so much more efficient than earlier machinery that large numbers of existing firms using older machinery and thus employing many men will be forced to close down: they will be too inefficient to compete.

The process can be summarized as follows: created demand will lead to purchases of highly efficient and productive machine systems that need few men to control them: i.e., to the installation of cybernation. Thus, in the relatively near future, a policy of forcing rapid growth in demand in order to increase employment opportunities will actually lead to the opposite result: it will raise unemployment rather than lower it.

The conclusion that massive unemployment is inevitable is still rejected by most economists and policy-makers, who argue that increases in demand brought about, if necessary, by federal intervention to balance the economy can *always* be large enough to ensure that all the available labor will be used. Unfortunately, however, there is no economic theory or contemporary evidence to support this conclusion. The neoclassical theorizing of the last part of the nineteenth century and the beginning of the twentieth assumed that men and machines would cooperate with each other; today, however, they are competitive. Keynes, who is presently used as the justification for the assertion that demand and supply can be kept in balance, and jobs provided for all, should not be used for this purpose because he excluded from his analysis those very factors that now threaten massive unemployment. "We take as given the existing skill and quantity of available labor, the existing quality and quantity of available equipment, the existing technique. This does not mean that we assume these facts to be constant, but merely that in this place and context, we are not considering or taking into account the effects and consequences of changes in them."

In effect, therefore, economists have no valid theoretical structure to support their contention that unemployment can be avoided by increases in demand. To the non-economist, such a statement will necessarily be shocking, but it is unfortunately valid. Economists, like many social scientists, have generally been far more concerned about theoretical rigor within a given pattern of assumptions than about the validity of the assumptions themselves; the development of theory has proceeded despite the ever decreasing relevance of the assumptions on which it is based. Economic predictions about unemployment rates will not be valid until the analysis from which they are drawn is based on a new and more relevant set of assumptions.

As minimum unemployment cannot be achieved in coming years, fundamental change in the socioeconomic system will be absolutely essential. As we have already seen, our present system is postulated on the belief that every individual who desires a job will be able to find one and that the jobs thus obtained will pay well enough to enable the individual to live with dignity. I am convinced that if we desire to maintain freedom, a guaranteed income will necessarily have to be introduced. In addition, during the period of transition from a scarcity to an abundance socioeconomy, we will have to consider the whole problem of income maintenance for those whose income level is above the minimum income floor in order to allow them to update their education and to minimize hardship when individuals lose their jobs because of further increases in technological sophistication. Although . . . this essay [cannot] deal with the issue of income maintenance, it is necessary to stress that the need for an income maintenance program is just as great as the need for a guaranteed income floor. . . .

For society at large, and especially for those creative individuals now shackled by the absence of a guaranteed source of income, the situation would seem to be analogous to that which obtained at the time of the introduction of limited liability in the nineteenth century. Limited liability was introduced to encourage risk-taking by those investing in companies. The concept of a joint venture was replaced by the concept that a stockholder's liability for company debts no longer put a lien on his total wealth but only on the amount he invested in the company. Limited liability was a precondition for the taking of risks: it did not ensure innovation or risk-taking, but it did make them possible, thus allowing the economy and society to benefit from the self-interested acts of individuals.

A guaranteed income provides the individual with the ability to do what he personally feels to be important. This will allow risk-taking and innovation in areas where the existing and emerging needs of society are not being met by an otherwise efficiently functioning free-enterprise system. The guaranteed income is not mediated through the offices of any other individual or organization within the market system and therefore does not bring with it built-in pressures for the recipient to continue doing what is already being done through the market system.

The guaranteed income therefore involves a major shift in rights and obligations. Today we demand of an individual that he find a job, but we then provide him with the right to "pursue happiness." Tomorrow we will provide him with the right to receive enough resources to live with dignity, and we will demand of him that he develop himself and his society.

The guaranteed-income proposal is based on the fundamental American belief in the right and the ability of the individual to decide what he wishes and ought to do. This is surely the basic meaning of the phrase "private enterprise": that the individual should have the right to obtain enough resources to do what he believes to be important. In the past, the individual could go into business for himself and thus obtain resources. Today all the evidence shows that neither the self-employed businessman nor the small company can compete with the large corporation. The ideal of private enterprise can, therefore, be preserved only if the guaranteed income is introduced.

The guaranteed income will, in fact, lead to the revival of "private enterprise." Once the guaranteed income is available, we can anticipate the organization of what I have called "consentives": productive groups formed by individuals who will come together on a voluntary basis simply because they wish to do so. The goods produced by these consentives will not compete with mass-produced goods available from cybernated firms. The consentive will normally produce the "custom-designed" goods that have been vanishing within the present economy. The consentive would sell in competition with firms paying wages, but its prices would normally be lower because it would need to cover only the costs of materials and other required supplies. Wages and salaries would not need to be met out of income, as the consentive members would be receiving a guaranteed income. The consentive would be market-oriented but not market-supported.

We can anticipate that small market-supported firms will be enabled to survive by transforming themselves into market-oriented consentives. The opposite process will occur as consentives that make significant profits automatically turn into market-supported firms. Thus the guaranteed income would help to bring about a reversal of the present trend toward similarity in type of goods and services, inflexibility in methods of production, and uniformity in productive organization.

At the present time we are committed as a society to the idea that we can and should provide jobs for all. This goal is no longer valid, and we should therefore provide everybody with an absolute right to a guaranteed income. This will, of course, mean that there will be far more unemployment in the future than there is today. We will, however, come to perceive unemployment as favorable rather than unfavorable. The individual and the society fear unemployment today for two reasons: first, because it usually involves the receipt of an inadequate income; second, because it threatens cessation of all activity that seems meaningful and indeed encourages antisocial activities. Once we have provided adequate incomes to all and have introduced the new policies required to develop each individual's potential, unemployment—which will then be redefined as the condition of *not* holding a job—will be seen to be highly desirable, for it will provide the individual with freedom to develop himself and his society.

The Negative Income Tax

Milton Friedman

The proposal to supplement the incomes of the poor by paying them a *fraction* of their unused income exemptions and deductions, which I termed a *negative income tax* years ago, has many advantages over present welfare programs:

1. It would help the poor in the most direct way possible.
2. It would treat them as responsible individuals, not as incompetent wards of the state.
3. It would give them an incentive to help themselves.
4. It would cost less than present programs yet help the poor more.
5. It would eliminate almost entirely the cumbrous welfare bureaucracy running the present programs.
6. It could not be used as a political slush fund, as so many current programs—notably in the "war on poverty"—can be and have been used.

In the course of advocating a negative income tax . . . I have repeatedly encountered the same objections time and again. Let me try to answer a few of them.

1. *By removing a means test, the negative income tax establishes a new principle in the relation between citizens and the government.* This is simply a misunderstanding. The negative income tax retains a means test—the straightforward numerical test of income rather than the present complex and demeaning test. It uses the same means test to decide who shall receive assistance from the government as the one we now use to decide who shall pay the expenses of government.

True, it guarantees a minimum income to all. But that is not a new principle. Present welfare arrangements guarantee a minimum income in practice, and in some states, even in law. The trouble is that these present welfare programs are a mess.

2. *The minimum levels of income proposed are too low.* We are talking about a Federal program and a *nationwide* minimum. The levels of assistance are decidedly higher than current levels in most states. They are decidedly lower than current levels in states like New York, Illinois, California. It would be absurd to enact such high levels as national standards. But there is every reason to encourage the more affluent states to supplement the Federal negative income tax out of state funds—preferably by enacting a supplementary state negative income tax.

3. *The poor need regular assistance. They cannot wait until the end*

From Newsweek, *October 7, 1968. Copyright Newsweek, Inc., 1968. Reprinted by permission.*

of the year. Of course. The negative income tax, like the positive income tax, would be put on an advance basis. Employed persons entitled to negative income tax would have supplements added to their paychecks, just as most of us now have positive taxes withheld. Persons without wages would file advance estimates and receive estimated amounts due to them weekly or monthly. Once a year, all would file a return that would adjust for under- or over-payments.

4. *The negative income tax destroys incentives to work.* Under present programs, persons on welfare who obey the law generally lose a dollar in relief for every additional dollar earned. Hence, they have no incentive whatsoever to earn the dollar. Under the negative income tax plan that I propose, such a person would keep 50 cents out of every additional dollar earned. That would give him a far greater incentive than he now has.

One additional point. A welfare recipient now hesitates to take a job even if it pays more than he gets on welfare because, if he loses the job, it may take him (or her) many months to get back on relief. There is no such disincentive under a negative income tax.

5. *The negative income tax will foster political irresponsibility.* If we adopt an open and aboveboard program for supplementing the incomes of people below some specified level, will there not be continued political pressure for higher and higher breakeven incomes, for higher and higher rates on negative income? Will the demagogues not have a field day appealing to have-nots to legislate taxes on haves for transfer to them?

These dangers clearly exist. But they must be evaluated in terms of the world as it is, not in terms of a dream world in which there are no governmental welfare measures. These dangers are all present now—and have clearly been effective. The crucial question is, how do we get out of the mess into which these pressures have driven us? The negative income tax offers a gradual and responsible way to work ourselves out of this mess. No other way of doing so has as yet been suggested.

Anti-Poverty Policy for the Seventies

A. Dale Tussing

A conflict of viewpoints is brewing in the field of anti-poverty policy, a conflict in which old ideological positions will be blurred with liberal set

Mr. Tussing is associate professor of economics at Syracuse University. His article is published here for the first time.

against liberal and conservative against conservative. What will be at issue will be the extent to which the welfare establishment will continue to control the lives of the poor and, thereby, to keep them powerless and dependent.

The conflict is not new, but the numbers, sophistication, and political muscle of those favoring substantial reform in anti-poverty policy have been gaining, and momentum is developing. This point of view is still sufficiently novel that it may be called a new wave in anti-poverty policy.

THE MEANING OF POVERTY

A discussion of this new wave requires, first, a digression into the nature of poverty in America. There is what will be called here an "economic fallacy" commonly employed in defining poverty, one which is easy to fall prey to, but one which leads necessarily into wrong conclusions and apparent paradoxes.

The first step in the fallacy is to define poverty as the inadequacy of means relative to needs. Since this definition is the most commonly accepted one, few people would object. Consequently, few people would resist being led into two inferences from this definition. First, poverty is to be defined in *income* terms—i.e., sufficiency of "means." Second, since the community's conception of "needs" changes over time, an income which would have provided amply for needs and even for comfort sometime in the past (say, at the turn of the century), or which would be adequate today in some other country, may be a poverty income today in the United States (when adjusted, of course, for price-level changes). America's poor are, it is often alleged, quite rich in worldwide terms or in historical perspective. American blacks, for instance, are claimed by the *New York Times* to be "economically the most prosperous large group of nonwhites in the world, enjoying a higher average income than the inhabitants of any nation in Africa, Asia, or Latin America."

Anyone who has accepted the argument thus far is in the trap of the economic fallacy. He is led to two conclusions which he knows are false:

1. He is led to accept the "poverty-line" definition of poverty, either the crude $3000 line first proposed by the Council of Economic Advisers, or the variable line (depending on family size and other indicators of budget needs) developed by Mollie Orshansky of the Social Security Administration. He is led to conclude, then, that the poverty group includes temporarily poor persons with irregular incomes; persons with considerable or even moderate wealth (e.g., retired homeowners with liquid savings) whose current incomes are low; graduate and medical students and others whose low incomes do not in any way constitute a social problem. But he may be troubled by these apparently false conclusions, and begin to be aware that the problem of poverty and problem of income are not identical.

2. He is led, further, to conclude that American poverty is only inequality,

i.e., only "poverty" in a relative and not an absolute sense. He is led to conclude that, in a worldwide or long-run sense, many American poor are, in fact, quite wealthy, owning automobiles, television sets, and having free medical care available to them, and having, then, a level of life reserved in other countries only for a small elite. But he knows how American poor live, and he knows that they are not wealthy. He knows that, despite their apparent prosperity, they tend to be caught in a vicious or cumulative circle which freezes them at the bottom of the social and economic ladder; that dependency and apathy not only are their salient characteristics but tend to be inherited; that their rates of criminality, suicide, mental illness, alcoholism, narcotics addiction, and other measures of despair reflect no position of wealth but rather of hopelessness; that social and family disorganization are endemic; that, in short, they share most of the characteristics of what Oscar Lewis has called the "culture of poverty," a worldwide phenomenon, though their material means exceed those of the Mexican or Puerto Rican poor.

It is this pathology of poverty that is of social concern, and this pathology tends to be associated with, but is not the same as, insufficiency of means.

Some of the difficulties with the economic definition of poverty may be removed if we use greater sophistication in its specification. For example, we can measure income over a longer time span so as to exclude the temporarily poor (and hence those not demoralized by their low incomes). We can include accumulated wealth as well as current income in the poverty definition. We can recognize that a given level of income can mean poverty in a rich society but not in a poor one.

This last statement is widely accepted in a relative sense, but it is also true in an absolute one. A few examples will illustrate. Failure to own an automobile in Ecuador, Malaysia, or even the Soviet Union is no particular hardship; those societies are not organized around the automobile, and occupations, shopping, and social life are not dependent upon automobiles. In the United States, by contrast, the organization of society is highly dependent upon the automobile, and is becoming more so. Critical problems have developed where public housing projects have been constructed without attention to providing for grocery and other shopping; project planners apparently had tacitly assumed that the residents (many of them non-automobile owners) would simply hop in their cars and drive to the shopping center every week or so. Similarly, failure to own a television set where live entertainment flourishes on streetcorners is not poverty; failure to own one in the McLuhanist society of the United States probably is. Failure to own a telephone where no one else has one either, and where other means are provided for communication, is not poverty; failure to possess one in the United States makes it impossible to conduct the ordinary business of life, which is heavily dependent upon the telephone. There are endless examples. Any absolute level of real income provides greater hardship where the fabric of society has adjusted to a considerably higher level of income. Many of the poor of other countries would feel little richer living among America's poor, despite nominally superior means.

Such modifications in the concept of poverty would clarify the role that income plays; but they would not resolve the fundamental problem, which is that income is far too narrow a concept to comprehend all the social problems that go under the heading of poverty. It is possible we need a new word, in place of "poverty," to describe those conditions; it is certain that the conditions which have attracted so much humane attention in recent years reflect a phenomenon that is not coterminous with insufficiency of means relative to needs. Our concern is with the dynamics, or the pathology, of the problem: the self-generating cycles, the drop-outs—not alone from school but from ambition and productive life. As psychologist Warren Haggstrom has pointed out, "the problems of the poor are not so much of poverty as of a particularly difficult variety of situational dependency, a helplessness to affect many important social factors in their lives, the functioning or purpose of which they do not understand, and which are essentially unpredictable to them."

In other words, the poverty of the poor is measured in power, not money. The power referred to is of the most essential sort, control over one's own destiny. The poor of America and of other countries are those whose lives are, or seem to them to be, controlled by forces outside their own control—by other people who are in positions of authority, by perceived evil forces, or by "hard luck." In America, where material success is important, and where commonly accepted mythology holds material success to be within reach of everyone if only he merits it, the poor are, by a definition even they seem to accept, failures. Their survival often depends on others, and their apathy in social matters can only be heightened by their economic vulnerability. They are in a trap which they can't break out of. Part of that trap, perhaps most of it, is economic; but it is not exclusively economic.

COMMUNITY ACTION AND WELFARE RIGHTS

The definition of poverty as powerlessness has a number of important implications.

First, it implies that even the *economic* aspects of poverty are ill-measured by income and wealth. The poor are separated from the non-poor by their greater vulnerability to economic catastrophe. Two persons, with identical current incomes, are not equally poor when one but not the other is protected by social insurance, job security, the availability of family resources, or by such wealth as money in the bank or canned food in the cupboard. Economic poverty, then, must be measured not only in terms of the relationship of means to needs but also in terms of vulnerability. Parenthetically, it might be noted that most of the income-maintenance and income-security programs of the American welfare state are unavailable to many poor, and serve primarily to keep the non-poor from falling below the poverty line. Unemployment compensation, social security, minimum wage laws, union security, disability, and the other welfare-state programs are not universal but exclude large categories of persons, and most commonly those who are excluded are among the poor.

Second, it implies that many of the most productive measures to solve the problem of poverty can come only from the poor themselves. The "welfare rights" movement of George Wiley and others, the type of community action associated with the name of Saul Alinsky, the CORE-sponsored cooperative movement, and even "black capitalism" have considerable promise not alone because they provide vehicles for increasing the means of the poor, but also because they involve approaches to reducing their psychological dependency and increasing their power. This does not mean, however, that the affluent white community can have no role to play in working to end poverty. Indeed, the new wave of anti-poverty thought concerns the role of government and social agencies, as will be seen. But it does mean that the paternalistic "let's help the poor" approach can have no useful role.

And third, it implies that some ostensible "anti-poverty" programs in fact act to reinforce dependency and powerlessness, while others may work to reduce them. It is axiomatic that whenever a byproduct of a program is to control patterns of life of the poor, the effect is to increase dependency and to stultify personal development.

NEW ANTI-POVERTY THOUGHT

It is this last point that has suggested new techniques for abating poverty. It is hard to define the new approach in a few words, though its most salient characteristic is to revise programs for the poor so as to provide for more freedom. It has appealed to many on the left who have come to emphasize power, including but not limited to "black power," and who view the bureaucratic establishment with emotions ranging from suspicion to hostility. It has also appealed to many conservatives who come to their anti-bureaucratic views from the right, out of their reverence for *laissez-faire* and the free market.

Four examples will make clear the nature of the new thinking, and will point up the areas of conflict between the new viewpoint and the conventional position: housing, medical care, food, and income maintenance.

Housing. The conventional approach to providing for the housing needs of the poor is the construction of large public housing projects in poor (and typically ghetto) neighborhoods. Only those satisfying a means test are eligible, and rent is based on income. A tenant whose income rises above the maximum for eligibility is required to move. Tenants may also be evicted for other reasons, such as improper upkeep of the apartment, or an immoral personal life. Project managers have wide discretion. Some view themselves as parent surrogates; others act more like wardens.

The objections to public housing are considerable. First, the projects are easily identifiable, and tenants are easily recognizable as dependents. Second, the control exercised over tenants' lives by managers is inconsistent with personal freedom. Third, projects tend to be located in undesirable sites, such as adjoining (or *under*) freeways and superhighways. Fourth, they involve segregation, not only of a racial sort, but also of an economic and social sort that is more subtle but quite pernicious. Recalling that many of the poor view themselves and each other as dependents and as failures, consider the effect of grouping massive numbers of such persons together in projects. How it could be other than demoralizing, nurturing and encouraging the self-generating characteristics of a poverty culture, is hard to imagine. Fifth, project construction has involved a net reduction in the quantity of low-income housing, as the quantity of (admittedly substandard) low-cost housing that has been demolished to provide sites vastly exceeds the amount of new housing created in the projects themselves.

And, finally, their administration provides a disincentive, rather than an incentive, to success. Anyone who works with the poor at all knows of families who purposely limit their incomes (and, when possible, conceal parts of them) in order to avoid eviction. Since there almost never is a "halfway house" between subsidized public housing and the high rents of the ghetto, a family with a rising income which is evicted may find that its standard of living actually falls on account of better pay.

Executives and professionals are prone to object to the high marginal rates of the personal income tax on incentive grounds, claiming that effort and investment are deterred. But vast loopholes (which provide for an average tax rate of less than 30% for those in the 70% bracket) protect the rich. The poor have no loopholes to protect them from what may amount, for practical purposes, to a marginal tax rate in excess of 100%. That incentives should be impaired is not surprising.

The alternative suggested by the new wave of thought is the rent supplement. No more housing projects would be constructed. The poor would seek their own housing from private landlords, who (contrary to practice) should not know that their tenants were being subsidized. The poor would live among the non-poor, thus avoiding both the stigma and the apathy-reinforcement of project life. As incomes rise, the subsidy would decline and eventually disappear, without the tenant being forced into the trauma of eviction. Tenants would simply refuse to live under freeways or next to garbage dumps, and no homes would be built in such locations. Most important, no administrator would be in a position to control the lives of the poor.

It is hard to understand the opposition of much of Congress and of the middle class to rent supplements. Public housing projects, after all, are outright socialism; the rent supplement program would rely on the free market, and strengthen the private housing industry. One can only conclude that many of those who oppose "bureaucracy, regimentation, and loss of freedom" under government programs are in fact insincere, and that they really want regimentation of and control over the lives of society's poor.

Medical Care. The conventional approach to provision of medical care for the needy, which is the medical clinic approach, shares many of the characteristics of public housing. It involves stigma, segregation, and disincentive, and some special indignities of its own. The ill or injured are viewed by classes of medical students, who often treat them with the same deference as they do their cadaver-bank "patients." And in a series of sensational charges, New York State Senator Seymour Thaler has claimed that public clinics and hospitals have used the poor for medical experimentation, without, of course, the consent of the human guinea pigs.

Suggestive of the new thinking on medical care for the poor are the nationwide Medicare program for the elderly, and some of the Medicaid programs enacted by states with Federal assistance. Of the latter, the New York State program, until its emasculation in 1968, was most noteworthy. Like the rent-supplement program in housing, these allow a maximum of free choice. Patients use their own private physicians and choose their own drug vendors (who, unfortunately, are told that their patients are Medicare- or Medicaid-supported, and who can refuse such patients, as some doctors have done), receiving potentially the same type and quality of medical care as do others. The New York program is especially noteworthy, for despite its sharp reduction in 1968, its original design provides the model for what should become, eventually, a national health program. The application procedure was and is relatively simple, and does not involve either the delays or the indignities of, say, public assistance, even though Medicaid is, unhappily, administered by local welfare departments. Standards of eligibility were quite liberal (thus arousing conservative . . . wrath) : for instance, families of four with incomes of less than $6000 were eligible for full assistance. (It is these standards that have been severely restricted.) Patients choose their own physicians, hospitals, etc. (if the latter accept them); payment is made by the welfare department to the institution or practitioner. Funds come in part from the Federal government, under a section of the Medicare law, in part from the state, and in part from local sources.

Substitution of a medical-aid plan for medical clinics would help to remove one of the major sources of poverty—the birth of unplanned and unwanted children. Study after study has shown that poor families (contrary to accepted mythology) want smaller families than the affluent, not larger ones. The major difference is that, through their physicians, the non-poor have access to adequate birth-control information and devices. Where the poor are forced to rely on clinics, law or regulations often prohibit the dispensing of birth-control information and devices. In this crucial instance, as in many others, their poverty requires the poor to give up rights and freedoms available to everyone else.

Food. The CBS documentary "Hunger in America" has made much of America familiar with the advantages and disadvantages of the food-stamp program, which represents, at least in part, the new approach. The conventional food-distribution program distributes surplus food commodities acquired by the government under the price-support programs of the Department of Agriculture. Not only is this program subject to the criticism that it selects *what* food poor people may have, thus helping determine the patterns of their lives, but further that the types of food distributed are not determined according to any nutritional criteria but rather are chosen according to farmers' needs for price supports. Farmers who have supported the program . . . are aware that some means must be found to dispose of whatever surpluses are acquired by the government in their price-support program in order to allay public opposition to that program. The food-distribution program serves the needs of the well-to-do farmers; that poor people should benefit is only a coincidence.

Moreover, food is distributed in such a manner as to injure the dignity of the recipient. States and localities administer the program and determine their own eligibility criteria, which vary around the nation. Typically, food is distributed on a determined date, at a warehouse or some other central spot, and recipients queue up to wait, perhaps for hours. Often they bring children's wagons or supermarket shopping carts, for the foods distributed—lard, flour, dried milk, cereals, etc.—are quite bulky; and the infrequency of distribution dates (usually monthly) requires stocking up.

Under the relatively new food-stamp program, eligible poor (still determined by the states) are permitted to buy food stamp coupons whose value, when exchanged at grocery stores for food, exceeds the purchase price. The advantages of this approach are considerable. Like the rent supplement program, it replaces an all-or-nothing program with one in which the degree of public support can vary according to need. It lets the poor choose among retail outlets, giving them some degree of control over merchants—the same kind of control now exercised by any discriminating shopper. And it permits the poor to select virtually any food product (so long as it is domestically produced—the farmer cannot be altogether forgotten). . . .

In spite of these advantages, the structuring and administration of the food-stamp program have contained such grave weaknesses—weaknesses for the most part not inherent in the food stamp device *per se*—as to have led the National Welfare Rights Organization to oppose further spread of the program and to prefer surplus-foods distribution. Food stamps must be purchased in predetermined amounts, and the amounts are often such as to require families to commit a larger fraction of their incomes to food than they had previously, thus reducing rather than increasing budgetary freedom. The stamps are purchased only monthly, and families must come up with the entire month's food allotment (as much as $80 or more) at one time. Actually, this is less difficult for the welfare family, which receives a monthly check, than it is for the weekly paid (or irregularly paid) working poor. There are even families so poor that they cannot afford to buy food stamps at all. Since food stamps always replace rather than supplement surplus-foods distribution, their introduction has typically denied all food assistance to thousands of technically eligible families, while admittedly improving the diet of thousands of others.

Finally, many poor have been humiliated when presenting food stamps in grocery stores, particularly when they mistakenly present them for such non-food grocery items as detergents, light bulbs, and toilet paper, for which the stamps cannot be exchanged.

Most of these defects can be repaired; but some are inherent in any form of restricted or in-kind assistance, and would disappear only where all assistance took the form of unrestricted cash grants.

Income Maintenance. Present housing, medical, and food-distribution programs for the poor all share a common defect: They substitute for the poor person's judgment the views of welfare technicians, legislators, and administrators. The [latter group's] judgment may be superior, though that is open to question; but this approach, at best paternalistic and at worst dictatorial, cannot provide the environment in which judgment and independence can develop. All three reforms discussed increase the poor person's power of choice and consequently his freedom.

But all three reforms suffer a common disadvantage: they continue, though within far broader limits, to enclose the range of choice open to poor people. Assistance which takes the form of rent supplements cannot be used for food, recreation, or night-school tuition. Medicare and Medicaid checks go directly to the vendor, and food stamps can be used only for food. Moreover, there are a great many other programs which provide either chosen goods and services or restricted-use transfer payments to the poor: "fresh-air" summer camp programs, symphony concerts and ballet performances for the "culturally disadvantaged," settlement houses and "community centers," and the like.

Perhaps such vestigial regimentation and paternalism is inevitable, though it stands in marked contrast to the "welfare programs" available to the well-to-do. No one establishes purposes for which farm price-support subsidy payments may be used, for instance; no caseworker investigates the suburban family to make sure the $600-per-dependent tax exemption has actually been spent on the child. Texas millionaires may use their depletion allowances for drink, if they choose.

Maximum freedom of choice would be provided by any one of the many income-support programs which are being proposed today: the negative income tax, under which the machinery and reporting system of the Federal internal revenue bureau are used to make transfer payments to the poor; the social dividend, under which a cash grant would be made to every family, rich or poor, but those with high incomes would, in effect, have their grants taxed back again by the government; family allowances, as used in Canada; the guaranteed income; or even comprehensive public assistance granted as a "right" (and not, as now, at the discretion of welfare commissioners). It is not a matter of indifference which of these is adopted; they have different side effects, whose nature is beyond the scope of this article. But each of them provides techniques for providing assistance according to need (not, as now, according to age, occupation, place of residence, and willingness to submit to humiliations); and the assistance they provide, taking the form of cash, permits maximum free choice and consequently power. Their very existence would reduce the economic vulnerability of the poor and further reduce the likelihood of today's non-poor ever joining the poverty ranks.

The program presently coming closest to an income-maintenance scheme is the array of public assistance programs, partly Federally and state financed but generally locally administered. Public assistance has all of the undesirable characteristics found in the other bureaucratic programs discussed above. There is a degrading application procedure, which itself deters more than half of those eligible from applying and receiving coverage. Benefits paid depend on demonstrated needs, so that a family may have a housing allowance, a food allowance, a clothing allowance, and so forth—the entire budget determined outside the family. Welfare department "caseworkers," who are actually investigators, check frequently on eligibility and on use of welfare checks. A recipient will know he or she is in hot water with the caseworker if the check does not come on time; the caseworker withholds the check as a way of forcing the recipient to come in for a lecture. The reason might be that there is a rumor the recipient, a woman, has a boyfriend living with her, or the recipient, a man, was seen in a poolroom. Recipients (called "clients" by the welfare establishment) often are not even trusted to do their own shopping; they are told where to buy. Anyone who thinks this kind of program is an anti-poverty program is sadly misled. It serves to satisfy the basic biological needs of the poor, but it also serves to perpetuate their dependence and the sense of failure. Recipients may be wealthy by contrast to Africans and Asians, but Africans and Asians are more likely to develop economically and socially than American welfare clients.

It is also under public assistance that the disincentives are the greatest. A family "on the welfare" which earns any money (through occasional jobs, teenagers' babysitting, or any other source) must report such income though there is, of course, a tendency to conceal it. The welfare check is reduced by a like amount. There is, in effect, a 100% tax on all earnings. The "family assistance system" of welfare reforms proposed by President Nixon in August, 1969, was to reduce this effective tax rate to 50%.

Some of the most pernicious effects have been found under the largest and most controversial program, Aid to Families with Dependent Children (AFDC). Before 1961, regulations governing this Federally supported program (then called Aid to Dependent Children, or ADC) made aid unavailable to the unemployed. Only where parents were incapacitated or were absent from home could support be given. In practice, this meant that aid went generally to families with a woman as the sole head. The effects were often tragic: a husband, unable to get regular work or work paying enough to support his family, would in despair leave home so that the wife could qualify for ADC. Often the wife opposed this move; and often she would refuse for some time to apply for assistance, both because of the fundamental indignities involved, and because to qualify she had to swear out a warrant against her husband for desertion. Moreover, she would then probably be hounded regularly by investigators, who might even make midnight raids to make sure she was not committing the crime of living with her husband. There is no doubt that welfare has created many broken homes. The Nixon proposal includes a provision that recipient families could include those headed by a father as well as those headed by a mother—provided, however, that able-bodied fathers and even mothers with no pre-school children accept suitable work or training.

Incidentally, disincentive effects such as these should make us more suspicious than we are of poverty statistics. Irving Kristol has written in the *New Leader* that unemployment cannot be a major source of poverty since only one-sixteenth of poor families are headed by an unemployed person. But, according to the same crude $3000 poverty-line figures used by Kristol, 25% of poor families have a female head; and the figures of course give no indication of how many instances of broken homes may have been initially caused by unemployment, which does not show up in the current statistics. . . .

Almost any income-maintenance program would be superior to public assistance. Most programs would require essentially no application procedure at all. The negative income tax, for instance, would require the poor person to do what virtually everyone does anyway—fill out an income tax return form. Perhaps Internal Revenue Service investigators would audit the returns, as they do now; but there would be no special investigatory procedure for poor people only. Payments would be based on need; and the 75% of poor families who today receive no assistance would be covered, thus raising all families above the poverty line. The cost of doing so is surprisingly low. For example, if income and corporate profits taxes had not been reduced in 1964, and the proceeds had been applied to such a transfer program, no families would have to be below the poverty line. Recipients, covered by a national program, could move from depressed areas and depressing circumstances, and seek opportunity, as so many did in the tight labor markets of World War II. Recipients would be permitted to spend their checks as they see fit and appropriate; and only special, emergency needs would lead them to require, for instance, food stamps or some other special benefit. Except under the guaranteed income plan, the poor person could always live better by working more or harder, thus weakening the disincentive effect of present programs. Families could stay together. And they would run their own lives.

It was once held that poor persons should be deprived of the vote. Today this idea is quickly dismissed as grossly undemocratic. Yet virtually every welfare program in the United States deprives the poor person of the "dollar vote" that economists are fond of speaking of. What is lost is, in fact, a good deal more freedom than would be lost through denying the vote, since the poor person loses control over his own life. As things stand today, the poor person gives up, as the price of his survival, his independence, his dignity, and his ambition.

And the loss of these will almost always keep him poor.

QUESTIONS FOR DISCUSSION

1. *Do you support or reject, in principle, the idea of income maintenance (a guaranteed annual income or a negative income tax)? On what grounds do you base your conclusion?*
2. *What kind of "new thinking" in anti-poverty policy does Tussing suggest?*
3. *In what sense might our attempts to "help" the poor and the economically crippled actually reduce their personal and public freedom? Cite some examples.*

Is There a
Military-Industrial
Complex?

Earlier in the readings we noted the problems which the Vietnam War has posed and the difficulties which must be faced in the eventual reduction of this military effort. War and its impact on the American economy is a much larger question than simply the Vietnam build-up and its impact on government spending and aggregate economic performance. Americans have now lived for three decades under the steady threat of war or cold war. This condition has had a profound, if not altogether clear, effect upon our private lives and upon our social, economic, and political institutions. The United States has spent more than $1 trillion on war and defense during this period, which gives some measure of the importance that war has played in the economy. Such spending is not neutral in its effects. Over the years large segments of the industrial structure, millions of workers, and whole regions of the nation have grown dependent upon military spending. To many social scientists and thoughtful citizens, the situation is alarming. The institutionalization of war, which was once considered only a temporary, abnormal condition for a society, is seen as a threat to our traditional values. Indeed, as we become more and more dependent upon the economy of war, critics ask: "Can we afford peace?"

It was along this line of thought that President Eisenhower, in his farewell speech to the Union, urged that Americans should be vigilant against the threat of a military-industrial establishment. Today, very few Americans would hold that such an establishment does not exist. The obvious dependence of many firms upon defense contracts and the common interest of large defense contractors and military men make a denial nonsense. However, it is not commonly agreed that the existence of such an "establishment" is clear proof of a serious threat to the economy and society.

The first of the following articles, by Fred J. Cook, a well-known journalist, argues that the establishment is a threat and attempts to show how war spending dominates and controls local economies. The second article examines the size of the "chiefly military" industry and its interconnections with the Pentagon. The last piece, by a leading defense contractor, argues that the firm could easily make the transition from war and defense-related activities to peace if international events took a different course.

The Warfare State

Fred J. Cook

The economies of 22 of our 50 states depend in abnormal degree upon the maintenance of military spending. This was a major finding by a panel of economic experts, headed by Professor Emile Benoit, of Columbia University, in a report they presented in January, 1962, to the new United States Arms Control and Disarmament Agency. The report was described as the first comprehensive inquiry ever made into the effect on our national economy that major arms cuts might be expected to have; and in an attempt to assess this, it probed deeply into the question of our present dependence on the arms race.

"In some areas of the country the dependence on defense production is already very tangible and a serious source of concern," the committee reported. ". . . Certain States are clearly subject to disproportionately heavy impacts because of the relatively heavy dependence of their manufacturing on major items of procurement."

The committee found that in 14 states war industries accounted for a heavy percentage of total manufacturing employment. In seven states—and in five of these the figures admittedly were incomplete—war industries accounted for more than 20 percent of all manufacturing jobs. The states and their percentages: Utah, 20.4; Arizona, 20.6; Connecticut, 21.1; California, 23.3; New Mexico, 23.8; Washington, 28.6; Kansas, 30.2.

Startling as these figures are, they were not the whole story. The committee reported that eight other states and the District of Columbia showed "exceptionally heavy dependence on Department of Defense payrolls to sustain their income." Military payrolls at camps, forts, bases and various installations comprised from 10 to 26 percent of all payroll income in Alaska, Hawaii, the District of Columbia and Virginia. Alaska and Hawaii topped this list with percentages of 26.5 and 18.2 respectively.

"It is disquieting to note," the committee added, "that several of the States with heavy dependence on major procurement for employment are also well above the average for dependence of income on Department of Defense payrolls. This is notably true for New Mexico and Utah, but it is also true to some extent for Kansas, Washington and California."

The committee's figures showed that the Military supplied 9 percent of all payroll income in New Mexico—this in addition to 23.8 percent of all manufacturing jobs that depended on procurement. In Utah, military bases accounted for 6.7 percent of all payrolls, in addition to 20.4 percent of all manufacturing jobs.

Such heavy concentrations of military spending power spell almost total dependence, especially when one takes into account the multiplier factor—the number of jobs and businesses that are sustained by the military payrolls and the war plant jobs. However, more than the economy of entire states, the economy of the entire nation is bound up in the same dire equation. Secretary of Labor Arthur Goldberg has reported that one out of every six jobs in all America is held in three states—Texas, California and Florida. All of these states rank high on the list of Military dependents. In Texas, 5.5 percent of all payroll income comes from the Military and 10 percent of all manufacturing jobs; in Florida, 3.8 percent of all payrolls, 14.1 percent of all manufacturing jobs; in California, 3.7 percent of payroll income comes from the Military, 23.3 percent of all manufacturing jobs.

The picture that emerges is the picture of a nation whose entire economic welfare is tied to warfare. Our livelihoods, our homes, our families depend on the jobs that depend on the armament race. And the longer the race continues, the greater will be the dependence; for the Benoit committee estimated that, on the basis of current trends, armament spending will climb to $60 billion annually by 1965. This would be almost one-third more than the figures of 1959 from which the committee drew its dreary picture of a war-based national economy. [By 1969, the total had grown to over $80 billion annually for defense.]

To change this base, to alter this trend, would require the most far-sighted and courageous political leadership. Even supposing a softening of international tensions should make change possible—a highly unlikely development in an atmosphere in which our weapons maintain tension in Russia, hers maintain tension here—we would have to be prepared to accept the loss of multi-billion-dollar war contracts, at least a temporary level of high unemployment, and a decided reduction of the prosperity that comes from high consumer consumption and plant expansion in a burgeoning economy. We would have to be prepared, in other words, to endure hard times unless a well-geared government program could swing swiftly into action to finance the jobs of peace as the government has financed the tasks of war. Such a program would include, it would have to include, many of the very kind of government-sponsored public works projects that are symbolic of the Welfare State—and that is a prospect to make even a hardy man shudder. Since it is, since one can almost feel the tremors of alarm that course along the spines of the military-industrial caste at the mere suggestion of such heresy, it seems obvious that there is almost no chance that we shall have, within the foreseeable future, the kind of dedicated political leadership that would prepare the people and the country for the uncertainties of peace.

This hard fact of modern political life, in rare and precious moments of utter frankness, is even acknowledged by the politicians themselves. In one unusual "Town Meeting on World Crisis" in York, Pennsylvania, early in 1962, Representative George A. Goodling frankly told his constituents: "No political party can afford to disarm. I'm sorry to say that. I wish we could." He explained that the national economy simply could not stand disarmament, a position that was supported by a former Congressman from the district, Chester H. Gross, who declared that arms cutbacks would bring a wave of unemployment.

Almost as the Congressmen spoke, the accuracy of their analysis was emphasized in a dramatic way. The Navy decided to "phase out" a jet fighter plane, and when it did, a vast section of Long Island was confronted suddenly with the prospect of becoming a depressed area.

The plane was the F-105 D Thunderchief, a 1400-mile-an-hour fighter-bomber manufactured by Republic Aviation Corp. in Farmingdale, Long Island. The Navy decided to switch production to what is evidently considered a better plane, one being manufactured in the Midwest. This meant that Republic, which had virtually all of its production eggs in the Thunderchief basket, wouldn't have any work for its workers. This meant that some 13,000 men might lose their jobs. This meant that a number of sub-contractors making parts for the plane would be out of business. All together it meant that perhaps 20,000 men would be thrown out of work; that home owners would be unable to pay their mortgages; that car time payments would lapse; that television sets and appliances of all kinds would have to be repossessed. The only salvation from such disasters was to see that the Defense Department came through with new orders for Republic Aviation.

Justin Ostro, president of Republic Lodge 1987, International Association of Machinists, AFL-CIO, rallied the workers to meet the crisis of the moment. Eight thousand of them gathered in the Levittown Arena and heard Ostro urge a letter-writing campaign to the White House to save their jobs. "The only area we can hope to get any help at all is the White House and the President of the United States," he said. "You must let him [President

Kennedy] know you are in trouble; he promised you an expanding economy and full employment."

Governor Nelson A. Rockefeller charged down to Long Island from Albany to back up the workers' plea. The layoffs, he said, might make all of Long Island a depressed area, and certainly the federal government could not permit this. Congressmen and United States Senators, newspapers and business organizations whose businesses would suffer if the war plant payroll that supported them suddenly dried up, all bombarded the White House with pleas to save the warplane jobs at Republic Aviation. The issue was even injected into one of President Kennedy's televised press conferences. The President assured everyone that the administration didn't want to see any man lose his job; that the layoffs would be considerably less than 13,000; that he had already talked to Secretary McNamara, the Defense Department was already re-examining its production schedules, and he was "hopeful" some other tasks could be found to buoy up Republic, Republic's workers and the economy of all Long Island.

This was the story of just one plane and just one cancelled war contract. Multiply it by the thousands of contracts and the billions of dollars involved in projects much more massive in scope than the construction of a fighter-bomber, and you begin to get some dim idea how completely the seemingly prosperous American economy is dependent on the war race. For the outcry that arose on Long Island over the demise of the Thunderchief is typical of the outcry that arises anywhere and everywhere any time an effort is made to slash any part of the defense budget.

Consider the tempest that was generated throughout the nation when, on March 30, 1961, Secretary McNamara announced plans to close down 52 military installations in 25 states and 21 overseas bases in the next three years. McNamara's order was based upon a sane re-examination of reality in the age of missiles. Some depots were too close to major cities and too vulnerable; some sprawling air bases covering hundreds of acres of flat, sandy soil did not lend themselves to the need of the missile age for concealed launching sites, founded upon and protected by solid rock formations. These were doubtless sound military considerations, but nothing short of economic devastation impended for many local areas to whom the nearby installations represented the only hope of business prosperity. Inevitably, screams of protest resounded across the nation and in Congress.

In Del Rio, Texas, a businessman went to his cash register, punched it open, and took out $50.00. This was his contribution, based on an assessment of $1.00 for every foot of business frontage, to the expenses of a four-man delegation that Del Rio hustled off to Washington to fight the scheduled closing of the Laughlin Air Force Base. Del Rio has a civilian population of 18,612, and the Laughlin base is its one big industry. The base payroll, civilian and military, has been running at $10.5 million a year; some $42,000 annually has been spent with local businessmen for such odds and ends as office supplies and pest-control services; Laughlin accounted for 20 percent of the town's electric and telephone services; some 1700 Laughlin families shopped in Del Rio stores. It takes no imagination to visualize the economic impact on Del Rio if it should suddenly be deprived of Laughlin.

In Tacoma, Washington, the owner of a shoe store fitted three small children for shoes. The father gave him a twenty-dollar bill, and when the proprietor handed back the change, the father presented a small card. It read: "You have just done business with a Mount Rainier Ordnance Depot employee. How much money will you lose when the $14 million payroll goes to Utah? Write your Congressman, Senator, Governor if you want to protest this move."

In Benicia, California, a town of 6000, officials were aroused by the announcement that the Benicia Ordnance Depot would be closed down by April, 1964. Mayor James Lemos was wroth because the municipality had just constructed a $1.6 million sewage plant, about three times as large and expensive a project as would have been needed if the depot hadn't been there. He estimated that the town would lose in sales-gas-beverage taxes alone some $21,500 a year; and it would lose, too, the trade of the 2400 civilian workers at the depot. In response to the local outcry, Representative John Baldwin, Republican Congressman from the district, sent a vigorous letter of protest to President Kennedy, contending that the Benicia Depot was just what the nation needed for Kennedy's plan to have "an army trained to meet a limited war crisis."

So it went across the nation. Kansas protested the shifting of a naval air technical training unit from Olathe to Glyngo, Georgia. Olathe sent a delegation to Independence, Missouri, to visit former President Truman and see what could be done about it. Truman received the delegation graciously, but he was his usual blunt self. "The basis of the shift is political," he told the delegates. "Kansas didn't vote right." Kansas, it may be recalled, had cast its eight electoral votes for Richard M. Nixon; Georgia, on the other hand, had better bargaining power. It is the home state of Senator Richard B. Russell and Representative Carl Vinson, chairmen respectively of the Senate and House Armed Services Committees. Coincidentally, of course, Georgia was crammed with nineteen military installations—so many that an indiscreet general is said once to have remarked, "One more base would sink the state." This prediction, it seemed, was about to be put to the test. Not only was Georgia not to lose any of the bases that she had, but she was to gobble up one more in the shift of the training unit from Olathe.

This entire sequence illustrates the host of problems that arise any time the most gentle of waves rocks the boat of the Warfare State. When a cutback on military bases threatens adjacent towns and cities with economic collapse, it becomes fairly obvious what would happen if violent hands should ever be laid on the fantastic billions that are being poured into military procurement contracts. Then entire states would be prostrated.

Business Week on February 27, 1960, headlined a feature article: "Missile Industry Carries Utah." The article explained that, for generations, Utah's prosperity had been built around two basic industries, steel and copper. In 1959, both of these bellwethers of the Utah economy had been closed down by strikes. "Without missiles," wrote *Business Week*, "these strikes might have put much of the state flat on its back. But the growth of missiles more than offset the strikes and helped to give Utah its biggest year. Today, the industry employs over 10,000 workers—a gain of 5000 during 1959."

What missiles are to Utah, the whole aircraft-missile-space complex is in an even larger way to the powerful State of California. California, of course, has Hollywood, but Hollywood is a piker beside the ganglion of war industries on which the prosperity of the state has come so much to depend. *The Los Angeles Times* reported in February, 1960, that in the Los Angeles metropolitan area alone twenty-seven out of every hundred manufacturing workers were employed in aircraft, missiles or space. The area had a backlog of military contracts exceeding $3 billion.

Still, there was serious concern. It was obvious to everyone that missiles rapidly were making the warplane obsolete—and a heavy cutback on plane orders would make things very, very bad. The Southern California area had had a taste of this kind of hardship in 1957, when federal orders for the huge sky birds were cut back some 40 percent. Plants had shut down, thousands of workers had been laid off. California had snapped back smartly from this period of temporary trial. Most of its airplane manufacturers had had the foresight to see the handwriting on the wall; they were already shifting their production to missiles, the weapon of the future, and soon missile contracts took up the slack of lost plane contracts. By November, 1958, aircraft-missile payrolls on the West Coast had mounted to about *$42.4 million a week,* with more than half of this—$23.1 million—concentrated in the Los Angeles area. Still, there was unhappiness. The plane cutback had struck a severe blow at Douglas Aircraft: there were heavy layoffs in the Santa Monica and El Segundo-Torrance plants. Alarmed, the International Association of Machinists bombarded California's Congressional delegation with telegrams of protest and demands for an investigation to discover what had caused this unjust cutback of war orders at Douglas.

Such agitation and alarm in the midst of still-flowing plenty give but a faint idea of the utter chaos that inevitably would result from any serious de-emphasis of the military staff of life. A few years ago, the Southern California Research Council, a private association of prominent businessmen and academicians, drew up a widely circulated report entitled, "The Effect of a Reduction of Defense Expenditures upon the Los Angeles Area." It concluded that if "a 50 percent cut in defense expenditures should occur . . . [while] business conditions and investment remain high, the estimate would be for total unemployment of about 200,000 or 12 percent of the entire labor force. Or, if business conditions and investments are lower, unemployment might approximate 350,000 or 20 percent." This, remember, is the kind of disaster that a cut of just one-half, *not* a total cut, would bring down on the Los Angeles area. Obviously, it cannot be allowed to happen. . . .

As Eisenhower Was Saying: "We Must Guard Against Unwarranted Influence by the Military-Industrial Complex"

Richard F. Kaufman

Eight years have gone by since President Eisenhower opened the door on the military-industrial skeleton in the closet. Yet only recently has research started to hang some real meat on his bony, provocative phrase, "military-industrial complex." What is emerging is a real Frankenstein's monster. Not only is there considerable evidence that excessive military spending has contributed to a misallocation of national resources, but the conclusion seems inescapable that society has already suffered irreparable harm from the pressures and distortions thus created.

Military and military-related spending accounts for about 45 percent of all Federal expenditures. In fiscal 1968, the total Federal outlays were $178.9-billion. The Defense Department alone spent $77.4-billion, and such related programs as military assistance to foreign countries, atomic energy and the Selective Service System raised the figure to $80.5-billion. The $4-billion program of the National Aeronautics and Space Administration and other activities intertwined with the military carry the real level of defense spending considerably higher.

To place the defense bill in perspective we should note that 1968 appropriations were less than $500-million for food stamps, school lunches and the special milk program combined. For all federally assisted housing programs,

From The New York Times Magazine, *June 22, 1969.* © *1969 by The New York Times Company. Reprinted by permission.*

including Model Cities, they were about $2-billion. The poverty program received less than $2-billion. Federal aid to education was allotted about $5.2 billion. The funds spent on these programs and all those categorized as health, education, welfare, housing, agriculture, conservation, labor, commerce, foreign aid, law enforcement, etc.—in short, all civilian programs—amounted to about $82.5-billion, if the space and veterans' programs are not included, and less than $70-billion if the interest on the national debt is not considered.

The largest single item in the military budget—it accounted for $44 billion in 1968—is procurement, which includes purchasing, renting or leasing supplies and services (and all the machinery for drawing up and administering the contracts under which those purchases and rentals are made). Procurement, in other words, means Government contracts; it is mother's milk to the military-industrial complex.

The Pentagon annually signs agreements with about 22,000 prime contractors; in addition, more than 100,000 subcontractors are involved in defense production. Defense-oriented industry as a whole employs about 4 million men. However, although a large number of contractors do some military business, the largest share of procurement funds is concentrated among a relative handful of major contractors. Last year the 100 largest defense suppliers obtained $26.2-billion in military contracts, 67.4 percent of the money spent through contracts of $10,000 or more.

Similarly, the Atomic Energy Commission's contract awards tend to be concentrated in a select group of major corporations. Of approximately $1.6-billion awarded in contracts last year, all but $104-million went to 36 contractors. As for NASA, procurement plays a larger role in its activities than in those of any other Federal agency. More than 90 percent of its funds are awarded in contracts to industry and educational institutions. Of the $4.1-billion worth of procurement last year, 92 percent of the direct awards to business went to NASA's 100 largest contractors.

In terms of property holdings, the result of almost two centuries of military procurement is a worldwide and practically incalculable empire. An almost arbitrary and greatly underestimated value—$202.5-billion—was placed on military real and personal property at the end of fiscal year 1968. Weapons were valued at $100-billion. Supplies and plant equipment accounted for $55.6-billion. Most of the remainder was in real estate. The Pentagon says the 29 million acres it controls—an area almost the size of New York State—are worth $38.7-billion. (The official Defense Department totals do not include 9.7 million acres, valued at $9-billion, under the control of the Army Civil Works Division or additional property valued at $4.7-billion.) The arbitrariness of those figures is seen in the fact that they represent *acquisition* costs. Some of the military real estate was acquired more than a century ago, and much of it is in major cities and metropolitan areas. The actual value of the real estate must be many times its acquisition cost.

But the important fact about procurement is not the extent of the Pentagon's property holdings; it is that defense contracting has involved the military with many of the largest industrial corporations in America. Some companies do almost all their business with the Government. Into this category fall a number of the large aerospace concerns—such giants as General Dynamics, Lockheed Aircraft and United Aircraft. For such other companies as General Electric, A.T.&T. and General Motors, Government work amounts to only a small percentage of the total business. But the tendency is for a company to enlarge its share of defense work over the years, at least in dollar value. And whether defense contracts represent 5 percent or 50 percent of a corporation's annual sales, they become a solid part of the business, an advantage to maintain or improve upon. A company may even work harder to increase its military sales than it does to build commercial sales because military work is more profitable, less competitive, more susceptible to control through lobbying in Washington. The industrial giants with assets of more than $1-billion have swarmed around the Pentagon to get their share of the sweets with no less enthusiasm than their smaller brethren.

The enormous attraction of military and military-related contracts for the upper tiers of industry has deepened in the last few years as military procurement has increased sharply. For example, General Electric's prime-contract awards have gone up from $783-million in 1958 to $1.5-billion in 1968; General Motors went from $281-million in 1958 to $630-million in 1968. While much of this increase can be traced to the Vietnam war boom and many contractors would suffer a loss of business if the war ended, there was steady growth in the defense industry during the fifties and early sixties (in 1964 and 1965, before the Vietnam build-up, there was a decline in prime-contract awards). In the five years from 1958 to 1963—five years of peace—the value of General Electric's prime contracts increased $217-million and General Motors' rose $163-million. The same trend can be shown for many of the large corporations in the aerospace and other industries.

What seems to be happening is that defense production is gradually spreading throughout industry, although the great bulk of the funds is still spent among relatively few companies. Still, as the defense budget increases the procurement dollars go further. The geographical concentration of defense production in the industrialized, high-income states also suggests that military contracts have come less and less to be restricted to an isolated sector of the economy specializing in guns and ammunition. Military business has become solidly entrenched in industrial America.

Considering the high degree of mismanagement and inefficiency in defense production and the tendency for contractors to want more sales and therefore to support the military in its yearly demands for a larger budget, this is not a healthy situation. The inefficiency of defense production, particularly in the aerospace industry, can hardly be disputed. Richard A. Stubbing, a defense analyst at the Bureau of the Budget, in a study of the performance of complex weapon systems, concluded: "The low over-all performance of electronics in major weapon systems developed and produced in the last decade should give pause to even the most outspoken advocates of military-hardware programs." He found that in 13 aircraft and missile programs produced since 1955 at a total cost of $40-billion, fewer than 40 percent of the electronic components performed acceptably; two programs were canceled at a cost to the Government of $2-billion, and two programs costing $10-billion were phased out after three years because of low reliability.

And the defense industry is inefficient as well as unreliable. Albert Shapero, professor of management at the University of Texas, has accused aerospace contractors of habitually over-staffing, over-analyzing and over-managing. A. E. Fitzgerald, a Deputy Assistant Secretary of the Air Force, in testimony before the Joint Economic Subcommittee on Economy in Government, described poor work habits and poor discipline in contractors' plants. In the same hearing, a retired Air Force officer, Col. A. W. Buesking, a former director of management systems control in the office of the Assistant Secretary of Defense, summarized a study he had conducted by saying that control systems essential to prevent excessive costs simply did not exist.

In a sense, industry is being seduced into bad habits of production and political allegiance with the lure of easy money. And industry is not the only sector being taken in. Consider conscription (3.6 million men in uniform), the Pentagon's civilian bureaucracy (1.3 million), the work force in defense-oriented industry (4 million), the domestic brain drain created by the growth in military technology, the heavy emphasis on military research and development as a percentage (50 percent) of all American research, the diversion of universities to serve the military and defense industry. These indicators reveal a steady infiltration of American values by those of the military establishment: production for nonproductive use, compulsory service to the state, preparation for war. In the process, the economy continues to lose many of the attributes of the marketplace. In the defense industry, for all practical purposes, there is no marketplace.

The general rule for Government procurement is that purchases shall be made through written competitive bids obtained by advertising for the items needed. In World War II the competitive-bid requirements were suspended. After the war the Armed Services Procurement Act was passed, restating the general rule but setting out 17 exceptions—circumstances under which negotiation would be authorized instead of competition. The exceptions, which are still in use, are very broad and very vague. If the item is determined to be critical or complex or if delivery is urgent or if few supplies exist and competition is impractical or if emergency conditions exist or if security considerations preclude advertising, the Pentagon can negotiate for what it wants.

When President Truman signed this law in 1948 he saw the possibilities for abuse and wrote to the heads of the armed services and the National Advisory Committee for Aeronautics. "This bill," he said, "grants unprecedented freedom from specific procurement restrictions during peacetime. . . . There is danger that the natural desire for flexibility and speed in procurement will lead to excessive placement of contracts by negotiation and undue reliance upon large concerns, and this must not occur." Unfortunately, Truman's apprehensions were well justified. Last year about 90 percent of the Pentagon's and 98 percent of NASA's contract awards were negotiated under the "exceptions."

What this means is that there is no longer any objective criterion for measuring the fairness of contract [costs or] control over the costs; quality and time of production, insofar as they resulted from competition, are also lost. Negotiation involves informal discussion between the Pentagon and its contractors over the price and other terms of the contract. It permits subjective decision-making on such important questions as which firms to do business with and what price to accept. The Pentagon can negotiate with a single contractor, a "sole source," or it can ask two or three to submit proposals. If one later complains that he had promised to provide a weapon at a lower price than the contractor who obtained the award, the Pentagon can respond by asserting that the price was not the major factor, that the Government simply had more faith in the contractor who won. This, in effect, is how the Army responded to the Maremont Corporation's recent challenge of a contract award to General Motors for the M-16 rifle. The Pentagon, because of its almost unbounded freedom to award contracts, can favor some companies. And over long periods, this practice can lead to a dependence by the Government on the technical competency of the suppliers on whom it has come to rely. For example, the Newport News Shipbuilding Company has a virtual monopoly on the construction of large aircraft carriers.

Typically, the Pentagon will invite a few of the large contractors to submit proposals for a contract to perform the research and development on a new weapon system. The one who wins occupies a strategic position. The know-how he gains in his research work gives him an advantage over his rivals for the larger and more profitable part of the program, the production. This is what is meant when it is said that the Government is "locked in" with a contractor. Because the contractor knows he will obtain a lock-in if he can do the initial research work, there is a tendency to stretch a few facts during the negotiations.

Contractor performance is measured by three factors: the total cost to the Government of the weapon system, the way in which it functions and the time of delivery. During the contract negotiations over these factors the phenomenon known as the "buy-in" may occur. The contractor, in order to "buy-in" to the program, offers more than he can deliver. He may promise to do a job at a lower cost than he knows will be incurred or to meet or exceed performance specifications that he knows are unattainable or to deliver the finished product long before he has reason to believe it will be ready.

Technically, the contractor can be penalized for his failure to fulfill promises made during the negotiations, but the Government rarely insists on full performance. The contractor knows this, of course, and he also knows the "get-well" stratagem. That is, he can reasonably expect, on practically all major weapon contracts, that should he get into difficulty with regard to any of the contract conditions, the Government will extricate him—get him well.

The contractor can get well in a variety of ways. If his costs run higher than his estimates, the Pentagon can agree to pay them. (Cost increases can be hidden through contract-change notices. On a typical, complex weapon system, the changes from original specifications will number in the thousands; some originate with the Pentagon, some are authorized at the request of the contractor. The opportunities for buying real or phony cost increases are obvious, so much so that in defense circles contract-change notices are sometimes referred to as "contract nourishment.") The Government can also accept a weapon that performs poorly or justify a late delivery. If for some reason it is impossible for the Pentagon to accept a weapon, there is still a way to keep the contractor well. The Pentagon can cancel a weapon program for the "convenience" of the Government. A company whose contract is canceled for default stands to lose a great deal of money, but cancellation for convenience reduces or eliminates the loss; the Government makes reimbursement for costs incurred. An example of this occurred recently in connection with the F-111B, the Navy's fighter-bomber version of the TFX.

Gordon W. Rule, a civilian procurement official who had responsibility for the F-111B, said in testimony before the House Subcommittee on Military Operations that General Dynamics was in default on its contract because the planes were too heavy to meet the height or range requirements. Rule proposed in a memorandum to Deputy Secretary of Defense Paul H. Nitze that the contract be terminated for default. At the same time, Assistant Secretary of the Air Force Robert H. Charles and Roger Lewis, the General Dynamics chairman, proposed that the Navy reimburse the company for all costs and impose no penalty. Nitze's compromise was to make reimbursement of $216.5-million, mostly to General Dynamics, and to impose a small penalty.

In a memo written last year Rule made this comment on the attitude of defense contractors: "No matter how poor the quality, how late the product and how high the cost, they know nothing will happen to them."

There are many other ways to succeed in the defense business without really trying. The Pentagon generously provides capital to its contractors; more than $13-billion worth of Government-owned property, including land, buildings and equipment, is in contractors' hands. In addition, the Pentagon will reimburse a supplier during the life of his contract for as much as 90 percent of the costs he reports. These are called "progress" payments, but are unrelated to progress in the sense of contract objectives achieved; they correspond only to the costs incurred. The progress payments are interest-free loans that provide the contractor with working capital in addition to fixed capital. They minimize his investment in the defense business and free his assets for commercial work or for obtaining new defense work.

Investigations by the General Accounting Office have revealed that the Government's money and property have been used by contractors for their own purposes. The most recent incident involved Thiokol Chemical Corporation, Aerojet-General (a subsidiary of General Tire & Rubber Company) and Hercules, Inc. From 1964 through 1967 they received a total of $22.4-million to be used for work on the Air Force Minuteman missile program. The Government accountants found that the three contractors misused more than $18-million of this money, spending it for research unrelated and inapplicable to Minuteman or any other defense program.

The defense industry is perhaps the most heavily subsidized in the nation's history. Thanks to Pentagon procurement policies, large contractors find their defense business to be their most lucrative. Although no comprehensive study of such profits has been made, the known facts indicate that profits on defense contracts are higher than those on related nondefense business, that they are higher for the defense industry than for manufacturing as a whole and that the differential has been increasing. In a study that compared the five-year period from 1959 through 1963 with the last six months of 1966, the General Accounting Office found a 26 percent increase in the average profit rates negotiated. Admiral Hyman G. Rickover has testified that suppliers of propulsion turbines are insisting on profits of 20 to 25 percent, compared with 10 percent a few years ago, and that profits on shipbuilding contracts have doubled in two years.

The figures cited by Rickover relate to profits as a percentage of costs, a measure that often understates the true profit level. The more accurate measure is return on investment. An example of the difference was demonstrated in a 1962 tax-court case, North American Aviation v. Renegotiation Board. The contracts provided for 8 percent profits as a percentage of costs; the tax court found that the company had realized profits of 612 percent and 802 percent on its investment in two succeeding years. The reason for the huge return on investment was the Defense Department policy of supplying both fixed and working capital to many of the larger contractors. In some cases the amount of Government-owned property exceeds the contractor's investment, which is sometimes minimal. It is no wonder that contractors prefer to talk about profits as a percentage of costs.

Murray Weidenbaum, recently appointed Assistant Secretary of the Navy, found in a study that between 1962 and 1965 a sample of large defense contractors earned 17.5 percent net profit (measured as a return on investment), while companies of similar size doing business in the commercial market earned 10.6 percent.

The Pentagon has attempted to answer the critics of high defense profits by citing the findings of the Logistics Management Institute, a think tank that has done a study showing declining defense profits. The trouble with the institute's study is that it used unverified, unaudited data obtained on a voluntary basis from a sample of defense contractors. Those who did not want to participate simply did not return the questionnaires; in fact, 42 percent of those contacted provided no data. There is no way of knowing whether the group of contractors who refused to participate in the study included the ones making the highest profits.

There is almost no risk in defense contracting except that borne by the Government. If a major prime contractor has ever suffered a substantial loss on a defense contract, the Pentagon has failed to disclose his name, although it has been requested to do so by members of Congress. On the other hand, the disputed Cheyenne helicopter and C-5A cargo plane projects could conceivably result in large losses for Lockheed, the contractor in both cases. Lockheed asserts that it might still make a profit on the C-5A (which is being produced in a Government-owned plant), and denies that it is at fault in the cancellation of latest proposed changes in armed services procurement regulations. The Industry Advisory Council until recently was called the Defense Industry Advisory Council. Dropping the word "Defense" from its name suggests its concern over public relations. The council's membership at the time of the October meeting included the presidents or board chairman of Boeing, General Electric, Brown and Root, Western Electric, duPont, Lockheed, Newport News Shipbuilding, Northrop, General Dynamics, Olin Mathieson, Tenneco, Litton and Ford.

The immediate outcome of the October meeting was an outline of major problems facing the Pentagon and industry. The outline and a memorandum from Assistant Secretary of Defense Thomas Morris were circulated to officials on the assistant-secretary level of the Defense Department and each of the armed services. The subject was: "Fundamental Problem Areas: Key areas worthy of joint exploration by Department of Defense and industry in calendar year 1969."

Four major problem areas were listed. The first was how to "maintain public and Congressional confidence in the integrity and effectiveness of defense procurement and contractor performance." Others were how to obtain full compliance with procurement policies by both Pentagon and industry officials; how to maintain a healthy defense-industrial base; and how to increase the effectiveness of the major-weapon-system acquisition process.

The memo, in discussing how to shore up lagging public and Congressional confidence in the defense procurement process, listed some more specific "detailed problems," including these: uniform-accounting-standards legislation; excess-profits hearings; the Truth-in-Negotiations Act; General Accounting Office investigations and audits; investigations of such specific programs as the TFX and the M-14 rifle and statutory profit limitations. In other words, the chief worries of the industry and Pentagon representatives in 1969 are legislation that would tighten controls on procurement and defense profits, the investigation of specific weapons programs and investigations and audits by Government accountants.

The danger of the military-industrial complex lies in its scale. Reasonable men will tolerate a war machine as a necessary evil. It is the size of the machine and its claim on national resources and individual lives that is at issue. What is alarming is the growth of the complex.

The great leap of the military budget in the last few years, from about $50-billion to $80-billion, and its earlier growth, beginning with the Korean War, have helped to bring about serious stresses in the economy. Although no one factor can be identified as the sole cause of inflation, it is no accident that the three most recent price surges accompanied sharp increases in military spending, between 1950 and 1953 (the Korean War period), between 1955 and 1957 and since the build-up in Vietnam began. Defense expenditures have contributed substantially to these inflationary trends. The consequent reduced value of savings and fixed-income assets during each of these periods is an indirect cost of defense; the 10 percent tax surcharge made necessary by the Vietnam build-up is a much more direct one.

More ominous than the economic consequences of a bloated defense budget are expanding and sometimes furtive military activities in such areas as foreign affairs, social-science research, domestic riot control and chemical and biological warfare. In hearings last year on Pentagon-sponsored foreign-affairs research, Senator Fulbright quoted from a 1967 report of the Defense Science Board (a scientific counterpart to the business-advisory groups): "The D.O.D. mission now embraces problems and responsibilities which have not previously been assigned to a military establishment. It has been properly stated that the D.O.D. must now wage not only warfare but 'peacefare' as well. Pacification assistance and the battle of ideas are major segments of the D.O.D. responsibility. The social and behavioral sciences constitute the unique resource for support of these new requirements. . . ."

Fulbright's reminder that the military's responsibility is "to prosecute war or to provide military forces which are capable of defending against an external attack" might have sounded like naïveté to the Pentagon, but his point is important. Social-science research conducted in foreign countries by foreigners should, if it is to be supported at all, be supported by the State Department, not the Pentagon. Research into socio-cultural patterns or the social organization of groups or processes of change should not be a military responsibility. Yet the Pentagon does support foreign research all over the world, awarding contracts to General Electric to make projections of "future world environments" and to McDonnell-Douglas to do a study entitled "Pax Americana," later retitled "Projected World Patterns, 1985."

The Army's new domestic "war room" in the basement of the Pentagon is also of doubtful legitimacy. This "operations center" is supposed to help dispatch and coordinate troops for urban riots (maybe that's "pacification assistance"). Even assuming the need for this kind of activity, one can raise the same question that disturbs Senator Fulbright with regard to social-science research: Is this a proper military responsibility?

The most recent example of the Pentagon's "independent thinking," brought to light by the efforts of Congressmen Richard D. McCarthy and Cornelius Gallagher, is the controversial Army plan to transport about 27,000 tons of obsolete poison gas across the country by train to New Jersey to be loaded onto old hulks, towed out to sea and sunk. Both the State Department and the Interior Department have a direct interest in this project, yet the Army did not bother to coordinate its plans with them until long after the plans were formulated.

Such incidents as the construction of the domestic war room and the independent decision to ship poison gas across the country symbolize the drift of power in the executive branch to the Pentagon and show the extent to which military authority has exceeded its traditional limits. Swollen by overgenerous appropriations, the defense budget has become the source of frightening political as well as economic power. Practically freed of the fiscal limitations that restrain other agencies, the Pentagon seems to be able to exercise its will in almost any area it chooses, foreign or domestic, from negotiating a new lease for bases and promising military assistance to Spain (as it was recently alleged to have done) to launching programs of social reform.

The nature of the problem was simply stated, recently at a hearing of the House Subcommittee on Military Operations. Testifying was Phillip S. Hughes, deputy director of the Bureau of the Budget. Representative William Moorhead had charged that the bureau was unable to scrutinize Defense Department expenditures to the same extent that it reviews nondefense spending. The budget requests of Government agencies, except the Defense Department, are subjected to an independent analysis and review, which is then submitted to the Budget Director. The Director makes his recommendations to the President, subject to challenge by the Cabinet officer concerned. But the Defense Department is treated differently. In the Pentagon, Moorhead said, Budget Bureau analysts must work alongside their Defense counterparts, not independently. The results of this joint review are submitted to the Secretary of Defense, who sends it to the President, subject to challenge by the Budget Director.

The result is that the burden of persuading the President to change the budget he receives is shifted from the agency head to the Budget Director in the case of the defense item, but only there. (The Nixon Administration's Budget Director, Robert P. Mayo, testified recently that the defense budget would be transmitted to the President in the future just as other departmental requests are.)

"The most relevant consideration," Hughes testified, "is, in blunt terms, sheer power—where the muscle is—and this is a very power-conscious town, and the Secretary of Defense and the defense establishment are a different group to deal with, whether the Congress is dealing with them or whether the Budget Bureau is dealing with them. . . ."

The military-industrial complex has become a massive tangled system, half inside, half outside the Government. Like the Gordian knot, it is too intricate to be unraveled. But like the dinosaur, its weakness lies in its great size. If its intricacy rebuffs us, its grossness is vulnerable; it can be reduced by substantially cutting the defense budget.

This is the only viable immediate solution, for innovations in contractual procedures, regulatory statutes such as the Truth-in-Negotiations Act and such watchdog agencies as the General Accounting Office have not been able to cope effectively with the major excesses in military procurement. The Bureau of the Budget has been in a subordinate position, notwithstanding its recent success in challenging the Manned Orbiting Laboratory funds and its claims to more power over the defense budget. The deck is stacked against those who would sit down across the table from the military-industrial complex.

The only way to change the game is to cut the budget.

From War to Peace

Lockheed Aircraft Corporation

We welcome the opportunity to express our views to the Subcommittee in connection with its studies of the utilization of aerospace technology and

From Nation's Manpower Revolution, Hearings, Part 9 (Washington, D.C.: United States Government Printing Office, 1964). This statement was made to the U.S. Senate Committee on Labor and Public Welfare, November 1963.

manpower, and we want to assure the Subcommittee's members of our continuing interest in this subject and our support of their efforts.

Although we believe that foreseeable changes in government procurement practices will not have an immediate, drastic effect upon either the level of the aerospace industry's business or its manpower requirements, we believe it is wise to continue planning against even a remote possibility that these changes may become more severe than anticipated. Even apart from this consideration, the advantages of speeding the application of aerospace technology to the civilian economy seem to us sufficiently great to warrant a study of the type you are undertaking.

We believe that there are several public and community needs to which aerospace technology could be almost immediately applied and many others to which it could, in varying periods and with varying degrees of supplementation, be made to apply. We believe, further, that such an application would serve to sustain the impetus of our present scientific and technological drive and capture many of its benefits for the civilian economy. Aerospace technology, redirected in part to civilian ends, could aid in the development of new products and industries, assist in the solution of a wide variety of current public problems, and provide, in effect, a new avenue of national growth and new and more satisfying patterns of living.

It is obvious, of course, that in the event of large cutbacks in defense business, such a program would help to maintain aerospace industry strength to meet new defense demands in the future—demands that our experience indicates are very likely to be made again, as they have been so many times in the past. It would provide the basis for a standby industry and technology that could be quickly mobilized to meet possible threats to our security—either those employing existing weapons or those involving technological surprises. To guard against this latter contingency, of course, it is important that a high research and development effort be maintained even during the most apparently tranquil periods. Civilian programs that would sustain this research effort and keep research and development teams together should have a high priority.

We recognize that the application of aerospace research and technological resources to civilian areas of the economy will pose difficult questions regarding the proper roles of government and industry and will require new patterns of government-industry cooperation to achieve social gains without damage to the enterprise system that has been a traditional source of our national strength. Nevertheless, we are hopeful that these new patterns can be further developed. Some of them have already begun to emerge in the government's relationships with the aerospace industry, and it is certainly possible that they can be refined and extended to other than aerospace areas.

In summary, we believe the need is not immediate, since we do not anticipate drastic or sudden reductions in government defense contracting. Nevertheless, we believe it is wise to plan against the contingency. And, even in its absence, we believe the advantages of applying aerospace technology to civilian needs are sufficiently intriguing and compelling to justify this planning.

Following are more specific and detailed comments. We have felt they could be most useful to the Subcommittee if we offered them as answers to what seemed to us four basic questions.

1. *What may be the nature and scope of the manpower problem resulting from possibly changed procurement levels in our industry in the years to come?* Briefly, we do not believe the prospect for great manpower loss to be as serious as it has been represented to be in some quarters. Governmental purchases of the things our industry sells—airplanes, missiles, space vehicles, electronics, rocket fuels, instruments, ships, and related services—are now in excess of $20 billion a year. While current defense and space appropriations bills are somewhat under the totals requested by the President, they provide funds to continue this rate of expenditures. Our own forecasts all point to a continued high level of defense and space spending in view of the basic realities of the present world situation.

It seems to us reasonable to expect a nearly constant level of combined defense and space spending over the next few years or, at the most, only a slightly declining one. Recent estimates of a $5 billion decline in defense spending over the next five years appear to us as a valid but perhaps outside figure, more likely subject to downward rather than upward revision. We should think that civilian space spending may hold steady or perhaps increase.

Translated into our own company expectations, future governmental procurement practices should have only a moderate effect upon our company's manpower. Our experience leads us to believe that, if we can continue to maintain our traditional portion of available government business, normal employee turnover plus our regular adaptive measures will help us keep any manpower disruption and dislocation to normal levels.

Of course, it is not simple. Much of our historic turnover occurs among new employees, and very little of it occurs within certain key groups of highly skilled or senior employees. Some dislocations of these latter groups would unquestionably occur. Yet because of past fluctuations in our business, we have a long experience in cushioning dislocations of this type. The normal vicissitudes to which we are constantly exposed in the phasing out of old programs and the buildup of new ones have accustomed us to a certain amount of organizational restructuring and reassignment of personnel.

We are confident that, so long as the decline in defense expenditures is gradual and is accomplished by orderly procurement and contract-termination policies and actions on the part of the government, we can keep manpower disruption to moderate levels. It is the sudden, unexpected, or drastic cutback or cancellation that provides us with a problem we cannot handle in a normal and orderly manner and that is likely to flood the community with large numbers of laid-off employees.

It is worth noting that the problem of this kind of manpower surplus is more likely to be a community than a national one, since even seemingly minor changes in procurement levels or types tend to have profound effects upon single companies or single plants. This is a problem that exists even under conditions of rising government expenditures, as companies fail to obtain particular kinds of new business. It would, of course, be accentuated under declining defense expenditures.

2. *What planning and actions are appropriate and possible for a defense company such as Lockheed in adapting to changed conditions?* Change has been an outstanding characteristic of our industry from almost the beginning, and our company, as have most others in the industry, has a long experience in anticipating change and adapting to it. The most notable example in recent years is the transition the industry made from the manufacture of airframe to the design and development of missiles and space vehicles and the corresponding transition from an industry of high production to an industry oriented to research, development, and weapon-systems integration and management. We have also, of course, had long experience with changing procurement levels.

To accommodate to these recurring changes in both the levels and types of our business, Lockheed has developed a variety of techniques that have served to cushion the shocks and lessen manpower dislocations—techniques that work well when the changes are gradual and when we are forewarned but are less than adequate in the face of sudden, unannounced, and drastic cutbacks.

These techniques include such things as pre-established orderly transfer, layoff, and recall procedures, designed to retain vital skills and longer-service employees. They also include procedures providing for extensive transfer of people from project to project or division to division, and a high degree of support of various manpower-development and training programs that include retraining and conversion-training activities. We encourage the development of a wide variety of skills through employee tuition-reimbursement programs, in-plant training programs, and other educational activities designed to provide a work force of flexible skills and talents.

We also try to anticipate changes and new opportunities through extensive long-range planning and diversification studies. Our development planning group has been making master long-range plans since 1953 and, in these and other ways, tries to help us plot our course as far ahead as ten or twenty years. We believe much of our success in adapting to present-day space and defense needs . . . [arises from] these long-range planning efforts.

On the diversification side, we have also been successful in recent years in extending our competence into new fields through the acquisition of ship-building, propulsion, and electronics companies. Although much of this diversification has been limited to the defense field, we have also developed and marketed a number of nonmilitary products—commercial jet airplanes, flight recorders, fuel-oil registers, bridges, commercial ships, salt-water anticorrosion systems, new metal alloys, airport-fueling services, and many others. . . . [Although] our total sales volume in these areas is relatively small, it represents penetrations into a number of civilian fields where growth potential exists.

Nevertheless, with nearly 96 percent of our current sales going to United States and foreign military customers, we cannot yet claim any great success in diversifying into nongovernmental areas. We believe this is not the result of inadequate foresight or lack of planning but rather reflects the great difficulties that we, in common with other aerospace companies, have in entering commercial fields in spite of our desire to do so and our constant exploration of promising possibilities.

These difficulties stem from a variety of causes. Our industry is technologically oriented toward the very sophisticated product or system involving very high degrees of reliability, quality control, and advanced engineering. Such products, and the techniques and safeguards involved in developing them, are likely to be competitive only in those commercial markets where extremely high-quality and state-of-the-art advances likewise are placed at a high premium.

Then, too, the aerospace industry has little experience in competing for markets in most commercial fields and suffers not only from this inexperience but also from the lack of the kind of organization it needs to compete—extensive dealership organizations, for example, or other commercial outlets for its products.

Behind these problems—problems subject to solution with sufficient time and effort—has lain the persistent inability of the industry to give them the time and attention they require for solution. Our first responsibility has always been to our governmental customers, and we have always felt the strong obligation to devote our best talents and facilities to defense programs, often at the expense of commercial diversification efforts.

Whatever the reasons, the industry has not been notably successful in developing extensive commercial markets, even though it has long recognized the desirability of doing so. Lockheed has made several forays into unrelated commercial fields—aluminum curtain walls, for example—with little success. Other companies have had similar experiences, many of them dating back to the period just after World War II.

All this suggests there is no lack of concern in the industry with establishing commercial markets to balance military ones. It does suggest serious but not insurmountable limitations on the part of aerospace companies to enter many commercial fields under existing conditions.

3. *What can the government do to assist in devising and implementing plans for constructive adjustment to possibly changed procurement levels?* We believe the government might well consider joining with industry [in] studying methods of continued employment of defense industry engineering, scientific,

and other manpower resources. We hope that an objective of such studies would be to insure the retention of technological-team competence against the time that it might again be needed for rapid conversion back to future defense work. And we would urge that the research and development sector of the industry be permitted to continue to devote a major share of its attention to defense problems even under the most stringent cutbacks in order to maintain its ability to cope with new technological threats to our security. Experience proves that the finest research results are obtained when a strong and continuing level of effort is maintained.

We, therefore, look with favor on such efforts as that contemplated in the recent bill Mr. Hart and Mr. Humphrey introduced before the Senate to establish a commission on the application of advanced technology to community and manpower needs and are glad to observe that this bill provides for an advisory panel to include representatives of government, private industry, and educational and technological institutions.

We believe this kind of approach may prove a valuable supplement to tax-cutting measures . . . [because] it will have the effect of preserving defense competence while partially directing it into other useful areas. It can also be pinpointed to specific community needs in ways that tax cuts cannot.

4. *What other areas of activity show promise for utilization of the defense industry's technological resources?* As part of our own company's present long-range planning, we are now conducting a study of broad areas of national, community, and human needs that might be served by the application of our own company's technology. For the most part, private enterprise has not yet undertaken these tasks, largely because they are marginally uneconomic in our present state of development. Many of them are very large in scope. They represent potential areas of promise to the aerospace industry as a whole because they can make use of existing aerospace technological and productive skills, because they will benefit from the application of aerospace research resources, or because they involve the extensive systems-engineering ability that is to be found within the industry.

We have not yet completed this study, and the following list is incomplete and certainly not definitive. But it will serve, we hope, to suggest some of the kinds of areas in which the broad competences of the industry might beneficially be employed under conditions that would make this employment economically feasible. These conditions would probably require varying degrees of government support, until the programs become economically self-sustaining.

The following projects or programs may well serve as examples of commercial areas in which aerospace technology, with varying degrees of conversion effort, might be applied:

1. *Supersonic transport.* This, of course, is a current project for which Lockheed is now competing. It is mentioned here merely to identify it as a type

of peacetime conversion effort that is already underway and that may be regarded as setting a precedent.

2. *Transport helicopters.* The short-haul use of helicopters can be greatly expanded, particularly in areas of high-density population. New helicopter developments, some of them within our own company, are producing more efficient and more economical vehicles. Concentrated effort in this field, as well as in the whole area of vertical take-off and landing craft, could produce substantial transportation improvements.

3. *Facilities for general aviation.* These involve such items as improved communication and navigation aids, cargo-handling devices, air-traffic-control systems, more and better terminal facilities, and so on, all contributing to the ease and safety of flying and stimulating commercial air travel and private flying alike.

4. *Integrated transportation systems.* These are vast systems-engineering projects involving the coordination of rail, road, air, and even sea facilities to avoid duplication and expedite travel. Perhaps one way to visualize such a system is through the concept of an integrated terminal, fed locally by rail, bus, or private automobiles arriving at different levels; fed from medium distances by helicopters, feeder planes, bus, or rail service; and fed from larger distances by subsonic or supersonic transports and ultimately, perhaps, even rocket-powered aircraft.

5. *Satellite programs.* This is an area already under exploitation for civilian ends by NASA [National Aeronautics and Space Administration] and, in the case of the communications satellite, by private enterprise. The utility of the communications satellite in relaying voice, video, or pulse information is well-known. Other satellite projects offer similar advantages. Weather satellites, for example, can furnish large national benefits in the accurate prediction, and possibly even control, of weather. Greater emphasis on these practical satellite programs is worth considering.

6. *Harbor development.* This area may have more application to our own company than to others in the industry because of the construction, dredging, and other skills of our ship-building subsidiary. However, we see it as a possible outlet for our capability, particularly in connection with the project following.

7. *Merchant-marine improvement.* American ships and the shipping industry may be substantially benefitted by application of aerospace technology. New types of high-speed vehicles with which we are now experimenting include hydrofoil craft and interface vehicles that skim above the water. Anticorrosion systems, protective coatings, and cargo-containerization systems are already under development or being produced by Lockheed with the expectation that the number of commercial marine products can be extended in the future. In addition, we are currently expanding our shipbuilding facilities to permit the construction of large commercial oceangoing vessels.

8. *Underwater systems.* This is a field whose potential is still largely

unknown. For the past several years, Lockheed has supported an oceanographic research program which includes the operation of a fully equipped oceangoing research vessel. Our present investigation of underwater mining and exploration is but one outgrowth of this research effort.

9. *Air-pollution control devices.* The importance of air-pollution control to public health and welfare needs no comment. This is a large-scale project requiring intensive research efforts and perhaps developing into large hardware production programs. Aerospace technology is engaged in a portion of this area now in connection with investigation of closed ecological systems for space travel.

10. *Water-conservation systems.* Integrated water systems involve dams, pipelines, antipollution treatment, and so on. They are of particular interest to our company because they make use of our heavy construction experience.

11. *Waste-disposal systems.* These systems could provide more efficient collection and disposal methods than currently in use, perhaps with recapture of waste products. Lockheed already has some experience in this area, involving construction of a pilot plant to convert waste materials into economically useful gases and solid products such as soil conditioners.

12. *Automated-materials-handling systems.* There are many systems of modern living, such as hospitals, warehousing, and consumer food distribution, in which the extensive or inefficient use of human labor suggests room for improvement through electromechanical handling systems and automatic controls.

13. *Power conversion and storage.* The industry has long been exploring new and unusual sources of power for space propulsion and auxiliary power supply to spacecraft. Of particular commercial interest is the fuel cell, still under development, that converts chemical to electrical power directly and may serve a number of highly useful purposes in the future, possibly even to the extent of replacing the gasoline engine.

14. *Nuclear electric power.* Already competitive in some areas of the world, nuclear power should become even more widespread in the future with the development of reactors capable of producing lower-cost power, and with the development of fast breeder reactors, and ultimately through the control of thermonuclear reaction. Small nuclear reactors for marine and space propulsion, long-endurance space power sources, and remote site operations represent an area where continuing research efforts will be needed. Many aerospace companies maintain a nuclear capability that can be put to work to speed this process. Our own company operates a nuclear research laboratory that does radiation studies, and builds training reactors and radioisotope power sources.

15. *Information systems.* The industry's high competence in advanced military electronic systems offers great potential for the future development of commercial information systems of various kinds. These range from large command and control systems (air-traffic control is a familiar example) through

various data storage and retrieval systems (automated libraries, medical information systems, and so on) to smaller management information systems or business systems for industry. Indeed, it can be stated that the growth and vitality of the nation's commercial electronics industry owe much to past military electronics research and development efforts. And current studies underway in the areas of microminiaturization and high-reliability components will be of great benefit to commercial users in the not-too-distant future.

16. *Salt-water conversion.* Perhaps the ultimate answer to the nation's need for water, salt-water conversion, although not directly related to present aerospace research efforts, offers such positive public and community benefits that it might well warrant attack by aerospace research and technical teams.

Aerospace companies today have a widespread research competence ranging over most of the physical and mathematical sciences and many of the life sciences. They have, in fact, the highest research and scientific competence to be found anywhere in the nation and represent our chief reservoir of assembled scientific talent. When you add to this the industry's high proportion of skilled labor, its productive abilities and facilities, and its outstanding systems-engineering skill, it appears to be ideally suited to create and develop massive engineering programs that can add greatly to the public good.

To some, programs such as those listed above may appear visionary. Perhaps they are. But on reflection it is possible they may be no more so than was the concept of the earth satellite ten years ago. To insure constructive planning and selection of such ventures, each will need careful appraisal, balancing considerations of technical feasibility, economic practicality, and usefulness in meeting the nation's public and community needs. We are confident, however, that among these and other programs and projects there exist opportunities in which the scientific and engineering resources of defense industries may be directed effectively, at the same time mitigating the consequences of possible future cutbacks in defense production.

QUESTIONS FOR DISCUSSION

1. *Do you think a "military-industrial complex" exists in America today? If so, do you see this as a threat? Why or why not?*
2. *Does your community depend in any significant way upon military spending? How?*
3. *If peace were to once again become the "normal" condition, what economic problems might it pose?*
4. *How might we deal with these problems?*

Can We Save the
Environment?

President Nixon has announced that the decade of the seventies shall be devoted to the protection and resuscitation of the environment, and, according to scientists and conservationists, the dedication comes none too soon. (Indeed, some say it comes too late.) Pollution and the problems of dwindling land space are not really new issues. The question of dwindling land supplies was at least implicitly raised in Parson Malthus' writings nearly two hundred years ago, and Americans have long been aware of the water and air pollution resulting from industrial development. The recent concern is sharpened for two reasons: (1) the problem is frankly worsening, and (2) the filth and starvation of our environment present a clear paradox alongside our obvious material wealth.

The issue of environment in one way or another strikes at the heart of traditional American economic philosophy. Americans have generally approached their land and resources as if they were inexhaustible, to be used or misused simply as profit motives determined. To obtain coal and other minerals, they fouled their streams and destroyed their forests, and to manufacture goods, they have discarded, without thought, their waste products in the air and water. If the environment can be protected and improved, at least to some degree, the obvious question is: Who should pay for this resuscitation? The easy answer would seem to be that polluters should pay for pollution. But how and how much? What would prohibit industries that pollute from passing on abatement costs to consumers?

Answers to these problems are obviously difficult. They involve the calculation of the social and economic costs of environmental decline. They may require the use of direct regulation, subsidy payments, and incentive pricing and taxation to control pollution. While this brief section can answer few of these questions, it should raise

them for the student, and he should begin to apply some of the economic concepts with which he is familiar to obtain some possible solutions.

The first of the following articles surveys the crisis in land use and the
second studies the destruction of our water resources as seen in the problems of
the Great Lakes. The last article supplies an analytic framework to look at these
problems.

The Crisis in Land Use

Department of Research, AFL-CIO

America contains a fixed amount of land which is being subjected to
increasing demands of more and more people. The onrushing technological
revolution, increasing living standards, greater consumption, more leisure time
and the new age of transportation are placing enormous burdens on the bounty
of the land and sharpening competition and controversy over its control and
use.

Every day, somewhere in the country one can glimpse bits and pieces
of the problem:

The urban center that rises in aluminum and glass splendor while the displaced poor burrow deeper into the wretchedness of the ghetto.

The water course running brick-red or chocolate brown with the topsoil
washed off a suburban housing development or from farms being mined for
money crops.

The farmland and woodland sliced up by freeways.

The shopping centers and massive apartment complexes mushrooming on
land better suited for city dwellers' recreational needs.

The desolation and poverty of cutover timber land and the ruin that remains in the wake of strip mining.

The hideous wasteland of auto junkyards and the unsightly strings of
service stations and factories leading into major cities.

In 1900, each American had the equivalent resources of 25 acres of
land; by 1950, this was down by one-half to 12.5 acres; in 1966, there were
9.7 acres of land per capita. When the year 2000 rolls around, there will

From the AFL-CIO American Federationist, *February 1967. Reprinted by permission.*

be less than 6 acres of land per capita. And the price of land mounts as intense competition for its uses grows and speculators add to the upward price spiral.

These figures do not reveal that seven of every ten Americans now live in urban areas which occupy only about 1 percent of the continental area of the United States. It is estimated that eight of every ten Americans will be living in metropolitan areas by the end of the century. Most of them will live in three supermetropolitan areas that stretch from Boston to Washington, from Buffalo and Pittsburgh to Milwaukee and from San Francisco to San Diego.

It seems like only yesterday that hunger for land and freedom drew the first colonist here. It seems like only yesterday that the settlement of the continent was accomplished with the ebullient optimism that the bounty of the American earth was boundless and there would be no tomorrow.

From colonial days to the atomic age, control and use of the land were issues that have moulded the lives of generations of Americans. It has been and continues to be conditioned by the long battle between differing philosophies of property rights and ownership and the nature of government.

The Republic in its infancy was precariously situated between the Atlantic and the Alleghenies, looking westward across a vast continent that national imperatives demanded be taken and subdued.

Early United States land policy laid the basis of survey and settlement in family-sized parcels, characterized, in the words of Daniel Webster, by ". . . a great subdivision of the soil and a great equality of conditions, the true basis, most certainly, of popular government."

The 1.8 billion acres of land in the public domain were disposed of in the form of grants to aid schools and colleges, for the improvement of stock raising and agriculture, for roads, railroads and canals, for extraction of metals and minerals, for commercial timber and for formation of new states.

By 1900, the axe had cleared more than 300 million acres of virgin forest. The plow had ripped open nearly 300 million acres of virgin grasslands. The rich store of metals and minerals was being exploited to provide the raw material sinews of an urbanizing industrial society. The country was linked together by transcontinental railroads. Agricultural abundance was serving regional, national and world markets. Immigrants from abroad, as well as rural and small town people, were pouring into the cities.

The nation was painfully awakening from its blissful dream of eternal abundance. It found that creation of an industrial giant and an emerging world power had run up some enormous due bills. It began to appraise its land resource with new and uneasy eyes.

Coming of age as a nation carried with it a heavy price. Timber and grasslands had been ruthlessly exploited. Wasteful mining had gutted huge areas. Whole species of wildlife had been wiped out or were in danger of extinction.

America was brought into the modern conservation era by Theodore Roosevelt and Gifford Pinchot at the turn of the century. Looking at the land through the eyes of the new breed of conservationists, the public saw 1904 billion acres of land within the continental limits of the United States containing a wide range of productive capacity, with climate (including precipitation), topography, soil and river systems the most important controlling factors and producing great differences in its potential.

The public was being taught that the resources on this land, taken in their entirety, were great but not limitless, that many of them were not renewable—such as metals and minerals. The public was being taught that the strength and well-being of the country required careful resource preservation, development and management and strong protection against monopolies.

The role of the federal government in resources was being sharply redefined to deal with a problem of national scope and new dimensions. No longer was it to be a passive instrument for giving away the public domain, but the principal planner, investor, steward, researcher and regulator. The new public policy guideline was that all possible benefits stemming from the use of the land be attained and shared by all the people.

From Teddy Roosevelt's era came the new concept which has been the yardstick of all conservation programs on the land—comprehensive, multipurpose development and use, with the river basin as the operating unit, reaching its fruition in the Tennessee Valley Authority.

This concept grew out of Pinchot's insight that all separate resources questions were merely parts of ". . . the one great central problem of the use of the earth for the good of man."

By the time the New Deal came in, the bottom had fallen out of everything for farmer, city dweller and the nation.

Franklin D. Roosevelt loved the land like no other President. He had put 10,000 unemployed men to work on New York's forests while governor of that state. In his inaugural address, he talked of putting a million men to work restoring United States timber and rangelands.

What the New Deal did to restore the people and their land is familiar history: the Civilian Conservation Corps, uniquely FDR's idea; TVA, whose work to conserve the soil, change the farm practices of the region and restore the forests was as important but less known than its dam building and electric power programs.

In 1935, Congress passed the Soil Erosion Act, creating the Soil Conservation Service, with Hugh Bennett its first director. By 1940, there were 314

Soil Conservation Districts on 190 million acres and, by 1960, nearly 3000 located in every state and operating on 98 percent of total U.S. croplands.

The Taylor Grazing Act in 1934 regulated use of public domain for cattle and sheep, established user fees and created the Grazing Service out of the old General Land Office in the Department of the Interior.

More land and money was made available for protection of fish and wildlife, for national parks, monuments, recreational and primitive areas. The Biological Survey was shifted to the Department of the Interior and became the Fish and Wildlife Service.

The private timber industry began to emphasize modern forestry management during this period, while new lands were added to national forests and programs to aid state and private forestry programs were begun. The Great Plains shelter belt of trees, conceived by Ferdinand Hayden 75 years previously, was instituted by Franklin D. Roosevelt. By 1955, it extended 2000 miles, from Canada to Texas.

In the cities and towns, land was acquired under federal programs for low-cost public housing. Efforts to establish self-contained "greenbelt" communities were begun on a pilot basis. The goal was to buy up cheap land around cities, tear down city slums, relocate their former inhabitants in well-planned garden towns and establish cultural centers and parks in the city cores. This concept of Rexford Tugwell had a perverted result in the unplanned suburban sprawl of the post-Korean era, but it also was the genesis of President Johnson's demonstration cities program.

By 1960, it was evident that problems of population increase, the growth of great metropolitan areas and the galloping technological revolution no longer could be ignored. The increase of leisure time from shorter hours of work, cheaper travel and higher wages and salaries were bringing the need for more places to play for Americans. There was a mounting drain on non-renewable resources of the land, enormous problems of the future of cities and their ability to function effectively for people and their needs, and a slow but pervasive poisoning of the environment by the waste products of industrial technology.

Since the 1930s, there had been little change in the pattern of land uses, but the competition among uses—for highways, suburban and city housing, for commerce and industry, for recreation—was increasing. There was enormous unplanned land waste and there was unconscionable speculation in land.

The New and Fair Deals developed federal mortgage insurance programs for middle-income people and for detached suburban homes. It resulted in enormously expanded home ownership and construction, but also caused unplanned urban sprawl—a disarranged flight to the suburbs from city centers and an intensification of local and regional land use problems.

The 1949 Housing Act, which authorized federal aid for urban redevelopment, was intended to retain the vitality of the central city by rebuilding its decaying framework. This program, too, has accentuated the problems of the poor and middle-income families by removing them from condemned housing and giving them the choice of leaving town or finding even worse accommodations.

The land retirement program to reduce production of soil destroying crops was expanded under President Truman and carried on by the Eisenhower Administration.

By the 1960s more than one-third of America's land was still publicly owned, most of it federally, but large areas also were held by the states. Most federal land had never been in private ownership, particularly in the 17 western states and Alaska. On the other hand, the states [had] disposed of more than 65 percent of their land holdings over the previous years.

Land acquisition by public agencies for public uses is on the rise again. This trend will increase, particularly for recreation, with emphasis on nearby facilities to serve the great metropolitan regions. There will be greater use of the power of government for public undertakings—eminent domain, easement, police power and power of the purse.

The Kennedy and Johnson Administrations ushered in a new conservation era. The frontiers are the city. The emphasis is on quality, development and preservation, esthetics, recreation, population, environmental hazards. Here are some of the major problems involving land use and the federal programs enacted to deal with them:

Cities and towns: Community Facilities Act, the new Department of Housing and Urban Development and the Economic Opportunities Act. The newly enacted Demonstration Cities program to be administered by the Department of Housing and Urban Development establishes the basis for a broad attack on the most crucial metropolitan problems—the slums, housing and recreation needs, urban blight and mass transportation—but lacks adequate financial resources.

Special regions: Appalachian Regional Development, Area Redevelopment and the Public Works and Economic Development Acts.

Outdoor recreation: Land and Water Conservation Fund, Open Space and Wilderness Preservation Acts. The largest addition in history to America's national parks system [is planned], with several proposed areas awaiting final action. Also enacted was the Highway Beautification Program and legislation making recreation a part of any decisions on multi-purpose water development projects.

Fish and wildlife: Congress empowered the Secretary of the Interior to use stronger measures, including land acquisition, to protect species of wildfowl in danger of extinction.

The federal public domain: The Land Classification and Multiple Use Acts.

Agriculture: The Conservation Reserve, Rural Areas Redevelopment and Food for Freedom programs.

The environment: Amendments to the Water Pollution Control Act; the Clean Air Act and amendments; the Solid Wastes Act.

Passing legislation is only the beginning. How it is administered and how adequately it is financed are crucial to its success. It is difficult to assess either the immediate or longer-range value of the manifold federal programs affecting the land which have been established since 1961. There is a mixture, both of concrete achievement and of mere reshuffling of programs. Duplication of functions, programs at cross purposes and tight-fisted budgeting continue to block meaningful progress. There is no integrated land policy.

THE CITY

America's new frontier is the city—with its rapidly growing population and deteriorating pockets of slums and poverty.

The conflict in land uses is a massive roadblock to the orderly development and improvement of the life of people in towns, cities and larger metropolitan areas.

Much land is not being used at all. Much is being misused and not assigned to its best function. Speculative forces freeze land-use patterns into profits instead of the public interest. Urban governments are enclosed in a trap of constantly expanding public service requirements which are outpacing available local revenues. Their planning and zoning agencies are subjected to enormous political and speculative pressures.

Planning for urban land use must change its emphasis. There is a great need for an adequate supply of decent housing for poor and middle-income families. There is also the need for schools and hospitals, clean air and water, transit systems and highways, libraries and museums, parking areas and recreation facilities. Meanwhile, urban sprawl, loss of good land to freeways, vehicular congestion and polluted air and water problems grow more serious. Horse and buggy political institutions as reflected in the maze of local jurisdictions cannot cope effectively with land-use problems.

The price of land, particularly in urban areas, has been in an upward spiral since the 1930s. In the downtown areas of major cities, land is sold by the square foot and speculators amass fortunes each year from putting together land parcels for luxury office and apartment buildings. And in the suburbs, too, land prices soar. The average price of lots of federally-insured one-family homes skyrocketed 200 percent in 1951–1965. Unless this problem is solved, it will become increasingly expensive and most difficult to rebuild American cities.

How much longer can the great metropolitan areas grow and retain their ability to perform their essential functions? What changes are necessary to enlarge freedom of choice for the poor and for minority groups? What is the effect of this haphazard growth on the quality of living and the creative human spirit?

The AFL-CIO policy resolution on urban America "urges the federal government to undertake a massive effort to rebuild our cities." Labor's program includes several key proposals which involve changes in land-use patterns: an increase in low-rent public housing, including equal housing opportunity without regard for race; increased federal capital grants for urban renewal programs and community facilities, with higher matching funds for the largest cities where needs are greatest and increased federal assistance to achieve forward-looking metropolitan area planning.

How effectively large urban areas plan for land use will in large measure determine whether the big cities will continue to sprawl formlessly over the landscape while the cancer of urban blight gnaws away their central cores. Now is the crucial time for the cities to resume their historic roles as seedbeds of creative ideas and fruitful associations of people.

THE FARM AND THE FOREST

Since the 1920s, the technological revolution on the farm has made it possible for a super-abundance of crops to be produced without any significant addition to the nation's cropland area.

This tremendous changeover in farming methods has taken the form of mechanization—replacing millions of draft animals and millions of farm workers through rural electrification, pesticides, fertilizers, better strains of plants and a constant input of new information from governmental and private research.

Between 1940 and 1963, farm production rose 60 percent while the number of farm workers dropped from 11 million to 6.5 million and the farm population fell off precipitously from 30.5 million to 17.1 million. Most of the displaced rural people migrated into the towns and cities.

In 1900, one farm worker produced enough to feed 7 persons. In 1940, he could feed 17. Now his productivity can feed 31.

To raise all a nation requires year in and year out has been a goal sought by peoples since the beginnings of history.

The United States stands between famine and enough to eat in developing nations around the world. The Food for Peace program has expanded to the point where Secretary of Agriculture Orville Freeman has declared 60 million acres of land in the "conservation reserve" eligible for planting in wheat and feed grains for next year's harvest.

The American farmer over the next several years increasingly becomes a key man in the subsistence future of much of the world. The ability to continue to increase his productivity on a limited amount of cropland is of enormous importance.

Yet erosion and faulty drainage remain serious problems on substantial areas of farmland. Too many farmers regard their land as a capital asset and concentrate on raising productivity at the expense of soil conservation.

A keystone of the nation's land policy since 1785, the family-operated farm has been actively and consistently supported by organized labor since the 1870s. The AFL-CIO continues its strong efforts to prevent the weakening of the 160-acre restriction provisions of federal reclamation law in California and Arizona under the less than forceful administration of the Secretary of the Interior and the pressures of the powerful farm corporations of those states.

From 1949 to 1964, there has been a sharp decrease of 1.8 million in the number of farms—from 5.2 million to 3.4 million units. This drop took place almost entirely among the small part-time, technologically inefficient and non-commercial holdings with less than $2500 annual sales. Those with more than $2500 annual sales remained about the same in number over this period.

Relatively large farms are increasing in number and relatively small farms with marginal income are decreasing. Family farms are getting fewer and larger, but there is no strong trend toward their replacement by the huge factories in the field.

The main problem of land use for commercial timber is the expected deficit in forest products by the year 2000 as related to supply. The U.S. Forest Service estimates that requirements for timber products will increase by 80 percent between now and 2000 and, by that time, supply could fall short of this demand by 16 percent or some 13 billion board feet. While some wood products are likely to be imported, most will come from domestic forests.

Continued population growth could lead to demand far in excess of the Forest Service projections. It proposes more intensive forest management procedures—timber stand improvement, access roads, planting and reseeding, protection against fire, insects and disease and timber salvage. It also urges increased sustained yield production by farmers and miscellaneous smaller private owners who control 60 percent of U.S. commercial forest land.

Forest land provides an invaluable additional function of protecting soil and stabilizing water flow on the headwaters of river basins. It also will increasingly serve as a recreational resource. A substantial amount of marketable timber already has been withdrawn in many areas of the wilderness system.

Until there are strong programs to assist small timber owners to grow and market trees, the heaviest demands will be exerted on the timber companies and the public forests, particularly those in the Far West.

If more land is required for tree raising, there will be an increasing conflict with other land uses, particularly recreation and fish and wildlife.

THE PUBLIC DOMAIN

There are 180 million acres of residual federal public domain lands in the continental United States and an additional 270 million acres in Alaska.

These lands are administered by the Bureau of Land Management, within the Department of the Interior, under a maze of laws which date back to the 1860s and hamper modern multiple-use management.

The present and future value of public domain lands is enormous. Revenues from minerals leasing, sale of land and timber and grazing fees total $3.5 billion since 1875, of which $1.3 billion has been received between 1961 [and] 1965. The public lands not only are important for conserving land and water, but can be managed to help finance other needed federal resources programs.

Retention of the Classification and Multiple Use Act as a permanent program should result in decisions as to what land should be retained for the American people for economic and recreational benefits and what land should be reclassified for sale or exchange with other federal, state and local agencies.

Repeal of the Homestead, Desert Land and Mining Acts of 1872 is called for. No public domain land is left for agricultural settlement. The Mining Act simply keeps the Bureau of Land Management in constant administrative and judicial snarls. The Public Land Law Review Commission created by Congress in 1964 is to make recommendations on existing laws and policies by December 31, 1968.

The remaining 150 million acres of land intended for retention as a national heritage should be guarded well. It contains $300 billion worth of oil shale rock, hundreds of millions of dollars' worth of coal, natural gas, phosphates, uranium, timber and other resources. It also protects vital river headwaters.

LAND FOR MINING

While mining does not account for a large proportion of total land use, placer, strip, auger and open pit operations in the United States have ruined or seriously damaged about 1.75 million acres of once beautiful land, of which 900,000 acres are in the Appalachian region.

Timber interests already had done immense damage to the land. The open pit coal mines of recent years have done an even more brutal job. They have blighted surrounding areas. Sulphur in the soil prevents anything from growing. Acid washes into the streams, killing all marine life. Landslides occur; tons of silt are washed into streams.

TVA has developed economically feasible techniques of reclamation of stripped land and at last is requiring such restoration as part of its new coal supply contracts. Kentucky and other states have passed laws requiring mining operators to reclaim the damaged areas. The recent Interior Department report on strip mining recommends that all affected states enact strong laws requiring mine operators to restore the land. Cooperative state-federal programs are proposed to correct past damage and develop recreational and other uses in the recovered areas.

LAND FOR RECREATION

In 1960, recreation not only gave pleasure to millions of Americans who made 4.4 billion visits to all kinds of places, but generated a $20 billion demand for associated goods and services.

Demand for recreation land and the recreation business are expected to triple by the end of the century—the former from 44 million to 134 million acres, the latter from $20 billion to more than $60 billion. More than 12 billion visits are forecast by the year 2000.

The two principal problems to be solved are competition in land uses, particularly in urban areas, and rising land costs due in large part to speculation.

If the necessary land is found for the needs of [the year] 2000, it will leave a 50-million-acre deficit nationally. This means that other lands—farm, timber, grazing—would yield to recreational uses if these were considered of higher national priority.

The needed acres should be close to where the people are. City dwellers can only occasionally travel hundreds of miles or more to recreational areas. They need places where they can take their families for afternoon or weekend outings.

The slowness of federal and state governments to acquire recreational land makes possible the tremendous price escalations. The $169 million provided by Congress for the Land and Water Conservation Fund is already short $87 million in 18 areas. In 22 others, the Bureau of Outdoor Recreation does not know if the properties can be purchased with available funds.

Proposals to get around land price hikes have included giving authority to river basin commissions to issue bonds for land purchases; stronger land zoning, both urban and rural; private foundations holding land by option until federal money becomes available; and special taxes for recreational land.

Workers have a tremendous stake in the use of the nation's land. Workers, in common with all other citizens, have both needs and responsibilities. The needs are for land which will be developed, managed and conserved to yield them the fundamentals of a good life in all of its aspects, [land] to be handed to the next generation in just a little better shape. The responsibilities are those of citizens who will consistently work to help reach those goals.

It is necessary to understand the American condition no longer permits the luxury of doing with land just exactly what any person wills, regardless of how it affects others.

The Great and Dirty Lakes

Gladwin Hill

Whatever a honeymoon visit to Niagara Falls was like in the days when Blondin was crossing on his tightwire, it's different now. Something new and unpleasant has been added. Sightseers boarding the famous *Maid of the Mist* excursion boat are likely to find themselves shrouded in a miasma that smells like sewage. That's what it is—coming over the American falls in the Niagara River and gushing out of a great eight-foot culvert beneath the Honeymoon Bridge. As the little boat plows through the swirling currents to a landing on the Canadian side, it has to navigate an expanse of viscous brown foam— paper-mill waste out of the culvert—that collects in a huge eddy across the river.

While aesthetically shocking, this annoyance is hardly factually surprising. The falls in effect are the funnel through which the water from four of the Great Lakes passes on the final leg of its trip to Lake Ontario, the St. Lawrence River, and the sea. . . .

The Great Lakes constitute the largest reservoir in the world, containing about 20 percent of the fresh water on the face of the earth. They are the principal water source for one of the nation's largest concentrations of population and industry. If their waters became corrupted, it would be a calamity of unprecedented magnitude. And it would involve not one but two nations, for the Canadian boundary bisects all the lakes except Lake Michigan.

If you stand on the shore at Duluth, Minnesota, and look out over the endless expanse of Lake Superior, it seems impossible that such a vast body of water could ever become tainted. Yet the flow of industrial pollutants alone from Lake Superior into Lake Huron has been measured by the International Joint Commission in hundreds of millions of gallons a year. The contamination gets rapidly worse as you move eastward along the chain of lakes to Michigan and Erie. . . .

Chicago, at the southern tip of Lake Michigan, has spent more than half a century and billions of dollars developing a good water system. The city draws a billion gallons a day from the lake, to serve 4,400,000 people. Its sewage, treated to remove most of the pollutants, is channeled southward into tributaries of the Mississippi, so that it does not affect the lake.

But around Chicago, extending past the Indiana line only ten miles to the southeast, is a network of small, sluggish waterways—the Grand Calumet River, the Little Calumet River, Wolf Lake, and various canals—that serve as a drainage system for a dense industrial complex sprawling for more than twenty miles along the shore, from Chicago through Hammond, Whiting, and Gary, Indiana. The complex includes ten steel mills, five oil refineries, and dozens of other plants ranging from paper mills to soap factories. Six major plants discharge a billion gallons of waste a day that includes 35,000 pounds of ammonia nitrogen, 3500 pounds of phenols, 3000 pounds of cyanide, and fifty tons of oil. A good deal of this finds its way into Lake Michigan. There it has spoiled some of Chicago's best beaches, exterminated much aquatic life, and recently defied city water officials' best efforts to provide a supply free of objectionable tastes and odors.

Reporting on a typical incident, Chicago alderman Leon Despres said, "In December 1964 we found millions of mysterious polyethylene pellets washed up on our two miles of breakwater. We learned that they represented just one flushing from a chemical plant, and that on the Michigan shore part of the same flushing made up thirty or forty miles of windrows."

"The southern tip of Lake Michigan," comments Wisconsin's Senator Gaylord Nelson, "is turning into a cesspool." He is concerned because similar troubles are developing one hundred miles up the west shore of the lake at Milwaukee.

Last March the Department of Health, Education, and Welfare initiated, as it had in thirty-four previous major pollution situations across the country, a formal abatement proceeding for the Chicago area, with Illinois and Indiana as parties. In conference with representatives of the Public Health Service, officials of the two states agreed to a corrective program based on detailed studies and recommendations of federal investigators. The program, which is enforceable by federal court action, prescribed waste treatment methods and standards to be instituted within a year.

Pollution from the western Great Lakes is augmented to a repulsive level as their waters come down through the Detroit River—actually an interlake strait—and flow into Lake Erie.

"These waters," the Public Health Service summarizes, "are polluted bacteriologically, chemically, physically and biologically, and contain excessive coliform (intestinal bacteria) densities as well as excessive quantities of phenols, iron, ammonia, suspended solids, settleable solids, chlorides, nitrogen compounds and phosphates."

Michigan has prided itself on enforcement of its pollution regulations throughout most of its 11,000 lakes and 36,000 miles of stream. But Detroit, with its great industrial complex and a surprising horse-and-buggy municipal sewage system, has long been a stumper.

Apart from relatively minor contributions from Canadian communities just across the strait, the Detroit area dumps twenty million pounds of contaminant materials into Lake Erie every day, in a waste flow totaling 1.6 billion gallons.

About two-thirds of this is from industry and one-third is municipal sewage. Detroit gives the sewage of three million people only "primary" treatment, which means just the settling-out of grosser solids; standard sewage treatment today includes a "secondary" stage of chemical and biological neutralization of up to 90 percent of the contaminants.

Late in 1961 Michigan asked for federal help in cleaning up the Detroit situation. The Public Health Service spent two years on an exhaustive investigation of pollution sources. The report named some of the nation's leading automobile, chemical, and paper companies as major offenders. A cleanup program similar to the Chicago one was arrived at in hearings this spring.

Michigan waters account for only about 1 percent of Lake Erie's surface area. Conditions like Detroit's are repeated in various degrees at Toledo, Cleveland, Erie, and Buffalo. No one knows the total amount of pollution pouring into the lake. But there is plenty of other evidence, both visual and scientific, that the aggregate pollution has long since passed the danger point. It has transformed the 240-mile-long lake, Senator Nelson remarked, "from a body of water into a chemical tank."

Because documenting interstate pollution, as the basis for involuntary federal intervention, is laborious, the Public Health Service had resigned itself to proceeding from one metropolis to another in voluntary intrastate actions, as with Detroit. But by this spring, public disgust at the lake's deterioration had reached the overflow point. A one-man crusade by David Blaushild, a Cleveland automobile dealer, alone elicited hundreds of thousands of signatures of Ohio citizens on protest petitions.

Feeling the heat, Ohio's Governor James Rhodes in June formally requested the federal government to initiate an interstate abatement action. This automatically involved Michigan, Ohio, Indiana (which contributes pollution via the Maumee River, running through Ohio), Pennsylvania, and New York.

Two weeks of federal hearings in Cleveland and Buffalo last August laid the groundwork for a cleanup program. It will cost upward of $100 million just to bring Detroit's sewage system up to standard. The outlay confronting industry there for adequate waste treatment facilities is probably several times that. Along the whole lakeshore, comprehensive remedial measures will probably run into the billions.

These programs, under federal law, are not just pious declarations of intent. The Secretary of Health, Education, and Welfare is empowered both to prescribe performance schedules and to reconvene the parties, customarily at six-month intervals, to review progress. At these sessions the Public Health Service regularly gets impressive moral and technical support from other federal agencies, such as the Fish and Wildlife Service, and from militant lay organizations such as the Izaak Walton League and the League of Women Voters, which has made water pollution reform one of its major national projects.

There are those who gainsay the severity of Lake Erie's pollution. Mainly they are state and local water and health officials parrying implicit criticism of their activities and defending their areas against stigma. Life would be simpler for everybody if their position were substantial. But it is negative. They are arguing matters of degree. They can't and don't contend that conditions are getting any *better* or that there's any prospect, without action, of their getting anything but worse. Their argument against corrective steps is that "we have no assurance of what they'll accomplish." This is rather like arguing against transferring from a sinking ship to a lifeboat on the ground that one doesn't know where the lifeboat is going.

Pollution abatement officials concede that they cannot tell to what extent remedial measures can restore Lake Erie to its pristine cleanliness. The accumulation of contaminants down the years has disrupted its biological metabolism to the point where it has the limnological equivalent of cancer. Oxygen-absorbing chemicals have so sapped its supply of free oxygen, essential to the normal plant-fish-insect life cycle, that there is a 2600-square-mile patch in the middle of the lake, equal to more than one quarter of its area, where the water for up to ten feet from the bottom is devoid of oxygen. The lake's general oxygen deficiency has set in motion a devolution of fish life from desirable species toward primeval anaerobic sludgeworms and fingernail clams. Whitefish and pike, once the basis of a multimillion-dollar fishing industry, have vanished; in their place are inferior species such as carp that require less oxygen.

The disruption of normal processes has been aggravated by a runaway growth of algae, the plant life that in a healthy lake is microscopic; in Lake Erie it grows like seaweed, in great swatches up to 50 feet long. The dominant type is *cladaphora,* a coarse growth that looks as if it had dripped off the Ancient Mariner and smells terrible.

Algae growth is promoted by phosphates, which come particularly from municipal sewage. Detergents are composed up to 70 percent of phosphates. Millions of pounds of waste detergent pour into the lake every year. Each pound will propagate 700 pounds of algae. The algae absorbs more oxygen. When it dies, it sinks to the bottom as silt and releases the phosphate to grow another crop of algae. Copper sulfate will kill algae in a small volume of water, such as a pool. But biologists know of no chemical that can exterminate it on a scale such as is found in Lake Erie.

Even if the flow of pollution into Lake Erie were stopped entirely tomorrow, the reversal of this accelerating deteriorative cycle would be problematical. "All we can do," the scientists say, "is try."

Lake Erie contracted this disease rapidly because it is quite shallow. Its maximum depth of 210 feet is only one-eighth that of Superior, the deepest of the lakes. But Erie's fate obviously is simply a preview of what awaits all the lakes if pollution is not stemmed.

As Erie's turbid waters flow into the Niagara River, they pick up a final spate of pollution from around Buffalo. The Buffalo River is another industrial and municipal sewer, so polluted that it will not even support anaerobic creatures: slime samples pulled up from the bottom are lifeless. The coliform intestinal-bacteria count recurrently exceeds 1,500,000 per 100 milliliters—1500 times the safe level for human contact.

The conspicuous streaks that visitors a few miles away see in the water as it pours over Niagara Falls are described by Public Health investigators as "high phenol concentrations, oils, and high coliform counts [in a] polluted zone which extends about 400 feet from Bird's Island in the vicinity of Buffalo's sewage treatment plant, and widens to about one third of the river's width near Strawberry Island." . . .

Laymen aware of the Great Lakes' pollution, and their binational status, are often moved to suggest a massive international attack on the problem. This has logic but is impractical. Most of the pollution comes from the American side. The International Joint Commission, which deals with boundary problems, is inherently cumbersome and slow. Its basic function is to advise the foreign affairs divisions of the two governments, and it can only take up matters formally referred to it after lengthy consideration on both sides. It took eight years of prodding by New York governors for the Lake Erie-Lake Ontario situation to be referred to the commission, and another two years before commission committees formally went to work on the matter last spring. Meanwhile, Canadian provincial authorities have been pursuing pollution abatement programs roughly paralleling United States efforts.

"The crux of pollution abatement," observes Murray Stein, the Health, Education, and Welfare Department's enforcement director, "is establishing individual pollution sources, defining corrective steps, and then following through to see that they're carried out. The Great Lakes situation is the biggest problem we've ever tackled. But the important thing is that it has now been tackled, and with reasonable cooperation it should be possible to clean it up. In the meantime, we've just got to hope for scientific advances that will make possible the undoing of the damage that's been done already."

The Economics of Pollution

Edwin L. Dale, Jr.

Now that environment has become a national concern, it might be well to clean up some of the economic rubbish associated with the subject. There are, alas, a few "iron laws" that cannot be escaped in the effort to reduce the pollution of our air and water, in disposing of solid waste and the like. The laws do not necessarily prevent a clean environment, but there is no hope of obtaining one unless they are understood.

We have all become vaguely aware that there will be a cost—perhaps higher monthly electric bills, perhaps higher taxes, perhaps a few cents or a few dollars more on anything made from steel—if there is a successful and massive effort to have a better environment. But that is only a beginning. There are other problems.

This article will describe the three iron laws that matter. There is no point in hiding that all three are very depressing. The only purpose in adding more depressing information to a world already surfeited with it is a small one: to avoid useless effort based on false premises. A classic example has already arisen in wistful Congressional inquiries into whether we might think of a future with somewhat less electric power, or at least less growth in electric power.

In shorthand, the three laws are:

1. The law of economic growth.
2. The law of compound interest.
3. The law of the mix between public and private spending.

THE LAW OF ECONOMIC GROWTH

Whether we like it or not, and assuming no unusual increase in mass murders or epidemics, the American labor force for the next 20 years is already born and intends to work. It is hard for any of us—myself included—to imagine a deliberate policy to keep a large portion of it unemployed. But that simple fact has enormous consequences.

For more than a century, the average output of each worker for each hour worked has risen between 2 and 3 percent a year, thanks mainly to new machines, but also to better managerial methods and a more skilled labor force. This increase in what is called *productivity* is by far the most important cause

From The New York Times Magazine, April 19, 1970. © *1970 by The New York Times Company. Reprinted by permission.*

of our gradually rising standard of living—which, pollution aside, nearly all of us have wanted. In simplest terms, each worker can be paid more because he produces more and he consumes more because he earns more. Inflation only increases the numbers and does not change the facts. Machines increase the productivity of an auto worker more than a barber, but both rightly share, through the general rise in real income, in the expansion of productivity in the economy as a whole.

It is difficult to conceive of our society or any other wanting to halt the rise in productivity, or efficiency, which has made real incomes higher for all of us. But even if "we" wanted to, in our kind of society and economy "we" couldn't. The profit motive will almost always propel individual, daily decisions in the direction of higher productivity. A business will always buy a new machine if it will cut costs and increase efficiency—and thank goodness! That is what has made our standard of living—and we do enjoy it—rise.

It is not a matter of enjoying it, however. By any fair test, we are not really affluent; half of our households earn less than $8,500 a year. Apart from redistributing income, which has very real limits, the only way the society can continue to improve the well-being of those who are not affluent—really the majority—is through a continued increase in productivity. Anyone who wants us to go back to the ax, the wooden plow, the horse carriage and the water wheel is not only living a wholly impossible dream, he is asking for a return to a society in which nearly everybody was poor. We are not talking here about philosophical ideas of happiness, but of what people have proved they want in the way of material things. This society is not about to give up productivity growth. But every increase in productivity adds to output. Now consider the next step:

We can count on the output of the average worker to continue to rise in the years ahead, as it has in the past. Nearly all current forecasts put this rise in productivity much closer to 3 percent than to 2, and 3 percent has been about our average in the years since World War II. So without any change in the labor force at all, our national output will go on rising by some 3 percent a year.

What does output mean?

It means electric power produced—and smoke produced.

It means cans and bottles produced.

It means steel produced—and, unless something is done about it, water and air polluted.

It means paper produced—with the same result as for steel.

And so on and on.

But that is not the end, for there will not be a static labor force. As noted, the force for the next 20 years is already born and it is going to grow year by year (with a caveat, to be described below).

Obviously, we want to offer these people employment opportunity. So, in addition to a 3 percent productivity growth, there will be an added growth of at least 1 percent a year in the number of workers. The result is that we are almost "condemned" to a rise in our total output of 4 percent a year. The only escape, it seems, would be a national decision either to have high unemployment or to try to be less efficient. Both are absurd on their face.

The law of economic growth says, then, that we already know that the national output in 1980 will be, and almost must be, some 50 percent higher than it is now. President Nixon has said so publicly, and he is right. That is the result of an annual rate of real growth of about 4 percent, compounded. It is terrifying. If an economy of $900-billion in 1969 produces the pollution and clutter we are all familiar with, what will an economy half again as large produce?

Is there no escape from this law? The answer, essentially, is no. But there is one possible way to mitigate the awesome results. We might reduce the labor input (but, we hope, not the productivity input), without creating mass unemployment.

Each working person has a workday, workweek, workyear and worklife. Any one of them could be reduced by law or otherwise. We could reduce the legal workweek from the present 40 hours. We could add more holidays or lengthen vacations to reduce the workyear. We are already shortening the worklife, without planning it that way: increased participation in higher education has meant later entry into the labor force for many, and retirement plans, including Social Security, have brought about earlier retirement than in the past for others.

If, by chance or by law, the annual man-hours of employment are reduced in the years ahead, our output will grow a little less rapidly. This is the only way to cut our economic growth, short of deliberate unemployment or deliberate inefficiency.

There is a cost. It is most easily seen in a union-bargained settlement providing for longer vacations without any cut in annual wages, or a legal reduction in the workweek from 40 to 35 hours, with compulsory overtime payments after that. In each case, more workers must be hired to produce the same output, and if the employer—because of market demand—goes on producing at the same level, wage costs for each unit of output are higher than they otherwise would have been. Prices will therefore be higher. This is widely recognized. Maybe we would be willing to pay them.

But we cannot guarantee less output. Only if employers produce less— because of the extra cost—would that happen. And in that larger sense, the cost of a reduction of our annual labor input is simply less production per capita because the labor force is idle more of the time.

But less production was the objective of the exercise—the antipollution exercise. If we start with the proposition that the growth of production is the underlying cause of pollution, which has merit as a starting point, the only way we can get less growth in production, if we want it, is to have more of our labor force idle more of the time. In that case, we will have more leisure without mass unemployment, as we usually think of the term. Our national output, and our standard of living, will rise less rapidly.

That last idea we may learn to take, if we can cope with the leisure. But under any foreseeable circumstances, our output will still go on rising. With the most optimistic assumptions about a gradual reduction of the workday, workweek, workyear and worklife, we shall undoubtedly have a much higher output in 1980 than we have in 1970. To a man concerned about the environment, it might seem a blessing if our economic growth in the next 10 years could be 2 percent a year instead of 4 percent; he cannot hope for zero growth.

The law of economic growth, then, tells us a simple truth: "we" cannot choose to reduce production simply because we have found it to be the cause of a fouled environment. And if we want to reduce the rate of growth of production, the place to look is in our man-hours of work.

THE LAW OF COMPOUND INTEREST

It is a fair question to ask: Why weren't we bothered about pollution 12 or 15 years ago? In October, 1957, to pick a date, the Soviet Union sent the first earth satellite into orbit. The American economy had just begun a recession that was to send unemployment to 7 percent of the labor force. The late George Magoffin Humphrey, who had just resigned as Secretary of the Treasury, was warning of what he saw as vast Government spending, at that time $77-billion, and saying it would bring "a depression that would curl your hair." There were plenty of things to think about.

But nobody was worried about pollution. Conservation groups were properly bothered about parts of the wilderness (the Hell's Canyon Dam in Idaho, for example), but that was an entirely different thing. That was an issue of esthetics, not health. Nobody seemed to mention air pollution or waste that might overwhelm the space in which to put it. In a peculiarly sad irony, the late Adlai E. Stevenson had fought and lost an election against Dwight D. Eisenhower in 1956 partially on a "pollution" issue—radiation in the atmosphere from the explosion of atomic weapons.

The question, to repeat: Why didn't we worry about pollution then? The answer is that, relatively speaking, there *was* no pollution. Yes, there were electric power plants then, too. Yes, there were paper mills polluting streams. Yes, there were tin cans and paper and bottles. Some snowflakes, though we didn't know it, were already a bit black, and Pittsburgh got national attention because it tried to do some cleaning up.

But here we come to the law of compound interest. In 1957—*only 13 years ago*—our gross national product was $453-billion. In 1969, in constant dollars, it was $728-billion. That is an increase of nearly $300-billion in tin cans, electric power, automobiles, paper, chemicals and all the rest. It is an increase of 60 percent.

So what? That was not the result of an unnaturally rapid growth rate, though a bit more rapid than in some periods of our past. The *so what* is this: in the preceding 13 years the growth had been *only $100-billion*. We were the same nation, with the same energy, in those preceding 13 years. We invested and we had a rise both in productivity and in our labor force. But in the first 13 years of this example our output rose $100-billion, and in the second 13 it rose $300-billion.

In the next 13 it will rise more than $500-billion.

That is the law of compound interest. These are not numbers; they are tin cans and smoke and auto exhaust. There is no visible escape from it. Applying the same percentage growth to a larger base every year, we have reached the point where our growth in one year is half the total output of Canada, fully adjusting for inflation. Another dizzying and rather horrifying way of putting it is that the real output of goods and services in the United States has grown as much since 1950 as it grew in the entire period from the landing of the Pilgrims in 1620 up to 1950.

Most investors know the law of compound interest. There is a magic rule, for example, known as the Rule of 72. It says, with mathematical certainty, that money invested at a 7.2 percent rate of interest, compounded each year, doubles in 10 years. Our G.N.P., happily, does not compound at 7.2 percent. But it compounds at between 4 and 5 percent, and it has been compounding. The result is that the same, routine, full-employment, desirable, nationally wanted, almost unavoidable percentage increase in our national output in 1970 means precisely twice as many extra tin cans, twice as much additional electric power, and so on, as the same rate of growth in 1950. And that is only 20 years ago! We are not doing anything different, or anything awful. We are the same people. Granting approximately the same amount of human carelessness and selfishness, we are the victims solely of the law of compound interest.

THE LAW OF THE MIX BETWEEN
PUBLIC AND PRIVATE SPENDING

Robert S. McNamara, the eternally energetic and constructive former Secretary of Defense and now president of the World Bank, gave a speech in February about the plight of the poor countries. In the speech he understandably criticized the United States for reducing its foreign aid effort. But in supporting his point he adopted, almost inadvertently, a piece of partly fallacious conventional wisdom:

"Which is ultimately more in the nation's interest: to funnel national resources into an endlessly spiraling consumer economy—in effect, a pursuit of consumer gadgetry with all its senseless by-products of waste and pollution— or to dedicate a more reasonable share of those same resources to improving the fundamental quality of life both at home and abroad?"

Fair enough. It means tax increases, of course, though Mr. McNamara did not say so. That is what the "mix" between public and private spending is all about. But for our purposes the point is different. Let us look more closely at the phrase: ". . . a pursuit of consumer gadgetry with all its senseless by-products of waste and pollution. . . . "

As it stands, it is true. Private consumption does create side effects like waste and pollution. But now, assume a Brave New World in which we are all happy to pay higher taxes and reduce our private consumption so that the Government may have more money with which to solve our problems—ranging from poor education to poverty, from crime to inadequate health services. We shall not examine here the issue of whether more Government money solves problems. It is obviously more effective in some areas than in others. But anyway, in our assumption, we are all willing to give the Government more money to solve problems, including pollution.

Now let us see what happens.

The Government spends the money to reduce pollution. Sewage plants are built. They need steel. They need electric power. They need paperwork. They need workers. The workers get paid, and they consume.

The Government spends the money on education. New schools are built, which need steel, lumber and electric power. Teachers are hired. They get paid, and they consume. They throw away tin cans.

The Government spends the money on a better welfare system that treats all poor people alike, whether they work or not. Incomes among the poor rise by some amount between $4-billion and $20-billion, and these people consume. Electric power production rises and appliance and steel production rises, and so on and on.

The point is obvious by now. A shifting in our national income or production between "public goods" and "private goods" hardly changes the environment problem at all because it does not reduce total spending, or output, in the economy.

Lest a careful economist raise a valid objection, a slightly technical point must be conceded here. Government spending is done in three categories:

Purchase of goods (tanks, typewriters, sanitation trucks and school buildings).

Transfer payments to people outside government (Social Security, veterans' benefits, welfare).

Purchase of services, meaning the services of the people it employs (teachers, policemen, park rangers, tax collectors).

To the extent that a shift to more public spending, through higher taxes and a resulting reduction of private consumption, involves the first two of these categories, the point stands as made: there will be just as much production of steel, tin cans, electric power and toasters as before. To the extent that the higher public spending goes to the third category, employment of more teachers, policemen and the like, there will be slightly less production of goods even though these people spend their paychecks like everyone else. Essentially what happens in this case is that the society has chosen, through higher taxes, to have more services and fewer goods. If we assume that goods production brings pollution, a society with fewer auto- or steelworkers and more cops will crank out less pollution.

But this remains a relatively minor matter. Hardly anyone who proposes a solution to our problems thinks in terms of vast armies of Government workers. Reforming welfare through the President's new family-assistance plan is the perfect example; this will be a simple expansion of transfer payments. And, for that matter, building more sewage plants will be a purchase of goods. The overriding fact is that we can spend 30 percent of our G.N.P. for public purposes, as we do now, or 50 percent, and the G.N.P. will still be there. The law of compound interest will apply, forcing the G.N.P. upward. To the extent that the environment problem is caused by ever-expanding output, the third law says that it will not be essentially changed by altering the mix between private and public spending.

CONCLUSION

Three nice, depressing laws. They give us a starting point for any rational discussion of the environment problem. Our output is going to go on growing and growing under any conceivable set of choices we make.

But the starting point does not mean despair. It simply means that trying to solve the problem by reducing output, or the growth of output, is waste of time and energy. It won't and can't work.

How is the problem solved then? The purpose here is not, and has not been, to solve any problems. It has been to try to head off useless solutions. But a few things can be said:

There is, first, technology itself. The very energy and inventiveness that gave us this rising output—and got us to the moon—can do things about pollution. A fascinating case is the sulphur dioxide put into the air by coal-burn-ing electric power plants. A very strong argument can be made that under any foreseeable circumstances we will have to burn more and more coal to produce the needed growth of electric power. And the ground does not yield much low-sulphur coal. Thus, somebody is going to have to have the incentive to develop a way to get the sulphur out before it leaves the smokestack; and if this costs the utilities money, the regulatory commissions are going to have to allow that cost to be passed along in electric bills.

Next, there is the related idea—being increasingly explored by economists, regulators and some legislators—of making antipollution part of the price-profit-incentive system. In simplest terms, this would involve charging a fee for every unit of pollutant discharged, with meters used to determine the amount. There would be an economic incentive to stop or reduce pollution, possibly backed up with the threat to close down the plant if the meter readings go above a specified level. The company—say a paper company—would be faced with both a carrot and a stick.

There is also the simple use of the police power, as with poisonous drugs or, lately, D.D.T. It is the "thou shalt not" power: automobiles can emit no more than such-and-such an amount of this or that chemical through the exhaust pipe. Once again, if the engineers cannot find a way out, the car simply cannot legally be sold. There will be, and should be, all sorts of debate "at the margin"—whether the higher cost of the different or improved engine is worth the extra reduction of pollution. The argument exists now over D.D.T.; there are clearly costs, as well as benefits, in stopping its use. But the "thou shalt not" power exists.

Finally, there are many possibilities for using a part of our public spending for environmental purposes. Sewage plants are the obvious case. President Nixon has proposed a big expansion of the current level of spending for these plants, though not as much as many interested in clean water—including Senator Edmund Muskie—would like to see.

In this case, and only in this case, a greater effort at curing pollution must be at the expense of some other Government program unless we pay higher taxes. It is proper to point out here the subtle dimensions of the issue. There are all sorts of possible gimmicks, like tax rebates for antipollution devices for industry and federally guaranteed state and local bonds. One way or another, spending more for pollution abatement will mean spending that much less for something else, and the something else could mean housing or medical services. Every local sewage plant bond sold means that much less investment money available for mortgages, for example.

A final reflection is perhaps in order, though it is almost banal. Our rising G.N.P. gives us the "resources" to do the antipollution job. These resources include rising Government receipts. Our technology, which has given us the rising G.N.P., might find the way out of one pollution problem after another—and they are all different.

But, in the end, we cannot be sure that the job will be done. Growth of total output and output per capita will continue. The long-term relief is perfectly obvious: *fewer "capita."* That sort of "solution" might help, in our country, by about 1990. If we survive until then, the law of compound interest will be much less horrifying if the population is 220 million instead of 250 million.

QUESTIONS FOR DISCUSSION

1. *How can certain external economies for firms actually produce external diseconomies for the society?*
2. *What are social costs? How do they differ from economic costs?*
3. *How has our ideological commitment to laissez faire affected the utilization of our environment?*
4. *Cite a pollution problem in your community. How would you solve it?*

Can We Make Cities Livable?

Most Americans live in cities; therefore, most of us have a personal stake in what is going on currently and what will take place in the future in urban or metropolitan areas. The present "crisis" of American cities is probably the most distressing and confusing economic and social problem that confronts this nation. We find most of the other pressing issues of contemporary America, such as poverty, racism, and economic opportunity, tied in part or wholly to our urban problems.

Americans have been criticizing their urban centers almost from the nation's beginning. Cities seem to have been always dirty, crowded, crime-ridden, and impoverished of adequate public funds. Over the last two or three decades, events have intensified urban problems. The auto and the freeway have pushed the cities' economic limits farther out into the countryside, far beyond the municipal legal limits, creating serious jurisdictional problems for city governments on such questions as tax collection, providing adequate education, water and sewage, and meeting the needs of urban planning. Meanwhile, the old inner-city, once the commercial hub and the population center, has been undergoing a revolutionary change. Industry has been fleeing, stimulated in part by rising taxes and also by technological changes which no longer make central location so essential. The old residential locations in the central city have often deteriorated into hopeless slums or ghettos, populated by men and women who now find it increasingly difficult to find work and, as a result, slip deeper into economic despair. Even the distant affluent suburbs are not without their problems. Rising taxes, greater commuter difficulties, and a growing fear of the junglelike conditions of the central city contribute to much uneasiness even beyond the cities' municipal limits.

The first of the following articles, by the President's Council of Economic Advisers, takes a general look at some of the more pressing urban problems and argues for a new direction in federal policy toward urban areas. The last article surveys the state of city planning and argues that Americans must become more committed to planning if cities are to be saved.

The Urbanization of Our Society

Council of Economic Advisers

Today, America is an urban nation. In 1960, 125 million people, 70 percent of our population, lived in urban places—places with a population of 2500 or more. Half a century earlier, less than half of our people resided in urban areas. And the forces promoting urbanization are not likely to abate. By the year 2000 over 250 million people, 4 out of 5 of the population, are likely to be urban.

Moreover, the urban population is increasingly concentrated in metropolitan areas—clusters of cities and suburbs and their nearby hinterlands. New York, the largest, had 10.7 million people in 1960. All together, one-third of the United States population lived in 24 metropolitan areas containing a million or more people. Another 30 percent lived in the remaining 188 metropolitan areas. But 10 million of the urban population still live in the smaller towns that are not part of metropolitan areas.

The urbanization of our society has been greatly accelerated by immigration from abroad and migration from farm to city. Most of the European emigrants to this country poured into the rapidly growing cities of the late 19th and early 20th centuries. This population movement came to an abrupt halt with World War I and the subsequent introduction of immigration quotas.

As the great immigrations from abroad reached their peaks and receded, an equally massive internal migration from rural to urban areas began. In many ways it has produced social and economic effects as far-reaching as the earlier waves of immigration.

Although the movement of people from the land to the cities is not new, it has reached new proportions in recent years. Indeed, the size of this internal migration is not generally appreciated: over one million a year have

From "Annual Report of the Council of Economic Advisers, 1965," Economic Report of the President (Washington, D.C.: United States Government Printing Office, 1965).

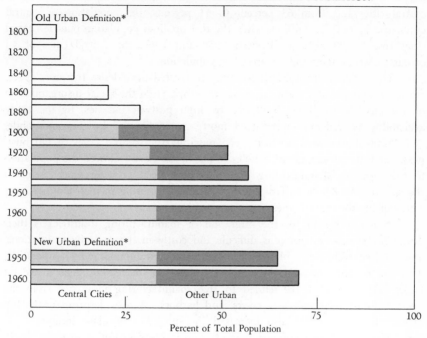

*For Definition of Urban, See Department of Commerce, Bureau of the Census,
  1960 Census of Population, Volume 1, Part 1.

Source: Department of Commerce

left the farm since 1940. A minority of the migrating farm families have found new opportunities in rural communities. The vast majority have sought new jobs in urban areas. And others besides farmers have left rural areas, bringing the total influx to the urban areas [to] 25 million.

Finally, the high birthrates of the postwar period have contributed as much to the absolute growth of urban populations in the last two decades as has the migration of people from rural areas.

CHANGING STRUCTURE OF URBAN AREAS

The rapid growth of population in our metropolitan areas has been accompanied by major changes in the locational patterns of life and work. The growth of cities has long taken place primarily by outward movement at the fringes. During the postwar period this process has been characterized by its speed and its tendency to take place beyond the boundaries of central cities.

Between 1940 and 1960, the share of the metropolitan population living in central cities fell from 63 percent to 51 percent; the population of central cities rose by only 12 million, while the metropolitan population outside central cities rose by 28 million. Between 1950 and 1960, the central cities of 14 of our 15 largest metropolitan areas lost population.

The flight to the suburbs has been motivated by a desire for more space, fresh air, and privacy, and by a desire to escape from the social disorganization of the city. It has been facilitated by high postwar incomes, by the ready availability of federally guaranteed mortgage credit, and by the automobile.

Many businesses also have been moving from central cities. Retail businesses and, to a lesser extent, wholesale businesses have followed the population to the suburbs. Manufacturing industries have been growing much faster in the suburbs. By 1960, half of the jobs in manufacturing in metropolitan areas were outside the central cities.

A major reason for the migration of manufacturing industries is their desire for space. Expansion is difficult and costly in the central city locations, and modern technology places a premium on continuous one-floor operation. The rise of trucking and, in many instances, the decreasing dependence on bulky raw materials have tended to free manufacturing industries from the need to locate near railroads, rivers, and harbors. More widespread ownership of cars by workers has also increased the flexibility of plant location.

There has been continued concentration in central cities of financial, legal, and specialized business and consumer services. Cultural and educational facilities, central office administration, and governments have also shown preference for expansion in central city locations.

By and large, the transformation from rural to urban and from urban to metropolitan areas has been consistent with the search for greater economic opportunity and higher economic rewards. Urban areas offer far more opportunities for high-paying jobs and urban people enjoy higher incomes. With some exceptions, our largest metropolitan areas rank near the top in this respect. But in the wake of this transformation have come serious problems of adjustment: for the rural areas, adjustment to decline; for the central cities, adjustment to change in population structure and economic base; and for the suburbs, adjustment to rapid growth.

PROBLEMS AND UNMET NEEDS OF URBAN AREAS

Existing institutions have responded only partially to the rapid growth and changing economic structure of our large cities. Many public and private efforts are already devoted to our urban problems, but the time is ripe for a more comprehensive response.

Our concern is both with the disadvantaged in the city and with the quality of the physical environment. . . .

Human Problems of the Cities. Rural-urban migration has created problems of adjustment for the migrants and for the areas receiving them. Existing urban educational systems, social groupings, and economic structures have been unable to absorb smoothly the rapid influx of the poor, uneducated, and unskilled among the rural migrants.

Many have found it difficult to adjust to the new economic and social environment. Because they lack skills, they are handicapped in an industrial society which is increasingly replacing unskilled labor with skilled labor and machines. They become victims of impersonal business fluctuations which affect most heavily the younger, the less skilled, and the nonwhite workers. And if unemployed, they cannot fall back for food and shelter on the extended family system of a traditional rural society.

As middle- and upper-income groups have fled to the suburbs, central cities have been left with a disproportionately large share of the poor. This situation has been aggravated by racial discrimination which often restricts nonwhites to the older neighborhoods of central cities.

Poverty, lack of education and skills, and irregular employment stifle incentives for self-improvement and lead to social disorganization. Family breakup, alcoholism, drug addition, rising crime rates, and illegitimacy have become major problems in our cities. Children in such environments, left to their own resources at an early age, quickly assume the ways of the preceding generation, perpetuating the process of poverty. Society must pay the costs through waste of human resources, increased public welfare expenditures, and decay of our social fabric.

The human problems are aggravated by the inadequacies of the physical environment. The accommodation of a large population at very high densities in cities which were shaped in an earlier technological era produces living conditions with little privacy or amenity.

Urban Decay. The blight and decay that afflict large parts of central cities are clear and visible. Part of what we see is another reflection of poverty: poor people cannot afford adequate, attractive housing. Another part results from the decreased dependence of industry and trade on central city locations.

But blight in cities tends to be cumulative. The older structures concentrated near the city center lose their economic usefulness as the functions of the downtown areas change. Extensive conversion, rehabilitation, and reconstruction are needed. If a few buildings need to be replaced or renovated in an otherwise prosperous area, the market provides private developers and builders with sufficient incentives to undertake the work. However, when a pattern of decay permeates a large area, the dilapidation of neighboring buildings reduces the profitability of improving a particular property. A large area must then be improved as a single unit, and the cost and difficulties of acquiring and redeveloping a large tract of central city land are likely to deter private investors from the undertaking. In such cases, there is need for public policies to assist the private market in developing property for new and improved uses.

Although inadequate housing is by no means the only aspect of urban blight, it is the most important. Ten percent of all urban households—about 3.8 million families—live in housing that is dilapidated or lacking such amenities as plumbing facilities, piped hot water, and kitchen or cooking equipment. Inadequate housing is particularly acute for nonwhites: only 7 percent of urban white families live in inadequate housing, compared with 32 percent of urban nonwhites.

In many United States cities, the process of urban blight is worsened by discrimination against nonwhites. Discrimination in housing markets provides a captive market for dilapidated slum dwellings. Large profits can be made by undermaintenance, since Negroes are virtually deprived of access to adequate housing. The situation is sometimes aggravated by inadequate enforcement of building codes and public health statutes. The success of any effort to upgrade urban housing standards will depend on the elimination of racial barriers.

Commercial and industrial structures also become obsolete. The failure to maintain these facilities reflects in part the greater attraction of suburban locations. Here, too, it is sometimes difficult for normal market processes to avoid cumulative deterioration and achieve conversion to new uses.

Area-wide Problems. The large metropolitan area typically consists of a central city and several smaller suburban communities. In dealing with many of the public services of the metropolitan area, it is desirable to take a broad view encompassing the needs and preferences of all the constituent communities. This is true in some instances because there are important economies that can be achieved by acting in concert; in others, because decisions taken in isolation by a particular community may have undesirable side effects on its neighbors. Thus, as metropolitan areas grow in size and diversity there is greater need for some area-wide coordination and planning.

LAND USE. Efficient use and aesthetic development of the limited land resources are major problems facing almost all urban communities. Private uses compete with each other and with public facilities for space. Individual land use decisions affect the value of neighboring properties and the general environment. These effects can be given adequate weight only if a broader social view is taken, through appropriate taxation, zoning, and other regulations.

In metropolitan areas, zoning and other land use restrictions need to take into account the needs of the area as a whole, together with the special problems of the individual communities. Each community in isolation will zone its land use to suit itself, frequently banishing the less desirable uses to outskirts remote from its center and residential areas, but possibly near the living areas of neighboring communities. If the area is to have an efficient transportation system and if enough land is to be set aside for recreational purposes in convenient locations, a metropolitan perspective must be added to local land use decisions.

TRANSPORTATION. The movement of people and business to the suburbs has greatly increased the burdens on our urban transportation systems. Part of this increase has been due to commercial traffic—the result of expanded economic acitivity. The greatest part, however, has been due to the growth of commuting between places of residence and employment. People are commuting longer distances, and more are crossing city boundaries. During the 1960 Census week, nearly one-fourth of the 39 million workers employed in our metropolitan areas commuted across the limits of the central city.

By no means all urban traffic moves into the city in the morning and out in the evening. As much as 29 percent of commuting across central city limits takes place in the opposite direction. The decentralization of retailing, manufacturing, recreation, and other activities has meant that travel patterns have increased in variety and complexity.

Commuters in most areas travel to and from work by automobile. This has led to massive investment in streets and highways and in parking facilities. As roads have been extended and improved, more individuals have been encouraged to commute by automobile, and congestion has continued. This has stimulated a revival of interest in mass transportation.

An effective transportation system involves a combination of individual and mass transit. The advantage of the automobile is its flexibility and convenience in terms of time and place of travel, number of people, and cargo. The advantage of public transit lies in its lower cost, more economical use of space, and broader availability to persons unable to rely on automobiles. But no one system can do the job alone.

In many areas, patronage of public transportation has declined drastically; between 1952 and 1962, revenue passengers carried by buses and streetcars in the United States dropped by 41 percent; and 194 transit companies were abandoned between 1954 and the end of 1963. The loss of patronage raises unit costs, requiring higher fares to break even, and leading to further shrinkage of patronage. Railroads subject to the same process have abandoned many commuter routes. With the advent of the automobile, some decline in patronage of public transportation was inevitable. Yet it might not have been as great under a program of more balanced public development of individual and mass transportation. While billions of public funds have been spent on roads and streets, the mass transit systems have not been able to attract private capital, nor have the central cities been able to invest sufficiently to keep them from deteriorating.

Clearly, the transportation problems of a metropolitan area transcend individual communities, whether they be the central city or the suburbs. An effective transportation system for the metropolis should permit people to move easily both between and within the suburbs and central city. Individual communities working in isolation to solve their local traffic problems are more likely to provide a patchwork than a logical system of connecting routes. Thus, area-wide planning is required if an effective transportation system is to be devised and coordinated.

WASTE DISPOSAL AND WATER POLLUTION. The growth of urban population, commerce, and industry has led to a rapid rise in the use of water. Little water is actually consumed in most uses for which it is withdrawn. Most of it is returned to some natural body of water, usually with some waste or other deterioration in quality. If the quality has not deteriorated too much, the water is available for reuse. Water in major rivers is reused several times before it reaches the sea.

Since most of the costs of pollution are borne by downstream users rather than by those who generate the wastes, municipalities and industry have little incentive to treat waste adequately before discharge. The result is that the collection and treatment of waste lag behind water use. In 1962, about 20 million more people were served by municipal water supply than by waste treatment systems. Much industrial waste is discharged without treatment, and between 1950 and 1960 the discharge of industrial organic waste to streams increased by 30 percent.

The discharge of pollutants is concentrated in urban areas and is increasing as time passes. More effective regulations and enforcement will be necessary to achieve cleaner streams and lakes. Another policy instrument that may be of value is a system of fees for the discharge of effluent. Such fees, if feasible, would confront polluters with the social costs of their actions and would encourage them to reduce pollution.

AIR POLLUTION. Air pollution, like water pollution, results from excessive discharge of wastes, often the result of incomplete combustion. Pollutants are discharged into the air by industries, households, and municipalities. The automobile is probably the largest single source of air pollution; California has adopted a law prohibiting the sale of cars without pollution control devices, and other states are considering similar action.

Discharge of pollutants has increased rapidly with the growth of population and industry. More than half of all United States urban communities are affected by air pollution. One-quarter of the population live in communities in which air pollution is a major problem.

Air pollution is at best a public nuisance, at worst a source of serious damage to health and property. Although more research is needed, relatively inexpensive methods are already available for the control of most pollutants. As with water pollution, economic incentives are lacking. The cost of air pollution is borne mainly by the community at large rather than by those responsible for the pollution. It can be reduced by more effective regulation or, for major polluters, by discharge fees.

OPEN SPACES AND OUTDOOR RECREATION. Although people value open spaces in urban areas, there is no market on which they can register these preferences. It would not be feasible to create such a market because of the difficulty of imputing or confining benefits from urban open spaces to particular individuals. There is a strong temptation for hard-pressed local governments to maintain their tax base by abandoning open spaces to developers, by routing new roads through parks rather than through developed areas, and by making inadequate additions to the available open space as the population expands.

The amount of open space per person is small and probably declining in the larger metropolitan areas. In addition, the provision of State and county parks within driving distance of metropolitan areas is lagging behind the growth of these areas, and most of our Federal recreational facilities are remote from the major population centers.

But with incomes rising and leisure time increasing, the demand for outdoor recreation is growing rapidly. Many city parks are now used nearly to capacity, and visits to State parks have increased by 123 percent in the last decade. The Outdoor Recreation Resources Review Commission projects a tripling of over-all demand for outdoor recreation facilities by the year 2000.

Federal Programs for Urban Areas. During the past thirty years, the Federal Government has been developing programs of assistance—to individuals, to business, and to State and local governments—that contribute to the improvement of the urban environment and to the alleviation of the social, developmental, and financial problems of urban areas. Among the most important of the existing programs to improve the physical environment are aids to public housing, urban renewal, highways, mass transit, waste treatment, airports, and hospitals. The human problems of the city are approached through national programs for education, health, welfare, and social insurance, and to combat poverty.

These measures have made great contributions to the development of urban life. But the rapid growth of metropolitan areas has compounded or changed the nature of many of these problems and created new ones. New knowledge—partly gained from the mistakes of the past—can be brought to bear. It is now evident that new directions in Federal policy are needed in these efforts.

Most important is Federal encouragement of area-wide metropolitan planning, to assure the development of integrated systems of land use, of transportation, water supply, sanitation, and pollution control. Some Federal programs now require local coordination in the provision of physical facilities. But even if some area-wide coordination is achieved in individual functions such as transportation or sanitation, an effectively integrated pattern of development cannot emerge unless the several functions are brought into a common focus. This can only be achieved if there is some method of taking an area-wide, comprehensive point of view, which brings together all levels of government and pertinent private organizations to evolve a metropolitan area plan.

Metropolitan area planning is no panacea. Each community has its own preferences and problems, and its local government is best able to discern them. Nor does metropolitan planning directly augment the resources available to meet the rapidly increasing needs. It is clear, however, that fragmentation of legal jurisdictions has proceeded too far in many of our metropolitan areas. The Federal Government has a responsibility to promote planning to assure that public needs are met efficiently and that the federally aided local public programs will, indeed, produce a more livable and efficient urban environment.

Because the allocation of land to various purposes is so fundamental to the future pattern of a metropolitan area, the Federal Government should continue to give some help to promote better land use planning. While decisions about land use will remain mainly a local matter, research and the spreading of information to improve zoning techniques are desirable.

As the metropolis grows in area and density, it is particularly difficult to preserve open spaces for recreational and aesthetic purposes. The Federal Government already aids localities to acquire open lands, and this program is a logical part of a greater emphasis on metropolitan planning.

One way of avoiding congestion in the metropolitan area is to bring homes, community services, and jobs closer together in smaller and more self-contained communities. Federal aids to urban areas need to be adapted to this promising new approach.

The Federal Government has a responsibility to reexamine and improve its existing programs. Urban renewal is rapidly transforming many of the blighted downtown areas of our cities to new and more productive uses, thereby helping to reverse the downward spiral of malfunction and decay. However, despite an increase in the efforts to find adequate housing for the persons displaced by the tearing down of slums, it is evident that these efforts are still not wholly successful. Experience has shown that much of the land made available through urban renewal in downtown areas is drawn into commercial and high rent residential uses. The Government therefore must take further steps to augment the supply of low and medium rent housing in the city. The recent emphasis in urban renewal on rehabilitation of existing residential units should make a contribution to this need; and the Federal sharing of costs of code enforcement begun last year should help to stem the decline of gray areas.

The FHA and VA mortgage guarantee programs have greatly increased the supply of middle-income houses and are among the main forces behind the growth of suburbs. The public housing program has sought to provide low-income housing, and in recent years housing assistance for middle-income families has been a major program innovation. But we need to test out more flexible methods of providing housing assistance for families of different incomes, under which families are not forced to move out of their homes when their incomes rise above a specified level.

The impact of governments on the private decisions which mainly determine the development of metropolitan areas is large. The value of land in alternative uses depends on government decisions on zoning and transportation. The commuter's decision to use a particular transportation system depends on the cost he must pay. The extent of air and water pollution depends on the willingness of governments to impose regulations. Federal, State, and local methods of taxation help to determine the profitability of slums and of their rehabilitation.

As public policy seeks to improve the livability of metropolitan areas, it must be keenly aware of its effects on private incentives and behavior. The development of our metropolitan areas will always be primarily determined by private actions. Wise government policies will promote private efforts that improve the quality of urban life and will provide incentives which channel private decisions toward an efficient use of resources.

. . . And Civic Foresight

Mitchell Gordon

It took the Black Plague to get London to lay its first underground sewer system, though the need had long since been proclaimed by those anxious for the city's health. Even then, the experience failed to frighten other cities with open sewers running through their streets into similar action. Naples began confining its public filth only after suffering a cholera epidemic of its own decades later. In France, waves of the disease sowed death and dissension before housing standards finally were established to inhibit the scourge.

Civic myopia rarely takes its toll in human life in developed nations today. Modern man has conquered infectious disease in most civilized parts of the world. But he has not learned to cope with many of his other urban ills. Possibly because their alleviation is no longer a question of life or death but of lost opportunities and unvisualized benefits, civic ailments tend to be tolerated as the inevitable consequences of a more crowded urban existence.

As a result, the exercise of civic foresight in metropolitan affairs is rare. Urban giants gobble up open space with scant regard to nature's spiritual worth to man. Populations smear themselves across the landscape, but no effort is made to cultivate the lines of destiny capable of nourishing new transit systems into being and old ones back to health. City centers are strangled by thickening congestion and shattered beyond the walker's scale by ruthless expressways and land-gluttonous parking facilities, yet schemes for rescuing these strategic areas are rarely taken seriously by the populace whose support is necessary to bring them into being.

With the exception of the early colonial period, Americans have given almost no communal direction whatsoever to their urban development. Until the mid-1920's, in fact, exceedingly few cities had even zoning controls to prohibit the intermingling of factories and residences. Some big cities still lack them: Houston is one. As recently as 1954, only fifty American cities had housing codes to establish minimum standards in construction. Even today, a number of large cities lack these rudiments of control over urban development. Before the Wagner Housing Act was passed in 1937, there was not a city in the country with the power to condemn slum properties, clear them, and make their salvaged land available to private investors for redevelopment.

It is ironic, perhaps, that Americans, who are notorious for their nonsupport of better civic design, are nevertheless among the most ardent admirers of European cities, often those which owe their beauty most to some ambitious plan. It is true, of course, that much Old World planning was done under circumstances considerably more conducive to success than those which prevail in the United States. Well-planned cities of the past were customarily laid out by strong central governments or rulers for the relatively easily determined purpose of facilitating military movement; even Baron Haussmann's boulevard-ing of Paris in 1870 had the easy flow of armies largely for its purpose. It is a good deal more difficult, on the other hand, to mold a city to suit the varied tastes and needs of its populace, let alone the economic and techno-logical changes which affect them and so rapidly alter the urban scene. When those preferences are to be interpreted, further, not by a strong central govern-ment but by a variously-composed and relatively easily-swayed democratic gov-ernment, the task becomes infinitely more difficult. . . .

In the United States, where the old could always be left behind and the principles of individualism were not to be contained in any sphere of endeavor, what few exercises were conducted in city planning were the products of relatively halcyon periods. William Penn's gridiron pattern for the city of Philadelphia, now regarded as so wasteful of land and inefficient for traffic, was presented in 1682. Pierre L'Enfant's plan for a monument-showcasing Washington dates from 1791. And the blueprint Mormon leader Brigham Young used to lay the form for Salt Lake City in 1847 had been drawn up thirteen years earlier by Joseph Smith in envisioning "the city of Zion."

American interest in city planning (but not yet action) was first widely stirred by the Columbian Exposition in Chicago in 1893. Daniel Burnham, architect of that world's fair, aroused the nation's imagination by expressing in visual layout a philosophy which exhorted planners to "make no little plans" because they did not have the "magic to stir men's blood" and therefore probably "would never be realized." To this day, the beauty of Chicago's lakefront development attests to the boldness of the Burnham vision. Ugly waterfronts and reviled natural assets of so many cities hold the docket for practical expediency.

Only a negative version of Burnham's brand of urban thinking ever got through to the public and their hardheaded city councils: the zoning authority to prohibit undesirable mixtures of land use. Even this principle was bitterly fought, though it had been used from time to time in the past, once to prohibit the location of storage places for gunpowder in the center of Boston. Back in the seventeenth century, there was even some attempt to "zone" the location of people, when, in an effort to fashion a more perfect democracy, the General Assembly of Massachusetts required its inhabitants to live within a half-mile of their respective Commons. The theory: they would then be more likely to participate in local government and perform their civic duties.

Walter Gropius, the German-born architect, has criticized the development of American cities as having been guided "only by zoning laws that merely forbade the worst." The American city, he maintains, "is not a product of necessity but of municipal habits. There is no lack of good planners and designers who really know what could be done to bring about a new unity of design," says he, "but they have no power."

In a democratic society, that power can come from only one source: public persuasion. Unless the planner is to be made the autocrat of city design, final decisions as to the city's form and shape must inevitably rest with the electorate or its representatives, however buffeted they may be by the political winds that happen to be blowing at the time.

The planner, to be effective, must be capable of putting across the merits of his plan while setting forth the advantages and disadvantages of alternative plans. Thus, he must also be something of a salesman. The community owes him, and itself, however, a platform for the purpose.

"Planners have been too timid up to now in presenting their ideas to the public, or else they have presented them too much on a take-it-or-leave-it basis," asserts David F. Bramhall, a Baltimore city planning consultant and a member of the faculty at Johns Hopkins University. The local citizenry, he argues, must be brought in on plans from their inception and solicited for ideas at various stages if the plan that is finally presented is to have its support. . . .

No section of the metropolitan area is immune to the ill effects of failing to plan for the motorcar. Vehicular approaches to the nation's greatest cities, almost without fail, are trimmed with ugliness. Known as "strip development," their strings of ramshackle enterprises with oversized signs smear the rouge of commerce over what might otherwise have been scenic or soothing vistas. Their metamorphosis, which might be accomplished through the use of setbacks and approved landscape design, could make motoring pleasanter, roadside rest more refreshing, and, probably, business more profitable through improved environment. When competition runs rampant, however, the premium generally goes to the enterprise that can snatch the motorist first.

The absence of planning tends to produce a free-for-all among municipalities no less than among enterprises. Their vying for industry, subdivisions, and other development often works to the detriment of the communities involved by causing them to lower minimum standards on such features as the width and quality of roads, the type of streetlights to be provided, the width of sideyards, the number of trees to be planted on a given length of frontage, and the provision of other amenities that tend to preserve property values.

Planning might as well be nonexistent where planning agencies are too profuse. Montgomery County, Ohio, recently counted twenty-six different planning and zoning commissions operating within its confines, none of them with authority over the area as a whole. A citizens' committee from the largest city in the county, Dayton, found that little or no planning preceded the enactment of zoning ordinances even at the municipal and township levels, much less at the regional level. Frequently, cities which zone for single-family residences on one side of the line, and begin to get that type of development, suddenly find cities next door permitting commercial or even industrial development right alongside.

One reason city planning stirs more vigorous opposition than communal support, of course, is that it imposes a certain discipline on development. In instances where the developer's immediate profit is at odds with the best long-term interests of the community as a whole, it tends to pit existing interests, sometimes powerful but always very much in existence, with an amorphous mass that has yet to come into being. Planning also tends to force the resolution of problems in advance of the discomforts which might ultimately yank those decisions loose; it is a good deal easier to get the patient to take his medicine when he is writhing in pain than when he is feeling just a little uneasy. The delay may be dangerous in human beings, in fast-developing cities it is at least costly.

The dictates of planned discipline may be somewhat demanding. Homebuilders in picturesque Palos Verdes Estates, just south of Los Angeles, have been prevented for years from roofing their structures with anything but red tile, according to a trust indenture laid down to preserve the area's Mediterranean-like character. The architectural fidelity may be irksome to those who prefer to put their dollars into fancier automobiles or finer china, but it is a source of pride to its "regimented" residents and a deliverer of character that is reflected in property values.

Communities do not have to go to such lengths for urban conservation. The city of Beverly Hills, in California, a good part of which is only modestly developed, goes a long way toward keeping up appearances by outlawing billboards, junkyards, and used-car lots within its borders. Palm Springs defends its dignity by prohibiting drive-ins, hot-dog stands, open markets, and auction yards. Some cities which permit these enterprises require them to "deblight" themselves; thus, junkyards are frequently required to fence themselves in, and sometimes to foreground themselves as well with pleasing shrubbery. A number of cities prohibit the posting of advertising signs on rooftops or hanging over streets.

More and more cities are causing unsightly power and· telephone lines to go underground. In picturesque Santa Barbara, California, a citizens' committee has agreed to pay half the cost of undergrounding utilities to get utility companies to go along with the project. In Oakland, California, where utilities are having to bear the entire load, residents must content themselves with two miles a year of new pole-cleared streets.

Building restrictions in the Florida community of Royal Palm, where lots are priced upward of $35,000 each, prohibit the use of outside clotheslines.

The city of Evanston, Illinois, for its part, has taken to diking itself against deterioration by planting trees on its downtown sidewalks, bathing the surfaces of its more interesting civic and commercial buildings in light, and employing more enforcement officials to ensure the effectiveness of its housing code.

Planning has more than practical ends to serve. It has ideals to lift aloft as well. Dr. Gulick of the Institute of Public Administration, and a lifelong missionary for better cities, puts it this way: "People who live and work in an urban area have a deep emotional need to have 'their city' stand for something worthwhile in the world and to present to themselves and to mankind a strong physical image of this spiritual ambition in the structure of the city, in its vistas and in its major monuments. Through these," says he, "men venerate the past, remember the achievements of those who have gone before, reach for the future and affirm their self-respect and idealism."

QUESTIONS FOR DISCUSSION

1. *What would you list as the chief problems that your city faces today? How is the city dealing with these problems?*
2. *What role has the auto played in creating current urban problems?*
3. *Do you support or oppose the idea of urban planning? Why?*
4. *Why do you think Americans have had so little success with attempts at planning in the past?*

DATE DUE

GAYLORD			PRINTED IN U.S.A